THE UNIVEF

Mar

ARCHAEOLOGY OF THE MILITARY ORDERS

During the twelfth and thirteenth centuries the Military Orders played an active role in the defence of the Latin States in the East (modern Turkey, Syria, Lebanon, Israel and Cyprus) and administered various urban and rural properties. They were also significantly involved in the various activities relating to the welfare of the Frankish populace and of the pilgrims visiting the Holy Land.

This book presents a detailed description of the archaeological evidence for the five Military Orders active in the Latin East – the Hospitallers, Templars, Teutonic Knights, Leper Knights of St Lazarus and Knights of St Thomas. The three principal sections of the book consist of chapters relating to the urban quarters of the Orders in Jerusalem, Acre and other cities, their numerous rural possessions, and the tens of castles built or purchased and expanded by them in the twelfth and thirteenth centuries. The distinctive architecture relating to their various undertakings (such as hospitals in Jerusalem and Acre) is discussed in detail, with emphasis on the important role of the Military Orders in the development of military architecture in the Middle Ages.

Adrian J. Boas is Senior Lecturer at the University of Haifa. He has published several articles and two books on Crusader archaeology.

ARCHAEOLOGY OF THE MILITARY ORDERS

A survey of the urban centres, rural
settlement and castles of the Military
Orders in the Latin East (*c.* 1120–1291)

Adrian J. Boas

Routledge
Taylor & Francis Group

LONDON AND NEW YORK

IN MEMORY OF MY FATHER
NORMAN SAMUEL BOAS

First published 2006
by Routledge
2 Park Square, Milton Park, Abingdon, Oxon OX14 4RN

Simultaneously published in the USA and Canada
by Routledge
270 Madison Avenue, New York, NY 10016

Routledge is an imprint of the Taylor & Francis Group, an informa business

© 2006 Adrian J. Boas

Typeset in Garamond by
RefineCatch Limited, Bungay, Suffolk
Printed and bound in Great Britain by
TJ International Ltd, Padstow, Cornwall

British Library Cataloguing in Publication Data
A catalogue record for this book is available from the British Library

Library of Congress Cataloging in Publication Data
A catalog record for this book has been requested

ISBN 10: 0-415-29980-2   ISBN 13: 978-0-415-29980-0

CONTENTS

CONTENTS

FIGURES

The Commander of the City of Jerusalem should have ten knight brothers
under his command to lead and guard the pilgrims who come to the River
Jordan; and he should carry a round tent and the piebald banner or flag, for as
long as his authority lasts.[12]

A second incentive for the establishment of the Orders was to provide troops to
participate in campaigns for the expansion and defence of the Crusader states. Prior to
the establishment of the Templar Order, knights who could be mustered for a campaign or even for regular defensive needs were in short supply. Fulcher of Chartres
recorded that few knights remained in the East after the capture of Jerusalem in 1099.
Baldwin I had, at first, no more than 300 knights in his service.[13] Following the
establishment and rapid expansion of the Templars in the twelfth century, they alone
numbered around 300 knights by the 1170s.[14] Together with the Hospitallers, they
came to provide about half of the entire fighting force of the Crusader army.[15]

From its foundation the Templar Order benefited from royal and ecclesiastical pat-
ronage. King Baldwin II supported the new organisation to the extent of providing
(temporarily, according to William of Tyre) a wing in his palace, the Templum
Salomonis (al-Aqsa Mosque) in the south of the Temple Mount in Jerusalem.[16] The
Augustinian canons of the neighbouring Templum Domini gave them a square nearby.
The Templars, who took their name from their new residence, were organised under a
Master in three classes: knights, sergeants and chaplains. They took vows of obedience,
personal poverty and chastity, established a communal coenobitical life and organised
their day according to a monastic daily routine which was based on the Benedictine
Rule and, under the guidance of Bernard of Clairvaux (St Bernard), were probably
influenced by the ascetic and anti-materialistic Cistercian reforms.[17] They slept in a
common dormitory, ate in a communal refectory and divided their time, according to
the canonical hours, between prayer, various household tasks, military training and care
of their equipment. They adopted a white tunic symbolising chastity, like that of the
Cistercians, adding a red cross in order to distinguish them from the monks. They wore
their hair short and avoided all contact with women. The fourth decade of the twelfth
century witnessed rapid recruitment to the Order, due in no small part to the enthusiastic support of Bernard of Clairvaux. Bernard wrote a treatise, *De laude novae militiae
ad milites templi* (In Praise of the New Knighthood), in order to silence criticism of the
foundation by those who regarded warfare as ungodly and incompatible with a
religious vocation.[18]

The Templar Rule is believed to have been composed by Bernard at the time of the
Council of Troyes in January 1129.[19] Two years later Patriarch Stephen of Jerusalem
(1128–30) completed its form. In 1139 Pope Innocent II (1130–43) granted the
Templars extensive privileges in a bull (*Omne datum optimum*).

The foundation of the Military Order of the Hospital of St John

The Order of the Hospital of St John, commonly known as the Hospitallers, was
the second Military Order to be established in the Holy Land. As an institution, it
existed much earlier than the Templars, not as a Military Order but rather as a welfare
institution providing care for the needy and treatment for the ill. Its origins may

possibly go as far back as the beginning of the seventh century, when in the year 603 Pope Gregory the Great called for the establishment of a hospice for Latin pilgrims. Though Christian pilgrimage to the Holy Land entered a period of decline under Islam, by the mid-tenth century it was on the rise again, despite the difficulties faced by Christian travellers in the Holy Land under Muslim rule. At this time an institution which can be considered the precursor of the Hospitallers was established by a group of Amalfitan merchants in Jerusalem. An anonymous Amalfitan chronicler records that while on pilgrimage to Jerusalem around 1080 Archbishop John of Amalfi (c. 1070– 81/2) visited the new establishments, which included a hospital/hospice for men and another one for women.[20] William of Tyre writes that the Amalfitans built two institutions: a monastery dedicated to the Virgin Mary, which was known as the monastery of the Latins, and a convent of nuns dedicated to St Mary Magdalene.[21] These were set up on a plot of land to the south of the Church of the Holy Sepulchre and followed the Benedictine Rule. The monastery had a hospital (*xenodochium*), which according to William was dedicated to St John the Almoner, but which modern scholars prefer to see as having been dedicated from the beginning to John the Baptist.[22]

These institutions were devoted to the care of poor and sick Latin pilgrims who arrived in Jerusalem. Towards the end of the eleventh century the hospice/hospital was under the astute leadership of a certain Gerard, possibly himself of Amalfitan origin, although there is no clear evidence for this.[23] Gerard's wisdom and foresight enabled the hospital to survive the traumatic events of 1099 and to continue to function and expand under Crusader rule in the early twelfth century. Gerard persuaded Duke Godfrey and his successor, Baldwin I, to support the hospital. The king gave the institution grants of properties in and outside of Jerusalem and, following the Battle of Rama (Ramla) in 1101, a tenth of all the spoils.[24] In 1112 Patriarch Arnulf of Chocques (1112–18) and Archbishop Evremar of Caesarea exempted the hospital from paying tithes.[25] In 1113, the Hospitallers received recognition and privileges in a bull (*Pie postulation voluntatis*) from Pope Paschal II (1099–1118). They were recognised as an independent Order. The privileges granted the Order papal protection, confirmed its possessions, and allowed the brothers to elect their own Master without being required to confer with any other lay or ecclesiastical authority. Pope Calixtus II (1119–24) confirmed Paschal's grants and Popes Innocent II and Anastasius IV (1153–54) extended their privileges. The Order began to expand its holdings, acquiring property in the West where it received extensive grants before 1113. Hospices were established in Italy, the Iberian Peninsula and southern France.[26]

Like that of the canons of the nearby Holy Sepulchre, the Order's Rule, which was drawn up by Gerard's successor Raymond du Puy (1120–58/60) and later added to by subsequent Masters, was based on the Rule of Saint Augustine.[27] In both East and West the Order remained primarily involved in the care of the needy and sick. However, Raymond du Puy, an energetic and effective organiser, led the Order to pursue an active military role. As early as 1123 an emergency unit of mounted knights was formed against the Fatimid threat. From 1136, the Hospitallers were given the castle of Bethgibelin by King Fulk and thus began their important role as castle-owners.

In Jerusalem the Hospitallers continued to occupy the area to the south of the Church of the Holy Sepulchre, expanding their holdings to include the entire plot of land from the church to David Street on the south and from the Street of the Patriarch (modern Christian Street) in the west to the triple market on the ancient

Cardo in the east. They began a monumental building programme in Jerusalem and in Acre.

The Teutonic Knights

The Teutonic Order was established in Acre in the last decade of the twelfth century.[28] Its origins lay in the collapse of the German contingent of the Third Crusade. In the spring and early summer of 1190, the Germans led by Emperor Frederick Barbarossa, who formed the largest faction of the Crusader army, crossed Asia Minor on the way to Tyre. However, the emperor was drowned while crossing the Saleph River on 10 June 1190, an incident which led to the total collapse of his army. Many of the Germans returned to Europe and others fell victim to an epidemic which broke out amongst the regrouping forces at Antioch. Despite these disasters, many Germans did arrive to participate in the siege of Acre, joining the other contingents of the Crusader armies from England and France. According to a contemporary text known as *Narracio de primordiis ordinis theutonici*, a fleet of fifty-five ships of German Crusaders had joined King Richard I of England, who occupied Acre on 12 July 1191 after an extended siege.[29]

Richard went on to recover the coast as far as Ascalon, but failed to retake Jerusalem. Consequently Acre's importance rose as the interim administrative capital of the rump kingdom. During the siege of Acre in 1190, some members of the German army, citizens of Lübeck and Bremen, established a makeshift hospital outside the eastern walls of the city near the Cemetery of St Nicholas, using a ship's sail for shelter. When the city fell to the Crusaders, the Germans purchased a garden inside the walls near the Gate of St Nicholas and built a church, hospital, tower and other buildings there. The hospital was dedicated to the Virgin Mary.

In 1197/8 a meeting of German ecclesiastical and lay leaders in Acre decided that the Germans should model their care of the poor and sick on the example of the Hospital of St John of Jerusalem, while taking the Templars as the model for their religious and military activities.[30] A papal bull of Pope Innocent III confirmed these decisions in February 1199, and the Teutonic Knights adopted the Templar Rule (which they later modified for their own needs) and its white mantle.[31]

The name subsequently adopted by this Order, the Hospital of St Mary of the House of the Teutons in Jerusalem, appears only about two decades later. It served as the basis for the successful claim of the Grand Master, Hermon von Salza (1210–39), to Frederick II in 1229 that the Order should receive the property formerly held by the German hospital in Jerusalem.

As latecomers to the scene, the aspirations of the Teutonic Order to expand and to gain possession of rural properties required them to centre their activities in the Galilee, which was less intensely occupied by the Hospitallers and Templars than most of the other fertile farmland in the Kingdom of Jerusalem. In order to do so, they set up a rural headquarters in Castellum Regis (Chasteiau dou Rei), a castle located on the crest of a hill overlooking farmland in the hills of the western Galilee. In 1226 the Order acquired extensive rural property in the region. Probably in the following year, work began on a new castle, Starkenberg, more commonly known by its French name, Montfort, which subsequently (by 1244) replaced Acre as the central headquarters of the Teutonic Order in the Latin East.[32]

The Leper Knights of St Lazarus

Like the Order of St John and the Teutonic Order, the Order of St Lazarus began not as a Military Order but as a hospital. Its origins go back to a leper hospital established outside the walls of Jerusalem in the third century AD (or possibly to the founding of an institution outside the walls of Caesarea by St Basil in the late fourth century).[33]

In the Crusader period, the Order of St Lazarus is first recorded in a document dating to between 1128 and 1137 referring to a leper hospital located outside the northern wall of Jerusalem between the Tower of Tancred and St Stephen's Gate. The Order was headed by a *magister* (*le maister de Saint Ladre des Mesiaux*), who was a suffragan of the patriarch of Jerusalem and who, Clermont-Ganneau suggested, may be the mitred figure appearing on the seal of the Order (Figure 80).[34] The brothers wore a green cross on their mantles and followed the Rule of St Augustine. Although, like the other Orders, the Knights of St Lazarus received many grants and privileges, papal recognition was achieved only in 1255.[35] Like the larger Military Orders, the Leper Knights began acquiring landed holdings quite early on. However, we lack information as to when they first took on a military role. The first reference comes only in 1244, when knights of the Order fought at La Forbie. Six years later they took part in the campaign of Louis IX in Egypt.

In the twelfth century a leper hospital was established by the Order in Acre, located well outside the walls. When the city expanded north and was refortified the leper hospital came within the walls. In 1240 land was rented to the Order by the Master of the Temple, Armand of Perigord, for an annual payment of 15 bezants.[36] There are records of other leper hospitals in the kingdom, including one at Castellum Regis (Mi'iliya) in the western Galilee and another dedicated to St Bartholomew in Beirut; but not all leprosaria were connected to the Military Order.[37]

Perhaps not all the brothers of the Order of St Lazarus were lepers. Statute 429 of the Rule of the Templars states: 'Nor may any brother of the Temple enter the Order of St Lazarus unless he becomes a leper.'[38] This would seem to suggest that in the past some Templars who were not lepers had joined the Order. Why they should have done so is difficult to tell, but there would be no reason to make such a rule if this was not a possibility which had to be prevented.

The Order of St Thomas of Canterbury

The Order of St Thomas of Canterbury is another institution that did not begin its existence as a Military Order. It was founded as a religious house of regular canons around the time of the Third Crusade (1189–92) and, perhaps not surprisingly, Richard I has been said to be its founder.[39] Ralph de Diceto (the dean of St Paul's) wrote that its first prior was William, his former chaplain. The new foundation received the support of the family of St Thomas Becket. The Order adopted the Rule of St Augustine and evolved into a Military Order towards the end of the third decade of the thirteenth century. When the Order of St Thomas became a Military Order under Bishop Peter, he chose to adopt the Rule of the Teutonic Knights.[40] Papal approval and support came in 1236 from Gregory IX, and in 1256–57 from Alexander IV.[41] Edward I of England became a patron of the Order in the late thirteenth century.

Expansion in the twelfth and thirteenth centuries

During the twelfth century the Military Orders went through a phase of rapid development and expansion. They acquired properties by various means, through grants, donations and purchases and through exchanges between the Orders themselves, each of which was attempting to build up its own consolidated areas of land-holdings. Most of the properties were acquired before 1187. Of a total of 858 Frankish sites in the Kingdom of Jerusalem alone that have been identified by Prawer and Benvenisti, 171 are known to have belonged to the Military Orders at various times.[42] These include urban sites, rural properties and castles. In even more detail, Riley-Smith lists the Hospitaller estates as including some 224 identified sites in the Kingdom of Jerusalem and some 47 unidentified sites, as well as some additional unnamed properties.[43] In the County of Tripoli he lists 53 identified sites, 29 unidentified sites and two unnamed *casalia* (villages). In the Principality of Antioch, the County of Edessa and the Kingdom of Armenia he lists 79 identified estates, 59 unidentified estates and a few unnamed *casalia*. In Cyprus there are nine identified Hospitaller estates and four unidentified sites. There are also some 13 Hospitaller sites in the Latin East whose location is entirely unknown, and several unnamed *casalia* and other properties. Although they suffered a major setback with the loss of their inland properties and their headquarters in Jerusalem in the aftermath of the Battle of Hattin in 1187, the Military Orders recovered and in the thirteenth century made new acquisitions and strengthened their fortifications.

Cyprus came into Crusader hands within a month after the arrival of King Richard I of England, leading a contingent of the Third Crusade, on 6 May 1191. The ill-treatment of his sister by the Byzantine ruler of Cyprus, Isaac Ducas Comnenus, served as the justification for the occupation of the island by Richard. He subsequently sold Cyprus to the Templars for the sum of 100,000 gold bezants (40,000 to be paid in advance and the promise of an additional 60,000 to be paid in the future from the island's revenues). However, the Templars appear to have made an error of judgement by purchasing Cyprus at a time when their resources were stretched to the limit. Consequently, lack of manpower (they could assign fewer than twenty knights to its garrison) and finances (they were not able to make the promised payment of 60,000 bezants), as well as the lack of local support resulting from their harsh rule and heavy taxation, forced them to abandon the island by April 1192. In their place Richard sold the island to Guy of Lusignan, who had been displaced as King of Jerusalem.[44] However, the Templars did retain holdings on the island and expanded them in the thirteenth century. They had properties in Famagusta, Limassol, Nicosia and Paphos, and the castles and estates of Gastria, Khirokitia, Phasouri, Psimolophou (and the dependent settlements at Tripi and Kato Deftera), Temblos and Yermasoyia until the 1270s, when the Templar Master's support of Charles of Anjou as King of Jerusalem over the rival claims of Hugh III of Cyprus cost them their Cypriot holdings.[45] Though these were apparently returned in 1282, whatever remained passed to the Hospitallers in 1308 after the suppression of the Templar Order.

The Hospitallers held the tower of Kolossi near Limassol, which served as their Grand Commandery from *c.* 1210, and a second Commandery at Khirokitia, which was destroyed by the Mamluks in 1426.[46] Kolossi was in a sugar-growing district and a sugar refinery was located adjacent to the tower.[47] In Limassol they had a tower and in

Nicosia a fortified or semi-fortified house. Other estates held by them in the thirteenth century included Plataniskia, Monagroulli, Phinikas, Palekhori, Kellaqkli, Louvaras and Trakhoniu, and property at Mora, as well as additional unidentified properties.[48]

The Teutonic Knights and the Knights of St Thomas of Canterbury held very little property in Cyprus. The German Order probably found little support on the island because of their unpopular patron, Frederick II. The impoverished English Order had few possessions anywhere, but did have an estate near Limassol and a church dedicated to St Nicholas in Nicosia.[49]

The Military Orders played a role in the defence of Armenian Cilicia from an early date. By 1131 or 1136/37 the Templars had established a march in the Amanus Mountains north of Antioch.[50] The Amanus Mountains form a natural barrier between Cilicia and Syria. Two routes pass through the mountains: the pass of Hajar Shughlan, located north of Alexandretta (Iskenderun), and, further south, the celebrated Belen Pass (the Syrian Gates). The Templar march controlling these two routes included the castles of La Roche de Roissol (generally identified with Chivlan Kale) and La Roche Guillaume (of uncertain location) guarding the northern pass. Gaston (Baghras) guarded the southern pass, and Trapesac (Darbsak) played an important role, being located between the eastern approaches of both passes.

Armenian control in Cilicia reached its peak under the Roupenid Levon (Leon) II, who was crowned on 6 January 1198. In this period the involvement of the three great Military Orders in the defence of the Kingdom of Armenia also greatly increased. Despite his attempts at annexing the Frankish Principality of Antioch, Levon had close ties with the Frankish states and granted the Military Orders lands and castles to aid in the defence of the kingdom. The Hospitallers had been established in Cilicia from 1149. Levon II strengthened their position in the region by granting them Silifke Castle as well as nearby Norpert (or Norbert, Castellum Novum) and Camardesium, thus effectively creating a Hospitaller march in the west of Cilicia which could bolster the weakening defences of his kingdom against attacks by the Seljuks. The grant was formalised in 1210. In exchange, the Hospitallers were to pay an annual tax and provide a cavalry support of 400 lancers.[51] Levon also ceded castles in the Giguer and along the Antiochene frontier to the Hospitallers.[52]

Possibly in order to find favour in the eyes of Otto of Brunswick, Levon II decided to support the German Order of St Mary and declared himself to be a *confrater* of the Order. The Teutonic Knights received Cilician villages from him, including Combedefort (Cambedeford) and Heion (Ayun) which have not been identified.[53] By 1211 the Order held a castle in the foothills in the north of the Amanus Mountain range, Amuda (Adamodana) on the road to Anazarbus and Sis. Levon made an important grant to the brothers throughout the kingdom by exempting them from sales and purchase taxes on victuals, various goods and horses for their own use. It is possible that the Teutonic Grand Master, Hermon von Salza, who visited the region in 1212, resided in Cilicia for a period.[54] After Levon's death relationships remained close and Hetoum I, king of Cilician Armenia (1226–69), appears to have supported Frederick II against the barons in the Kingdom of Jerusalem. In January 1236 he gave the Teutonic Knights their second castle, Harunia (Haruniye). Hetoum also became a *confrater* and enhanced the relationship between the Order and the kingdom.

The armies of the Military Orders

The Military Order was a highly efficient institution for the organisation and training of fighting men. Its wealth ensured that its knights were well equipped. The monastic lifestyle was ideally suited to promote discipline and a high level of training. The outcome was that both the Templars and the Hospitallers gained a well-deserved reputation as the best-disciplined and bravest fighting element in the Crusading army. The organisation of the troops of the Military Orders was under the control of the Master, who was dependent on the Chapter in declaring war, arranging a truce, alienating land, taking over the defence of castles and appointing commanders and chief officers, but had sole responsibility for strategy.[55] The Marshal commanded the castellans and, in times of war, the Turcopolier (commander of the Turcopoles, an office held by a brother under the orders of the Master, first recorded in the Hospitaller Order in 1203) and the Admiral, and had command over all the knights and sergeants of the Order. He was in charge of discipline in the *auberge* (knights' residence).[56] He controlled the acquisition and distribution of military equipment for the knights and sergeants and horses for the knights.

The Marshalsy of the Hospital (and probably that of the Templars on which it was largely based) contained two sub-departments: the arsenal and the stables.[57] The arsenal stored, issued and repaired armour and weapons (except for crossbows, which were in a separate department known as the arbalestry which was under the control of the Grand Commander). The stables issued horses, replaced at royal expense horses that were killed or injured in battle, a practice known as *restor*, and probably supplied saddlery as well. The *Ordenbüch* (containing the statutes of the Teutonic Order) records the Marshal's responsibilities to include horses, mules, weapons, tents, the saddlery and the forge.[58]

The Rules of the two major Orders, which throw a good deal of light on conventual life in general, are remarkably reticent on the training of knights and sergeants. In the Hospitaller establishments the afternoon was generally given over to military exercises. Although we learn little from the contemporary statutes, later statutes in the Rule give us some information on this. According to these, on three afternoons a week the knight brothers were required to attend gymnastics, wrestling, drill exercises in arms and shooting with the arbalest.[59] To encourage the archers a prize was given for marksmanship every two months.[60] Much of the training probably took place within the castle walls and, in the case of urban centres, within or near the Order's compound. Thus al-Idrisi mentions the archery grounds outside the compound, which apparently reached the church at Gethsemane.[61]

The Rules are much more informative with regard to the arms and equipment used by the knights and sergeants.[62] Of particular value is the Rule of the Temple, which gives a detailed list of the knight's and sergeant's equipment. Statutes 138–41 (from the Hierarchial Statutes dating to around 1165) give a detailed list of items in the possession of knight brothers. These included three horses and one squire, and a fourth horse and second squire. A knight wore a hauberk (suit of chain mail), iron hose and mail shoes and had a shield. He wore a white surcoat over the armour and an arming jacket (a padded jerkin) under the armour, and he had a *chapeau de fer* (helmet). His arms included a sword, a lance and a Turkish mace. Other equipment included three knives (a dagger, a bread knife and a pocket knife), a caparison (cloth cover for a horse), two shirts, two pairs of breeches, two pairs of hose, a small belt, a jerkin with tails in the front and back, a fur jacket, a white mantle and in winter a second one with fur, a cope, a tunic, a leather belt, three pieces of bed linen (a mattress bag, a sheet and a light blanket), a rug (white, black or striped, to be used to cover the bed or his hauberk when he is riding), two small bags (one for his nightshirt and one for his surcoat and arming jacket), a leather or wire mesh bag for the hauberk, a cloth for eating, a washcloth, a rug for sifting barley, a blanket for his horse, a cauldron, a measuring bowl for barley, an axe and grinder, three saddle bags, two drinking cups, two flasks, a strap, a buckled girdle, a second girdle without a buckle, a horn bowl and spoon, a cloth cap, a felt hat, a tent and a tent peg.

A sergeant had the same, except for the equine equipment (he had no horses or squires), the tent and the cauldron. His surcoat was black with a red cross on the front and the back and his mantle was black or brown. He had a *chapeau de fer* and could have sleeveless chain mail, though without mail hose.[63]

Contemporary sources

The archive of the Order of the Hospitallers of St John is an invaluable source of information on the possessions of the Order. The *Cartulaire général de l'ordre des Hospitaliers de St. Jean de Jérusalem*, which was published by Joseph Delaville Le Roulx in four volumes from 1894 to 1906, is a mine of information on the possessions of the Hospitaller Order. Another useful source which throws much light on the workings of the Order of the Hospitallers is the Rule of the Hospitallers.[64] This is a collection of works beginning with the Rule of Raymond du Puy (1120–60), to which a series of compilations of statutes, judgements and customs were added by the subsequent Masters of the Order throughout the later twelfth century and the entire thirteenth century and into the early fourteenth. The information in this work covers most aspects of conventual life, including daily requirements in prayer and during campaigns, conduct within and outside the convent, food, dress, required equipment and the possession of property, finances, privileges and care of the sick in the hospital of Jerusalem and elsewhere, the holding of chapters and punishments for breaches of the Rule.

The archives of the Templars did not survive the persecution and suppression of the Order in the early fourteenth century, but information can be gained from other sources which include charters or other material relating to the Templars. The most valuable surviving contemporary source on the Templars is the Rule of the Temple; a compilation composed of six sections: the Primitive Rule, the Hierarchical Statutes, Penances, Conventual Life, the Holding of Ordinary Chapters, an additional section on Penances and a section entitled Reception into the Order.[65] The Primitive Rule was a Latin text drawn up following the Council of Troyes in 1129, which was later translated into French. It contains an introduction to the foundation of the Order and the Council of Troyes and discusses in broad terms the requirements and duties of brothers. The Hierarchical Statutes, which date to around 1165, discuss the hierarchy of the Order and other aspects of conventual life and of military matters. The section on penances describes the infringements which could result in expulsion from the Order, or the less drastic but none the less severe penalty of the temporary loss of the habit. The section entitled Conventual Life deals with the basic requirements concerning behaviour in the convent and during campaigns. The next section, the Holding of

Ordinary Chapters, relates to the appropriate sentences to be given to brothers who are accused of or who confess in chapter to breaches of the Rule. The final section, Reception into the Order, details the stages of the ceremony which a candidate underwent in order to be admitted to the Order.

A collection of documents based on the Cartulary of the Teutonic Order, the *Tabulae ordinis theutonici ex tabularii regii Berolinensis codice*, edited by Ernst Strehlke, was published in 1869.[66] A compilation of the statutes of the Order, known as the *Ordenbüch*, was published in 1890 and was translated into English in 1969.[67] A few fragments have survived from archives of the Leper Knights of St Lazarus.

Narrative accounts are another valuable contemporary source on the properties of the Military Orders. Travel accounts (*itineraria*) were written by pilgrims who passed through the Crusader states and visited the holy sites. They sometimes wrote detailed reports, which include descriptions of the urban possessions and castles of the Military Orders.[68] An important and unique source which records the reconstruction of the castle of Saphet by the Templars from 1240 is the short tract known as *De constructione castri Saphet*.[69] This text discusses why, when and how the building of the castle began, the nature of the water supply (always an important factor in castle planning), the nature of the construction, the qualities of the castle and its location.

Archaeological research of the Military Orders

The awakening of interest in the history of the Crusader period that occurred in the mid-nineteenth century has gone hand in hand with an interest in its monumental archaeological remains. A considerable amount of archaeological research has been carried out at sites associated with the Military Orders. Important early surveys were carried out by Emmanuel Guillaume Rey (1837–1916) and the Survey of Western Palestine headed by C. Conder and H. Kitchener. Rey made three expeditions to Syria between 1857 and 1864, and in 1871 published his *Études sur les monuments de l'architecture militaire des Croisés en Syrie et dans l'île de Chypre*.[70] The Survey of Western Palestine studied and recorded remains from a number of sites, including the major castles of Montfort, Chateau Pelerin ('Atlit), Toron (Tibnin), of which not very much survives, and Saphet.[71] These works are still useful, although the descriptions are often out of date and many sites that received only minor mention or no mention at all have been surveyed or excavated in more recent times.

In 1899 Conrad Schick made a detailed study of the remains of the vast Hospitaller complex in Jerusalem shortly before it was dismantled in 1905.[72] Subsequent sporadic work carried out over the years in this area has rarely been published. In 1926 a brief season of excavations was carried out by a team from the Metropolitan Museum of New York at the Teutonic castle of Montfort. This excavation, headed by Bashford Dean, was the subject of a small publication in 1927.[73] An updated survey carried out in 1984 was able to trace the position of the outer enceinte.[74] From 1927 to 1929 Paul Deschamps began to clear the village houses that had been built within the castle of Crac des Chevaliers in Syria, and in 1932/33 he headed a team that carried out restoration and conservation of the site. This work was published by Deschamps in 1934 in what Kennedy justifiably described as 'perhaps the finest account of the archaeology and history of a single medieval castle ever written'.[75] Deschamps also surveyed Beaufort Castle above the River Litani.[76]

The excavations of Chateau Pelerin ('Atlit), carried out by British archaeologist Cedric N. Johns on behalf of the Palestine Archaeological Museum, took place in a series of short annual seasons between 1930 and 1934. Johns excavated the castle and its faubourg and published the results in a series of informative papers in the *Quarterly of the Department of Antiquities of Palestine (QDAP)*.[77]

The Hospitaller castle of Belvoir, located above the Jordan Valley south of the Sea of Galilee, was surveyed and entirely excavated in the 1960s, but a full account of the excavations has never been published.[78] Here, as elsewhere, excavations revealed that the castle was of a far more complex and remarkable design than had been believed.[79] Though it was previously thought to be a typical basic enclosure castle with a central keep, it proved to be of a superbly compact design with two enclosure castles, one within the other, unique in the Latin East except for the smaller and later castle of Saranda Kolones in Paphos, western Cyprus.[80]

Since 1992 extensive excavations have been carried out at the Hospitaller castle of Bethgibelin.[81] The excavations have exposed the castle, the adjacent church and a series of outer fortifications, and showed that the defences were considerably more complex than they were previously believed to be. A short description of the castle and its components has recently been published.[82] It shows for the first time the intricate gate system leading from the outer fortifications to the inner castle. This system was perhaps the prototype for the more advanced gates at Belvoir and Crac des Chevaliers.

In 1993 excavations began at the Templar castle of Vadum Jacob; they have continued on a small scale ever since.[83] Here as well archaeology has revealed a very different structure from what had been believed prior to the excavations. In this case, not only was the form of the castle different but, of more consequence to the study of medieval castles, the excavations showed that the construction of the castle was never completed. Thus this site affords a unique opportunity to study castle construction methods.

Excavations of the Hospitaller castle of Belmont west of Jerusalem were carried out in the years 1986 to 1988.[84] The nearby rural Hospitaller courtyard building known as Aqua Bella has been partially restored by the National Parks Authority.[85] As in other projects carried out primarily in order to develop sites for tourism, little attention was paid to the archaeological evidence, publication was minimal and consequently much information has been lost. Surveys by the British School of Archaeology in Jerusalem (BSAJ) include that of Qalansuwa in the Sharon Plain, which was carried out in 1983 as part of a regional survey of medieval settlements in the Sharon Plain.[86] The Red Tower (Turris Rubea, Burj al-Ahmar) was excavated by Pringle in 1983 and a detailed excavation report was published in 1986.[87] The BSAJ carried out a survey of the Teutonic castle of Judyn in the western Galilee from 1990 to 1992.[88]

In urban sites the quality of recent work varies greatly. In Jerusalem sporadic small-scale excavations have revealed fragments of the buildings of the Military Orders. Excavations in the Hospitallers' Quarter have added nothing new to the detailed descriptions of Schick. Now and then fragments of this monumental complex have come to light. In 1999 the foundations of the central apse of the Church of St Mary Major in the Hospitallers' Quarter in Jerusalem were re-exposed during renovations carried out in a shop in a street in the Muristan south-west of St Mary Latin.[89] Because of the sensitivity of their location, the remains of the Templar headquarters on the Temple Mount have not been the subject of archaeological study apart from the work carried by R.W. Hamilton in the al-Aqsa Mosque,[90] although the numerous examples of architectural sculpture which may have once decorated the buildings of this complex have been examined by various art historians, notably Helmut Buschhausen, Jaroslav Folda and Zehava Jacoby.[91] The so-called 'Templar Wall', a barbican wall extending from the south-east corner of the Temple Mount in a south-westerly direction and providing a forward line of defence to the southern entrances to the Templar Quarter, was exposed during excavations in the Ophel in the early 1970s.[92]

Archaeological research in Akko (Acre) began during the period of the British mandatory government in Palestine. An examination of Frankish and Turkish structures and ruins, known as the Winter Report, was carried out in 1942.[93] Between 1958 and 1963 archaeological excavations were carried out in the Hospitallers' compound in the north of the Turkish city, exposing three vaulted halls (part of the so-called 'Knights' Halls' complex), a narrow passage and the refectory (known as the 'Crypt').[94] Intensive excavations in the city have been carried out continuously since 1992.[95] These have concentrated on the Hospitallers' compound, which was largely well-preserved beneath the late eighteenth-century citadel of the governor of Akko, al-Jazzar. Several additional sites relating to the Military Orders have been excavated in and around the walls of the town. They include the subterranean passage leading east from the Templar palace and part of the city walls which may have been held by the Hospitallers. A joint team from Haifa University and the Deutcher Orden recently carried out two seasons of excavations (1999 and 2000) on a site to the east of the Turkish fortifications of Akko, but within the walls of Frankish Acre which may have been the Quarter of the Teutonic Knights from the end of the twelfth century.[96]

Several seasons of excavations have been carried out in the Crusader town of Arsuf (ancient Apollonia) since 1977. Large-scale excavations commenced in the citadel in 1999.[97] These excavations have uncovered remains of the city fortifications and domestic buildings, as well as considerable remains of the remarkable castle in the north-west of the town.

In Cyprus Camile Enlart carried out a monumental survey of Frankish architecture which includes descriptions of the few buildings of the Military Orders on the island.[98] A.H.S. Megaw refers to the 'scant remains' of fortresses of the Military Orders in Cyprus.[99] These include the Templar castle of Gastria on the north side of Famagusta Bay, of which only the rock-cut ditch survives, fragmentary remains of the tower at Khirokitia and the rebuilt Hospitaller tower at Kolossi.[100]

Robert W. Edwards's extensive survey of the castles of Armenian Cilicia, published in 1987, includes a number of castles built or possessed by the Military Orders.[101] The most important of these are the Templar castles of Baghras, La Roche de Roissol (Chivlan) and Trapesac in their march in the Amanus Mountains; two Teutonic castles, Amuda and Harouniya north of the Cilician Plain; and Silifke of the Hospitallers in the West.

Part I

URBAN ADMINISTRATIVE CENTRES

Before they began to acquire and construct fortresses and rural establishments, the Templars, Hospitallers and the smaller Order of St Lazarus already held important urban properties in Jerusalem (Figure 2). They later expanded into other cities, Acre being the principal centre of their urban activities. The Hospitallers possessed property in Jerusalem and Acre long before they became a Military Order,[1] and the Order of St Lazarus had a leper hospital outside the northern wall of the Holy City. The Templars were established as a Military Order in Jerusalem with property on the Temple Mount and later acquired Quarters in Acre and possessions in other towns. The Teutonic Knights and the Knights of St Thomas of Acre, both Orders that were founded in Acre after the fall of Jerusalem in 1187, had their headquarters in the city. After the recovery of Jerusalem by treaty in 1229, the Teutonic Knights were granted property in Jerusalem which they held for the short period of Frankish rule until the final fall of the city in 1244.

Their vast resources and the important functions they fulfilled made the Military Orders an important, indeed an essential, element in Crusader urban society. They played a vital role in the economic and consequently the demographic revival of the cities, and they assumed roles in social welfare, urban politics and defence, as well as other aspects of social life.[2] Their presence, in particular the presence of the Hospitallers, was one of the major contributing factors in the revival of Jerusalem after the Crusader siege and capture of the city in 1099. This conquest had been followed by the slaughter and expulsion of the entire local non-Christian population. It was the Hospitaller Order, more than any other institution in the city, which induced the economic revival and resettlement of the city by providing for the needs of pilgrims and thereby enabled them to come to Jerusalem, to spend their money there and sometimes to remain in the city. They also encouraged and participated in an expanding commerce centred on pilgrimage, including the exchange of money and the establishment of workshops and specialised markets manufacturing and selling goods specifically for pilgrims.

The role played by the Military Orders in other cities was varied, but in some cases of considerable impact. They provided the citizens with hospices and hospitals and occasionally built fortifications and took an active part in the defence of several towns.[3] In some of these towns at certain times they took over the defence of whole sections of the walls, including gates, towers, barbicans and moats,[4] while in others their fortresses provided refuge for the citizens in times of invasion. In some cases entire towns came into their possession: in 1152 the Templars were granted the city of Gaza and around

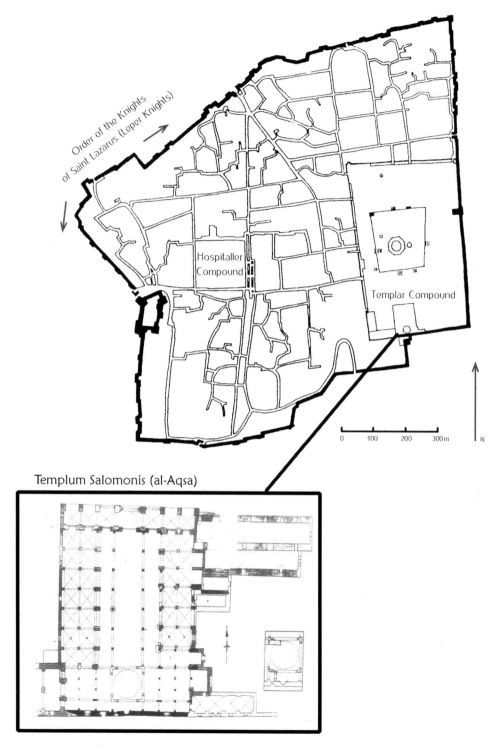

Order of the Knights
of Saint Lazarus (Leper Knights)

Hospitaller
Compound

Templar Compound

0   100   200   300m

N

Templum Salomonis (al-Aqsa)

Figure 2 Map of Crusader Jerusalem showing the Quarters of the Military Orders (inset:
Templum Salomonis).

the same time Tortosa also became a Templar possession, in *c.* 1260 the Hospitallers took over Arsuf in its entirety and in that year the Templars acquired Sidon. As a result of their experience and extensive connections, the Military Orders came to play an important role as advisers in matters of state and in the strategic and tactical planning of battles. They participated in war councils such as that which advocated the march on Hattin in 1187, the council held by Amaury II in 1197 which decided to attack Beirut, the council of 1210 which declined to renew the truce with Egypt, and a council discussing the refortification of Jerusalem held by Frederick II in 1229.[5] Their connections with the enemy also gave them an important role as mediators and treaty negotiators.[6] Naturally enough this activity also extended into local urban politics, in which they became both active participants and intermediaries in disputes between different factions in the Crusader cities. In the War of St Sabas, a violent conflict which broke out between the Italian communes in Acre in the mid-thirteenth century, the two major Orders took opposite sides, the Hospitallers supporting the Genoese camp while the Templars sided with the Venetians and Pisans. However, in the aftermath of the war they both became mediators, attempting to reconcile the opposing parties.[7] The Masters of the Hospital and the Temple had particular tasks in state and urban ceremonies; their special status in Jerusalem is reflected by the fact that they were given the privilege of holding the keys to the crown jewels.[8]

As organisations concerned with welfare, the Hospital of St John and the other hospitaller orders carried out the important task of providing care for the needy and the ill. They set up hospitals and hospices which could house hundreds of people. The Hospital of St John in Jerusalem provided medical care, though this was limited by the abilities of the medieval doctor. The Orders, however, did not have a monopoly on hospitals; most monastic establishments had an infirmary and there were also privately established hospitals. Raymond of St Gilles established a hospital for the poor (*hospitale pauperum*) on Mons Peregrinus in Tripoli and Count Bertrand, who followed Raymond as Count of Tripoli, gave rich endowments to this hospital.[9] Near Rafaniya, further to the north, Raymond and Bertrand established a similar endowment.[10] A hospital at Turbessel in the Principality of Edessa was annexed to the Church of St Romanus and was apparently endowed by Joscelin I de Courtenay and by Baldwin of Bourcq prior to his ascending to the throne of Jerusalem in 1118. On the other hand, the Military Orders' hospitals were large, well run and available to everyone, including the large numbers of poor and ill in the cities – and even, it would seem, Muslims and Jews.[11] In time the independent hospitals either disappeared or were absorbed into the Hospitaller network. On 28 December 1126 both of the establishments in the County of Tripoli were transferred to the Order of St John.[12] In 1134 Joscelin ceded the hospital at Turbessel to the Hospitallers; it no doubt ceased to function with the loss of the city to Zengi in 1144.

With regard to defence, the Military Orders played an important role in strengthening and defending the walls of several of the towns in the Latin East, including Jerusalem, Acre, Arsuf, Caesarea, Gaza, Jaffa, Sidon, Tortosa, Tripoli and Tyre. The Hospitallers helped to fortify Caesarea in 1218, and the Templars and Hospitallers possibly advised Louis IX about reconstructing its defences between March 1251 and May 1252.[13] The Hospitallers also appear to have been involved in the construction of the barbican (or a section of it) in Acre during the last decades of Crusader rule.[14] By that time the Military Orders were the only local organisations with the financial and human resources to carry out major works of construction.

1

THE URBAN QUARTERS OF
THE TEMPLARS

It is perhaps ironic that, like the Templar Order itself, the urban headquarters of the Templars have almost entirely disappeared. The irony lies in the fact that the destruction of the Templar buildings had nothing to do with the fate of the Order in the early fourteenth century.[1] The destruction of the Templar Quarter in Jerusalem was carried out by Saladin in 1187 as an act of purification of the Muslim holy site. As the Temple Mount was not returned to the Franks in 1229 when the treaty signed between the Egyptian Sultan al-Kamil and Frederick II gave them control over the rest of the city, the Templars never rebuilt their quarter in Jerusalem. In Acre substantial remains of the Templar Quarter survived the Mamluk destruction of 1291, but these were dismantled with the Turkish resettlement from the middle of the eighteenth century. The Bedouin governor Dahr al-Umar used the Templar palace as a source of building stone. It was almost completely demolished by 1752 and only minor fragments have survived the destruction of the last three centuries.[2] In addition, a rise in the level of the sea has inundated the area of the Templar palace.

The Templars' Quarter in Jerusalem

In 1220, after the Order was established, Baldwin II gave the Templars a wing in the royal palace (Templum Salomonis) on the southern end of the Temple Mount. According to William of Tyre: 'Since they had neither a church nor a fixed place of abode, the king granted them a temporary dwelling place in his own palace, on the north side of the Temple of the Lord.'[3] This might seem a remarkable act, and it would be difficult to find a precedent for a king parcelling out parts of his palace in this fashion, although William of Tyre did refer to this as a temporary grant. However, the king was perhaps not particularly satisfied with the royal residence in the Templum Salomonis (the al-Aqsa Mosque), which he himself had only recently occupied and which had certainly not been built to serve as a residence. It must have been rather uncomfortable, and, as I have suggested elsewhere, he may already have been contemplating a move to a more convenient location prior to the foundation of the Templar Order.[4]

For the first decade of its existence the Templar Order remained static in its development, numbering no more than nine brothers.[5] However, after the Council of Troyes in 1129, in which the Order received papal support, financial aid, grants and recruitment began in earnest and the Order entered a process of rapid expansion. It was probably around this time that Baldwin II, or perhaps King Fulk in the early years of his reign (1131–43), handed over the entire palace to the Templars and moved elsewhere.[6] The Order was now in possession of the entire southern part of the Temple Mount, and around the middle of the twelfth century began a programme of construction which, to judge from pilgrim accounts, was to transform the area entirely. Much of this construction must date from around the sixth decade of the twelfth century, as suggested by two facts. Firstly, there is the large corpus of Romanesque sculptural decoration which may have come from these buildings, which has been dated by art historians, on analogy with contemporary works from Apulia, to the second half of the twelfth century.[7] Unfortunately none of these pieces are *in situ* and consequently their source of origin remains unclear. More secure evidence is the fact that the Templar buildings, according to the German pilgrim John of Würzburg, were already largely standing at the time he described them in *c.* 1160 (or *c.* 1165) and the new church was under construction. His description of these buildings gives us a fairly good idea of the extent of the Templar construction works on the south side of the Temple Mount:

> On the right hand [after entering the western gate] towards the south is the palace which Solomon is said to have built, wherein is a wondrous stable of such size that it is able to contain more than two thousand horses or fifteen hundred camels. Close to this palace the Knights Templars have many spacious and connected buildings, and also the foundations of a new and large church which is not yet finished.[8]

A similar, but much more detailed description is given by another German pilgrim, Theoderich, writing around 1169 (or 1172):

> the palace of Solomon, which is oblong and supported by columns within like a church, and at the end is round like a sanctuary and covered by a great round dome so that, as I have said, it resembles a church. This building, with all its appurtenances, has passed into the hands of the Knights Templars, who dwell in it and in the other buildings connected with it, having many magazines of arms, clothing and food in it, and are ever on the watch to guard and protect the country. They have below them stables for horses built by King Solomon himself in the days of old, adjoining the palace, a wondrous and intricate building resting on piers and containing an endless complication of arches and vaults, which stable, we declare, according to our reckoning, could take in ten thousand horses and their grooms. No man could send an arrow from one end of their building to the other, either lengthways or crossways, at one shot with a Balearic bow. Above it abounds with rooms, solar chambers and buildings suitable for all manner of uses. Those who walk upon the roof of it find an abundance of gardens, courtyards, antechambers, vestibules, and rain-water cisterns; while down below it contains a wonderful number of baths, store-houses, granaries and magazines for the storage of wood and other needful provisions. On another side of the palace, that is to say, on the western side, the Templars have erected a new building. I could give measurements of its height, length and breadth of its cellars, refectories, staircase, and roof, rising with a high pitch, unlike the flat roofs of that country; but even if I did so my hearers would hardly be able to believe me. They have built a new cloister there

in addition to the old one which they had in another part of the building. Moreover, they are laying the foundation of a new church of wondrous size and workmanship in this place, by the side of the great court.[9]

Despite some obvious embellishments, particularly in Theoderich's account, these two sources are more informative about the Templar construction works than any other. We can conclude from these accounts that the Templars were investing heavily from the vast sums of money that were pouring into their coffers in the West in order to transform their headquarters in Jerusalem into an appropriately magnificent complex. According to the Jewish traveller Benjamin of Tudela, whose account of his visit to Jerusalem dates to about the same time as that of Theoderich (between 1166 and 1171), the Templar Quarter in Jerusalem housed some 300 knights who 'issue therefrom every day for military exercise'.[10] However, William of Tyre, writing not very much later, gave the same number as being that of the entire population of Templar knights in the kingdom.[11] Nonetheless, Benjamin of Tudela's account does give us an idea of the importance of this compound. The number of 300, if it has any basis in fact, may refer to the entire population of the quarter, including sergeants, squires, clerks and others, as well as knights.

The construction project on the Temple Mount was of a magnitude equal to and perhaps exceeding the other two great building projects of the time: the construction of the new Church of the Holy Sepulchre and the building of the hospital and convent of the Order of the Hospitallers of St John. However, of all the buildings constructed by the Templars only fragmentary remains have survived. When Saladin recovered the city in 1187 one of his first acts was to restore the Muslim shrines and 'purify' the Temple Mount. This apparently entailed removing all physical evidence of the Christian presence. This included not only the more obvious signs of Christian activity, such as the gold cross on the Templum Domini (Dome of the Rock) and the frescoes and inscriptions decorating its walls, but also the entire complex of conventual buildings of the Augustinian monks in the north and almost all of the Templar buildings in the south of the Temple Mount. According to the account of Imad ad-Din:

> When Saladin accepted the surrender of Jerusalem he ordered the *mihrab* to be uncovered, and issued a decisive command to that effect. The Templars had built a wall before it, reducing it to a granary and, it was said, a latrine, in their evil-minded hostility. East of the *qibla* they had built a big house and another church. Saladin had the two structures removed and unveiled the bridal face of the *mihrab*.[12]

From this description we can learn something more of the Templar works. To some extent, it tallies with Theoderich's description. The church 'East of the *qibla*' is probably that mentioned by both John of Würzburg and Theoderich; Charles Wilson recorded the remains of the apse of a church to the east of the al-Aqsa Mosque which would accord with Imad ad-Din's reference to it.[13] However, the 'big house' was probably the palace which Theoderich describes as being on the western side.[14]

The methodical removal of these buildings was so thorough that today very little archaeological evidence of them remains. If some of the numerous sculptural fragments scattered on and around the Temple Mount and incorporated in secondary use in mosques, fountains and other buildings originated in the Templar buildings, these would convey more than a hint at the remarkable quality of the work carried out here (Figure 3). These pieces have in the past been considered the produce of a great workshop labelled by some modern scholars the 'Temple Area Atelier',[15] although their origin in the Templar Quarter remains unsubstantiated. Because of religious sensitivities only limited archaeological exploration has been carried out on the Temple Mount and were it not for the detailed accounts of the two German pilgrims, as well as other contemporary visitors, we would have no idea of the extent of the Templar work in this area in the twelfth century. However, there are a few remains of Templar buildings which somehow survived Saladin's 'cleansing'. On the basis of these remains, and evidence from the sources, we can attempt to describe the quarter.

The Templum Salomonis (Figure 2 inset) remained the central and most prominent building in the Quarter. As noted above, probably in the third or fourth decade of the twelfth century the Templars gained control over the entire building, and there is evidence of quite extensive structural changes made at this time. Since, as we have noted, the Crusader kings apparently did not maintain the structure, it is likely that these changes date from the period of Templar possession, though some of them may have been made when Baldwin I first occupied the building and converted it into a royal residence in 1104. A study of the al-Aqsa Mosque carried out by R.W. Hamilton from 1938 to 1942, when the building was restored following the earthquake of 1937, has thrown considerable light on the Templar work. On the east side of the building, south of the transept, the Templars added 12 groin vaults in two ranges of six bays

Figure 3 Architectural sculpture on the Temple Mount area, Jerusalem (photograph by the author).

each.[16] The six southern bays in these aisles are somewhat different from the six to the north. They are of poorer construction and slightly larger (rectangular rather than nearly square), the piers are somewhat shorter and broader, and the transverse ribs have chamfered edges and spring from profiled brackets whereas those in the north are plainer and have no brackets.[17] The southern bays, which peak in a small round aperture, were apparently constructed earlier than the northern bays. They were originally open on the west, south and east but cut off on the north by a partition wall which was later removed, presumably when the six northern bays were added.[18] They are firmly dated to the twelfth century on the basis of their structural relationship to the adjacent eleventh-century construction, the typically Frankish style of the ribs and brackets, the diagonal tooling and the use of masons' marks.[19] Their Crusader use is evidenced by a graffito of a heraldic shield sketched on one of the piers in charcoal.[20] According to Hamilton, this southern part of the construction was a porch facing east.[21]

The construction of the six northern bays was the latest addition, post-dating not only the southern bays but the barrel-vaulted annexes to the east.[22] They were built as a closed construction to the north and east. The two small chambers in the south-east (now the Jami' al-Arba'in and the chamber containing the Mihrab Zakariyya) were also constructed in the Crusader period, probably by the Templars and perhaps to serve as chapels, although neither of them has an apse. The Mihrab Zakariyya is formed of panels and capitals of fine Templar workmanship.[23] High in the east wall is a wheel-window with six spokes set on a hexagonal base and miniature pillars with Romanesque Corinthian capitals supporting six arches.[24]

The three central bays of the mosque's western porch were constructed in the Crusader period.[25] In the thirteenth century they were restored by al-Malik al-Mu'azzam 'Isa (1217–18) using sculptural fragments from the Crusader period. Amongst other sculptural pieces found in secondary use in al-Aqsa are those used in the remarkable *dikka* and additional pieces used in the *qibla* wall, including panels and the *mihrab* capitals. These works are non-figural and therefore did not infringe the Muslim religious precepts against human representations. The pieces used in the *dikka* are in the graceful curved and spiralling 'Wet-Leaf Acanthus' style favoured by the Frankish artisans who produced most of the sculptural work found in this area.[26]

It is quite likely that the Templars found the Templum Salomonis no more convenient as a dwelling than did the Crusader kings, and it is likely that as soon as they were able to do so they built a more comfortable residence nearby. This was possibly Theoderich's 'new building' constructed to the west of the mosque with its cellars, refectories, staircases and high-pitched roof. As there is not a great deal of space to the west of the mosque, it is probable that the building now partly occupied by the so-called Women's Mosque (Jami' an-Nisa),[27] occasionally identified as the Templar armoury,[28] was in fact a part of this new palace. It is clearly a Crusader building; stonework on the north face of the wing that runs east–west between the south-west corner of the Temple Mount and the southern end of the mosque has typically Frankish diagonal tooling and many masons' marks.[29] The door at the centre of the north side is also Crusader, having masons' marks on all of the voussoirs. The southern and western façades seen from outside the Temple Mount were largely constructed of marginally drafted ashlars with pronounced bosses. On the southern wall there is a row of windows with flat lintels and relieving arches (ten in all). The hall has nine free-standing piers that support the vaulting of the two aisles, each consisting of ten groin-vaulted bays. The westernmost bays are slightly broader than the others and are cut off by a partition wall. Two piers stand at the east end of the building where it adjoins the al-Aqsa Mosque. If this building was indeed Theoderich's new palace it would have had additional storeys and the tall gabled roof that he described, and may perhaps have been higher than the mosque.

The Templars' massive building programme included the construction of a new church. Both John of Würzburg and Theoderich mention the foundations of a large new church, which was not completed at the time of their writing (the 1160s) but perhaps was by the time of the Ayyubid conquest in 1187. Imad ad-Din, apparently referring to this church, makes no mention of the fact that it was incomplete but merely notes that Saladin had it removed.[30] Theoderich refers to this church as being of remarkable size and workmanship.[31] Possibly some of the fine examples of sculpture found on the Temple Mount came from this church.

The locations of the brothers' dormitory and refectory, and their service buildings, are not mentioned with any precision in the written accounts and are not known from surviving buildings or archaeological remains. A hint at their general location is given by Ibn al-Athir: 'The Templars had built their living-quarters against al-Aqsa, with storerooms and latrines and other necessary offices, taking up part of the area of al-Aqsa',[32] but this does not tell us whether these buildings were on the east or west of the Templum Salomonis. However, as it appears that the church built by the Templars was on the east, it is quite likely that the Templars had constructed on that side a typical monastic complex with church, dormitory, latrines, kitchen, refectory and other elements located around a cloister. As previously noted, according to Theoderich the Templars built 'a new cloister in addition to the old one which they had in another part of the building'.[33] This seems to suggest that there was a cloister on either side of the Templum Salomonis. The present square to the west of the al-Aqsa Mosque, which is bounded on its east by the mosque itself, on its west and south by the present Islamic Museum and on the eastern continuation of the south side by the 'Women's Mosque', a Crusader structure, certainly constitutes one of the two cloisters. The other, Theoderich's 'new cloister', would most likely have been located east of the mosque, an area in which there are no constructions above ground today.

Theoderich's account of the Templar compound mentions magazines for the storage of wood and other provisions.[34] It is probable that a group of three barrel-vaulted annexes attached to the northern half of the east side of the al-Aqsa Mosque served for storage. These vaults survived intact until 1937, when they were dismantled during repairs made to the mosque after an earthquake.[35] The three vaults varied in size. The northern vault was 45 metres long (Hamilton believed that it was originally considerably longer, extending west into the present area of the eastern aisles of the mosque) and 8 metres wide (internally).[36] As these were barrel vaults, the walls were quite massive; the northern wall was 2.5 metres thick and the southern wall 2.8 metres thick. There was a door on the northern wall near its west end (i.e. near where it joined the porch of the mosque) and six embrasures, inwardly splayed with slightly pointed arches. An external staircase on the north wall led up to a door halfway up the wall from which one could reach another level of the store.[37] The middle vault was 37 metres long and 7 metres wide internally. It had two windows in the south wall and three in the north wall between it and the northern vault. A broad opening (6.5 metres wide) led into the northern vault opposite the latter's north door. The small southern vault was only *c.* 10.2 metres long and *c.* 5.3 metres wide. These vaults were constructed from a combination of well-cut, smoothly tooled ashlars (several of which had masons' marks) for the piers, window and door frames, and roughly shaped fieldstone for the walls. The lower two courses of the walls were also built from well-cut ashlars. The vaulting was of rubble and had cylindrical shafts with square-shaped lower openings in the crown of the vault.

Another reference by Theoderich is to baths.[38] The bathhouse was a common establishment in Crusader cities and there were bathhouses in both of the Hospitaller compounds in Jerusalem and Acre. We should not be surprised to find bathhouses in sites occupied by the Military Orders. The Rules of the Orders are not opposed to the brothers attending baths, although the Rule of the Hospital does state that they should not go 'except of necessity'.[39] There are bathhouses in some of the larger castles of the Military Orders such as the Hospitaller castle of Belvoir and Templar Chateau Pelerin. The ancient water supply system that had carried water to the Temple Mount was still at least partly in use in the Middle Ages. A conduit carrying water from Artas, south of Bethlehem, was still in working condition. It entered the city walls near the Tanners' Gate and extended adjacent to and occasionally beneath the buildings at the bottom of the eastern side of Mount Zion until it reached the bridge on which Temple Street crossed the Tyropoeon Valley onto the Temple Mount.

One of the surviving structures on the Temple Mount which was used by the Templars is the large subterranean vaulted structure known since medieval times as Solomon's Stables. On the twelfth-century Cambrai Map this building is shown in its correct location in the south of the Temple Mount, where it is labelled 'Stabuli Salomonis'.[40] The vaulted halls probably originated in the Herodian expansion of the Temple Mount in the first century BC. They were apparently intended to raise and level the podium without creating too great a pressure on the enclosure walls. The vaults possibly underwent additional construction or reconstruction in the Byzantine period and they were reconstructed again in the Middle Ages, perhaps in the Fatimid period. Certainly they do not appear to be Frankish work, neither in the round form of the barrel vaults nor in the vault construction of small squared stones with closely placed putlog holes, though some stones in the structure have Frankish tooling.

The structure comprises 13 rows of elongated barrel vaults, 9 to 10 metres high and of varying length (from 56 metres long in the eastern aisles to 17.6 metres in the western aisles) and width (between 3.5 metres for the narrowest span to 7.4 for the widest). They are supported on 12 rows of piers (88 piers in all) and cover an area of roughly 4,500 square metres. Rectangular putlog holes are placed at close intervals along either side of the vaults at the level of the vault spring. The piers are 1.2 metres thick and are constructed of large ashlars, many of which are Herodian marginally dressed stones in secondary use. The floor level is *c.* 12.5 metres below the surface of the Temple Mount and slopes down slightly from west to east. In 1891 the Muslim authorities levelled the floor, raising the eastern part and in the process burying the interior of the Single Gate and a number of mangers as well as the holes drilled in the corners of some of the piers to tie animals.[41] These holes and mangers are evidence of the medieval use of the building.

When he visited Jerusalem Benjamin of Tudela was duly impressed by the stables, which he referred to as: 'forming a very substantial structure, composed of large stones, and the like of it is not to be seen anywhere in the world'.[42] As noted above, Theoderich was duly impressed by its proportions.[43] According to John of Würzburg the stables housed more than 2,000 horses and 1,500 camels, a high estimate but closer to reality than Theoderich's 10,000 horses together with their grooms.[44] Pierotti, visiting the structure in the mid-nineteenth century, noted splayed loopholes in the south and east walls and iron rings fastened to the masonry.[45]

The importance of horses to an order of mounted knights is obvious. In one source there is a suggestion that the founding of the Templar Order was associated with the protection of horses. According to Walter Map, when the Burgundian knight Paganus was on pilgrimage in Jerusalem, he undertook the defence of a horse pool near the city[46] which was under attack by the Saracens, and he founded the Templar Order to carry on the work.[47] The reference to camels by John of Würzburg is interesting. They were probably mainly used as pack animals and perhaps were also used in battle by Turcopoles.[48]

Other possible evidence for Templar activity on the Temple Mount may have been exposed in excavations carried out in 1891 adjacent to the inner portal of the Golden Gate (Porta Aurea), where a large number of stone-lined graves were uncovered, aligned east–west and covered with stone slabs.[49] This cemetery, possibly used for burial of Templar brothers, may have included the tomb of Frederick, Advocate of Regensburg, who, according to Otto, Bishop of Freising, was buried near the Templum Domini at Easter 1148 after his death during the Second Crusade.[50] According to al-Idrisi there were archery grounds outside the Temple Mount extending down to the area of Gethsemane.[51]

Although it was located above the city on the Temple Mount and surrounded by the ancient walls of the Temple enclosure, the Templar Quarter suffered from a certain vulnerability on the south, where there were two gates giving access directly into their complex: the so-called Single Gate near the eastern end of the southern wall, which gave access into the subterranean Stabuli Salomonis, and the Double Gate, through which it was possible to enter the lower level of the Templum Salomonis. In order to protect this approach and defend these entrances, the Templars built a barbican or forewall, on the sloping hill outside the southern wall of the Temple Mount, the area known as the Ophel. This barbican, which is sometimes referred to as the Templar Wall, ran from the south-east corner of the Temple Mount across the slope in a south-westerly direction. It was obviously the intention of the Templars that this barbican would improve the defence of the gate area and enable a better control of the access to both the Double Gate and the Single Gate, further to the east. Theoderich is the only medieval source that refers to this defensive work. He writes:

> one goes southwards from this church or from the angle of the city itself, down the sloping side of the hill, along the outwork which the Templars have built to protect their houses and cloister . . .[52]

From his reference we know that this defensive work was in use by 1169, although it could have been built considerably earlier. Remains of the wall were exposed during excavations in the Ophel carried out by Benjamin Mazar during the 1970s. Unfortunately, since they were not recorded and were subsequently dismantled, the only surviving record is in photographs taken prior to and during the excavations. It was a fairly substantial wall, 2.8 metres thick. On a photograph taken by the German air force (Squadron 303) in 1917, the wall can clearly be seen extending from just east of the south-east corner of the Temple Mount. It runs first at a slight angle and then at a sharper angle towards the south-west, eventually turning west and seemingly reaching the line of the city wall which runs south from the Double Gate (i.e. a total distance of nearly 200 metres).[53] The section exposed in the excavations was only about 20 metres, the rest, according to Mazar, having already been destroyed.[54]

The Double Gate was accessed through a gate tower complex which the Templars used and expanded.[55] It was constructed against the southern wall of the Temple Mount directly below the al-Aqsa Mosque. Only the western portal of the Double Gate was in use at this time, the eastern portal being partly outside the new gatehouse and blocked. The gate tower is a confusing mixture of medieval masonry, including pre-Crusader and later construction but also incorporating Crusader work.[56] Schick published a plan showing a gate on the western side of the complex close to the southern wall of the Temple Mount. Through this gate one entered, via a passage running east, a large north–south chamber formed of three groin-vaulted bays. Three arched openings on the east wall of this chamber gave onto the area before the open portal of the Double Gate. At some stage these openings were blocked by a thin wall and at that time the only access would have been via a gate in the eastern wall of the eastern tower and from there through the Double Gate into the Templum Salomonis.[57]

The pointed-arched Single Gate, which is now blocked, can be identified as Frankish work by the use of the typical Frankish diagonal tooling on all of the stones of the door frame.[58] This gate was essential as a direct access to the stables. Pierotti suggests that it may also have been intended as a postern gate for sorties, but this could only have been the case prior to the construction of the above-mentioned outworks.[59]

Architectural sculpture from the Templar Quarter in Jerusalem

A sculptural workshop may have been active on the Temple Mount preparing sculptural works for the huge building project carried out by the Templars in their quarter around the middle of the twelfth century.[60] If such a workshop existed it also would have supplied sculptural pieces for other buildings in Jerusalem and its vicinity and even further afield.[61] There are no known archaeological remains representing the site of a workshop here and, at present, no way of knowing if and exactly where it would have been located, although we can assume that if it did exist it would have been in the southern part of the Temple Mount, near to or within the complex of new buildings constructed by the Templars, possibly in the area to the east of the Templum Salomonis where there was more open space and where it would have been convenient but somewhat less obtrusive.

In opposition to the existence of a Templar workshop, some art historians have dated these sculptural works to the late twelfth century and, mainly, to the thirteenth, on a stylistic basis.[62] If so these works could not have come from a Templar workshop in Jerusalem as the Templars never returned to the Temple Mount after 1187. According to Pringle they probably in fact date earlier, but he none the less opposes the idea of a Templar workshop, noting that virtually all of the works found on or around the Temple Mount are in secondary use and were clearly placed in their present locations by the Ayyubids and Mamluks.[63] While this is certainly true I would not entirely dismiss the existence of such a workshop. Most of these pieces clearly originated in a single atelier and would seem to date to a limited period rather than over much of the twelfth century. This, and the high quality of the pieces, suggests that they were produced for one of the major building projects carried out in the twelfth century rather than for various buildings throughout the city. The great Templar construction programme on the Temple Mount, which is described in *itineraria* of the 1160s, would then seem a likely source for these works. After Saladin 'purified' the Muslim holy places in 1187 by destroying the Frankish buildings, both he and later builders may well have used the conveniently located pieces from these structures to decorate their new buildings on and around the Temple Mount.

Inscriptions from the Templar Quarter in Jerusalem

Some interesting epigraphic evidence found in the Templar Quarter has been published. Two fragmentary inscriptions relating to the Templars were found during the restorations carried out in the al-Aqsa Mosque between 1938 and 1942. They are on two fragments of limestone and may have originated in the Templar Quarter. They were removed from the mosque during the renovations and are now located outside the Islamic Museum to the west of the mosque. Squeezes were taken of the two inscriptions, and a note recording their provenance in the mosque is preserved in the records at the Rockefeller Museum. These inscriptions have been published by de Sandoli and more recently by Pringle,[64] who established that these fragments probably come from at least three blocks of stone. One is from the first block (a space of 15 cm on the left side of the inscription suggests this). Diagonal tooling on the inscribed face of the stone is typical of the twelfth century. This fragment reads:

> .....]CTATOR : D[
> .....IH]C : XPO : Q(V)I[
> ....]M[:]WILL(ELMV)M : ERAT : T[
> MILITIA : TE(M)PLI : SIT : SE(M)[PER

The second fragment, possibly from the second stone in the sequence, reads:

>]T : EI : MIS[
>]CLAVDIT[:
>]MOTO : B(E)N(E) : [
>]THERA : LET[

Of the third stone no fragment survives, but its existence is suggested by the relatively straight right-hand edge of the second fragment, which also bears traces of mortar. The incomplete state of these inscriptions permits only a very limited reading. Pringle suggests that the text begins with '*O onlooker*' and '*to him/her/it*'; that the second line reads '*by/through/from Jesus Christ*', and '*he/she/it closes*'; the third line includes the name '*William*' or alternatively '*of the towns*' and perhaps, on very slim evidence, '*earthquake*' or alternatively '*at the noted time*'; and the fourth reads '*may the Knighthood of the Temple always be . . .*'

There is no way of knowing the source of these inscriptions and, in their fragmentary condition, we cannot even conjecture on the significance of the text.[65]

Coin hoard and seals found adjacent to the Templar Quarter

A hoard of at least 77 silver coins (76 from Chartres-Blois and one Islamic coin), a lead seal or bulla of Pope Alexander III (1159–81) and a bulla of Amaury, Latin Patriarch of Antioch (1142–94) were found in excavations carried out between 1968 and 1976 in the area to the south of the al-Aqsa Mosque.[66] The hoard was discovered in a channel in the courtyard of the easternmost of the group of Umayyad palaces which occupied the area to the south of the Temple Mount.[67] The papal and patriarchal seals were found 37.5 metres to the east in a room of Crusader date built on the south side of the tower outside the Double Gate. Of the 41 papal seals sent to Jerusalem by Pope Alexander III, more than half were addressed to the Templar Order, thus the example found here most likely originated in the Templar archives. These finds probably date from the second half of the twelfth century.

The Templars' Quarters in Acre

The Templars possessed at least three properties in Acre (Figure 4): the quarter with the palace on the coast in the south-west of the city, a property located outside the old northern wall of the city north of the Hospitallers' Quarter which appears on the medieval maps as the Templars' Quarter or Tower (Burgus Templi), and another property in Montmusard in the north-east of the suburb marked on the maps as the Templars' Stables (Bovaria Templi).[68] In addition they had custody of a section of the wall of Montmusard.

As the identifiable remains of the quarter are not very extensive, there is little that we can say with regard to its streets, squares and passages. However, there is one exception. An underground vaulted passage discovered by chance in 1994 was subsequently partially cleared and opened to the public in 1999. It led from the Templars' palace for a distance of about 350 metres under the Pisan Quarter in the direction of the port and to another northern exit. This passage is an extended, slightly pointed barrel vault, partly cut in the rock and partly constructed of well-cut and joined ashlars.[69] About 50 metres east of the present opening the passage divides into two smaller vaults, both of which continue east towards the port.

Just prior to this junction there is a section of the vault that is considerably larger than the passage leading to it and the two passages leading from it. Above this section to its east is an upper storey, a barrel-vaulted room in the northern wall in which are a door and two arched windows, one either side of the door. The walls of this room contain numerous iron pins which seem to have originally held a stone cladding which has not survived. From this room a staircase, now almost completely destroyed, descended into the passage below. Some kind of gate or grille which could cut the passage off appears to have been located here. This upper level was probably occupied by a guard who controlled movement in the passage below. The importance of these subterranean passages must have been considerable. As long as they were secure the Templars could pass freely from their quarter to the harbour, an ability which, in the thirteenth century, would have been of great importance. It is true that in the internecine dispute between the communes known as the War of St Sabas the Templars sided with the Venetians and the Pisans and would probably not have encountered any exceptional difficulty passing through the Pisan Quarter, which lay between their

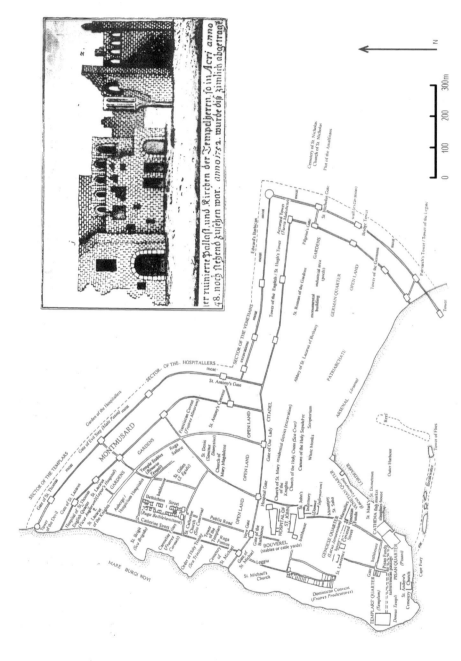

Figure 4 Map of Frankish Acre (drawn by Masha Caplan) (inset: ruins of the Templar Palace in Acre, drawn by Ladislaus Mayr in 1752).

quarter and the port. All the same, problems could arise and factions could change sides (indeed the Pisans did so, having originally supported Genoa against Venice). Access to the port was crucial and free passage to and from it made the underground route desirable. Later, as the territory held by the Crusaders shrank in the face of Mamluk conquests, this need became even greater. As the hinterland was lost to them, the Templars, like others in the disintegrating kingdom, came to rely to a greater extent on supplies transported from the West and arriving by their own ships at the port. Like the Hospitallers, they maintained a regular shipping service between Italy and the Kingdom of Jerusalem.[70]

It is generally accepted today that the Templar palace was located on the shore in the south-west of the city. This area is now under water, due on the one hand to its complete destruction and on the other to a rise of about 1.5 metres in the sea level since the Crusader period. Even in the Crusader period part of it was exposed to the elements.[71] Nothing survives of this remarkable building today except for some disappointing fragments which have been recorded in a recent survey.[72] Unfortunately, these are of virtually no use to us in our understanding of this complex. All that has survived of what was one of the most important and monumental structures in Frankish Acre is a section of a single wall, 50 metres long and 1.5 metres wide, preserved to a height of 70 cm. It runs roughly east–west across the southern part of the hewn sandstone shelf on which the Templar palace stood. It was built of ashlar stretchers (30 by 30 by 60 cm) laid in a foundation trench cut into the bedrock. Additional fragmentary walls on and near the edge of the sandstone shelf were constructed of headers and contain on their upper faces pieces of oxidised iron covered with a bonding agent, possibly remains of iron pins used to join the stones, an ancient method adopted by the Franks in certain structures.[73]

As to the appearance of the palace, although it has not survived and the attempts to represent it on maps of the thirteenth and fourteenth centuries are of little real value, there is an illustration made by Ladislaus Mayr in 1752 which, if not very detailed or accurate, at least gives us some idea of the appearance of this important structure (Figure 4, inset).[74] According to the legend beneath the illustration, it shows the ruins of the palace and church of the Templars in Acre in 1748, noting that it was completely demolished by 1752. This was at the time when the Bedouin Dahr al-Umar had begun to rebuild the town and stones taken from the Templar palace, together with many other Crusader remains, were used in the construction of the defences and buildings of Turkish Akko. In the drawing the palace appears as a stone structure of at least two, probably three, storeys with round-arched doorways and pointed-arched windows. A late thirteenth-century description of the palace has survived. The Master of the Temple, William de Beaujeu (1273–91), who was a cousin and supporter of Charles of Anjou, described the Templar compound as one of the strongest and most impressive buildings in Acre. William de Beaujeu's description, as recorded by his secretary, the so-called Templar of Tyre, presents it as a remarkable structure built like a castle with a tower which had four corner turrets on each of which was an enormous gilded lion *passant*.[75] The Master of the Templar Order was housed in a palace, apparently a separate building nearby, opposite the church and bell-tower of the nunnery of St Anne near the Pisan Quarter. The Templars had another old tower located on the shore which according to the Templar of Tyre had been built by Saladin in the previous century; here, according to this source, the Templars kept their treasury.

The strength of the Templar compound was also commented on by the fourteenth-century German pilgrim, Ludolf of Suchem.[76] On 18 May 1291, according to a contemporary chronicler from St Peter's Erfurt, 7,000 people fled there and held out for about twelve days after the capture of the city.[77] This was possible because, in the words of the German chronicler, 'it was located in a strong part of the city, overlooking the sea shore, and was surrounded by good walls'.[78] The castle was still standing when the entire city inside the walls had been destroyed; Ludolf of Suchem describes the Templars themselves as causing the great tower to collapse onto the mines dug by the Muslims, into which they had fled when the Templars got the upper hand.[79] Finally, however, the Templars agreed to abandon the castle.

Many pilgrims visited the Templars' church in their Quarter in Acre. Probably this was mainly due to the fact that it contained an important relic, a cross made, according to tradition, from a trough in which Christ bathed and which in times of bad weather was carried in procession through the streets of the city.[80] The only information that we have for the appearance of the church is once again the illustration of 1752. It appears to the right of the palace and, although the drawing is rather primitive and probably not very accurate, we can extract some information from it. A row of pointed windows, possibly the clerestory, can be made out quite high in the wall, and a small external pulpit is visible. One can also see, to judge from what appears to be a small minaret to the right, that by the eighteenth century the church had been converted into a mosque.

One of the Templars' pieces of real estate in the northern faubourg of Montmusard was the Templars' Stables (Bovaria Templi), located east of the Hospitallers' property and encroaching on what were probably open fields on the northern outskirts of Montmusard near the walls. This area is now buried under the houses of modern Akko. Their other property was the Burgus Templi, located in the south-west of the faubourg adjacent to the old northern city wall. The name 'Burgus Templi' could be interpreted as meaning either Templar Quarter or Templar fortress. Unfortunately, the nature of this property will probably always remain a mystery, as nothing in this area could have survived the excavation of the nineteenth-century moat. In addition to their properties in Acre, the Templars controlled a section of the city wall. On Marino Sanudo's map the north-western part of the defences of Montmusard is labelled as the Custodia Templi (Custody of the Templars), and the Templar of Tyre described this section as running 'from the sea to the Gate of St Lazarus'.[81] This section of the defences was guarded by the Templars; they may also have been responsible for its construction and maintenance.

The Templar faubourg in Chateau Pelerin

The faubourg at Chateau Pelerin ('Atlit), an example of a civilian settlement that developed in the shadow of a castle, was referred to by Prawer as 'the nearest the Crusaders came to founding new cities' (Figure 5).[82] The small size of this settlement (the faubourg within its walls covered an area of roughly 200 by 600 metres) would hardly justify its definition as an urban settlement. However, population and size are not the only parameters for categorising a settlement as urban, and indeed are of less importance than the presence of typically urban institutions. From the presence of a court of the burgesses in Chateau Pelerin, and consequently of the burgesses

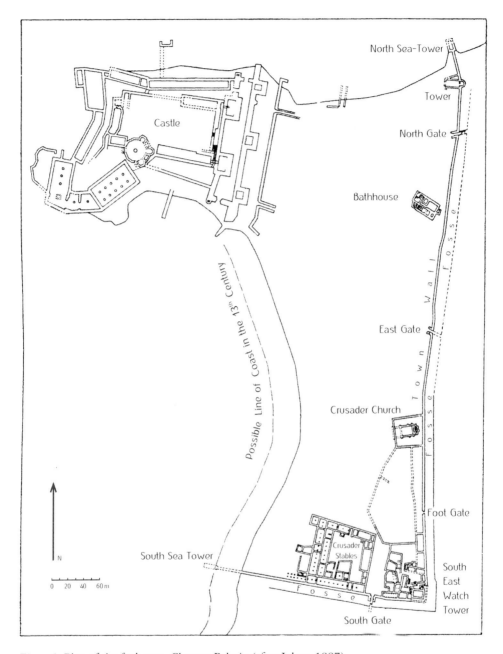

Figure 5 Plan of the faubourg, Chateau Pelerin (after Johns, 1997).

themselves, we can assume that this settlement had a permanent market. It also had fortifications, some sort of limited docking facilities, a bathhouse and a parish church. Although we know nothing about its inhabitants, there is no difficulty in regarding the settlement as a Templar establishment. The residents must have been dependants of the Order, servants, craftsmen and traders occupying Templar land, paying rents and tithes to the Order and providing it with services.

The town's fortifications and the south-east tower were excavated by Johns in 1930–31.[83] The tower which stood at the south-east corner of the faubourg was probably not as old as the tower known as le Destroit, which stood on the sandstone ridge to the east of the town and which was dismantled in 1217/18. Although it was similar in plan to le Destroit, the south-east tower probably post-dates the great fortress of Chateau Pelerin. No mention was made of it in the contemporary sources at the time of the construction of the fortress. Most likely it was built as a watch-tower at the outskirts of the faubourg as the latter developed in the thirteenth century. Eventually the settlement was also defended by a moat and wall with additional towers and gates. Johns suggests that the south-east corner tower served as the point from which these defences were drawn up when the need for them arose.[84] These defences were the subject of archaeological excavations carried out by Johns in 1930/31.[85] They had at least three other towers: one on the western shore at the end of the southern wall, one on the northern shore at the end of the eastern wall and an apsidal tower about 40 metres south of the latter. Of the two towers on the shore, Johns wrote that these were 'built far enough into the sea to make it difficult for an enemy to wade round'.[86] However, he did not take into consideration the rise in the sea level since the thirteenth century, which is considered to be somewhat over 1 metre, meaning that these towers were, in fact, on dry land in the thirteenth century.[87] Though the tower at the west end of the southern wall has been largely destroyed through erosion, the north tower, which was probably similar to it, has survived in somewhat better condition. This was an elongated, barrel-vaulted structure with a single entrance in its south wall against the inner side of the faubourg wall.[88] It had two windows in its east wall and apparently one on the west (the north wall has not survived). The roof or an upper floor was reached by stairs in the thickness of the east wall at its south end. The tower was constructed from large ashlars in courses 75 cm high at the base and decreasing higher up. The lower three courses had a batter which extended along the faubourg wall to the south. The few remaining stones of the south-west tower were held together by iron pins.

The apsidal tower in the east wall of the faubourg extended to the west in an elongated rectangular room which Johns believes was contemporary with the wall.[89] It contained a domed brick oven in the south-east corner and may have served additional functions apart from its military one. Another tower was located some distance to the south of the faubourg. It was isolated from the wall but was surrounded by its own moat. It may have been built at the same time as the south-east tower.

The moat of the faubourg was 10 metres wide throughout its length. The scarp and counterscarp were partly cut into the sandstone and partly constructed, the former with well-squared marginally dressed limestone ashlars, the latter using a dry-stone wall of fieldstones of varying size.[90] Four gates gave access into the faubourg, three in the east wall and one in the south wall near the south-east corner. The northern gate in the east wall (C in Johns) was 3 metres wide and was clearly intended for vehicular traffic, as were the central gate in the east wall (E) and the gate in the south wall (M). Gates C and E had side walls forming short corridors extending into the town for just over 6 metres. These walls probably supported barrel vaults that formed internal gate-houses. In Gate E there were arrow embrasures in the side walls, just in front of the doors. There were no embrasures in the side walls of the other main gates (C and M); Johns suggests that these gates may have been protected by machicolation, although he found no archaeological evidence for this. The south gate, Gate M, had an external corridor, possibly also vaulted, extending about half way across the moat. This effectively narrowed the moat at the gate entrance and allowed a wooden bridge, no doubt a drawbridge, to span the remaining 5.5 metres, supported on a wall at the half-way point. This gate had a portcullis about half way between the outer entrance and the doors (each of the other vaulted gates may also have had a portcullis). The doors of Gate M were bolted by a drawbar, apparently placed not in the usual position directly against the door but at some distance back and therefore seemingly resting against a second bar (*barre à fléau*) which pivoted on the centre of one of the door leaves. Inside the wall on the northern side of Gate E were two guardrooms. Gate H, southernmost on the east wall, was approached, unlike the others, from the floor of the moat. It was smaller than the others (*c.* 2.5 metres wide) and was identified by Johns as a foot-gate. It was locked by two drawbars.

The parish church was located in the south-east of the faubourg, close to the town walls. It was never completed, suggesting that construction had begun not long before 1265 when the faubourg was abandoned after being sacked by Baybars. This was a single-aisled Gothic structure, in design not unlike St George of the Greeks in Famagusta. It has been described in detail by Johns and more recently by Pringle.[91] It had a seven-sided choir and sanctuary to the east. The apse and single bay were both rib-vaulted. A second bay to the west may have been planned but was never constructed.[92] Single colonnettes in the apse and triple clusters of colonnettes in the bay supported the ribs of the vaulting. The apse apparently had lancet windows in each of its three eastern sides and on either side of the main bay.

Among the finds from the parish church, a hoard of 18 coins, nearly all of early thirteenth-century date, was recovered in 1934. These include four Amaury deniers, four from Damietta, one from Poitou, one from Dijon, one 'Star' denier from Tripoli and seven from Cyprus.[93]

The bathhouse excavated in the north-eastern part of the faubourg was restored following its excavation.[94] It was originally a dwelling house which was converted to serve as a bathhouse. An entrance was opened in the north wall of the house, which gave into a small groin-vaulted vestibule, leading to a larger groin-vaulted hall on its east side. This was the dressing room, in the centre of which stood a basin holding cold water. Around three sides were wide plastered benches. From the south-west corner of this room, a corridor led along the south side of the entrance chamber to the south wing of the bathhouse. This contained three small rooms: the cool room to the west, with the hot room built over the hypocaust to its east and beyond that the furnace. The floor of the hot room was paved with marble scraps laid in lime mortar. Ceramic vent pipes in the far corners of the hot and warm rooms forced a draught from the furnace. The furnace was in the east and the stoke hole was outside the east end. Water was supplied to the bathhouse by a covered conduit running from some unknown source and reaching it from the west. The layout of this bathhouse is similar to that of a Muslim *hammam* in that the largest room in the complex is the dressing room, whereas in a classical bathhouse the largest room is generally the *caldarium* (hot room).

Coins recovered from the bathhouse include one Amaury denier, two from Damietta, one Crusader imitative dirhem, one Dijon denier, a royal denier tournois of Phillip II (1180–1223), six Tripoli 'Star' deniers, one Cypriot denier and an Ayyubid fals.[95]

We have mentioned the brick-built oven in the room extending behind the apsidal tower on the faubourg wall. Two similar domed bread ovens, one built of stone and the other of brick, were located in a room constructed on the west side of the bathhouse. This room had a wooden roof supported on arches. On the south was a second small room containing a basalt rotary mill. Johns suggests that this bakery may have shared the heat and fuel supply of the bathhouse.[96] These bakeries would have supplied the needs of the settlers in the faubourg. In the castle there were additional ovens located at the southern end of the west hall, against the east wall of the kitchen (Figure 43).

In 1936 Johns referred to the stables in the faubourg as being intended for horses. However, in a later publication in 1947 he suggested that the stables excavated in the south of the faubourg were intended for cattle rather than horses, the latter being of too great a value to house outside the castle walls.[97] This stable was a large courtyard structure (84 metres n. by *c.* 100 metres s. by 70 metres e. by 77 metres w.) which had stabling for over two hundred animals. Roofed ranges supported on square beams (except in the central part of the north range and the western part of the south range, where the roof was supported on arches) surrounded the complex on three sides (north, west and south). In the west were two parallel ranges.

The walls of the stable buildings were constructed using masonry of sandstone quarried on the site. Johns describes it as: 'squared rubble in courses from 25 to 45 cm. backed with small un-squared rubble, with ashlar dressings at the doors and windows and perhaps at the quoins, also of sandstone'.[98] Mud-mortar was used except for the ashlars, which were bedded in hard lime mortar. The chambers were ventilated and lit by windows, and in the shared wall of the two western halls there were small loopholes at the level of the animals' heads. The outer windows had iron grilles (indicated by sockets in the jamb stones). The floors of the stables were constructed from yellow sandstone except for alongside the troughs, where there was paving of undressed flags for the animals to stand on. Other rooms also had stone flooring.[99] Carbonised beams, plaster and large wrought iron nails between 20 and 25 cm in length, were found in the rooms, evidence of the flat roof which was described by Johns as being built in the local tradition from beams supporting boards on which was a thick layer of concrete (*nahate*) coated on either side with plaster. In addition to pine, some of the charcoal remains here proved to be of cedar, which does not grow in the region and must have been imported from Cyprus or Lebanon.[100] As the need arose, more space within the courtyard was roofed to shelter animals. Additional stables were uncovered in the north-west corner of the yard of the adjacent corner fort.[101] These consisted of two rooms, the outer one having two stone plaster-lined troughs or mangers each of which could have served three or four horses. Iron rings set in lead tubes were attached low on these troughs at irregular intervals of 25.5 cm or 1 metre. Another shallow trough in the yard was raised to a height of 1 metre; Johns suggested that, together with stone water butts found here, it may have been used to water the horses or to wash the harnesses.[102] North of the stable and the south-east tower was a large walled area surrounded by a low boundary wall extending as far north as the church (*c.* 110 metres), which was used as a cattle enclosure.

Several interesting small finds were uncovered in the stables, many of them found under the collapsed superstructure and therefore belonging to the pre-destruction level (i.e. before 1265).[103] Amongst these were local and imported pottery vessels: amphorae, jugs, a herb or medicine jar (*albarello*), cooking pots and pans, antilliyah jars (jars used on a mechanism drawing water from a well) which Johns identified as jars for preserving syrup, and glazed and unglazed bowls. Glass finds include some blue-stained glass quarries found together with their lead cames and fragments of typical medieval long-necked jars, bowls and other vessels. Metal finds, mainly iron, include various tools, amongst them a spade, a chisel, a hammer and an axe, various hooks, strap hinges and brackets from a door, a bronze object (possibly part of a lock), harness rings, chain links and nails, horseshoes, buckles, bronze scabbard tips, some Western-type arrowheads and an iron or steel spear-head. Lead tokens or *jetons* were found in the stables, on one of which was the Templar sign (an inverted 'T' within an isosceles triangle).[104] On the floor, underneath the debris which consisted mainly of the burnt roof beams, Johns recovered 28 coins. These include most of the main categories of thirteenth-century coins in use in the Latin East: coins from Egypt (Damietta), Cyprus (Henry I) and Burgundy, a coin of Frederick II, a coin of Lucca, a coin of Amaury, deniers of Tripoli, a denier tournois and two coins of Sidon, as well as four Ayyubid copper coins and one Mamluk copper of Baybars.[105] These coins, particularly that of Baybars, together with the coins found in the wind-blown sand layer above the roof beams and concrete (dirhams and fals dating from the thirteenth and fourteenth centuries), support the proposal that the destruction of the stable (and probably of the other buildings in the faubourg, since these are the only coins recovered from a stratified deposit in the faubourg) dates from the raid of Baybars in 1265 rather than the abandonment of the castle in 1291, as Johns suggested.[106]

A few courtyard houses in the faubourg were exposed by the excavators, but were not published in detail in the report.[107] From the scanty information on domestic buildings published by Johns in his report, and from the short references to these structures in his unpublished field diaries, they appear to have been simple courtyard houses, somewhat irregular in plan and similar to contemporary houses excavated in Caesarea, Yoqne'am, Arsuf and Jaffa.[108]

Outside the castle on the north-east is the largest and best-preserved Frankish cemetery known to date. It is located just outside the southern end of the faubourg's east wall and contains some 900 graves, most of them now covered only by piles of plastered stones forming flat or gable-shaped tomb covers, on some of which are endstones with simple crosses. Others have monolithic tombstone slabs cut from the local sandstone. The largest of these is a sandstone monolith decorated with an elaborate cross, measuring 1.05–1.25 by 2.60 metres and 30 cm thick. Another monolithic tombstone slab, now located in the Rockefeller Museum in Jerusalem, measures 0.80–1.00 by 2 metres and is also 30 cm thick. It too has a large cross carved on it, beneath the arms of which are carved representations of the tools of a builder, a hammer and a set-square; another smaller tombstone, also of a builder, has no cross but only a set-square and a plumb. Yet another tombstone, one of the few examples of upright tombstones found in the cemetery, apparently marked the tomb of an archer or of a worker in the arbalestry (the workshop in which crossbows were made and repaired). It displays a representation of a crossbow (arbalest) below a simple cross. Most of the other tombstones have only decorative crosses – in one case the patriarchal double-armed cross. One stone has a heraldic shield which lacks its design, probably originally rendered in paint. None of the tombstones has an inscription. The same is true for the Frankish cemetery next to the Mamilla Pool in Jerusalem, perhaps indicating that these stones too originally had painted inscriptions which have not been preserved. Examination of aerial photographs of the cemetery of Chateau Pelerin reveals an interesting feature which cannot easily be observed on the ground. There appear to be clusters of burials which stand out from the general mass of graves as if they belong to families or groups of people who died at the same time, perhaps in battle, and were buried in orderly rows.[109]

In the small bay to the south of the castle was a harbour with a jetty on its north (the southern shore of the castle peninsula), well protected from currents and storms. This was the port for all goods arriving or leaving the castle by sea. It was also used for embarkation and disembarkation, and from here the last Crusaders embarked for Cyprus in August 1291. The small size of the jetty would have prevented it from replacing the port of Acre as the principal naval facility of the Templar Order in the Kingdom of Jerusalem, although such an arrangement would have been very desirable for the Templars in the thirteenth century.[110]

Templar possessions in other towns of the Latin East

The Templars had less substantial holdings in several other coastal towns in the Kingdom of Jerusalem. According to Theoderich, they built a castle on the top of Mount Carmel at Caifas (Haifa) which was used as a landmark by mariners.[111] Its remains can be seen on the illustration of Haifa and the Carmel Range by Cornelius Le Bruyn.[112]

A Templar castle is recorded at Gaza in the twelfth century. Gaza was in a state of ruin until 1149, when King Baldwin III decided to fortify it. According to William of Tyre, the Franks did not have the resources to rebuild the entire city and the king had to make do with erecting a castle consisting of strong walls and towers on part of the ancient city. On completion the castle was handed over to the Templars, together with the surrounding possessions.[113] This action proved its worth when, shortly after its fortification, Gaza successfully repulsed an attack from Ascalon. Within four years Ascalon was occupied by the Franks and the city of Gaza enjoyed a revival. Settlers established a faubourg outside the Templar castle and some defensive works were constructed on the remainder of the ancient city, although these were not very substantial, William of Tyre describing them as *humili et infirmo* (insignificant and weak).[114]

The Templars occupied Gaza (with a brief break in 1170) until 1187, when they turned the castle over to Saladin after the capitulation of Ascalon. Though its fortifications were destroyed by Saladin, in 1192 they were restored by Richard I and returned to the Templars. However, later that year the castle was again dismantled according to the terms of the Treaty of Jaffa.[115] The location of the Templar walls and castle remain unknown, and the only known remains of the Crusader period are two churches discussed in detail by Pringle in the first volume of his gazetteer of Crusader churches.[116]

In Jaffa, the Templars' house was located in the north of the city against the sea wall. It had a postern in the wall which was reached by a winding staircase through which Richard I entered the city in August 1192.[117]

The Templars held a house in Sidon by 1173,[118] perhaps the same house that the Master of the Temple, Thomas Berard, granted to the Hospitallers in May 1262.[119] By this time the Templars had purchased the entire lordship of Sidon in 1260 and had moved their headquarters in the town to the Sea Castle. Work on the construction of the Sea Castle began in 1228/29, when the Franks reoccupied the town after it had remained abandoned for over three and a half decades following the Ayyubid conquest. The castle was strengthened by Louis IX in 1253/54 and was held by the Templars until it was abandoned with the entire town in 1291. The Templars also had a presence in Tyre and Giblet (Jubail).

In the County of Tripoli the Templars based their presence in the castles of Tortosa and Chastel Blanc (Safita). Though there was a Templar house in the town of Tripoli itself, no archaeological remains of it have been identified. We are better acquainted with the Templar possessions in Tortosa (Figure 6). In 1101 Raymond of St Gilles occupied Tortosa (Tartus), located on the Mediterranean coast about 50 km north of Tripoli. In the spring of 1152 Nûr al-Dîn attacked and sacked Tripoli. Though he subsequently withdrew, Bishop William I of Tripoli, fearing a renewed attack, sought the support of the Templars, granting them extensive ecclesiastical privileges in Tortosa and property extending 'from the entrance to the port to the house of William of Tiberias and reaching on all sides to the Gate of St Helen'.[120] They occupied and rebuilt the castle, which had been previously held by a secular lord, Raynouard of Maraclea,[121] who probably could no longer afford its upkeep. It was located on the northern part of the shore against the northern town wall, very similar in position, and to a lesser extent

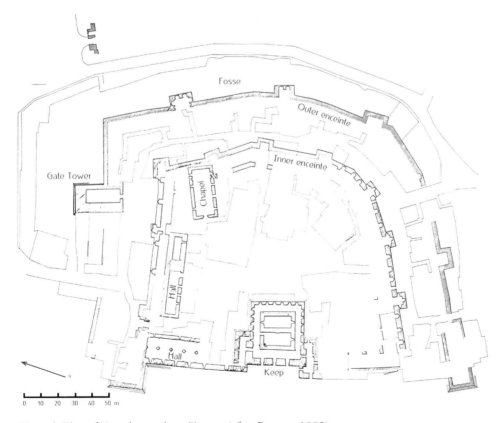

Figure 6 Plan of Templar castle at Tortosa (after Braune, 1985).

in layout, to the thirteenth-century Hospitaller castle at Arsuf. The Templars also received the nearby offshore island of Arwad. The traditional connection between Arwad (Crusader Ru'ad) and Tartus (Crusader Tortosa), which existed long before the Crusader period, was thus retained in the twelfth and thirteenth centuries.[122] Tortosa served as the Templars' regional headquarters. Count Raymond of Tripoli added to the property given to the Order by Bishop William additional lands, which Riley-Smith suggests might be the area covered by the late twelfth-century outworks as far as the northern gate (possibly the Gate of St Helen).[123] There were also a thirteenth-century hall and chapel in the town.

The castle, of which only fragments remain (albeit impressive ones), comprised a keep (*c.* 35 metres square) enclosed within a double line of walls and towers (Figure 7). The keep was massively constructed and proved strong enough to withstand the attack of Saladin in 1188, when he occupied the town and other parts of the fortress. Remains of this keep, built over by modern structures, still give a clear impression of its strength. Large marginally drafted ashlars, some with pronounced bosses, rise above a steep ashlar talus. At the time when it withstood the siege by Saladin it was a typical twelfth-century square keep, with the ground-floor basement divided in two rectangular chambers.[124] Improvements that were added later included a vaulted passage pierced with arrow slits at ground level, which would have served as a shooting gallery, and the addition of two oblong towers on the west where the keep met the sea walls of the castle.

In the early thirteenth century the castle appears to have served as the Templars' principal administrative centre and treasury.[125] It was damaged in the earthquake of 1202, but must have undergone repairs shortly afterwards. A decade later, when

Figure 7 Wall and rock-cut talus of Tortosa Castle (photograph by Denys Pringle).

Wilbrand of Oldenburg passed through, he described the town as 'not very fortified,' but he referred to the castle as 'a very strong castle with an admirable wall with eleven towers as if crowned with eleven precious stones'.[126]

Two lines of outer defences enclosed the landward side of the castle in a semicircle of curtains, towers and ditches. Substantial sections of the two curtains survive, in one place to their full height (25.5 metres). On the exterior they were constructed with the same large, marginally dressed ashlars found in the other parts of the castle, with smaller, smoothly worked stones lining the inner face. True to the conventions of concentric defences, the inner enceinte rises considerably higher than the outer enceinte and its towers are placed between those of the latter. Near the top it has a *chemin de ronde* with battlements above. The openings on both of these levels are square or rectangular in form, supplemented by the more usual embrasures narrowing to slits on the exterior. The square openings may have been intended for small mangonels.

The ground-floor level of the guard tower commanding the entrance to the castle from the north is well preserved. It is also constructed of large marginally dressed ashlars and is surrounded by a ditch with a partly rock-cut, partly constructed talus at its base, steeper than that of the keep. It is rib-vaulted and at floor level has a series of barrel-vaulted openings which, as in the outer defences, give onto rectangular windows rather than arrow slits.[127] The Templars' Grand Hall measured 44 by 15 metres (internal measurements). Two aisles of six rib-vaulted bays each were supported on five free-standing piers along the centre of the hall. The ribs were supported on triangular consoles, some of which were decorated with heads and leaves.[128] The Templars' chapel (not to be confused with the large cathedral in the town, which was apparently not built by them) measured 29.4 by 14.1 metres. It had a rib-vaulted roof (of which two bays survive) and a single door to the west with splayed jambs similar to those at Sebastia, Ramla and Gaza.[129] North-west of the chapel is a hall, perhaps the chapter house, also with Gothic rib-vaulting and an undercroft below. A hall to the west which has a central row of pillars may have served as the refectory.

In Cyprus, after the failed attempt to take over the entire island following its occupation by Richard I during the Third Crusade, the Templars came into possession of certain properties in the towns, including some in the port city of Famagusta. There is no detailed description of the Templars' properties here: it is known that the Templars of Famagusta owned some large merchant ships, but there are only vague references to their buildings. They possessed a house which was handed over to the Hospitallers in 1308, together with the Church of St Anthony. Documents listing the properties of the Templars refer to the *volta templi*.[130] Two small churches in Famagusta were designated by Enlart as the church of the Templars and the church of the Hospitallers.[131] This identification, which is speculative at best, was based on the presence on the taller but smaller of the two churches of a shield with a marble lintel carved with a cross similar to that of the Knights of St John found at Kolossi Castle. As this was the later of the two churches, appearing to be of fourteenth-century date, Enlart assumed that the other church to the north was that of the Templars whose property came into Hospitaller hands in the fourteenth century. This circumstantial evidence for the identity of the north church is rather weakly supported by an additional suggestion that the stone flagstaff holders on these churches are similar to those in the Hospitaller Street of the Knights (Strada Nobile) in Rhodes.

The northern of these two churches is possibly the Church of St Anthony. The style of this church suggests that it was built not long before 1308. It is a single-aisle church with three rib-vaulted bays springing from groups of brackets shaped like inverse pyramids with chamfered edges and ending in knobs at the base. The apse is roofed with a semi-dome with a single window. Three pointed-arch windows light the building and in the west wall above the door is a simple oculus with trefoil tracery. On the exterior there are buttresses with clasping buttresses on the corners of the west end, rather like those of a bridge. Stairs on the south side gave access to the roof. Enlart noted remains of an east–west wall joining the north-western buttress that may have once formed the perimeter of the conventual buildings, which have not survived.[132] Three doors in the north wall of the church would have given access to this enclosure.

In Nicosia the headquarters of the Templars were close to the royal palace.[133] Their church may have stood on the present site of Serai (Arab Achmet) Mosque, where there are some Gothic tombstones. This is the burial place of Guy of Lusignan and of Henry I (d. 1253).[134]

When the Templars prevented Hugh III of Cyprus from gaining control of Acre in 1276, he took revenge by destroying their house in Limassol and confiscating their other possessions in Cyprus.[135] They regained these properties only in 1284, after the death of Hugh. Though it has been claimed that Limassol Castle was built by Guy of Lusignan in c. 1193, another theory holds that it was a Templar castle which was seized by the king of Cyprus at the time of the suppression of the Order in 1308.[136]

2

THE URBAN QUARTERS OF
THE HOSPITALLERS

Like the Templars, the Hospitallers centred their activities in quarters in the two major cities of the Kingdom of Jerusalem: Jerusalem and Acre. However, they also had properties, including fortresses, convents, hospices and hospitals, in some of the other Crusader cities.

The Hospitallers' Quarter in Jerusalem and the Asnerie

The Hospitaller compound in Jerusalem developed out of an eleventh-century Amalfitan institution.[1] It was probably mainly towards the end of the fifth and into the sixth decades of the twelfth century that the remarkable group of monumental structures rose in the area to the south of the Church of the Holy Sepulchre.[2] The compound was within the north-west quarter of the city, the area known in the twelfth century as the Patriarch's Quarter (Figure 8). It extended south from the street on the south side of the Church of the Holy Sepulchre and the southern extension of its conventual buildings as far as David Street and east from the Street of the Patriarch as far as the western street of the triple market (the Street of Herbs) on the ancient Cardo.[3] Within this rectangular complex, which covered an area of approximately 130 by 130 metres, were the palace of the Hospitaller Master, three churches and their conventual buildings, possibly two hospitals, a bathhouse, storerooms, and no doubt stables and other essential service buildings. Remains of many of these structures survived until the late nineteenth century, and the early twentieth, and were recorded in photographs (Figure 9) and in the detailed plan published by Schick in 1902.[4] According to Benjamin of Tudela, the quarter housed some 400 knights,[5] though once again such a number is unlikely.[6] This should likewise perhaps read 400 brothers, including sergeants, grooms and others.

Though Schick's plan suggests the existence of a number of narrow streets in the quarter, only a few of them were located in his survey. A lane is shown exiting from a door on the east side of the hospital and passing north of St Mary Major. It turns to the south-east, crossing a north–south lane (or shops) and the adjacent street in front of St Mary Latin, and enters the northern aisle of the cloister of that convent as a covered lane. The north–south lane that it crosses appears to start from the street bordering the north side of the quarter. After it crosses the previously mentioned lane, it apparently turns west and then south, passing adjacent to the chevet of St Mary Major. How far south it extends is not clear, but there would probably have been a lane (possibly two adjacent lanes with shops between them) running in front of the large building south

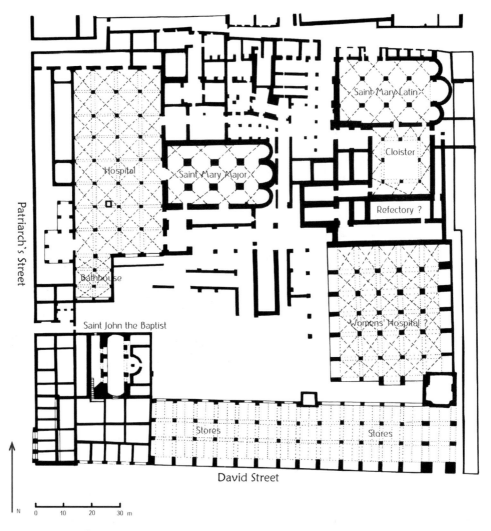

Figure 8 Plan of the Hospitaller compound in Jerusalem (after Schick, 1902).

of the cloister of St Mary Latin as far as the vaults north of David Street. It is likely that a lane ran along the northern face of these vaults. A covered street ran east–west at a point slightly south of St Mary Major and the southern end of the hospital, possibly leading to the bathhouse and to its southern exit. It may also have given onto a passage exiting the Quarter between the bathhouse and the Church of St John the Baptist.

There is no clear evidence, either written or archaeological, for the location of the palace of the Master. It was possibly located opposite the Church of the Holy Sepulchre in the complex of structures adjacent to the hospital on its east. On Schick's plan of the quarter, only the building identified as the hospital itself is on as grand a scale as the palace built somewhat later in the Hospitaller complex at Acre. Though the buildings adjacent to the hospital appear to have been less impressive, the location was certainly a prestigious one, directly opposite the Church of the Holy Sepulchre. Unfortunately, in

Figure 9 Nineteenth-century photograph of the Hospitaller ruins in Jerusalem.

his published survey Schick did not describe these buildings or speculate on their use. We are left only with the plan itself, which shows one structure consisting of six groin-vaulted rooms around a small courtyard, in which steps give access to an upper storey, and various other vaults with less regular layout to its east.[7]

Another building which we are unable to locate at present is the dormitory of the Hospitaller brothers. One possibility is that these quarters were located on a second-storey level above the row of vaulted shops and storage rooms running along the north side of David Street. A row of stone corbels above the arches on the façade of that structure suggests that this building had a second storey. However, this is purely speculative and the dormitory could have been located elsewhere.

The largest and most significant building in the Hospitaller Quarter was the hospital (*palacium infirmorum*). Unlike some of the other institutions in this quarter, the position of the hospital is well established, a consequence of its importance in the eyes of medieval visitors. It was located opposite the Church of the Holy Sepulchre and adjacent to the Street of the Patriarch, the north-west boundary of the Quarter. There is considerable documentation and archaeological evidence for this. The most reliable written evidence is the description in the anonymous early thirteenth-century French tract known as *Ernoul, l'estat de la Cité de Iherusalem* (The Condition of the City of Jerusalem).[8] This description leaves no doubt as to the identification of the large groin-vaulted structure in the north-west of the quarter as the hospital. According to this source there was a door on the right hand of the Street of the Patriarch, by which one could enter the House of the Hospital,[9] and the Master Gate of the Hospital was located to the right when coming from St Mary Latin.[10]

This building, located in the north-west of the quarter, was described by Schick in his publication of 1902:

> It consists of one large hall with three rows of piers still standing, seven in each row, and with those connected with the walls, and those of the southern prolongation, making forty-eight. The length of this chamber is about 230 feet, and its width about 120 feet, inside measurement; the arches in it are about 18 feet high. There is still *in situ* the base of a pillar, the shaft of which is lying on the pavement close by. To the east the vaulting is broken in, giving now light into the old vaults.[11]

John of Würzburg recorded that the infirm of both sexes were treated in the hospital, but elsewhere there are references to a separate hospital (*palacium*) for women. The anonymous Amalfitan chronicler recorded two *hospitalia* for the sick of each sex, and the anonymous Munich text refers to a separate hospital for sick women.[12] While it is possible that these were separate institutions in the same building, the hospital for women may have been located elsewhere. One location worth considering is in the south-east of the quarter, where a groin-vaulted structure survived until the end of the nineteenth century.[13] This building was large, though not quite as large as the hospital in the north-west of the quarter, and its substantial remains can be seen in a number of nineteenth-century photographs (seen in the foreground of Figure 9). It was certainly large enough to serve as a hospital and contained an oven, cisterns, communal latrines (*chambres*) and a sewage system.[14] However, one cannot rule out the possibility that it served as the dormitory of the knights or as a pilgrims' hospice.

Of the three known churches in the area of the Hospitallers' Quarter, two, St Mary Latin and St Mary Major, were independent Benedictine institutions founded in the eleventh century. The third church, St John the Baptist, the oldest of the three (indeed the oldest surviving functioning church in Jerusalem) and the only one to survive today, is located in the south-west of the Hospitallers' Quarter.[15] It was damaged several times and restored in the twelfth century, when it served for a short while as the conventual church of the Order of the Hospitallers until it was at some stage replaced by a new church. Adjacent to this church, to its north, stood a bathhouse. Although it was located within the Hospitaller compound, it apparently belonged to the Patriarch; hence the adjacent street was occasionally referred to as the Street of the Patriarch's Bath and in later times the bathhouse itself was known as the Hammam al-Batrak. However, its location would no doubt have made it convenient for the use of the brothers. The bathhouse survived the destruction of most of the other buildings in its vicinity and still functioned into the nineteenth century. Its location was apparently in the annexe at the south end of the hospital, where boilers are marked on Schick's plan. It was probably connected to the hospital and served the patients as well as the brothers of the Order. It received its water from the Pool of the Patriarch via an aqueduct which crossed the Street of the Patriarch.[16]

In the south of the quarter, along the northern side of David Street, is a row of 13 large, connected barrel-vaulted halls (14 including the somewhat larger vault at the eastern end of the building). These vaults probably served as magazines for storing the enormous quantity of supplies needed to run the hospitals and hospices and to supply the needs of the Order's houses elsewhere in the kingdom. As the broad open-arched entrances of these vaults face David Street, one of the principal thoroughfares of the city, they clearly also served as shops, probably occupied by merchants and craftsmen who paid the Order rent for their use. The craftsmen may have included the goldsmiths and silversmiths who are known to have been located in this general area. De Vogüé suggested that these vaults are the '*voltas concambii Hospitalis . . . in via quae ducit ad montem Syon*' recorded in the cartulary of the Church of the Holy Sepulchre.[17] Warren and Conder suggest that this name refers to the bazaar on the ancient Cardo to the east (apparently referring to the Triple Market north of David Street), and Pringle also suggests that it was possibly on the Cardo but south of David Street on Jewish Quarter Street (Suq al-Hussar) which in the Crusader period was known as the Vicus ad Montis Syon.[18] Structurally, this building is well preserved, although it appears to have lost an upper storey.[19] This upper storey could, as previously suggested, have served as dormitories of the brothers of the Order or to house the merchants who used the shops below, or for some other purpose. The ground-floor level has survived more or less intact, no doubt because it remained a useful, indeed necessary structure even after the rest of the quarter fell into ruin. However, today it is difficult to examine these halls since modern divisions and additions in the present shops on David Street, which were built within the vaults, hide most of the interiors. None the less, some of the halls have been cleared and reveal their original form. A typical hall measures 20.40 by 5.5 metres. Unusually for barrel vaults, instead of side walls they have piers rather than walls between each shop. The piers at the front (south) face of each vault are elongated (3/3.6 by 1.2 metres), and two free-standing piers (1.2 by 1.2 metres) support the vaults and pilasters on the back (north) wall. The vaults are strengthened by ashlar arches between the piers. Partition walls between the piers divide each vault from its neighbour. The fact that most of these vaults have their own cisterns (the six western vaults have cisterns under their centre and the eighth vault has a cistern in the north and extending out from its back wall) suggests that they were already separate units in Frankish times. However, the last four vaults to the east (west of the largest easternmost vault) remained open and still today form a large open hall.

The large vault at the eastern end of the David Street front, sometimes referred to as the 'khan', has two massive square piers (3.6 by 3.3 metres) on the street front and broad piers (2 by 1.2 metres) in the interior. At the back is a large cistern measuring *c*. 7.6 by 8.8 metres (internal). This vaulted hall and the adjacent vaults, which are open to one another, have sometimes been identified with the market referred to in *l'estat de la Cité de Iherusalem* where cheese, chickens, eggs and birds were sold.[20]

In Schick's survey of the ruins of the Hospitaller Quarter, about twenty cisterns are recorded and located and additional cisterns are suggested.[21] Each group of structures has its own cisterns. There were two under the hospital, two under the church of St Mary Major, one under St Mary Minor, three in the cloisters of the latter church, one in the large south-eastern structure, one in the south-eastern shop on David Street, seven in the other shops and one in the open space to the north of them. Though many of these cisterns undoubtedly predate the Crusader period, some of them, such as those located under the Crusader halls in the south of the complex, were certainly built at the same time as the superstructure.[22]

Returning to the *concambii hospitalis* which were mentioned in a charter of 1143, this

Hospitallers' exchange was located on the first floor of a house belonging to the canons of the Holy Sepulchre on Mount Zion Street above a bakery and below private apartments.[23] The Hospitallers must also have had stables in their quarter within the city walls. However, there is no evidence, archaeological or otherwise, for their location. They also had stables outside the city, located to the north of the city walls. This was known as the Asnerie (Anerie) or Asinaria.[24] It is first mentioned in 1163 in a document witnessed by one Bernardus de Asinaria,[25] and in the early thirteenth century it is referred to in *l'estat de la Cité de Iherusalem*:

> In front of this church [St Stephen which was located north of St Stephen's Gate, now Damascus Gate on the northern city wall], on the left hand, there was a large building, which was called the Anerie; here the asses and the sumpter-horses belonging to the Hospital were accustomed to be stabled, hence its name of Anerie ... The Anerie was not pulled down [in Saladin's siege of 1187 when the church was dismantled by the Franks to prevent the Muslims from using it as a position to attack the nearby walls], but was afterwards of service to the pilgrims who came to Jerusalem during truce, when it was in the hands of the Saracens.[26]

Two possible sites have been suggested for the Asnerie.[27] One site is located in the compound known as Gordon's Tomb or the Garden Tomb, a site identified by some as the true location of the Tomb of Christ.[28] At this site there is indeed evidence for a stable with rock-cut mangers, though these cannot be dated with certainty to the twelfth century. On the other hand, the second site was clearly of the appropriate period. It consisted of a group of large barrel vaults located near the remains of the Byzantine Church of St Stephen, which were discovered in 1873 but subsequently dismantled to make way for new buildings. However, plans and a description of the vaults and the small adjacent chapel were published by Claud Conder[29] and they can be seen in an unpublished photograph taken before they were destroyed.[30] After the Ayyubid conquest the Asnerie was used to house Christian pilgrims visiting the Holy City who were not permitted to reside within the walls.

A complex of buildings which came to be placed under Hospitaller authority was the German Hospital and the Church of St Mary Alemannorum, located in the south-west of the city in the present Jewish Quarter. A papal bull issued by Pope Celestine II in 1143 placed the newly established German hospital under the Hospitaller Master Raymond and future Hospitaller masters, with the stipulation that the priors and attendants must be Germans.[31] Three buildings were constructed for the German pilgrims.[32] That to the north was a courtyard building measuring *c.* 21 by 36 metres. It was surrounded on the ground floor by 19 groin-vaulted rooms and entered from the road on the south via a door and a groin-vaulted bay in the south-west corner. A small basilica was connected to it directly to its south, and south of the church was a two-storey building, possibly the administrative headquarters of the complex. Its lower level was a basement hall measuring *c.* 14 by 25 metres roofed by eight engaged and three free-standing piers supporting eight groin-vaulted bays. The upper level, of which little survives, was probably of similar layout but more decoratively treated with elbow consoles and capitals.

Partial remains of these buildings survive today, particularly those of the church and the building to its south. The church was first examined in 1872 by C.F. Tyrwhitt Drake[33] and in 1968 it was surveyed by Asher Ovadiah and Ehud Netzer.[34] It was subsequently excavated, together with the southern building, by Meir Ben-Dov.[35] The church is a triapsidal basilica divided by two rows of plain square piers. It measures 20 by 12 metres and has its main door to the west and additional doors to the two other buildings of the complex on its north and south.

We have some knowledge of burial sites of the Order in Jerusalem. On Schick's plan of St Mary Major a sarcophagus is recorded in an annexe on the south side of the church.[36] Additional tombs are recorded adjacent to the church of St Mary Latin in the northern and eastern aisles and in one of the vaults on the north side of David Street.[37] Amongst the bones (apparently of more than one body) was a skull with a deep sword cut across it. For pilgrims and the poor who died in the hospital, the Hospitallers had a large charnel house located to the south-west of the city at the traditional site of Akeldama (Field of Blood) on the southern slope of the Hinnom Valley opposite Mount Zion. It was here that they buried the more than fifty patients who, according to John of Würzburg, died each night in the hospital.[38] The charnel house was therefore an important institution, as it solved the problem of disposal of the bodies of destitute pilgrims who died in the hospital.[39] It is not known when it was built, but the land and a church which was under construction at the time were granted to the Hospital by Patriarch William in 1143.[40] The word 'Akeldamach' appears on the twelfth-century round maps of Jerusalem, but this does not necessarily mean that the charnel house was already in existence in the first half of the twelfth century (the probable date of the original round map).[41] An illustration of the structure itself appears only from the fifteenth century (on the Comminelli Map), and from then on it is found on many maps over the following centuries.[42] Descriptions of the structure begin in the late fifteenth century (Felix Fabri, 1480). In the nineteenth century the building was described by several scholars including Pierotti and Schick.[43] Most recently a survey of the structure was carried out in 1999.[44] The now largely collapsed barrel vault of the charnel house originally measured c. 19.5 by 6 metres (internal). It adjoins a number of rock-cut chambers to the south. In the crown of the vault there were originally nine square openings, with another two openings on the southern side of the vault; there were four more openings above the rock-cut section to the south. Through these openings the bodies of the dead were dropped.

The Hospitallers' possessions in Acre

The Hospitallers were granted properties in Acre early in the twelfth century: confirmation of early grants appears as early as 1110, six years after the Crusader occupation of the city.[45] These possessions were located adjacent to the northern side of the cathedral of the Holy Cross. They were abandoned by 1135, when the construction of a north portal to the cathedral required the demolition of their building.[46] They subsequently moved to a new site further west, close to the Porta St Johannis. The appearance of the name of this gate in a charter of 1194[47] supports a twelfth-century date for this move, but it may have taken place much earlier, soon after the destruction of their old building. As Riley-Smith notes, it had certainly occurred by 1149, in which year a charter of Queen Melisende refers to the Hospitallers' church, presumably the Church of St John the Baptist, located to the south-east of their complex.[48] There is no archaeological evidence for a Romanesque church at this new site (though it would certainly have been in this style if it predated 1149). All of the finds, including the most recent, belong to the Gothic church,[49] the ruins of which can be seen on the well-known seventeenth-century panorama of Acre.[50] The possibility therefore remains of a different location for the church referred to in the charter of 1149, or a complete rebuilding in the Gothic style.[51] Although it probably existed much earlier, the Hospitaller headquarters itself is first recorded only in 1169 by the German pilgrim Theoderich.[52] He notes that the Hospitallers had founded a splendid house in Acre.

The great expansion of the quarter began after the reoccupation of the city in the Third Crusade. The headquarters of the Order may have been temporarily moved to the castle of Margat in the Principality of Antioch but, according to Riley-Smith, at this time the Hospitallers added warehouses and stores to their complex in Acre and the conventual brothers were moved to the *auberge* in Montmusard.[53] The Order received grants from Guy of Lusignan (1192) and Henry of Champagne (1193),[54] and continued to expand in the early thirteenth century following the purchase of property up to the northern city wall.[55] A charter of Henry I Lusignan dated 1252 authorised the Hospitallers to construct two new gates to their quarter.[56]

During the War of St Sabas (1256–58) the Hospitallers supported the Genoese against the Templars and their allies, Venice and Pisa. Genoa invaded the Pisan Quarter in 1257. After they were pushed back the Venetians besieged both the Genoese and the Hospitaller Quarters.[57] By 1258 the Genoese were expelled from the city, but the Hospitallers managed to hold on to their property. In 1281 a dispute between the Hospitallers and the Pisans over the defence of the city walls was settled by Count Roger of San Severino (lieutenant of the King of Jerusalem and Sicily) in favour of the Hospitallers, who were given control over the section of the walls from St Antony's Gate to the Accursed Tower.[58] This evidence conflicts with the information given by the various versions of the fourteenth-century maps by Marino Sanudo (drawn by Pietro Vesconte) and Paolino of Puteoli. On these maps the title Custodia Hospitalis appears on the southern section of the outer wall of Montmusard, while the section from St Antony's Gate to the Accursed Tower is located on the wall that continues east of the walls of Montmusard, and it (or at least the western part of it) is described on the maps as Custodia Venetorum.[59] Either the maps, which were drawn up some four decades after the grant of Roger of San Severino (more in the case of Paolino), were inaccurate, or they reflect a change in the position of the Hospitallers' Custodia that may have taken place by the time of Sanudo's visit to Acre in 1285 or 1286, a few years before the final Mamluk siege of 1291.[60]

One and perhaps more of the few fragments of Acre's walls that have been rediscovered in archaeological excavations are part of the section of the defences which were described in the Hospitaller archives as being given to them by Roger of San Severino. In 1991 a salvage excavation was carried out at a site north-east of the north-eastern corner of the Turkish city walls.[61] The archaeologists uncovered the north-east corner of a tower and the counterscarp of the adjacent moat. The tower was constructed on the bedrock, its foundations beginning 1.50 metres below the base of the moat. These foundations consist of two to three courses of roughly shaped, poorly joined stones. The walls, which are stepped above the foundation, vary in thickness from 3 metres at their base to 2.5 metres above the floor levels. The construction, of local sandstone, is in the typical Crusader style of two faces of well-dressed and fitted ashlars.

Many of these have been robbed, probably in the time of al-Jazzar Pasha. The wall has an internal rubble and mortar core 1.9 metres thick. The interior faces of the walls are somewhat less carefully constructed, no doubt because they were covered with plaster. A postern (1.05 metres wide) was located 4.2 metres west of the surviving corner of the tower. A finely built well-shaft was exposed within the wall to the east. It was 0.95 cm in diameter and the archaeologists have estimated that it was originally 8.5 to 9 metres deep, extending down from the upper storey of the tower to the medieval ground water level.[62] Inside the tower were a partition wall and a pilaster which possibly supported a wooden staircase which led up to an upper level, since burnt wood was found around it. The moat here was 13 metres wide. A section of about 15 metres of the counterscarp was exposed opposite the tower. Though its ashlar facing had been robbed, evidence of it could be observed in the imprint of the missing stones in the core and the strips of mortar which had once joined the ashlars. Amongst the small finds from the ground floor of this tower were a number of cooking and storage vessels, which led the archae-ologists to conclude that the ground floor of the tower was used as a kitchen.[63] The discovery at this site of a number of the unglazed bowls known as 'Acre Bowls', which were apparently manufactured in the Hospitallers' Quarter[64] and which appear to have been used by pilgrims or brothers of the Military Orders,[65] while not conclusive, is further evidence of a Hospitaller presence at this site.[66]

An additional section of these defences, possibly also part of the Hospitallers' Custodia, was exposed in an excavation which took place in 1998/99.[67] This consisted of a section of a well-constructed retaining wall running north–south until it turns rather more than 90 degrees and continues roughly east–west. It was apparently a section of the counterscarp of the northern moat, east of the point where it joins the oblique fortifica-tion line of Montmusard. The sharp angle of this section suggests that the counterscarp here, like that of Caesarea, followed the offsets and insets of the city wall.

Of the three elements which appear in the Hospitaller Quarter on Paolino's map (the Hospitale, the ecclesia and the Domus Infirmorum), the Hospitale would appear to refer to the entire courtyard complex located to the north-west of the church and hospital (Figure 10). It included the palace of the Master (after the fall of Jerusalem) and all of the various conventual buildings. A number of narrow streets cross the complex, both above ground and below. The entrance street, which gives access to the courtyard, runs from east to west between the northern halls and the palace. It is 3.5 metres wide. Remains of structures from the Hellenistic period compelled the builders to raise this street to almost 2 metres above the adjacent buildings.[68] A second street located to the south of the refectory runs east-west along the southern side of the complex and then turns north. Beneath the compound are subterranean passages, some of which are part of a sewage network from the latrines in the north-west tower.

At the heart of the Hospitaller Quarter is the large courtyard, covering an area of 1,200 square metres (Figure 11). Like a monastic cloister, it is located at the centre of the complex with the dormitory, refectory and other communal buildings around it (although it is not in the usual position relative to the church). The courtyard is surrounded on all sides by elongated piers (c. 2 metres wide) supporting pointed arches that form deep recesses averaging c. 4 metres deep.[69]

The large rectangular building on the east side of the courtyard has been tentatively identified as the palace of the Master. This building (or the entire courtyard complex) is probably the building labelled 'Hospitale' on the fourteenth-century maps, and may

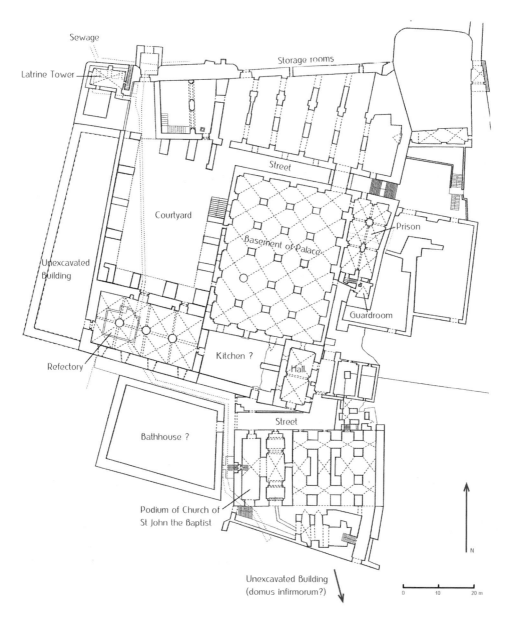

Figure 10 Plan of the Hospitaller compound in Acre (after E. Stern, 2000).

have been what was called the 'grand maneir' in a document of 1252.[70] It was constructed in conjunction with a group of barrel-vaulted halls to its north (the eastern part of the so-called 'Knights' Halls',[71] the prison to its east and part of the substructure of the Church of St John to the south. It appears under the name Palais du Grand Maître on the panorama of Acre drawn in 1686.[72] Although that designation was given nearly four hundred years after the destruction of Acre, it is none the less a reasonable identification considering the monumental proportions of this building.

Figure 11 Hospital compound in Acre (photograph courtesy of Eliezer Stern, IAA).

The panorama gives some idea of the external appearance of this structure in the Crusader period. At the time it was still standing (in part) to most of its original height. The southern and eastern façades can be seen rising high above the other ruins and the houses of Turkish Akka. On the ground level are large, blind, pointed arches, probably structural in nature. Above these can be seen two rows of windows of the first and second storeys and remains of part of the third storey. There appears to be a slightly projecting tower rather more than half way along the south side. A second illustration dating from 1698 is also invaluable in giving us an accurate picture of the appearance of the palace from within. It was drawn from the west, inside the courtyard, apparently (as the viewpoint is well above ground level) from a window of the building opposite which has not survived.[73] The illustration shows with considerable accuracy the monumental staircase leading up from the courtyard to the first storey and the ground-floor level with its blind arches, similar to what can be seen of the south façade on the 1686 panorama. This part of the complex has been uncovered in recent years by excavations.[74] In the background of the 1698 illustration a fragmentary wall stands to a considerable height. This was all that remained of the three upper storeys above the first-floor level. Thus the building was in much poorer condition than it had been a few years earlier in 1686.[75] The excavations have revealed that the ground floor of this building was a huge groin-vaulted hall consisting of four north–south aisles of six bays each supported by nine massive square piers and 20 pilasters, covering a total area of 1,107 square metres (internal). The vaults are about 6.5 metres high. Construction is of well-cut sandstone ashlars and there is no apparent decoration. This level would most probably have been intended for storage and perhaps for stables. A drainage channel runs along the external wall. On the west face are blind structural arches and a monumental staircase giving access to the first floor, where the living quarters must have been located. One way of reconstructing the palace is by comparing its remains to the somewhat later but well-preserved buildings of the Hospitallers in Rhodes. Two buildings in Rhodes, the new hospital and the Hospitallers' palace, both have courtyards with arched galleries and monumental staircases supported on arches. According to two inscriptions the hospital was built in the mid-fifteenth century.[76] The Grand Master's Palace, which was rebuilt from 1937 to 1940 after having largely collapsed in the mid-nineteenth century, has apparently preserved its original design. The great similarity between these buildings and the remains uncovered in Acre leaves little doubt as to it having being their model.

A group of nine connected barrel-vaulted halls on the north and north-east sides of the courtyard at Acre are today popularly known as the 'Knights' Halls'. They vary in size because the north wall, which predates the rest of the structure, is on a different alignment. That to the east is the shortest because part of its space is taken up by an annexe to the north-east tower. It is 14.5/17.5 metres in length. The second vault on the east is the longest (c. 25/26 metres), and the others shorten progressively to the west. Later vaults were added to the west in the early thirteenth century. The vaults average c. 7 metres in width and they are about 8 metres high. These vaults on the ground-floor level certainly served as warehouses. Riley-Smith has suggested that the Hospitaller 'vault' (the term used to describe the warehouse in which the principal stores of the Acre headquarters were kept) was located in the eastern range of the compound.[77] This is the groin-vaulted hall at ground level below the palace which, as we have noted, was probably used for storage and stabling. It is also possible that this term refers to the nine vaults of the northern range or to both of these structures. In these vaults the Hospitallers kept foodstuffs and other items for use in their Acre compound and in their other more distant houses. Riley-Smith mentions 'buckram, boots, canvas, soap, iron, wool, leather and imperishable foods as salted meat and cheese'.[78] To this list we can add one item revealed in the excavation of Halls VII and VIII (the two western halls of the northern range). Hundreds of sugar moulds were found on the floor of these halls, some of them placed inside one another. Ash found between them showed that they had been wrapped in protective layers of straw. These vessels apparently fell from shelves during or following the destruction of the building in May 1291.[79] These storage vaults were under the control of an officer known as the 'Commander of the Vault', apparently also known as the 'Petty Commander'.[80] His function seems to have been the equivalent, on a larger scale, of a monastic cellarer, providing the brothers and other residents of the quarter with food, clothing and other necessities. Above the vaults there was originally a second storey, and there are indications that this level contained living quarters. It is possible that a dormitory was located here, but if it was the dormitory of the knight brothers this was only the case until 1187, since after the Third Crusade they would have been housed in the auberge in Montmusard.[81] This wing could alternatively have housed a pilgrims' hospice or the hospital itself, although that institution is generally regarded to have been located further to the south.[82] A staircase on the south and west walls of one of the vaults towards the west gave access to this upper storey. Though this level has not survived, it may have run along the entire length of the vaulted halls and would probably have given access to the latrines in the adjacent western tower. In this, the complex would have followed the typical design of a medieval monastery, with the latrines located at the end of the dormitory wing. This wing was Gothic in style, as is indicated by the finds of vault ribs and a rosette decorated rib boss. Fragmentary finds of coloured (black, yellow and red) and incised fresco were recovered from the few remains of this upper level.

The latrines (chambres) were located on the ground and first floors of the north-west tower. The rooms on these levels contained parallel rows of stone seats placed over chutes around the walls which emptied the waste into a large subterranean chamber with a sloping floor. Rainwater was collected from the roof to wash the waste through the chutes into the underground chamber. From here the waste was flushed out into a system of well-constructed drains which carried it to the sea (possibly in the direction of the port, which is known to have been polluted in this period).[83] The examination of samples of soil from the latrines proved them to have come from people who suffered from whipworm (*Trichuris trichuria*), roundworm (*Ascaris lumbricoides*) and freshwater fish tapeworm (*Diphyllobothrium latum*).[84] As tapeworms were relatively common in the West, but not endemic to the Near East, the carriers were presumably Westerners. The presence of these intestinal parasites shows that there was a lack of hygiene amongst the residents. As these could not have been the knight brothers of the Order, who lived in the *auberge* in Montmusard, they were perhaps Western pilgrims.

The refectory (palais[85]) is one of the more remarkable buildings in the complex from an architectural aspect. This building, still occasionally known by the erroneous title the 'Crypt',[86] is a rib-vaulted hall measuring 30 by 15 metres and 10 metres high. The eight-bay vaulting is supported by three massive round piers, 3 metres in diameter. Rib consoles on the north-east and south-east corners are decorated with the fleur de-lis. These and oak-leaf patterned bossets are the only surviving decoration in the refectory.

There are a number of reasons for identifying this hall as the refectory. Its location in the centre of the compound, adjacent to the cloister, is typical of the position of refectories in medieval monasteries. The design of this hall is similar to that of monastic refectories. Moreover, the three chimneys in the northern part of the east wall (one built within the wall and two against it) suggest that the unexcavated room to the east is the kitchen. The unusual combination of massive piers typical of Romanesque architecture and Early Gothic rib-vaulting has led archaeologist Ze'ev Goldmann to suggest that in this building we may have the earliest example of Gothic in the East, attesting to the changeover from the Romanesque to the Gothic style in a single building.[87] Riley-Smith believes that it predates the fall of Acre to Saladin in 1187; Pringle dates it later, probably after 1194; and Stern has dated the walls, and perhaps the vaulting, to the early thirteenth century.[88]

A small Gothic hall is located on the eastern side of the unexcavated room which was probably the kitchen. It measures 7 by 13 metres (internal) and is well constructed, consisting of two groin-vaulted bays. It is entered from the street to the south and has lancet windows on each of the other walls, opening into the kitchen on the west and the palace. Narrow pilasters support the two bays and a transverse arch divides them.

A brother who committed a crime or breach of good conduct could find himself committed to confinement in prison. Unlike the Rule of the Temple, the Hospitaller Rule barely refers to this punishment, and the alternatives of *septaine* (seven days of penances) or *quarantaine* (forty days of penances), beatings, other humiliating chastisements and what may have been considered the most severe penalty of all, loss of the habit (expulsion), were the principal punishments. However, a term of imprisonment was inflicted, for example, on a brother who, despite suffering lesser punishments, repeatedly refused to obey the order of the commander. Committed to prison, he would be fed on bread and water alone and could be kept in chains.[89] The place of detention in the Hospitaller Quarter appears to have been a room located *c.* 2.5 metres lower than the level of the other buildings, on the east side of the palace (south of the entrance to the northern street). It was a vaulted hall consisting of six groin-vaulted bays, 8/10 by 20 metres and 5 metres high, supported on two free-standing rectangular piers, the northern one more massive and the northern bays slightly wider than the others. Along the walls, about 2 metres above the floor level, are small holes which may have been where chains to restrain the prisoners were attached to the walls.[90] A small annexe on the south of the south-eastern bay appears to have been a guardroom. It has an embrasure and a window which was blocked at a certain stage. There were no other windows, additional evidence supporting the identification of this hall as a prison.

The Church of St John the Baptist was located to the south of the castle. In this church Walter of Brienne, Count of Jaffa, who had been killed when in captivity in Egypt, was buried in *c.* 1250.[91] Other than unreliable representations of this church on different versions of the thirteenth-century map of Acre by Matthew Paris and the early fourteenth-century map of Paulinos of Puteoli, there is only one known depiction of this church[92] – on the panorama of Akko drawn in 1686.[93] Here the church, elevated on its podium, can be seen rising above all the other buildings except for the Palace of the Grand Master behind it to the north-west and the wall of what may have been the hospital to its east. At this time it was already in a very ruinous state. Five large recessed embrasure windows of trefoil form can be seen on its southern face. Above them rise a few fragments of an upper level, perhaps the clerestory.

A massive vaulted structure known as el-Bosta (the Turkish post office), located to the south-east of the castle, served as a podium above which stood the church. It consists of six parallel halls, the two western halls possibly including pre-Frankish (Fatimid?) remains.[94] The eastern groin-vaulted halls have massive 3–4 metres thick piers. The substantial construction of this building points to its only apparent function (the small, dark vaulted bays between the massive piers would have been of little use): to raise the church high above the surrounding buildings. Exploratory excavations were carried out in the Turkish serai above the Bosta in 1995/96.[95] After the removal of modern and Turkish period paving, the excavators exposed collapsed rubble consisting of sandstone ashlars, sand and light-coloured ash. Amongst the remains found from what was apparently the nave of the church were marble columns set in a floor constructed of rectangular light-grey marble tiles (25 by 40 cm, *c.* 4 cm thick), two painted marble capitals, on one of which was a cross painted in red on a black ground,[96] and finds included quarries of stained glass in a range of colours. Ceramic finds, some of which came from the bed of the tile floor, included thirteenth-century Port St Symeon ware and bowls from Cyprus which give a *terminus ante quem* of the third decade of the thirteenth century for the church.

The hospital ('Domus Infirmorum' as it appears on the fourteenth-century map of Paulino of Puteoli) may be the very large vaulted ruin to the right (south-east) of the Church of St John the Baptist on the seventeenth-century panorama.[97] A groin-vaulted structure to the south-east of the castle has been tentatively identified as this building. Excavations began here in the early 1990s, but had to be halted because of the poor state of the structure and its threat of impending collapse. The location of this structure to the south-east of the church and castle confirms the position of the Domus Infirmorum in relation to the palace and church of St John on one of the fourteenth-century maps.[98] As previously suggested, a possible alternative is that the hospital was located in the wing above the vaults known as the 'Knights' Halls' on the north side of the courtyard.[99] Here again, one may use analogy with later hospitals to reconstruct this building. Like that of Rhodes, the hospital in Acre may have been a similar building to the palace, but on a smaller scale with a central courtyard and a monumental staircase.

In the Hospitaller archives reference is made to a bathhouse adjacent to a tract of land which was the starting point of the procession of donates (noble laymen attached to the Order) when they were received into full brotherhood. A statute dating from 1270 commands that the new brothers:

> not be promenaded through the town [after receiving the robe of the House], but should come straight from the bath to our House or to the Auberge, and that there should be no trumpets nor tabors.[100]

This bathhouse may possibly have been located on the site of the Turkish bathhouse (*hammam*) which is to the south of the Hospitaller compound, west of the Church of St John the Baptist.[101]

On the various versions of the fourteenth-century map of thirteenth-century Acre there is a section of the city in the Montmusard suburb, adjacent to the sea and north of the Ruga Bethleemitana, that is marked 'Hospiticiu[m] Hospitalis, or, alternatively, 'Alb[er]ges Hospit[al]is'. This was the conventual lodging (auberge) of the brothers of the Order under the command of the Marshal.[102] The *auberge* in Acre is described in the *Gestes des Chiprois* as containing a 'very noble room, very long and very beautiful, which was 150 *canna* [*c.* 300 metres!] in length'.[103] The coronation of Henry II took place here in 1286, and this was the residence of the Marshal of the Hospital.[104] This building has not yet been traced.

The Hospitallers probably possessed a number of cemeteries in Acre and the surroundings. Beyond the need of a burial place for the knight brothers of the Order and other associates, in view of the nature of medieval medicine the Hospitallers would have needed to bury the many patients who must have died each day in their hospital. As we have seen, in Jerusalem the solution was in the form of a large charnel house. In Acre there may have been a similar solution, though there is no documentary or archaeological evidence for it. However, we do hear of Hospitaller ownership of more than one cemetery. In 1200 Theobald, Bishop of Acre, granted the Order a cemetery near Acre. The cemetery of St Nicholas in the north-east of the city, which together with its chapel is illustrated on the various versions of the thirteenth-century map of Matthew Paris, was apparently held by them, as were the chapel and cemetery of St Michael on the shore within the city walls.[105] An inscription on a slab of marble (180 by 50 cm) honouring the eighth master of the Hospitaller Order, Petrus de Veteri Brivato (Peter de Vieille Briude), and dated to 1242 was found in a hall beneath the Church of St John the Baptist.[106] Its original location was probably in the Church of St John the Baptist. It reads:

(ANNO AB INCARNACIONE DOMINI MCCXLII OBIIT FRATER
PETRUS DE VETERI BRIVATO / OCTAVUS MAGISTER SANCTE
DOMUS HOSPITALIS JERUSALEM POST OCCUPATIONEM SANC / TE
TERRE XV KLS OCTOBRIS CUIUS AIA REQUIESCAT IN PACE AMEN
(CUIUS TEMPORE COMES / MONTIS FORTIS ET ALII BARONES
FRANCIE A CAPTIUITATE BABILONIE LIBERATI FUERUNT DUM
RICH / ARDUS COMES CORNUBIE CASTRUM ERIGERET ASCALONE

'In the year 1242 after the Incarnation of the Lord, at XV calends of October
(17 Sept.), Brother Petrus of Vielle Briude passed away. He was the eighth
Master of the Holy Hospital of Jerusalem after the occupation of the Holy
Land. May his soul rest in peace. Amen. In his time the Count de Montfort and
other barons of France were delivered from captivity in Cairo while Richard
Earl of Cornwall was erecting the fortress of Ascalon.'[107]

Additional properties of the Order recorded in the thirteenth century included a hay
or oil store, ox stalls (possibly the bouerel that appears to the west of the Hospital on
the maps of Pietro Vesconte and Paolino Puteoli), woodsheds, a piggery, fowl houses
and a carpentry workshop.[108]

Hospitaller possessions in other towns of the Latin East

In 1261 Balian of Ibelin handed the town and castle of Arsuf over to the Hospitallers.
A mere four years later, in 1265, Arsuf fell to Baybars. It is none the less quite likely
that part of the remarkable fortress that dominates this small town on its north-west
dates from this brief period.[109] The town and its castle have been the subject of
intensive excavation over the past decade. The excavations carried out by Tel Aviv
University have exposed sections of the urban defences, including sections of the moat
to the south and east and a city gate on the east.[110]

The castle is surrounded by its own broad moat (up to 14 metres deep from the top
of its counterscarp and up to 30 metres wide) which was traversed by a drawbridge in
the south-east. The gate was protected by a portcullis and defended on either side by
horseshoe-shaped towers. As the apsidal wall of one of these towers faced east, it is
quite possible that (as at Saranda Kolones, Sidon and possibly Montfort) the castle
chapel was located in a tower, possibly on the first-floor level.[111] At the centre of the
castle was an open courtyard and to the west a polygonal keep (c. 8 by 8 metres
internally) rose above the wall, overlooking the cliffs above the sea and the small
harbour. At some stage, perhaps during the Hospitaller occupation, the keep was
modified by the addition of square corners on its north-east and south-east, giving it a
square form. North of the keep was the castle kitchen. This was a small room paved
with stone flags and containing two plastered basins and ceramic pipes on the east and
five ovens on the north (Figure 58). These were not unlike those of Belvoir. Their firing
chambers opened onto a passageway on the north. It is reasonable to assume that the
refectory was located nearby, perhaps in the hall just to the north. On the southern side
of the keep a broad staircase ascended to the upper storey of the keep, of which nothing
remains. Numerous mangonel balls scattered amongst the ruins dramatically illustrate
the final days of the siege here in 1265.

Early in the twelfth century Eustace Garnier, lord of Caesarea (1105/10–23), granted the Hospitallers houses in Caesarea.[112] By the middle of the twelfth century they had an auberge in the town.[113]

Shortly after the occupation of Jaffa in 1099, Godfrey of Bouillon granted the Hospitallers an oven, land and houses in the town.[114] Their property increased when in 1194 they received an entire quarter of Jaffa from Count Henry of Champagne. It was located in the north-west of the faubourg, extending from the Church of St Peter, below the castle, to the shore in the north, where they held two towers on the sea wall of the faubourg.[115] In the thirteenth century they further extended their holdings in the city, receiving additional grants of land in 1231 and 1238.[116] There was an auberge in Jaffa.[117] The Hospitaller Order also had a hospital and a hospice in Nablus, the former apparently a large courtyard building, fragmentary remains of which survive. Of the latter nothing is known. According to Benvenisti, the hospital was a large structure, 80 metres long (north–south).[118] However, Pringle notes that the remains of the hospital, as they survived until early in the last century (and were recorded in photographs by Creswell),[119] were of an elongated barrel-vaulted building on an east–west axis measuring 50 to 55 metres in length by 15.8 metres in width.[120] It had a slightly protruding turret on the north and several arched openings on the north and south walls. A now-lost inscription on a marble block was found here in 1564 and recorded by the Portuguese Franciscan, Pantaleone d'Aveiro. It read:

HOC HABITACULUM EDIFICATU[M] FUIT IN HONOREM
DEI ET BEATE MARIE
ET SANCTI JOHANNIS BAPTISTE AD HABITATIONE[M] PEREGRINORUM
ROGERIO, MAGISTRO HOSPITALIS HIERUSALEM,
ANNO AB INCARNATIONE DOMINI MCLXXX
BEATI QUI AMBULA[N]T IN DOMO TUA DOMINE:
IN SECULA SECULORUM LAUDEBANT TE.[121]

'This dwelling place was built in honour of God, the Blessed Mary and St John the Baptist for the habitation of pilgrims by Roger, Master of the Hospital in Jerusalem, in the year of the incarnation of the Lord 1180. Blessed are they who walk in your house, Oh Lord: they will praise you for ever more.'

In Tyre the Hospitaller house was located south of that of the Teutonic Knights which, as we know from a source dated 1264, was near to the city wall and the Butchery postern.[122] The Hospitallers possessed property in Sidon, and in 1162 Gerard, lord of Sidon, granted them part of the city's defences, a gate and part of the forewall extending from Baldwin's Tower to the Sea Tower, as well as a plot of land outside the walls.[123] A Hospitaller house (*mansus*) was recorded in 1262. A grant to the Hospitallers of a church dedicated to St John the Baptist on Mont Pelerin (Mons Peregrinus), close to Tripoli, was made by Bishop Pons of Tripoli between 1110 and 1113, and received papal confirmation in 1119.[124] In 1126 they were also granted a hospitale pauperum.[125] The Hospitaller church of St John, which was apparently consecrated in 1126, had a cemetery.[126] Excavations carried out here were published by Hassan Salamé-Sarkis and, more recently, by Pringle.[127] Two adjacent structures with a connecting passage and staircase were exposed. The smaller structure, the crypt, had benches and a basin with a conduit, and it appears to have served as a funeral chapel. Late in the thirteenth century the Hospitallers built a new tower in the town of Tripoli.[128]

In 1207 the Hospitallers received from Raymond Roupen of Antioch the coastal town of Gibel, south of Laodicea. This grant was only realised in 1218, but the town had also been granted to the Templars by Bohemond of Tripoli.[129] In Antioch the Hospitallers possessed a hospital, and in the early twelfth century Bernard, the first Latin patriarch of Antioch, granted them land in front of it on which to build a stable.[130]

The Order possessed certain properties in Cyprus. A Hospitaller house in Famagusta is referred to,[131] and in 1308, after the suppression of the Templars, they received the Templars' house.[132] The church which Enlart designated as belonging to the Hospitallers probably dates from the fourteenth century. It is a rather small building consisting of a single groin-vaulted bay (extended slightly at either end with the apse in the east), but is taller than the Templar church and resembles a small tower. It was constructed in a strange mixture of styles with Romanesque elements but also Gothic crocket capitals. There is Burgundian-type corbelling composed of grouped brackets, similar to examples found in Champagne.

The Hospitallers were also in possession of some buildings in Nicosia, including a fortified town-house, a tower and the Church of St John. The church had served as the burial place for the first Frankish kings of Cyprus: Hugh I in 1218 (and his wife Alice of Champagne, d. 1257) and Hugh II in 1267. The tower was renowned for an incident in 1229 when Philip of Novara took refuge in it after having escaped from an ambush by the bailies sent to Cyprus by Frederick II. Nothing remains of the conventual buildings at Limassol.[133]

3

THE URBAN QUARTERS OF THE
TEUTONIC KNIGHTS

There were no Teutonic possessions in twelfth-century Jerusalem, which fell to Saladin in 1187, before the Order was established in Acre after the Third Crusade. However, in the thirteenth century, following the reoccupation of Jerusalem in 1229, Frederick II granted the Teutonic Order the former German pilgrims' hospice and church (St Maria Alemannorum) in the south-east of the city, as well as a house in the Armenian Street, near the Church of St Thomas, and a garden and six acres of land.[1]

The German Quarter and tower in Acre

During the siege of Acre in September 1190, the newly founded German field hospital received from Guy of Lusignan a grant of a house within the city walls at the Gate of St Nicholas, another plot for building a permanent hospital and additional land located nearby.[2] The German Quarter which was thus established is recorded on the medieval maps of Acre as occupying land near the walls in the eastern part of the city and including a castle and a tower.[3] The Templar of Tyre describes the Germans' 'most beautiful hostel and most noble tower which was as large and as beautiful as that of the Temple'.[4] The Teutonic Quarter had a church which was burnt down by the Templars during internecine disturbances in 1242.[5]

Other sources reveal that in the last decades of Crusader rule, after they had lost their headquarters at Montfort to Baybars in 1271, the Teutonic Knights expanded their quarter in Acre through the purchase of considerable additional property in the north-east of the old city. A document in the state archives of Venice, which was authenticated on 1 September 1273, records that one Thomas of Bailleu, with the consent of King Hugh III, sold his heritage in Acre to the Teutonic Knights for 6,620 Saracen bezants, including 175 bezants and 22 corroubles in rent (censive) for a number of houses.[6] This property was situated between Ruga St Samuelis to its south, the moat of the citadel to the north, the heritage of a Syrian moneychanger named Brehin (Ibrahim) in the east, and the monastery of St Samuel in the west. From these parameters it is clear that by 1273 the German Quarter occupied much of the north-east corner of the old city up to the southern moat of the citadel.[7] This property extended their existing Quarter to the north and west into the open area south of the citadel.

Like the other Orders, the Germans were also given custody over a section of the town defences. In 1193 Henry II granted the Teutonic Order a *barbacana* at the Gate of St Nicholas, together with towers, walls, a moat and a vault at the town wall.[8] This was no doubt a section of the forewall extending from the Gate of St Nicholas to either the north or the south (or perhaps in both directions). In return the Order was required to keep these defences in repair.[9]

There are at present no remains in the east of the Crusader city that can be identified with certainty as belonging to the German Quarter. However, in 1999 and 2000 a group of structures was partly exposed in excavations outside and well to the east of the walls of the Turkish city (Figure 12). This may have been part of the German Quarter and headquarters, which appear with the titles 'Alamani' and 'Turris Alamanorum' on the medieval maps of thirteenth-century Acre.[10] This excavation, carried out as a joint project of the Deutcher Orden and the University of Haifa, uncovered evidence of several domestic structures as well as the fragmentary remains of a large rib-vaulted building.[11] These buildings were destroyed in the Mamluk conquest of 1291, as is evidenced by a destruction layer of ash and rubble which contained late thirteenth-century ceramics, glass and coins.[12] A later destruction of these remains can be dated to the eighteenth and early nineteenth centuries when, after the construction of the city walls of Turkish Akko, all structures outside the new walls were systematically dismantled in order to prevent their being used by assailants as shelters and in order to open an obstacle-free area before the walls.

Despite the fragmentary state of the remains exposed in these excavations, it is clear that they included both public and private buildings as well as industrial installations. Goldmann excavated a large public building here in 1961, and Moshe Dothan excavated the more substantial remains of a second building nearby in 1974.[13] The remains of the former building consisted of three courses of well-dressed stones, each half a metre high and some bearing masons' marks. Amongst the finds were some sculptural

Figure 12 Excavations at the possible site of the Teutonic house in Acre (photograph courtesy of Georg Phillip Melloni).

fragments. Goldmann identified the building as belonging to the Teutonic Order.[14] This was part of the rib-vaulted building excavated in 2000.[15] The building excavated by Dothan about 70 metres further to the north was constructed from well-dressed sandstone ashlars with plaster mouldings.[16] It had a loggia faced with marble on its south side. A conflagration destroyed both of these buildings in 1291.

Fragments of other structures uncovered in the recent excavations were of private houses, and the large quantity of ceramics found established both the residential and the industrial nature of this site. These were mostly cooking vessels and tableware, but in one building a quantity of moulds used in the refining of sugar were found. This site is located only a few metres from another site excavated by E.J. Stern in 1995, in which industrial installations, including two plastered pools (2.5 by 2.5 and 1.5 by 4.0 metres), were uncovered.[17] Additional excavations in this area carried out in 2003 exposed sewage works, which add to the likelihood that this was a residential area.[18]

Nothing is known of the appearance of the German Quarter's church. In this church Duke Frederick of Swabia and Alsace, son of Frederick I Barbarossa, was buried after his death on 20 January 1191. It was burned down by the Templars during the unrest of 1242.[19]

In summary, the archaeological and historical evidence points to a quarter consisting of fortified and non-fortified public and private buildings. These included a section of the city fortifications, open land or gardens inside the walls, a castle or palace, a large tower, a hospital, a church, private houses, industrial installations, possibly including a sugar refinery, and perhaps other workshops.[20]

Possessions of the Teutonic Knights in other towns of the Latin East

In 1206 Juliana, lady of Caesarea, granted the Teutonic Order two towers on the wall of Caesarea, together with houses and other possessions.[21] The grant was confirmed by Pope Innocent III in June 1209. The Order possessed houses in Ramla, Gaza and Ascalon.[22] They had a house in Sidon in the western part of the town near the sea, recorded in a document of 21 March 1253.[23] In Jaffa in 1196 Count Henry of Champagne gave the Order a plot of land in the city and Pope Celestine III confirmed the grant of a house, vineyards and other possessions.[24] A list of property held by the Teutonic Order which predates 1243 includes possession of a plot of land located near their oven and court (*curia*) in Jaffa.[25] In April 1195 Henry II presented the Teutonic Knights with a house in Tyre and land in the vicinity, outside of the city walls.[26] A document of 1264 refers to a house of the Teutonic Knights near the city walls of Tyre not far from the postern called *la Boucherie* (the Butchery).[27] Teutonic possessions in Tripoli which are recorded in documents include three towers.[28] The Teutonic Order had only limited possessions in Cyprus; in Famagusta, according to a Genoese document of 1300, there was a St Mary's Hospital of the Teutonic Knights.[29]

4

THE URBAN QUARTERS OF THE
LEPER KNIGHTS OF ST LAZARUS

Although the Church and the Crusader rulers were on the whole well disposed to the leper community,[1] the desire to distance lepers from the rest of the general population was as strong in the Latin East as it was elsewhere. The Third Lateran Council (1179) had ruled that lepers must be segregated from the community, have a separate church and be buried in separate burial grounds. Leper colonies in the Kingdom of Jerusalem were generally located outside city walls, as was customary in the West and in Eastern cities.

The leper quarter outside the walls of Jerusalem

The leper house in Jerusalem, the Maladerie, of the Leper Knights of St Lazarus occupied an area north of the city walls to the west of St Stephen's Gate. Though the exact location of this Quarter is unknown, there are indications from various sources, including archaeological finds. Two sources suggest a location outside the western city wall. One of these is the reference to a mill owned by the Order which was removed by Queen Melisende in 1151 because it was obstructing traffic into the city by David's Gate.[2] The other is the twelfth-century Cambrai Map, which shows the Church of St Lazarus near the north-west corner of the city on the western side.[3] Another source, *Ernoul, l'estat de la cité de Iherusalem*, locates the leper quarter outside the northern city wall on the right hand of St Stephen's Gate near the wall, pointing out that the postern of St Ladre connecting the Lepers' Quarter with the city was close to the hospital and that in the thirteenth century, when Jerusalem was again under Muslim rule, the gate was used by Christian pilgrims going with guides to the Church of the Holy Sepulchre.[4]

An arched portal constructed of typically Frankish diagonally tooled stones, located in the northern city wall some 2 metres below the modern ground level, was found in the late nineteenth century by the Franciscans, excavating to the north of their newly purchased property.[5] This was apparently the inner portal of the Postern of St Lazarus (i.e. that in the main wall). The discovery of steps in the moat nearby leading down from an outer portal and the threshold of the outer postern itself was published in 1895.[6] It seems that in order to enter this postern it was necessary to cross the moat and climb the staircase; clearly no vehicular traffic entered the city in this way. The discovery of these two posterns give an indication of the position of the Lepers' Quarter, which may have extended along a fair part of the northern wall and even along the northern section of the western wall, possibly as far as David's Gate.

Another source suggesting the northern location is a charter of 1177 which refers to a main road leading from the leper house towards the reservoir: '*Stratum regium que ducit a domo leprosorum Sancti Lazari versus lacum Legerii*'.[7] A second road continued north-east to the Church of St Stephen, which had in earlier times supported a leper colony. The location of the open reservoir known as the Pool of St Ladre (Lacus Legerii), which can still be seen to the north of the northern wall within the modern suburb of Morasha (Musrarah), also supports a northern location for the quarter. However, another source suggests that the lepers in fact occupied two areas outside the walls, at both David's Gate and St Stephen's Gate. This is the *Estoire d'Eracles*, which when discussing Saladin's siege of Jerusalem in 1187 describes the line of attack as being from the Maladerie for women at David's Gate to the Maladerie for men at St Stephen's Gate.[8] Thus we have two separate leper hospitals, one for each sex, and the Order's properties may have extended or been scattered along the space in between, with the Church of St Lazarus about half way between them near the corner of the wall, as it appears on the Cambrai Map.[9]

The leper colony would have been abandoned in September 1187 when Saladin opened his siege on the city in precisely the area which they occupied. The hospital was probably abandoned well in advance, for after the Battle of Hattin there could have been no doubt that a siege of the city was imminent and the lepers were entirely exposed and undefended. Where they would have gone at this time is an open question. Would they have been allowed into the city? If so, and it is reasonable to assume that this would have been the case in such circumstances, they would most likely have been isolated in one of the open fields on the periphery of the city within the walls. It may have been at this time that the colony, which in the Turkish period was located in the south of the city (against the inner side of the southern city wall to the east of the present Zion Gate), was established.

Nothing is known of the appearance of these buildings. In excavations carried out in 1989 in the area outside the western city wall archaeologists found a number of ashlars dressed with typical Frankish diagonal tooling, one of them bearing a mason's mark.[10] In 1988/89 buttressed walls and a quantity of ashlars were discovered during excavations on a site to the north of the north-west corner of the city, where the new Jerusalem municipality building was to be constructed. In the former case the stones were not found *in situ* and there is no means of knowing what building they came from or exactly where it was located. They could have originated in any of a number of other buildings near the walls, inside or outside the city. As for the latter finds, other than the fact that they were discovered in the general vicinity of the Quarter of St Lazarus, there is no evidence to support the excavator's suggestion that these may have been remains of the leper hospital.[11]

At the end of the nineteenth century the remains of a burial structure were discovered on a plot of land opposite the north wall of Jerusalem.[12] The position of this unusual building to the north of the city walls, slightly east of Porta St Stephan and adjacent to the area possessed by the Order of St Lazarus, suggests the possibility that it was owned by the Order and possibly served as a burial house for the lepers.[13]

The Quarter of the Leper Knights of St Lazarus in Acre

It is not known exactly when the Quarter of St Lazarus in Acre was founded or whether, as in Jerusalem, it existed before the Crusader period as a regular leper colony. If it existed by the mid-twelfth century, the lepers' quarter in Acre at that time would have been located well outside the city walls. However, as the city expanded north in the second half of the twelfth century the new settlements outside the walls would have approached it. By the thirteenth century it was contained within the new city walls, together with these new suburbs. On Matthew Paris's map it appears close up against the north-west corner of the suburb of Montmusard (Domus Militum Ecclesia Sancti Lazari).[14] On Marino Sanudo's map it is north of the Hospitallers' auberge and south of what were probably open fields adjacent to the inner northern wall, on the east side of a street running north–south from a gate in the old northern wall to the south (St Michael's Gate) to the Porta St Lazari in the wall of Montmusard.[15]

Other urban possessions of the Leper Knights of St Lazarus in the Latin East

In 1160 Hugh of Caesarea granted the Order of St Lazarus a garden and two adjoining houses, apparently to serve as a leper hospital.[16] They were to be held rent-free and free of other services as long as they housed members of the Order. This grant was motivated by the fact that Hugh's brother, Eustace, was himself a member of the Order. One of these houses had indeed previously belonged to Hugh, the other to one Arnald Gala who had also become a member of the Order.

In Nicosia there was a nunnery, recorded in 1310, which was dedicated to St Lazarus.[17] It appears to be the same institution as the one which received a legacy from Bernard Fayssa of Narbonne in 1310. In this will it is recorded as a hospital, 'infiirmis Sancti Lazari' – probably the leper hospital.[18]

5

THE QUARTER OF THE KNIGHTS
OF ST THOMAS

The houses of the Order of St Thomas were originally located on the eastern side of Acre, near the hospital of the Germans. On the instigation of Peter de les Roches, Bishop of Winchester, the Order moved in the 1220s to a new location in the north of the Montmusard faubourg near the Quarter of the Knights of St Lazarus (to its south on one of the medieval maps). The bishop built a church here for the Order. On the thirteenth-century map of Matthew Paris, above an illustration of a church, appear the words: 'La maisun de seint Thomas le mar[tir]'.[1] Along the length of the north-eastern wall of Montmusard appears the inscription: 'C'est le Burg ki est apelé Munt Musard: c'est tut le plus inhabi{t}é de Engleis'.[2] Prince Edward, later Edward I of England, visited Acre in 1271, at which time the Order was constructing a new church. When he subsequently came to the throne he supported the Order, giving them custody over the new tower (Turris Anglorum) that he had had constructed near the eastern end of the outer northern wall of the city.

This minor Military Order has, to the best of our knowledge, left no visible physical remains, unless they survive in some walls that can be traced on the present shoreline north of the old city of Akko and south of the offshore round tower, which defines the line of Montmusard's northern wall. The Order had few other properties. There was a priory of the Order of St Thomas of Canterbury in Nicosia which had a church dedicated to St Nicholas (later referred to as ecclesia S. Nicholai Anglicorum).[3] Enlart has suggested that this may be the surviving church of St Nicholas.[4] This church is situated on the south side of the cathedral *parvis* (square). Its plan is somewhat unusual, a large central nave terminating in a five-sided apse with one broad aisle on the north and a three-sided apse and two narrower aisles on the south, each with a round apse inset in a thick chevet. The rib-vaulted bays of the southern aisles are not aligned with the vaults of the central nave and the northern aisle. The second bay from the east of the central nave supports an octagonal drum (internally cylindrical) carried on pendentives and supporting a hemispherical dome lit by eight windows which, as Enlart notes, created a remarkable blending of Gothic and Byzantine.[5] The church contains work from the late thirteenth century (the crocket capital on a column between the southern aisles dates from about 1270) to the fifteenth or early sixteenth century. The main doorway on the north, with its squat Gothic gabling imitating the west doorways of St Sophia, is fourteenth century. The western front of the church has a porch of four rib-vaulted bays and has three doorways corresponding with the nave, the northern aisle and the southernmost of the two southern aisles. However, the main door was on the north side of the church, opening onto the *parvis*. A door on the south appears to have given access into the conventual buildings, of which only fragmentary remains survive. These may have been the conventual buildings of the house of the Order of St Thomas.

After the departure of the Order, by the early sixteenth century the church was adopted by the Greeks as their cathedral. By the beginning of the eighteenth century de Bruyn (1700) describes the church as being used as a bazaar, and in the nineteenth century it was used as a governmental tithe barn.[6]

In addition to the Church of St Nicholas, in the Cathedral of St Sophia there was a chapel, built on the instigation of John de Polo, which was dedicated to St Thomas of Canterbury. Enlart suggests that this may have been the upper chapel of the treasury, which is similar in style to other works in the cathedral ascribed to de Polo. He describes the chapel thus:

> The upper chapel of the treasury is lit on the east side by three lancets and on the north by only one. These windows have elegant colonnettes with round capitals ornamented with foliar crockets. On the south and west, above the flat roofs of the ambulatory and the transept, they have been replaced by *oeil-de-boeuf* windows with quatrefoil tracery.[7]

Part II

THE RURAL ACTIVITY OF
THE MILITARY ORDERS

6

EXPANSION INTO THE COUNTRYSIDE

With the exception of the crown and monasteries, the Military Orders were the principal landholders in the Latin East. Although the process of acquiring farm lands and rural settlements began early in the twelfth century, it took root in the thirteenth century as financial difficulties increasingly forced knights to sell their land. The Military Orders, with their almost unlimited resources, took over these properties, acquiring extensive tracts of land throughout the Kingdom of Jerusalem and the other Crusader states. They acquired land partly by occupation following conquest, but mainly by purchase and the receipt of grants. The Hospitallers began to establish a rural presence quite early in the twelfth century: in 1118 they were settling farmers in the County of Edessa.[1] With the establishment of a group of Templar castles in the Amanus Mountains north of Antioch in the late 1130s, the Templars may have come into their first landed holdings in the East. By the second half of the twelfth century both of the large Military Orders possessed extensive rural properties in the East and West. As a latecomer on the scene, the Teutonic Order began to acquire property only in the early thirteenth century, purchasing lands in the western Galilee and somewhat later in Cilician Armenia.

The acquisition of agricultural properties became an important activity of the Military Orders (Figure 13). The possession of farms and villages was essential as a means of providing food and other produce, both for the use of the garrisons of castles and for the maintenance of their urban quarters and institutions. Surplus goods could be sold in the town markets for cash. Taxes and tithes collected from their local villages and farms supplemented the finances pouring in from the Orders' possessions in the West. Thus we find the Military Orders competing with the barons and other land-owners, and of course with one another, for the ownership of an ever-dwindling supply of land. Not only was farmland acquired to supply castles, but the process was some-times reversed; some castles were built by the Military Orders in order to provide protection for their landed possessions.

Hospitaller rural possessions

From an early date all of the major Military Orders became involved in acquiring properties outside the cities and thus in various activities connected to the management of rural estates. As noted, well before they became a Military Order the Hospitallers received property grants which are mentioned in a confirmation given by Baldwin I in 1110.[2] These included lands and houses in the region of the Carmel Mountains:

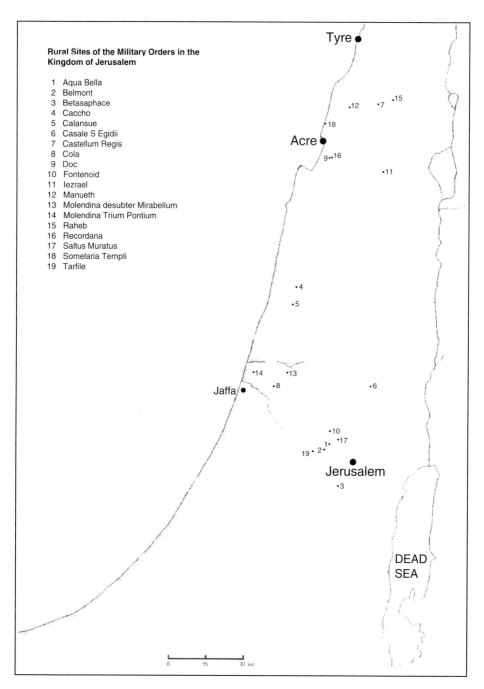

Rural Sites of the Military Orders in the Kingdom of Jerusalem

1   Aqua Bella
2   Belmont
3   Betasaphace
4   Caccho
5   Calansue
6   Casale S Egidii
7   Castellum Regis
8   Cola
9   Doc
10 Fontenoid
11 Iezrael
12 Manueth
13 Molendina desubter Mirabellum
14 Molendina Trium Pontium
15 Raheb
16 Recordana
17 Saltus Muratus
18 Somelaria Templi
19 Tarfile

Figure 13 Map of the rural sites of the Military Orders in the Kingdom of Jerusalem.

'*terris ac domibus in villa Cayphas et Capharnaum*'. Even before this they were granted properties, including a village near Jerusalem called Hessilia (es-Silsileh) by Godfrey of Bouillon. In 1136 King Fulk granted to the Order the small castle of Bethgibelin (see pp. 116–18), which he had built. It was located at the centre of a rural estate including several *casalia* (villages) in the vicinity.[3] The castle was part of a group of fortresses forming a ring around Fatimid Ascalon; these were intended to put an end to the incursions of Muslim raiders which since the beginning of the century had harassed the hinterland of the kingdom. By the early 1150s, before the fall of Ascalon, these fortresses had achieved their desired effect and had brought a degree of quiet and security that allowed the Franks to establish rural settlements.[4] Shortly before the fall of Ascalon to the Franks in 1153 a village was set up near the castle at Bethgibelin. A record of this event has fortunately come down to us in the form of an agreement reached between the Hospitallers and the settlers, preserved in a document dating from 1168.[5] It sheds considerable light on the way in which the settlement was founded and is perhaps typical of the agreements establishing such settlements in the twelfth century. Prawer referred to this settlement as a *ville neuve*, an increasingly common type of planned settlement in the medieval West, and to the charter granted by the Hospitaller Master, Raymond du Puy, as 'not less than a *carte de peuplement*, a real *carta puebla*'.[6] Although the village was sacked by the Muslims in 1158, by the 1160s it was solidly established and housed 32 families.[7] These settlers were Franks, all of them freemen and some from the local towns of Hebron, Jerusalem and de Ramis (Ramla or ar-Ram); one was from Edessa and the others from Europe (Auvergne, Gascogne, Lombardy, Poitou, Catalonia, Burgundy, Flanders and Carcassonne).

According to the terms of this charter, each of the villagers received a plot of farmland measuring two *carrucae* (an estimated 6–8 hectares[8]) in *tenure en bourgeoise*.[9] They paid the *terraticum* (tax paid in kind) and tithes (except on olive crops). In order to attract settlers the Hospitallers relinquished the usual right of pre-emption, granting the settlers the right to alienate their land in return for a minor payment to the Order.

Unfortunately, this valuable source of information on the arrangement between the Hospitallers and the settlers does not enlighten us at all as to the actual location of the settlement in relation to the fortifications. The archaeological work that has been so rewarding in recent years in exposing the castle and church has provided no clear evidence of the whereabouts of the village. Indeed, according to the excavators there was a remarkable absence of any apparently domestic remains in the excavated area within the outer fortifications. If we examine the plan of the complex (Figure 32), it would seem that the most likely location of the settlement would have been to the west of the inner castle, within the double outer walls and moat. As no trace of the village has been found there, it may be worth while to consider other alternatives. One possibility, suggested by the excavator, Amos Kloner, is that it was located outside the fortifications to the south, on the other side of the modern Ascalon–Hebron road. In the area that has not yet been examined can be seen the surface remains of a number of buildings which could be of medieval date.[10] Another possibility is that the rural settlement was located at a more distant location, perhaps at the site of the remains of the Byzantine church of St Anne at Khirbat Sandahanna, about 2 km to the south near the ancient tell and city of Mareshah.[11] In the twelfth century a smaller church was built here by the Franks within the Byzantine ruins, occupying the area of the old nave and incorporating substantial remains of the earlier church.[12] However, despite the lack of archaeological evidence, it would seem unlikely that the medieval settlement was not near the Hospitaller castle and enclosed by the impressive fortification works that have been uncovered. The Sandahanna site seems too distant and exposed. And yet, as the contemporary Frankish settlements with which we are acquainted were well-built stone constructions,[13] it would seem unlikely that the archaeologists have failed to notice the remains of houses within the walls. This question remains at present unresolved.

The outer fortifications of Bethgibelin appear to have been constructed at about the same time as those of other small castles in the south of the kingdom when they were similarly expanded. These improvements were probably carried out in the 1170s. With the Crusader occupation of Ascalon in 1153 these castles had lost their original function, and their defensive capabilities had declined as a result of the building of unfortified structures around and against them. This enhancing of the castles' defences was most likely carried out to enable them to face a renewed and growing threat of invasion from Egypt.

The outworks constructed at Bethgibelin (Figure 32) considerably enlarged the fortified area and strengthened the site. Two parallel lines of fortification were added. The outer wall is *c.* 3 metres wide, and is lined with a talus, and the inner wall is *c.* 2 metres wide. Both walls have a number of rectangular projecting towers and the inner wall has two polygonal towers in the south-west. A row of massive piers inside and adjacent to the inner wall appears to have supported a groin-vaulted passage.

The Hospitallers possessed property in the vicinity of Bethgibelin as far east as Bethsura. Further north, the Hospitallers received from John of Ibelin partial possession of a mill near the mouth of the Yarqon River known as the Molendina Trium Pontium, 'Mill of the Three Bridges', in 1241.[14] This mill survived into modern times and was still functioning in the early twentieth century.[15] A triple-arched bridge that gave the mill its name was destroyed in 1917.[16] A second mill on the Yarqon further upstream, Molendina desubter Mirabellum (al-Mirr), was a two-storey structure with a dam (Figure 14).[17] According to Y. Pinkerfeld, who examined the remains, it had originally been built in the Roman/Byzantine period and was restored by the Franks.[18] However, what can be seen today appears to be entirely of Ottoman date. Though there is no direct evidence that this mill was also in Hospitaller hands, it is possible that the Order was in control of all the mills in the region.[19]

The Hospitallers acquired several properties on and near the southern route between Jerusalem and Jaffa. Before September 1110 Baldwin I granted the Order the village of Bethasaphace (Bait Safafa) to the south of Jerusalem near the road to Bethlehem.[20] Ruins of the medieval complex that survive in the village include a rectangular enclosure fortified with a talus on three sides, perhaps with a gate on the north-east. Within this are a tower and adjacent vaults. The tower measures 18.2 by 13.7 metres with walls 2.5–2.9 metres thick, and has three floor levels, one of which was an inserted mezzanine supported by a rounded barrel vault; there are additional vaulted structures.[21]

West of Jerusalem was a Hospitaller possession named Saltus Muratus. This site is mentioned in the Hospitaller archives and is generally identified with the twelfth-century settlement at Qaluniya (Colonia), 6.5 km from the Old City of Jerusalem on the

Figure 14 Site of the Hospitaller mill, Molendina desubter Mirabellum (photograph by the author).

road to Tel-Aviv.[22] At this site are the remains of a Frankish rural settlement consisting of a number of barrel- and groin-vaulted structures. One of these is a well-built barrel vault, constructed of large field stones with marginally drafted ashlar quoins, which measures 15 by 30 metres (external). The walls survive on the interior to the height of the vault springing; the exterior of the south wall is preserved to a height of 5 metres or ten courses. Pringle suggests that it may have been a cistern,[23] but the presence nearby of a large underground vaulted cistern may point to another use for this building, perhaps as a first-floor hall house.[24] Fragmentary remains of groin-vaulting can be seen about 18 metres to the north-west of this structure. This appears to belong to a structure which measured *c.* 7.45 by 4.2 metres. It was constructed of fine limestone ashlars with typically Frankish diagonal tooling. An additional large barrel-vaulted building to the west, which was recently excavated by the Theological Institution of the University of Basel, demonstrates that this complex originally consisted of several vaulted structures, rather like the complexes at Qalansuwa and Cola.[25]

By 1169 the Hospitallers were also in possession of the village of Fontenoid or Castellum Emaus (Abu Ghosh) further to the west; they appear to have been responsible for the construction of the well-preserved tri-apsidal church in this village. Fontenoid was identified by the Franks as the Emmaus of the New Testament, the place where Christ appeared to two of the disciples three days after the Crucifixion and Resurrection. The attraction of this site for the Hospitallers included its location on the Jerusalem road near some of their other possessions (Aqua Bella, Belmont), the comparative fertility of the land, a good water supply and the identification of a holy event at this place. The latter made it an important pilgrimage site and consequently a source of income for the Order.[26]

The Church of the Resurrection at Abu Ghosh is one of the best preserved Frankish churches (Figure 15). It was constructed before 1165, perhaps well before that date.[27] Clermont-Ganneau points to the possibility of a date before 1137.[28] He based this on a passage written by a monk from Montecassino, Petrus Cassinensis (Peter the Deacon), which discusses the construction of a church at Kiriath Jearim. However, this was apparently a Byzantine church located not at Abu Ghosh but at Tell al-Azhar somewhat further to the west.[29] Most scholars date the construction of the church at Abu Ghosh to after 1141, when the Hospitallers received land to the west of Jerusalem known as *terra de Emaus*. Pringle also suggests an early date (*c.* 1140), on the basis of the similarity of the ground plan with that of the church of St Mary of the Germans in Jerusalem and the use in both churches of thick-leafed capitals on elbow consoles supporting transverse arches which span the nave.[30] An early date is also suggested by the fortified nature of the construction, with side walls over 2.5 metres thick and the western wall and chevet well over 3 metres thick. Such construction, which goes well beyond the usual proportions for Frankish rural church building, would be appropriate up to the fifth decade of the twelfth century, when the region was still under threat of Muslim incursions from Ascalon, and less necessary in the 1150s or 1160s when the threat had been removed.

The Church of the Resurrection was built adjacent to an early Islamic (ninth-century) caravanserai and partly over the ruins of a Roman cistern. It has a typical

Figure 15 Church at Fontenoid (Abu Ghosh) (photograph by the author).

Crusader basilical plan with three apses and measures 27.5 by 20.6/21.3 metres (external). A broad staircase leads to a tri-apsidal crypt containing the spring, the focal point of the site, above which is an altar.[31] Construction throughout is of local limestone fieldstones, with marginally drafted ashlar quoins and diagonally tooled ashlars for window and door frames and for the interior. The vaulting is roughly constructed of small fieldstones and is plastered over. Pilasters and six square free-standing piers support the twelve groin vaults of the church, with two massive free-standing piers supporting the six groin vaults of the crypt. A buttressed clerestory with eight windows, together with embrasure windows on the east and west and on the side walls, illuminated the church. The principal door (1.6 metres wide) is on the north, while a smaller door to its left gives access to a staircase leading down to the crypt.

Architectural sculpture is almost entirely lacking in this rather austere building. One exception is the row of elbow consoles with simple Romanesque thick-leafed capitals that supports the transverse arches in the nave. Another is the use of spiral *fleurons* in the hood-mould of the north door. The wall paintings in the church have been dated by Kühnel on stylistic evidence to *c.* 1170.[32] These frescoes, which have recently (2001) been restored, are an exceptional example of church decoration, being the best preserved and most extensive example of fresco painting in the mainland Crusader states.[33] A long period of neglect, some intentional damage, and use of the church as a stable have all contributed to the deterioration of these works, which decorate the three apses and the eastern bays of the aisles. Simple fresco decoration also decorated the vaulting in the crypt. The programme included the Anastasis (resurrection of Christ) in the central apse, the patriarchs in the southern apse, the Deesis (Christ between the Virgin Mary and John the Baptist) in the northern apse, a Koimesis (falling asleep of Mary) on the north wall and a Crucifixion scene on the south wall. In addition, there are representations of saints on the side walls. The workmanship is of high quality and the paintings belong to the so-called 'dynamic' phase of the Comnenian style.

To the east of the church are the remains of conventual buildings. These include a large structure on the eastern side of the ninth-century caravanserai which served as a water tank. In the Crusader period it was converted into a barrel-vaulted hall supported with a transverse arch at the centre. It was entered from the north-west and illuminated by embrasures in the north and south walls. This hall may have functioned as the refectory, though another possibility is that it served as a storage area and bakery. There is a large bread oven built into the east wall. A water tank below an adjoining room on the south-east (one of the small chambers around the caravanserai courtyard) was converted in the twelfth century into a latrine pit. There was apparently another building, which has not survived, adjacent to the east wall of the church. A staircase built within the northern wall of the church gave access to the upper storey of this building. This was possibly the dormitory wing of the Hospitaller brothers; the stairs would have been night-stairs giving them direct access into the church for night services.

On the other side of the modern highway are the remains of a two-storey structure known as Dair al-Banat at a spring known by the Franks as Aqua Bella (Figures 16, 17). This large courtyard building is situated in a small fertile valley with terraced fields and a good water supply from a spring. Along with Fontenoid and nearby Saltus Muratus (Qaluniya), Belmont (Suba) and Belveer (Castel), most of the land here was in the possession of the Hospitaller Order and the single twelfth-century reference (1168)

Figure 16 Hospitaller building at Aqua Bella (photograph by the author).

to this building refers to the Hospitaller Order as the owners. In this document the Hospitallers offered the income of these estates, together with that of Aqua Bella, to Duke Béla of Hungary (later King Béla III) to help support the duke and his wife, who were contemplating a move to the kingdom.[34]

This building has been variously interpreted as a convent, a farmhouse, a manor house or rural estate centre, and a hospital.[35] It was built on a hillside, the south side of the structure consisting of two constructed levels and the north side partly cut into the hill, partly constructed. The ground floor has three large barrel vaults surrounding the courtyard on the north, south and west. The fourth (east) side of the courtyard is enclosed by a high stone wall with a gate. The southern vault is entered via a door in its south wall and a second door in its north wall gives access to the courtyard. Windows on the west, east and south and the doors on the north and south provided light and air to this room, which not only served for storage but was an industrial area containing an olive press. In the east wall is a small square recess which held the press beam and a large millstone is still located in this vault. In the courtyard a staircase against the south wall gives access to the upper south range.

The upper level could also be accessed via a second entrance in a turret built over a cistern on the west. A gallery crosses the west side of the courtyard at this level. In the north-west corner is a small tower from which, as Pringle noted, the nearby Hospitaller fortress of Belmont could be seen.[36] The south range of the upper storey was a hall of three groin-vaulted bays with a small chapel on the east. A partition wall separated the

Figure 17 Interior of the Hospitaller building at Aqua Bella (photograph by the author).

chapel from the remainder of the hall. Near the centre of the south wall is a turret which contains pipes and may have served as a latrine. Enlart and more recently Pringle have suggested that this hall may have served as an infirmary.

By 1141 the landed estate referred to as *terra de Emaus* had also come into the possession of the Hospitallers.[37] A knight named Robert of Sinjil leased his property in this area to the Order for an annual rent of 500 bezants.[38] This gift was approved by the Patriarch in 1141. The Hospitallers were required to pay half-tithes from the estate to the Holy Sepulchre but could retain other revenues from these lands for their own use.[39]

North of Jerusalem the Hospital acquired properties in the region of Nablus, including Casale S Mariae ('Abud) south-west of Nablus at the eastern edge of the coastal plain next to the lands of the village of Bellfort. It was sold to them by the lord of Mirabel for 3,000 bezants and an annual payment of 200 bezants.[40] Further south on the road to Jerusalem they held lands near the village of Casale S Egidii or Saint Giles (Sinjil) which were granted to them by Robert of Sinjil, but not the village itself, which remained part of the royal domain and was settled by Franks.[41]

The castle of Bellfort (Bellifortis) itself stood at the high point of the village of Dair Abu Mash'al about 14 km south-east of Mirabel.[42] Its remains consist of a wall of marginally drafted ashlars enclosing an area *c.* 45 metres square.

Of the Hospitaller properties in the west of the kingdom, those in the southern part of the lordship of Caesarea have been discussed by Pringle.[43] The casale of Calansue (Qalansuwa) was granted to the Hospitallers by Geoffrey (or Godfrey) of Flujeac on 8

April 1128. Record of this donation charter appears only in an inventory of eighteenth-century date, where it seems to have been erroneously referred to as a castle.[44] The grant was confirmed by Baldwin II in 1129 in the royal court in Jerusalem and by Walter Garnier, lord of Caesarea, in 1131.[45] Lost to Saladin in 1187, Calansuc was subsequently recovered by the Franks following the Battle of Arsuf in 1191 and by 1207/8 was once again in Hospitaller hands. They may have established a commandery here around that time.[46] Calansue fell to Baybars in 1265.

Pringle has described in detail the group of medieval buildings at the centre of the village of Qalansuwa which probably constituted the commandery.[47] These included a tower and a first-floor hall, at least three other vaulted structures and a cistern. The tower, possibly the first structure of the complex, built when the Hospitallers occupied the site (or earlier),[48] survives only in a fragmentary state, since a groin-vaulted house incorporating the medieval remains was later constructed on the site. The northern and western walls of the tower are apparently all that survive, standing to a maximum height of 12.3 metres. The north wall is 12.05 metres long and *c.* 2–3 metres thick, built from roughly squared stones with quoins constructed of well-cut ashlars, some of which are marginally drafted.

The hall, located *c.* 40 metres north-east of the tower, measures 16.5 by 28(e.)/30(w.) metres (the difference in length is due to the sharp slant of the south wall). The basement and first floor of this building are composed of two rows of four groin-vaulted bays supported by three free-standing piers (1.65 metres square) and projecting pilasters (1.65 by 0.9 metres). Shallow transverse arches divide the bays. On the upper floor narrower pilasters with carved corbels support the transverse arches dividing the bays.[49] The internal measurements are 12.75 by 24.6/25.3 metres. The main entrances are in the well-preserved south wall. Here there are two doors: a smaller one with a pointed arch on the ground floor, 1.4 metres wide, and directly above it on the first floor a second doorway, 1.6 metres wide and 2.8 metres high, with a flat lintel set 40 cm within a larger pointed arch (2.33 metres wide). The larger, first-floor doorway was the principal entrance, apparently once reached by a wooden staircase or ramp. On the west side of the entrance passage is a staircase built in the thickness of the wall in a pointed barrel-vaulted passage which leads to the roof. Two lancet windows open onto it, one on the west wall and a second one higher up on the south wall. In the east wall in the second bay from the south of the ground floor is another door (now partly buried) which Pringle estimates as about 1.9 metres wide. One can still see additional lancet windows on the ground floor level in the west wall of the south-western bay and in the east wall of the north-eastern bay. These are 90 cm wide and 2.1 metres high (internally). On the first floor there is a double-splayed window in the west wall of the south-western bay. It is 1.05 metres wide internally, narrowing to 48 cm and expanding to 69 cm on its outer face. Pringle notes that it had a rebate for a shutter or glass and that it was intended only for illumination.[50]

Construction is of limestone and sandstone. The ashlars, extending several metres from the quoins, are 57 cm high and most of them have marginal drafting. The remaining walls between them (to judge from the surviving south wall) are constructed of smaller smooth ashlars in alternating courses of 31 and 26 cm. Smooth ashlars were used for the internal walls, vaulting and piers. The walls of the ground floor are *c.* 1.9 metres thick.

The first-floor hall house of Calansue constitutes a comparatively large and elaborate example of a fairly common type of rural administrative building in the Kingdom of Jerusalem. First-floor hall houses are found amongst other places at Bait 'Itab (Bethaatap), Khirbat Salman, Tel Hanaton (Tell al-Badawiya) and Khirbat al-Burj (Khirbat al-Kurum).[51] Such fortified or semi-fortified buildings were an appropriate type of residence for a landowner (or, as was probably the usual case, a representative of the landowner) in a countryside that was largely occupied by a peasantry which had little if any sympathy towards their Christian rulers. They have their counterparts in the European first-floor hall houses and *maisons-fortes*. They were perfectly adapted to the conditions and requirements of the Frankish East. The only thing that they lacked was enough covered space to contain the farm produce which was collected from the peasants as taxes paid in kind; this is why hall houses are almost invariably accompanied by additional vaulted structures to serve as storage and stabling and to contain related installations such as mills and presses. These additional buildings were often built together with the hall house enclosing a courtyard.[52] At Calansue the three additional vaulted structures do, after a fashion, form a courtyard complex, although not a very regular one. The south range consists of two rows of groin-vaulted bays (*c.* 5.30 metres e.–w. by 4.40 metres n.–s.) supported by a solid wall to the south and two rows of rectangular piers (1.4/1.7 by 1.8/2 metres). The remains of this building extend at least 25 metres east to west, but it clearly extended further in each direction and may possibly have joined the vaulted range to its east. Construction was of well-cut smooth ashlars on the north face (at least one with a mason's mark) and rubble vaulting with ashlar transverse arches.

Another groin-vaulted range is located to the east of the south range and to the south of the hall. It may possibly have been connected to the south range. Additional vaults, two joining barrel vaults, were located between the tower and the hall. The western vault is about 5 metres wide and the eastern vault is about 3.5 metres wide. Their length is unknown, and all of these structures would require excavation for a full understanding of how they relate to one another. A cistern is located on the south side of the barrel vaults and there were apparently additional cisterns south of the hall.[53]

Another Hospitaller estate centre at Qula, about 5 km south of Mirabel, was purchased from Hugh of Flanders in 1181.[54] It consisted of a tower-keep (*c.* 17 by 12.8 metres) with a barrel-vaulted ground floor and walls 3 metres thick, and a large barrel-vaulted storehouse (38 by 11 metres) with walls 2 metres thick. It was used by the Hospitallers for the production of foodstuffs for use in the Jerusalem hospital.[55] Throughout the twelfth and thirteenth centuries the Hospitallers acquired farmland and villages in the region. Early in the twelfth century they were granted land next to Caccho (Qaqun) by Eustace Garnier and by 1131 had received *curtileges* (farms), six *carrucae* of land and several houses, possibly including a house in Qaqun itself.[56] In 1141 Walter of Caesarea sold the Hospitaller Order a plot of land, together with a house and a threshing floor next to the communal cistern, for 800 bezants.[57] Pope Eugenius III confirmed the Hospitaller possessions at Qaqun in 1153 and Baldwin III confirmed them in the following year. At the same time they received from Hugh of Caesarea a threshing floor or corn mill located next to a garden already in their possession.[58]

All of these Hospitaller possessions were increased by additional grants later in the century. Income from the villages of Caphaer (Kafr ed-Dik) about 3 km east of Mirabel[59] and Sancte Marie ('Abud) was used by the Master of the Hospital, Jobertus, to supply white bread for the sick in the hospital.[60] In 1151/52 the Order purchased from Pisellus of Sinjil the casalia of Teira (at-Tira) north-east of Arsuf on the inland road between Lydda and Caco for 1,000 bezants (shortly afterwards they granted it to Robert of Sinjil in exchange for a reduction of 100 bezants on rent paid to him for land near Emmaus). Calosia (Kiludiya) was purchased in 1153 and Casale Moyen (Casale Medium/Madianum) (Majdal) was purchased from John of Arsur for 3,000 bezants in 1176.[61] In 1166 they purchased Casale Hadedun together with two *gastinae* (uncultivated lands), the *curtile* of Urrici Tendille and the Salina terris Gervasii with houses for the sum of 2,000 bezants from Hugh of Caesarea.[62] In 1182 Walter of Caesarea sold the Order lands, including a *casale* called Galilea located south-east of Caesarea for 5,000 bezants. Galilea included five *gastinae*: Gedida, Megar, Casale Rubeum, Gastina Fontis and Laasina. This grant was confirmed by Baldwin IV in 1182.[63] Walter of Caesarea also confirmed their possession of a tower called Turris Salinarum (Burj al-Malih) on the coast, located on Tel Tanninim, which had been granted to the Order by Hugh of Caesarea between 1154 and 1168. It probably guarded the salt pans at the mouth of the Crocodile River.[64] Before 1189 Casale Montdidier and Tour Rouge (Burj al-Ahmar) were leased to the Hospital by the Benedictine brothers of St Mary of the Latins and later, by 1236, to the Templars. They had previously been held by Eustace Garnier.[65] Casale Montdidier (Khirbat Madd ad-Dair), which was also known as Casale Latinae, was a village with a tower measuring *c.* 16 by 12.5 metres.[66] After the loss of this territory in 1187 and its recovery in 1191, it was rented to the Templars by the Abbey of St Mary. On 7 August 1248, about twelve years after an agreement was reached between the abbey and the Hospitallers, they vacated Casale Montdidier and Tour Rouge.

In 1207/08 the Hospitallers received from Lady Juliana of Caesarea the villages of Pharaon (Far'un) and Seingibis (Khirbat Nisf Jubail).[67] The village of Turcarme (Tulkarm), 32 km to the east of Caesarea, was given to the Hospitaller Order in November 1212 as pledge for a loan by Aymar de Lairon, lord of Caesarea, but later reverted to the lordship.[68]

Further east, to the south of Afula, is a fortified complex called Castellum Beleismum or Chastiau St Job (Khirbat Bal'ama), which was established by 1156[69] and was held by the Hospitallers by 1187.[70] It consists of the remains of a small tower (less than 8 metres square) within a rectangular enclosure (*c.* 60 metres e.–w. by *c.* 40 metres n.–s.) vaulted on the east and west sides. It had a chapel built above the ancient spring (Bir as-Sinjib) which was dedicated to St Job. The site was excavated by archaeologist Hamdan Taha.[71] In 1207 the Hospitallers received from Lady Juliana additional properties further to the north: three *carrucae* of land in Cafarlet and, somewhere between the *casale* of Roger de Chastellion and Cafarlet, the house of Robert Hohais (once belonging to George the Knight).[72] In 1213 they received the *casalia* of Cafarlet and Bubalorum as surety for a debt of 1,000 bezants from Aymar.[73] They also acquired lands in the east of the kingdom including the *casale* of Coquet, sold to them by Ivo Velos, where they built the castle of Belvoir, and probably the nearby castle of Forbelet ('Afrabala, at-Taiyiba), which they appear to have repaired after it was damaged by Saladin during his raid of 1183. Forbelet was a large, well-constructed tower, 26.3 metres square with walls 4.1 metres thick, of which only the southern part of the ground floor now survives. It was roofed by four groin-vaulted bays supported on a central pier (2.12 metres square). Moulded consoles supported transverse arches dividing the bays.[74]

In 1255 Pope Alexander IV gave the Hospitallers the monastery of Mount Tabor and its estates. The Hospitallers apparently intended to fortify the mountain and there was to be a garrison of 40 knights,[75] but there is no evidence for any building being carried out by them. However, a castellan was installed who was soon formally taking possession of part of the nearby lands of the monastery.[76] The monastery of Mount Tabor possessed a large rural holding between Nazareth and the Sea of Galilee as well as land near Tripoli and Jerusalem and in Oultrejourdain. The Order also acquired lands near La Hadia, a site located to the east of Acre. These included the estate of Johannes Marraim, a knight from Acre,[77] which was located west of La Hadia (Khirbat Utza).

In the village of Casale Album, also in the Plain of Acre, they acquired a house, three *carrucae* of land and a barn in 1245.[78] This was possibly the village referred to in 1208 as Casale Blanc, half of which had been granted by Beatrice, daughter of Joscelyn III de Courtenay, and her husband Otto of Henneberg.[79]

About 12 km south-east of Acre, the Hospitallers possessed a large courtyard building on the slopes of Tel Afeq (Tell Kurdaneh). This building, which probably served as a manor house, has never been excavated. It measures 90.5 by 53 metres. However, the nearby Recordane flour mills at the source of the Na'aman River (Flum d'Acre/Belus) have recently been discovered and examined (Figure 18). These mills are about 370 metres east (upstream) of the Templar mills at Doc.[80] They are mentioned in the twelfth century, together with the village, in a confirmation of a grant by Baldwin III dated 1154.[81] The mills on the Na'aman River were the grounds for a major dispute between the Templars and the Hospitallers early in the thirteenth century.[82] In order to power their mills the Templars constructed a dam across the river, substantial remains

Figure 18 Foundations of the Hospitaller mill of Recordana (photograph courtesy of Idan Shaked).

of which can still be seen. Their intention was to raise the water level so that it would flow into the wheel chambers and turn the mill wheels. However, by raising the water level they were endangering the Hospitaller mill, which was liable to be inundated. After negotiations in 1235 and papal intervention, it was agreed that the Templars would not raise the water level to an extent that threatened the Hospitaller mill. A line was marked on their mill above which the water should not rise. None the less, in 1262 the Hospitallers claimed that the Templars had reneged on this agreement and that the water had risen above the agreed line. The Templars countered with a claim that the Hospitallers had diverted the water to their sugar-cane fields, thereby putting the Templar mills out of action. It appears that the Hospitallers would also stop the flow of water, causing a build-up, and then suddenly release it. Though compromise was reached between the two parties,[83] in any case the mills were destroyed by Baybars shortly afterwards.[84]

The Hospitaller mill and its dam were recently identified to the east of Tel Afeq (Tell Kurdaneh) near the Na'aman springs nature reserve (Ain Afeq).[85] This discovery was made in the course of a long drought during which the water level dropped, exposing the previously unrecorded remains. Prior to this discovery it was generally believed that the Hospitaller mill was the existing mill and tower and that the Templar mill of Doc was located further downstream, possibly in the vicinity of Tel Da'uk.[86] It now appears that the mill with the tower (Figure 19) – now known as the Kurdaneh Mill and thus preserving the name of the Hospitaller mill, Recordane – is in fact the Templar mill (Doc) and that the Hospitaller mill was located further east, nearer to the spring. The first evidence for this came to light some years ago when, during drainage

Figure 19 The Templar mill of Doc (photograph by the author).

work carried out in the swampy land near the spring about 370 metres east of the mill and tower, a large number of ashlars and a basalt millstone (1.4 metres in diameter) were discovered. In 1999, following an extended period of drought, the Na'aman springs dried up. Salvage work carried out by the Society for the Protection of Nature in the area where the millstone had come to light exposed the foundations of a mill of Crusader date.[87] The structure is pentagonal in plan. One surviving corner consists of three courses of ashlars dressed with the typical Frankish diagonal tooling. The eastern side of the foundations of this mill rest on a well-constructed dam $c.$ 135 metres long. On the south of the structure the ashlar-built base of one of the chutes of the mill was exposed.[88]

To the north of Acre, 4.5 km to the south-east of Casale Imbert (Akhziv), is the rural estate of Manueth (Horbat Manot). It was held by the Tor (Tortus) family in the twelfth century and was sold to the Hospitallers by John of Brienne in 1212 for 2,000 bezants.[89] Manueth remained in Hospitaller hands, with a brief occupation by Baybars in 1260, until 1270, when it was leased to the Teutonic Order.[90] On a high point in the south-east are the remains of a courtyard building with a tower; below, near the modern Shlomi–Kabri road, is a structure comprising two ruined vaulted structures, the remains of a sugar refinery. The larger of the two vaults, which measures 13 by 35 metres, is aligned roughly east–west and originally had two storeys. Its main door was in the west and a second door was located in its east end. The smaller vault (9 by 18 metres), which is aligned roughly north–south, adjoins the eastern end of the northern wall of the large vault. The ground floor of the main vault contained the ovens for boiling molasses. Recent excavations have exposed remains of three ovens along its northern wall.[91] These opened outside the vault on its north side. A staircase built in the southern wall gave access to an upper storey or to the roof. It is perhaps unlikely that an upper storey would have served as living quarters because of the smoke and smell from the refinery.

Adjoining the east wall of the smaller (northern) vault is the mill, which was powered by water carried by an aqueduct from a spring to the east. A chute at the end of the aqueduct enabled the water to achieve the momentum required to turn the millstone. Further to the south-east of the aqueduct stood a press, probably converted from an earlier grape press, used to crush the cane. It consisted of a rock-cut press-bed and two mortises, one on either side of the bed, which apparently held the wooden uprights of the press frame which held the screw.[92] As is typical of such refineries, large quantities of ceramic funnel-shaped sugar moulds and handle-less molasses jars were found.[93] A ceramic study of these finds has shown that this refinery continued to function into the Mamluk and Ottoman periods.[94]

Near Tyre the Hospitallers acquired some orchards and, in the middle of the thirteenth century, three villages. In the east of the County of Tripoli, in the area around Crac des Chevaliers, the Hospitallers held rural property stretching in the north from Ba'rin to the Lake of Homs in the south. In Cyprus they received the fief of Kolossi from King Hugh I, as is recorded in a charter dating from 1210.[95] A clause in the Hospitaller Statutes of Fr. William de Villaret dating to after the loss of the Kingdom of Jerusalem (1296/1305), requires that 'Colosi be administered regarding expenses and all other things, just as were Manueth and Acre'.[96] Since at this time, prior to the move to Rhodes, Kolossi was intended to serve as the headquarters of the Order in the East, the comparison to Acre is understandable, but one might ask why the small property of Manueth is referred to. Manueth, located north of Acre, was indeed small, but it was lucrative for the same reason as was Kolossi: the presence of a sugar mill used to manufacture sugar from the cane grown in the region. Together with the locally produced wine, refined sugar was a significant source of income for the Hospitaller Order in both of these places.

The sugar mill at Kolossi consisted of a large barrel-vaulted mill-house and a water-driven mill-wheel powered by water carried on an aqueduct raised on a large stone wall. Kolossi was famous for its wines in the Middle Ages. Ludolf of Suchem mentioned the vineyard of Engaddi in the diocese of Paphos; it has been suggested that this may be a reference to the promontory near Limassol in the region of Kolossi.[97] According to Ludolf, this vineyard had once belonged to the Templars but had passed to the Hospitallers. He writes rather enthusiastically of the qualities of this vineyard:

> In this vineyard grow many grapes and vines of divers sorts, some of which yield grapes as big as great pears, and some yield grapes as small as peas. Some vines yield bunches of grapes as big as urns, and others exceedingly small bunches, and some vines yield white grapes, some black, and some red, some vines yield grapes without stones, and some oblong grapes, shaped like acorns and transparent, and countless other sorts of vines and grapes are to be seen in this vineyard.[98]

Templar rural possessions

Though the Templars were no less active than the Hospitallers in the acquiring of rural properties, we are very much in the dark about these because of the lack of documentation resulting from the loss of the Templar archives. However, it is possible to trace evidence for their rural activity in other sources and in the archaeological remains of some important Templar rural possessions which have been surveyed and excavated.

The Templars may have had possession of a vaulted spring on the road between Jerusalem and Nablus. At the Spring of the Brigands (or Spring of the Templars, Birket ed-Dawiyeh) in Wadi al-Haramiya there may have been a tower beside the vaulted cistern.[99] The Survey of Western Palestine described the Crusader structure built over the spring:

> The water of the spring comes from a hollow artificially scooped in the rock. There is also a rock-cut cistern and on the south a square tank of good-sized masonry, the corner stones drafted with a rustic boss . . . The work is most probably of the Crusading period.

About 12 km south of Acre, slightly downstream from the recently discovered Hospitaller mill of Recordane on the Na'aman River, is the Templar mill of Doc which is mentioned in thirteenth-century sources.[100] This building, which until the discovery of the Hospitaller mill was identified as Hospitaller Recordane (thus its Arabic name Khirbat Kurdana), is remarkably well preserved, the finest surviving example of a Crusader mill. It is built of local sandstone ashlars with diagonal tooling, several stones displaying masons' marks. The mill consists of two barrel-vaulted mill-rooms on either side of a two-storey keep. The northern mill-room, which is west of the tower and joins it at its north-west corner, held a single mill-wheel. The southern mill-room, nearly aligned with the tower to its south, contained two mills. An additional room of two mills was added to its south in the Ottoman period. It is easily distinguished by the poorer quality of masonry and the typically Ottoman use of double arches for the entrances of the wheel chamber.[101] The keep at the centre guarding the mills, measuring 11 metres (e.–w.) by 9.9 metres (n.–s.), has a single groin vault. It has three arrow-slits (with stirrup bases – see Figure 65) on the north and one on the south. Its entrance was on the west, and corbels over the large arched door show that it was defended with box machicolation. Inside the tower had a mezzanine floor supported on stone corbelling; at a later stage two levels of groin vaults were constructed, supported on corner pilasters. Pringle notes that these changes, which probably took place after 1267, blocked three of the tower's arrow-slits and necessitated the widening and lengthening of the central arrow-slit on the north.[102] The dam, much of which is preserved, is 325 metres long. It collected the water east of the mill and diverted it in the direction of the mill-rooms on either side of the tower. A type of horn work below the east wall of the tower guided the water towards the wheel-chambers.

Since there is no mention of the Templar mill in twelfth-century documents, it was probably not built before the beginning of the thirteenth century.[103] The machicolation also suggests a thirteenth-century date. It is likely that as soon as it was built the dam was the cause of the aforementioned dispute with the Hospitallers, which developed into a series of reprisals and counter-reprisals between the two Orders.

Casale Doc (Doke/Dochum), also a Templar possession, was located about 3 km north of the mill. The medieval remains on Tell Da'uk are of a rectangular courtyard building, apparently an administrative depot for Templar rural possessions in the region of the Na'aman River. The complex, which measures 70 by 40 metres, occupies the summit of the tell and consists of three long barrel vaults enclosing three sides; the vault on the north is 6 metres wide and 35 metres long.[104] Ellenblum calls this building a castle and refers to it as large and fortified (elsewhere he refers to this and the possibly similar structure on Tell Kurdaneh/Afeq as *maisons fortes*[105]). Benvenisti suggested that it was used as a storehouse,[106] and this type of courtyard plan without any apparent defensive work is typical of a rural estate centre or manor house. Ellenblum dates it to after the Battle of Hattin because there is no mention of a castle at Da'uq in twelfth-century sources, either Latin or Arabic.[107] As it appears more likely to have been a manor house rather than a castle, its absence from the sources is perhaps less remarkable.

The Templars possessed land near that of the Hospitallers outside the town of Acre.[108] They held a village and a large courtyard building on the coastal road north of Acre. This is on the estate referred to in contemporary sources as Somelaria Templi or le Semerrie (as-Sumairiya). A village is recorded here in 1277 as a possession of the Templars.[109] There is also reference to the Chapel of St George of Lesaumalaria, which in 1291 was granted an indulgence on the feast days of St George, St Julian and St Martin by Pope Nicholas IV.[110] Though this site has recently been cleared of vegetation and surface debris, it has never been excavated (Figure 20). However, surveys have been made of the surface remains.[111] It is a large rectangular complex (again referred to as a castle by Ellenblum[112]) measuring 60.5 metres (e.–w.) by 57 metres (n.–s.). The complex appears originally to have been enclosed on all four sides with barrel-vaulted galleries. That to the east is still standing, but considerable remains survive on the other three sides as well. The well-constructed eastern range has five intersecting vaults

Figure 20 Templar courtyard complex at Somelaria (photograph by the author).

on its western side springing from rectangular pilasters.[113] The recent clearance has shown that there were rooms constructed along the eastern side of the east wall outside the courtyard complex, and similar evidence can be seen on the south and west.

A few metres to the south-east of the complex, a thirteenth-century glass factory was excavated in 1968/69.[114] Excavations directed by Gladys Weinberg exposed a brick-built structure, including a furnace, two firing chambers, a glass-coated tank and a working area. The finds from this site included ceramic bowls in which glass was melted, waste glass and fragments of glass vessels including prunted beakers, a type of drinking vessel commonly found in local Frankish sites.[115] The close proximity (7 metres) of the glass factory to the Templar building makes it likely that it was they who were running the enterprise. The involvement of the Templars in the glass industry is not surprising. Their participation in one of the more lucrative industries in the Latin East is to be expected, just as was the better-known involvement of the Hospitallers and Teutonic Knights in the sugar industry.

To the east, on a hill overlooking the Plain of Esdraelon (the Jezreel Valley), was the village of Lezrael (Parvum Gerinum, ancient Jezreel). By the 1180s this village was apparently a Templar possession.[116] It was destroyed by Saladin in September 1183.[117] Crusader remains include a chapel, possibly a castle chapel (or a parish church). Nothing can be directly related to the Templars. A *casale* called Cafarsset near Tiberias was held by Templars until they exchanged it (also renouncing claims to possessions in the region of Valenia and Margat) for Hospitaller properties around Beaufort Castle in 1262 in order to establish an economic base for the castle.[118] The Templars had a few holdings near Tyre.[119]

At the manor of Khirokitia (Kheroidia) in southern Cyprus, east of Limassol, there was a Commandery of the Templars. With the arrest of the Templars in 1308, the Marshal of the Order was imprisoned here.[120] Enlart notes that the tower of the Templars seems to have been subsequently rebuilt, as the ruins are similar in style to the keep of the Commandery at Kolossi, which is of fifteenth-century date. The not-very-extensive ruins of the Commandery include the keep, various conventual buildings and a cloister. Enlart records 'remains of a handsome room with a pointed barrel-vault, constructed in fine ashlar masonry'. It has walls 1.6 metres thick and beneath it is a cellar (which at the time of writing was filled up). A wall 28 metres long and 70 cm thick extends at a right angle from this room; built into it (upside down) is a battered stone bearing the arms of the Hospitaller Order. Nearby is an enclosure within which is a rectangular structure containing a staircase leading down some 4.2 metres to a landing with a pointed arch opening onto a well fed by a spring.[121] Amongst finds in this area were remnants of fine French Gothic window tracery of thirteenth- to fifteenth-century date.[122]

A chapel known as the Chapel of Our Lady of the Field (Panayia tou Kampou), located to the south of the Commandery, was possibly the Templar chapel which, after the suppression of the Templar Order, was handed over to the Hospitallers in 1318 and restored by them. The chapel has a Byzantine apse and dome, but the other elements are French Gothic: pointed arches and hood moulding with a decorative finial.[123] Nearby is a bridge with pointed arches of uncertain date.

Teutonic rural possessions

The Teutonic Order concentrated on establishing a foothold in the Principality of the Galilee, in particular in the west (the east was less intensively settled). They also received and purchased estates around Tyre and between Sidon and Beirut. In 1193 Henry II gave them a *casale* called Cafresi in the district of Acre.[124] Not all of their rural possessions were in the north, and in 1196 they received from Henry II a vineyard outside Jaffa.[125] However, for the most part the Teutonic Order concentrated its efforts on gaining properties in the western Galilee. In the region of Acre, together with grants of properties in the towns, the German Hospital received from an early date royal grants of rural properties. Guy of Lusignan gave them four *carrucae* of land near Acre.[126] In 1198, they purchased from Amaury of Lusignan (Amaury II) a *casale* called Aguille in the district of Acre, together with its *villani* (villagers) and *gastini*.[127] All this was before the foundation of the Military Order. In 1200 the Order acquired two manors north of Acre, through grant and purchase from King Amaury.[128] This grant included the village of Le Bace (Lebassa) and the *gastina* of Missop (Massob), located to the north-east of Casale Imbert (Akhzib).[129] The Order subsequently acquired a complex of fiefs north of Acre, including 46 *casalia*, transferred by Beatrice von Henneberg, daughter of Joscelin III de Courtenay and his wife Agnes. This grant was confirmed by John of Brienne in May 1220 and Frederick II in January 1226.[130] In 1228 the Teutonic Order received a complex of fiefs, including 15 *casalia* and two parcels of wasteland. This grant included the castle of Montfort.[131]

The castle of Montfort is discussed below.[132] Ruins of a Gothic hall standing in the valley to the north of the castle, on the south bank of the seasonal stream Nahal Kziv (Nahr al-Qarn), have been described in detail by Pringle (Figure 21).[133] This

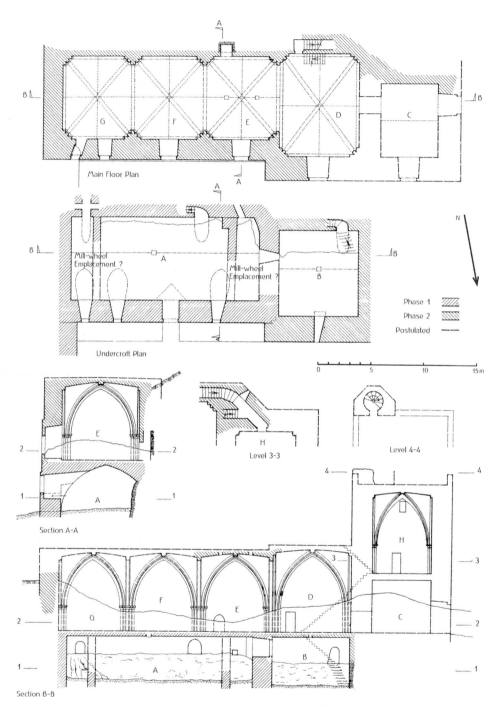

Main Floor Plan

Undercroft Plan

Mill-wheel
Emplacement ?

Mill-wheel
Emplacement ?

Phase 1
Phase 2
Postulated

Section A-A

Level 3-3

Level 4-4

Section B-B

Figure 21 Plan of the mill and guest house below Montfort (after Pringle, 1986b).

two-storey building, constructed against the base of the castle spur, is about 40 metres long and 10 to 12 metres wide. It consisted of an undercroft, a hall and a tower. The undercroft, partly cut into the bedrock (mainly its south wall) and partly constructed of masonry, was formed by two barrel vaults, the main one being some 18.2 metres long (internally), 6.5/7.6 metres wide and close to 4 metres high. The walls are 1.9 metres thick. It has a door in the centre of the northern wall and three splayed windows (originally with iron grilles), two to the east of the door and one to the west. Another splayed window is located in the wall between the two vaults. Internal partition walls at either end of the vault may have been emplacements for mill-wheels. There is a small opening at either end of the south wall and a third, larger opening near the west partition wall, which may originally have been a staircase (of which nothing survives).

The second vault at the west end appears to be a later addition, possibly built at the time when the hall (Pringle's D, E, F and G) and the tower (C and H) were added. It is only 7.5 metres long by *c.* 8 metres wide, its north wall 2.4 metres thick (its west wall, like the south wall, is rock-cut) and aligned slightly north of the larger vault. It has a staircase in its south wall and a splayed window in the middle of its north wall. Both of these chambers have rectangular vents in the crowns of the vaults.

Above the undercroft are the collapsed remains of a hall of four bays with quadri-partite rib-vaulting, extending slightly further east than the lower level. Its eastern bay (above vault B) was somewhat broader and higher than the others. The western bay (D) appears to have been the first to be constructed; the other bays were added thereafter but, as Pringle demonstrates in his detailed study, were planned when bay D was built.[134] Each bay had a single window with iron grilles in the north wall. In the eastern bay (G) there was also a door at the east end of the north wall, giving onto the dam which extends north from this end of the building across the bed of the stream. In the south wall of the third bay from the east (E) is a recess with a pointed arch, identified by Pringle as perhaps being a fireplace and chimney with a wooden mantel. A possible staircase on the south of vault D would have given access to the tower. The tower consists of two levels, a barrel-vaulted ground floor and a rib-vaulted first floor. Though the ground floor is largely covered with rubble, Pringle has esti-mated that it measured *c.* 6.8 (n.–s.) by 5.5 (e.–w.) metres (internally) and was at least 5 metres high.[135]

Pringle has identified this building as having begun its existence as a mill-house and later (between 1229 and 1266), with the addition of the upper storey and tower, being converted into a guest-house for important visitors.

In 1229 additional properties were restored to the Order in the region of Toron and Chateau Neuf.[136] In 1261 John II of Ibelin, lord of Beirut, granted the Order three manors north of Acre.[137] Of the earlier grant, there is a list of 21 other properties, which as Ellenblum has shown are all located in the vicinity of the *casale* of Castellum Regis (Mi'iliya).[138] Amongst these was St Jorge Labane/St George de La Baena (al-Ba'ina), part of a fief held by one Henri le Bufle in the twelfth century. It was later in the hands of Joscelyn III de Courtenay, and sometime between 1220 and 1249 was acquired by the Teutonic Order.[139] A large Frankish house (or two separate houses) can still be seen in the village. One of these has a door with slit-machicolation; Pringle suggests that it may have been part of a tower or hall-house.[140]

Another possession mentioned was Tarphile/Trefile/Tertille (Kh. el-Manhata). This was a *casale* about 1 km above the castle of Montfort on the road to Castellum Regis. It included mills and gardens,[141] and remains survive of a fortified courtyard with a broad gate, a tower and the quarry which supplied building stones for Montfort. The quarry was linked by two ramps to the road leading to Montfort.[142] The quarry itself covers an area of about 70 (n.–s.) by 90 (e.–w.) metres and a considerable area around it also contains medieval remains. A solid rock podium near the centre of the quarried area, which measures 13 by 10 metres, formed the base of the tower, smaller but similar in form to the podium of le Destroit (Figure 27).[143] A cistern was cut into the rock and on its south side there is a rock-cut staircase rising to the constructed first-floor level, of which only part of the west wall survives. Stairs were also cut in the rock sides of the quarry area.

Also included in this transaction were one-third of the fief of St George with seven *casalia*: Arket (Yirka), Yanot (Yanuh), Cabra (Kh. el-Qabra) and Meblie (Kh. Mibliya),[144] Saphet, elsewhere referred to as Saphet des Alemauns (which may be Kh. Safta 'Adi (2nd ref. 165.247) between Shefar'am and Doc[145] or Saphet lo Cathemon (Kh. Katamun, at 2nd ref. 184.274) which the Teutonic Order acquired in 1236[146]), Lemezera (possibly al-Mazra'a, just north of Somelaria, where there are remains of a tower of uncertain date) and Kemelye (unidentified).

Further to the north the Teutonic Order was also able to acquire a number of rural properties. In 1195 Henry II gave the Teutonic Order two *carrucae* of land at Sedinum north of Tyre.[147] In 1237 they held near Tyre a quarter of another village called Cabesie (al-Ghabasiya, at 2nd ref. 164.267).[148] Between 1257 and 1261 the Order was granted and purchased possessions in the region north-east of Sidon from Julian Grenier, lord of Sidon and Beaufort. This included about one hundred *casalia* in the region called Schuf (Souf), for which they made a partial payment of 23,000 bezants.[149] In 1258 the Teutonic Order purchased a manor from John de la Tour, constable of Sidon, and two manors from John of Schuf. From Andrew of Schuf they acquired a fief comprising several manors in 1258.[150]

The sources refer to certain rural estates held by the Teutonic Order in Cilicia and Cyprus.[151] For example, Ludolf of Suchem mentioned that near Limassol was a place called Pravimunt (Peninunt), occupied by brothers of the Teutonic Order and of the Order of St Thomas.[152]

Rural possessions of the Order of St Lazarus

Not a great deal is known about the rural holdings of the Order of St Lazarus. A *gastina* called Betana (Bethanam), probably to be identified with the village of Bait 'Anan west of al-Qubaiba (Parva Mahumeria, north-west of Jerusalem), was donated by Melisende to the Order according to a document dated 1159.[153] Some years earlier they had received from an Armenian monk a well which had previously belonged to Patriarch Warmund,[154] and five *carrucae* of land in the plain of Bethlehem were given to them in compensation for the loss of a mill outside Porta David in Jerusalem which Queen Melisende had removed in 1151 because it disturbed traffic into the city.[155] In 1186 the Order received a plot of land near Casale S. Egidii (Sinjil, between al-Bira and Nablus) from one Adam Magnus who lived in the village.[156]

7

SUGAR-CANE CULTIVATION AND THE SUGAR INDUSTRY

The role played by the Military Orders in the development and expansion of the medieval sugar industry seems to have been substantial. Considering the importance of this industry to the economy of the kingdom and the fact that the introduction to the West of cane sugar was apparently one of the few lasting contributions made by the Franks, this activity is worth examination. The Military Orders were central to the development of the industry for much the same reasons as they were important in the field of military architecture (the better-known area of contribution of the Military Orders, but one that had little influence on modern society). They were perhaps the only organisation financially capable of developing the industry to its full potential, constructing mills, refineries, aqueducts and warehouses, manufacturing – or more likely purchasing – the ceramic jars and moulds, and providing a workforce to cultivate and harvest the crop and to work in the refineries.

The Hospitallers stored refinery equipment at Acre and possessed mills and refineries such as those at Manueth[1] and Casale Rogerii de Chasteillon.[2] Sources inform us of the Hospitallers' need of sugar for use in their hospital in Jerusalem. In 1181 a General Chapter of the Hospitallers required the provisioning of the hospital with sugar from Mont Pelerin and Tiberias for the making of lectuaries, syrups and other medicines.[3] Sugar was used in the preparation of medications to treat asthma, diarrhoea, throat pains, eye diseases, coughing, chest pains, malaria, diseases of the urinary tract, skin diseases, and to strengthen the heart and to gain weight.[4]

Excavations carried out in 1997 in the northern halls (7 and 8) in the Hospitallers' Quarter at Acre have uncovered hundreds of conical ceramic vessels (sugar moulds) and molasses jars used in the refining of cane sugar.[5] In vault 7 excavations uncovered seven rows of sugar moulds, about 80 in each row. Sugar moulds and molasses jars have also been found at the Hospitaller refinery at Manueth.[6] Both of these types are wheel-made vessels of coarse, poorly levigated clay. The moulds are conical, a form which facilitated the removal of the end product of crystallised sugar. They have simple rounded and thickened rims and a hole in the base with a diameter of 1–2 cm. The molasses jars are handle-less with narrow mouths and ovoid bodies. The base is generally somewhat concave.

The method of manufacturing the sugar was fairly simple. When the liquid molasses gathered from the crushed cane had been refined by boiling, it was poured into these moulds which were placed in large ceramic jars. As it cooled and thickened, the liquid sugar dripped slowly into the jar while crystallised sugar began to form in the mould. By the end of the process the mould was full of crystallised sugar and the jar of molasses.

The Teutonic Knights were also involved in the growing of sugar cane and the manufacture of sugar. Sugar was grown on their lands in the Western Galilee in the region of their holdings at Castellum Regis and Judin. Numerous sugar moulds were found in the excavations of what may have been the Teutonic Knights' Quarter in the east of the Crusader city of Acre.[7]

Part III

THE DEFENCE OF THE LATIN EAST

The defensive role played by the Military Orders in the Latin East centred on two areas of activity: supplying the armies of the Crusader states with organized, well-equipped and experienced troops and constructing and maintaining castles which could serve as lookout posts, mustering points for armies in wartime, defensive positions, supply depots and, if necessary, refuges during a siege (Figures 22–24). In the latter activity the part played by the Orders was greater than that of other castle-builders in the East. Their vast resources enabled the Military Orders to build larger and more complex castles, to introduce innovations in defensive elements, and in general to lead the way in castle design. These activities culminated in the creation of buildings like Crac des Chevaliers, a structure which can take its place amongst the greatest achievements in architectural history.

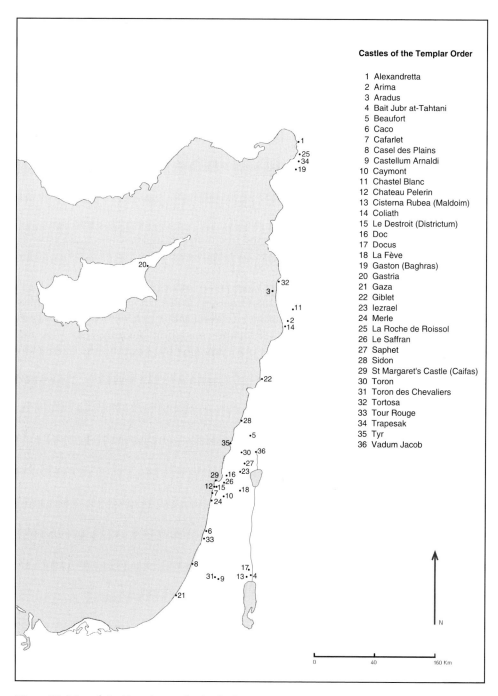

Castles of the Templar Order

1 Alexandretta
2 Arima
3 Aradus
4 Bait Jubr at-Tahtani
5 Beaufort
6 Caco
7 Cafarlet
8 Casel des Plains
9 Castellum Arnaldi
10 Caymont
11 Chastel Blanc
12 Chateau Pelerin
13 Cisterna Rubea (Maldoim)
14 Coliath
15 Le Destroit (Districtum)
16 Doc
17 Docus
18 La Fève
19 Gaston (Baghras)
20 Gastria
21 Gaza
22 Giblet
23 Iezrael
24 Merle
25 La Roche de Roissol
26 Le Saffran
27 Saphet
28 Sidon
29 St Margaret's Castle (Caifas)
30 Toron
31 Toron des Chevaliers
32 Tortosa
33 Tour Rouge
34 Trapesak
35 Tyr
36 Vadum Jacob

N

0   40   160 Km

Figure 22 Map of the Templar castles in the Latin East.

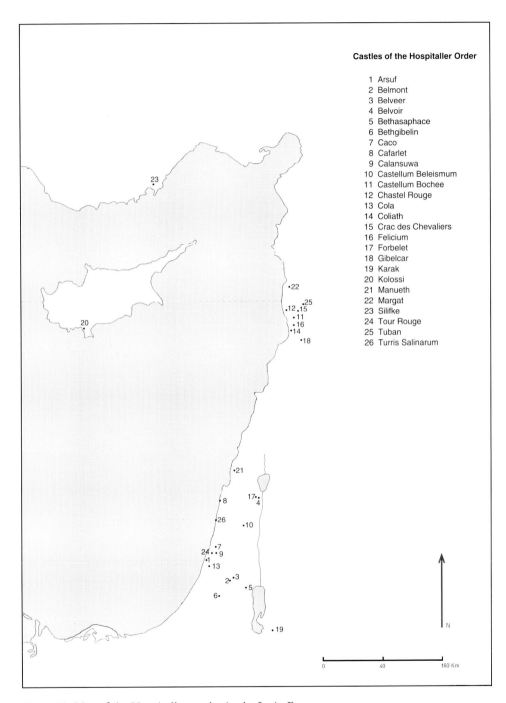

Castles of the Hospitaller Order

1 Arsuf
2 Belmont
3 Belveer
4 Belvoir
5 Bethasaphace
6 Bethgibelin
7 Caco
8 Cafarlet
9 Calansuwa
10 Castellum Beleismum
11 Castellum Bochee
12 Chastel Rouge
13 Cola
14 Coliath
15 Crac des Chevaliers
16 Felicium
17 Forbelet
18 Gibelcar
19 Karak
20 Kolossi
21 Manueth
22 Margat
23 Silifke
24 Tour Rouge
25 Tuban
26 Turris Salinarum

Figure 23 Map of the Hospitaller castles in the Latin East.

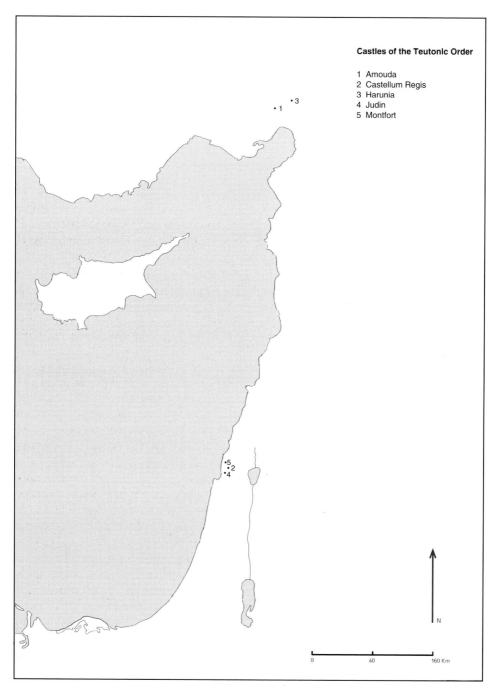

Castles of the Teutonic Order

1 Amouda
2 Castellum Regis
3 Harunia
4 Judin
5 Montfort

N

0   40   160 Km

Figure 24 Map of the Teutonic castles in the Latin East.

8

CASTLES AND THE DEFENSIVE
ROLE OF THE MILITARY ORDERS

The Crusader period was an important stage – indeed one of the most important stages – in the development of the medieval castle. The achievements of this period fall chiefly into two categories: castle design and the introduction or improvement of specific elements in the defences. Like most achievers, the Franks were enthusiastic adopters and innovators. They borrowed liberally from the Christian West, Byzantium and the Muslim East. While their innovations were mainly in the field of bringing together these borrowings in new and original combinations rather than inventing entirely new forms, the outcome was that in the Latin East the medieval castle evolved into a better-defended, more complex and more effective instrument of its varied tasks of defence and control.

From the beginning of their presence in the East, the Crusaders constructed stone keeps. Such castles, which were known in Western Europe at least from the middle or later tenth century, had become increasingly familiar there from the second half of the eleventh century.[1] Stone towers were appropriate to the early needs of the Frankish settlers, both as local administrative centres and as refuges. From fairly early in the twelfth century they also adopted the quadrangular enclosure castle with projecting corner towers, a castle type that was typical of the East for over a thousand years prior to the Crusades. The combination of the two types made a major original contribution, a simple form of concentric fortification, about which Smail wrote: 'Some observers may wish to regard this arrangement as a marriage of *turris and castrum* and as yet another demonstration of the integration of East and West which is said to have been a principal result of the Crusades.'[2] Their greatest advances came with the construction of the great spur and hilltop castles, mainly in the early thirteenth century.

The layout of castles was not the only sphere in which the Franks made great advances. They also enhanced their fortresses with Byzantine and Muslim defensive features such as complex gate passages and machicolation, which were used more inventively and extensively by them than by their inventors and were subsequently to influence Muslim and later Western fortifications.

At the forefront of this activity were the Military Orders, particularly the Templars and the Hospitallers. Something of their monopoly in this field is reflected in the words of Thoros of Armenia, who is said to have made the following comment to King Amaury during a visit to the Kingdom of Jerusalem in the 1160s:

'When I came to your land and inquired to whom the castles belonged, I sometimes received the reply: "This belongs to the Temple": elsewhere I was told: "It is the Hospital's." I found no castle or city or town which was said to be yours, except three.'[3]

Taking into account the fact that the three exceptions would probably have included Jerusalem and Acre, Thoros was clearly not intending this to be taken literally, but to some extent he was probably not far from the mark. Even in the cities the royal possessions had contracted, amongst other reasons because of the expansion of the properties of the Orders. We have already noted that the Templars had, long before the arrival of Thoros, taken over what had previously been the royal palace in Jerusalem itself. This situation became even more marked in the thirteenth century, when the expansion of the Military Orders came at the expense not only of the king but of the Frankish nobility in general. After the recovery of the land in the Third Crusade, many of the lesser nobles were forced to sell their recovered properties to the wealthy Military Orders. Consequently, the study of castle development in the Crusader period is primarily the study of the castles of the Military Orders, and particularly those of the Templars and Hospitallers. Among the castles built by the Military Orders we find most types of castle plans that were employed in the period and most defensive systems and mechanisms that were in use in medieval military architecture. While we cannot today accept T.E. Lawrence's conclusions regarding the differences between the architecture of the two great Orders and their individual building style, his statement that the establishment of the Military Orders 'meant a new era in Syrian castle-building' cannot be disputed.[4] Almost all the major castles in the Latin East, and many of the lesser ones, were built or rebuilt by them. This was above all due to the fact that they alone had the financial resources necessary to construct these enormous and complex constructions. No baron or prince, not even the King of Jerusalem himself, was capable of providing the money needed for the erection of such huge edifices as Saphet Castle, Margat or Crac des Chevaliers, not to mention their subsequent maintenance.[5] Consequently, when we consider the Crusader period in the development of castle construction, not only can we not ignore the contribution of the Military Orders but we must place the greatest emphasis on it, for the contribution of others was in comparison almost insignificant.

At the time of their foundation or shortly afterwards the Templars were given a specific role by Patriarch Warmund. According to William of Tyre:

> as far as their strength permitted, they should keep the roads and highways safe from the menace of robbers and highwaymen, with especial regard for the protection of pilgrims.[6]

One part of this assignment was the forming of armed guards to escort pilgrim convoys. The Rule of the Templars makes a direct reference to such an escort: 'The commander of the City of Jerusalem should have ten knight brothers under his command to lead and guard the pilgrims who come to the River Jordan.'[7] No doubt there were other such escorts on the pilgrimage routes and principal highways of the kingdom. But the main activity in this regard involved the construction of forts along the roads. The Templars were engaged in castle building (and the acquiring of existing castles) as early as c. 1137 in the Amanus Mountains. In the Kingdom of Jerusalem they built Toron des Chevaliers (Latrun) from 1137 to 1141[8] and received Gaza from King Baldwin III in 1149/50.[9]

The Hospitallers, on the other hand, had no such role. Their mission was to care for the sick and needy and consequently much of their activity was centred in the cities where they established hospitals and hospices (see pp. 43–60). This did not, however, prevent them from becoming castle-builders and, as they followed the Templars and evolved into a Military Order, they also became involved in this activity. Their castles were not oriented to the same extent to the protection of the roads and thoroughfares of the Frankish states but were rather intended to consolidate their hold over ever-increasing farmlands. The castles were needed to defend and administer these lands. The Hospitallers received Bethgibelin from King Fulk in 1136 and by 1170 they were in possession of the castles of Belmont and Belveer and the surrounding farmlands west of Jerusalem, of Belvoir and farmlands in its district, of other castles and farmlands in the Kingdom of Jerusalem, and of castles, villages and farmlands in the County of Tripoli including the castle of Crac des Chevaliers. By 1186 Margat Castle and large tracts of farmland in the Principality of Antioch were also in their possession.

If we consider the contribution of the Military Orders to the art of castle design and construction, the questions we must attempt to answer are not new but have been dealt with in varying degrees of success by several scholars over the years. One frequently raised question was whether there was a difference between the designs of the castles of the different Military Orders. Lawrence believed that the Orders developed individual distinctive types of castles, the Templars following traditional Byzantine models while the Hospitallers evolved more complex designs of interrelated defences based on contemporary French models.[10] However, Lawrence based his argument on an imbalanced group of examples; there are fewer well-preserved castles of the Templars than of the Hospitallers. The only important remains of large Templar castles are Chateau Pelerin and Beaufort, and Lawrence was writing before the excavations of Chateau Pelerin and Deschamps' survey of Beaufort, both of which took place in the 1930s.[11] Tortosa is difficult to understand because of later constructions which hide much of the Crusader work. The exposed remains of the enormous Templar castle of Saphet are fragmentary and, although we may have a better idea of its form when the current excavations have made some headway, it is so badly damaged from battle, years of neglect, stone robbing and earthquakes that it is unlikely to have any great impact on our understanding of this issue.[12] Vadum Jacob is a comparatively small castle and was never finished. Its intended final design thus remains ambiguous. The important castle of Toron des Chevaliers (Latrun), guarding the road to Jerusalem, has also been largely dismantled and, although the surface remains have recently been cleared and surveyed, it still awaits excavation. Arima and Chastel Blanc are not of the same complexity of design or scale as the great Hospitaller castles. Gaston (Baghras), the greatest of the Templar castles in the Amanus march, seems to owe less to Frankish than to Armenian design.

These complications make it very difficult if not impossible to make a conclusive statement on this subject. On Lawrence's suggestion that the Hospitallers evolved complex French-influenced defences (Crac des Chevaliers), while the Templars stuck to simpler Byzantine patterns, Boase pointed out that, while Chateau Pelerin and Tortosa are problematic as comparisons to Crac des Chevaliers and Margat (the former are located by the sea and the latter in the hills and thus they are fundamentally different in their layout), the defences of Chateau Pelerin are none the less 'as carefully devised in their system of support as anything worked out by the Hospitallers'.[13] Kennedy writes that there was 'a marked difference in style', but cites only one example of this difference: 'in contrast to the Hospitallers, but like their Muslim contemporaries, the Templars consistently preferred rectangular to round towers'.[14] This pronouncement is speculative at best. The number of Hospitaller castles possessing round towers that are definitely of Frankish construction is not much greater than the number of Templar castles.[15] Fedden and Thomson, commenting on this supposed difference between the architecture of the two Orders, noted that 'more emphasis than the evidence warrants has been put upon the alleged Templar use of square towers as opposed to the Hospitaller use of round towers'.[16] Without a larger body of examples, no argument can be made to support a distinction between the military architecture of the two Orders.

Defending pilgrim travel in the Kingdom of Jerusalem

As already stated, there were two means by which pilgrim traffic could be safeguarded: by providing armed escorts and by constructing and garrisoning outposts at sensitive positions along the roads. In the twelfth century the Templars constructed a number of castles and towers along important pilgrimage routes in the Kingdom of Jerusalem. Districtum (le Destroit) was built above a narrow pass on the sandstone ridge east of the peninsula at 'Atlit through which the coastal road passed. A large castle was built at le Saffran (Shefar'am) on the pilgrimage route leading south-east inland from Acre to Saphorie and Nazareth. Towers were built along the road to Jerusalem at Casel des Pleins (Yazur), Toron des Chevaliers (Latrun) and Castellum Arnaldi (Yalu). On the road from Jerusalem to the Place of Baptism on the Jordan River, the Templars constructed small towers at Maldoim (Figure 25) and possibly at Bait Jubr at-Tahtani.

Figure 25 Tower of Maldoim (photograph by the author).

Most of these castles were simple two-storey keeps. When the need arose, these were expanded or replaced by much larger fortresses; Toron des Chevaliers expanded from a small tower into a huge enclosure castle with concentric defences and Districtum was replaced by the nearby castle of Chateau Pelerin.

The establishment of marches and the defence of borders and passes

Our understanding of the role of castles in border defence has been transformed over the past decades. The belief held by some of the principal nineteenth-century scholars, and still popular for much of the twentieth century, was that Crusader castles formed a type of defensive ring around the Frankish territory, protecting it from the threat of invasion.[17] Only in 1956, with the publication of R.C. Smail's *Crusading Warfare, 1097–1193*, was the point (which now seems obvious) made that: 'when warfare was fought on a scale likely to endanger the Latin occupation, no fortress or group of fortresses could restrain the passage of an invading force'.[18] There was in fact no pre-planned defensive system. Frontier castles were generally no more than isolated, fortified, forward positions which could house large garrisons, contain stores of weapons, food and equipment, and serve as lookout positions and as refuges if necessary. None the less, these were significant roles which could be decisive in the success or failure of the field army.

This said, it is clear that there were localised defensive networks, marches defending border passes. The Military Orders played an important role in the establishment of these groups of castles in the frontier regions of the Crusader states. In the south, the castle of Bethgibelin, which was built by King Fulk in 1136, was intended, together with other royal castles (Blanchegarde, Ibelin, Gaza and perhaps Toron des Chevaliers), to put an end to incursions from Fatimid Ascalon. Though the king granted Bethgibelin to the Hospitallers, the other castles in this group were not held by the Military Orders. None the less, although before 1187 many of the castles located on or near the frontier between Christian and Muslim territory were royal or baronial establishments, in certain places frontier defence had largely, and sometimes entirely, passed into their hands. In the period 1142 to 1144 the Hospitallers received from Count Raymond II of Tripoli (1137–52) a group of fortresses on the frontiers of the County of Tripoli, including Crac des Chevaliers at the centre, Castellum Bochee, Lacum, Felicium and Mardabech.[19] This gave them control over the route between Homs and Tripoli passing through the Gap of Homs (the valley of Nahr al-Kabir). They also received rights over the towns of Ba'rîn and Rafanîyah, which at the time were in Muslim hands, and had been granted as an incentive to recover them. In the north of the county the Templars received Tortosa (between 1151 and 1169), Arima and Chastel Blanc.[20] Further south, in the Kingdom of Jerusalem, the Templar fortresses of Saphet and Beaufort faced the eastern frontier towards Damascus. Beaufort overlooked the Litani River and the southern approaches to the Beqa Valley. Vadum Jacob was begun by the Templars to defend and control the ford north of the Sea of Galilee. Hospitaller Belvoir Castle was ideally positioned to overlook enemy troop movements in the Jordan Valley south of the Sea of Galilee.

In Cilicia the Hospitallers, Templars and Teutonic Knights all played an important role in the defence of the Armenian Kingdom. The natural barrier surrounding Cilicia against invasion, the semicircle of the Taurus, Anti-Taurus and Amanus ranges, could be breached through a number of mountain passes. The Armenian kings therefore decided to employ the Orders in defending these passes through the creation of marches. A Hospitaller march was established by Levon II in the east of the kingdom to serve as a buffer between the Armenians and the Seljuks. Levon gave the Hospitallers the castles of Silifke, Camardesium and Castellum Novum and rights over Karaman, which was in Turkish hands.[21] North of Antioch, the Templars acquired a march in the Amanus Mountains where they were responsible for guarding the Belen Pass (the famous Syrian Gates) which served as a vital passage from south-eastern Cilicia into the region of Antioch, as well as the Çalan Pass 30 km further to the north.[22] The Teutonic Knights also played a role in guarding the northern–eastern approaches to Armenian Cilicia. They possessed two castles in Cilicia: Amuda and Harunia in the foothills to the north of the Amanus range.[23]

Castles controlling passage on the roads and serving as toll collecting posts

The Hospitallers built a tower (Burj as-Sabî) below Margat Castle to control traffic and collect toll payments from travellers along the coastal road (Figure 26). Another example of a tower serving as a toll collection post was the Black Tower, built by the Teutonic Knights on the southern border of their territory in north-eastern Cilicia.[24] The Templars also had a toll post, possibly also a tower, located 1 km south of Sari Seki near the road leading north to the Cilician plain, 7 km north of Iskenderun. It was

Figure 26 Tower of Burj as-Sabî below Margat (photograph by Ross Burns).

known as the Pillar of Jonah (the 'Portella') and was held by them for most of the twelfth and thirteenth centuries.[25]

Castles as central administrative headquarters of an Order

In some towns in the Crusader states where the Orders did not possess entire Quarters they built or occupied castles and used these as administrative headquarters. The castles at Sidon, Tripoli, Tortosa, Arsuf and Jaffa served this purpose. In addition, in certain rural areas the Military Orders built large castles to serve as regional administrative headquarters. In the thirteenth century Saphet and Chateau Pelerin certainly played an important role in regional administration of the Templar Order. The castle of Montfort was built by the Teutonic Knights in 1227 to replace their administrative headquarters in Acre and rural headquarters at Castellum Regis. The reason for this move appears to have been the desire to distance themselves from their rivals, the Templars and Hospitallers, who may have been making life difficult for the smaller Order.[26]

Castles used for the administration of rural properties

Many of the large and smaller castles built or occupied by the Military Orders combined their military role with rural administrative functions. In this role the castle was not only the residence of a castellan or commander and of the garrison but also was a depot for the storage of taxes paid in kind. Hence, there would have been not only a hall serving as residence and administrative headquarters but also vaulted storage rooms. In smaller castles of this type the administrative function may have surpassed the military function. The Red Tower is an example of a castle that had more in common with rural manor houses than with other Military Order castles.

9

THE CHOICE OF PLAN
Castle typology, design, location and function

When, in the early days of castle studies, T.E. Lawrence wrote that castles in the Latin East are 'a series of exceptions to some unknown rule', he was expressing a hesitancy that was understandable in view of the variety and individuality of Crusader castle architecture.[1] None the less, most castles follow certain basic rules of design and fall, in fact rather neatly, into a number of basic categories. The type of castle constructed at a particular site was decided by two main factors: the intended function of the castle and the nature of the terrain in which it was to be located. This is as true of the castles of the Military Orders as it is of other castles.

However, another factor must be taken into account which specifically affected the design of castles built by the Military Orders. This was the need to furnish both the spiritual and communal requirements of their occupants. The garrisons of these castles lived according to monastic rule and it was therefore obligatory that their castles include components that were not essential in lay castles, such as chapels, chapter-houses, cloisters and communal refectories and dormitories. This would explain why it seems that, as Kennedy notes, 'the twelfth century castles of the Military Orders were mostly enclosure castles rather than simple towers'.[2] An enclosure castle had space for all these elements.[3] At the same time an enclosure castle was best suited for military training and exercises.

Despite this, not all castles held by the Military Orders conformed to these requirements. Castles purchased by the Orders from lay owners were often limited to the most basic military and domestic arrangements, and it is clear that no sort of communal, monastic life could have been followed by the Templar and Hospitaller brothers in small forts like the Red Tower or the tiny castles of Maldoim and Beit Jubr at-Tahtani. Such castles may have been occupied by a small garrison of *confratres*, laymen associated with the Order but not full members and consequently not required to follow the monastic regimen of the Order's Rule. However, in some cases the castles purchased by the Orders underwent major rebuilding and expansion which would have made them suitable for the use of a garrison of knight brothers.

Something of an impediment to understanding the design of the larger castles is the lack of information on the state of these buildings prior to their coming into the possession of the Military Orders. It is often difficult to identify the remains of the earlier structures which were subsequently expanded by their new owners. For example, it would certainly be of interest to know what sort of castle the Hospitallers purchased at Belvoir in 1168 and whether the form of the original castle in any way influenced the remarkable final design. However, most of the larger castles were so completely rebuilt that the surviving structure is almost completely Hospitaller, Templar or Teutonic, and our lack of knowledge of the earlier castle, while unfortunate, is not greatly detrimental to our understanding of the later one. Where this lack of knowledge is more regrettable is in cases where the extent of construction by the Military Orders is less certain. It would be of value to know how much and which parts of the castle of Arsuf were built during the extremely brief Hospitaller possession of the castle and town between 1261 and 1265. In the castles of Cilicia as well, the extent of the contribution by the Military Orders to the existing structure is not always obvious.

A number of factors lay behind the choice of a location for the construction of a new castle. Clearly, before topographical and other natural advantages are taken into account, the castle-builders' first concern was to fulfil specific offensive, defensive or administrative needs. When we attempt to examine why a castle was built in a particular place, we must first ask which of these needs, or what combination of them, did the owner of the castle wish to answer. Like other castle-builders, the Military Orders' purposes included the need to defend problematic places such as roads passing from Muslim into Frankish lands, river crossings and mountain passes. Equally important was the need to position supplies for an army or to house a garrison in a region of warfare, to strengthen vulnerable places frequently subject to raids, to establish bases from which they could harass enemy strongholds and finally, but not least important, to set up centrally located administrative posts. The typical aim of these castle-builders is expressed in the thirteenth-century text describing the construction of Saphet Castle which, it was hoped:

> would provide defence and security against the Saracens and be like a shield for the Christians as far as Acre. It would also be a strong and formidable point of attack, and from here it would easily be possible to launch incursions and raids into Saracen territories as far as Damascus; and through the construction of the said castle the sultan would lose a lot of money and much support and service from the men who would be subject to the stronghold and from their lands. He would also in his own territories lose villages, agricultural lands, pasture and · other rights, because men would not dare to work the land for fear of the castle. His territories would be turned to waste and solitude, and he would have to undertake large expense and engage a considerable force of mercenaries to defend Damascus and the surrounding districts.

Secondary to the intended function of a castle, but still carrying considerable weight in the choice of a site, was the preference for occupying positions with topographical advantages as well as a good water supply and a local source of building material. Because of the defensive needs, there was sometimes no choice at all and a site was imposed on the castle-builders even if it lacked natural advantages. However, a topographically advantageous hill overlooking the surrounding terrain could almost always be taken advantage of and it is unusual to find a castle which does not occupy the highest place in its locality.

A good water supply was desirable, but if this was not available, as was often the case in the Near East, it could be substituted by the excavation or construction of huge cisterns which could hold winter rainwater. In many parts of the Near East the winter rain was substantial enough to provide a garrison's needs throughout the summer. A good supply of stone was generally not a problem in the East, although quality could vary considerably from place to place. Building stone was mostly quarried on site but occasionally stone was also imported from further afield. One example is at Belvoir, where the building stone used was the local basalt, a hard stone which is difficult to work. Here limestone was brought to the site from the Gilboa Mountains to be used for voussoirs and for decorative elements. The Crusaders favoured sites where there were ancient ruins which could be quarried for building stone, a fact which gave birth to the often-quoted Crusader axiom: 'A castle destroyed is already half rebuilt'.[4] Examples of such sites are numerous; indeed, most castles have at least some use of *spolia* and in some of them the reuse of ancient material is extensive.

Tower keeps

Square and rectangular keeps were one of the most common types of castles in the Crusader states. Pringle records some 75 towers known from archaeological remains and a large number of additional keeps recorded in historical sources in the Kingdom of Jerusalem alone.[5] This type of castle appears to have originated in the West.[6] A number of these small towers in the Latin East were possessed by the Military Orders. As noted on p. 100, the Templars built towers chiefly to protect pilgrims travelling on the roads, while other towers were built or purchased to serve as centres for the administration of rural properties.[7] An example of a tower that served the former function is that built by the Templars opposite the peninsula at 'Atlit on which they later built the large fortress of Chateau Pelerin. Le Destroit (Districtum) was, as noted, constructed on top of a sandstone ridge that runs parallel to the coast, at a point where the coastal road passed through a narrow trench cut into the rock (Figure 27). The narrowness of this passage, which gave the tower its Latin and French names, made it an ideal position for robbers to ambush travellers passing through.[8] Indeed, in 1103 King Baldwin I was attacked and wounded here.[9] In order to protect travellers and pilgrims the Templars built a tower here in the twelfth century. Utilising the easily quarried sandstone ridge, they cut a podium out of the rock to serve as the base of the tower, separating it from the ridge by clearing almost all the rock around it. The stone taken from around the podium served in the construction of the superstructure of the tower and the outer wall. The tower measured 15.5 by 11 metres. In 1120, after the construction of Chateau Pelerin, the Templars dismantled le Destroit so that it could not be used by the enemy as a defensive position from which to attack their new castle. Al-Mu'azzam 'Isa completed the destruction and all that remains today is the podium surrounded by a courtyard to the south and east and stables to the east. However, we can safely reconstruct the structure itself from these remains and comparison with other towers.[10] A wooden staircase supported on two rock-cut plinths gave access to the main doorway of the tower in the south wall. The interior of the ground floor was probably barrel-vaulted, since there is no evidence for piers to support groin vaulting (had they existed there would certainly have been evidence for them, as they would have been rock-cut). The width of the walls (2.4 metres) would suggest the usual two storeys, but as it was built on the rock podium this tower was perhaps somewhat higher than was usual. Its position on the sandstone ridge (the highest natural feature west of the Carmel Mountains) would have made it a valuable look-out position along

Figure 21 Remains of the Templar tower of Le Destroit (Districtum) opposite 'Atlit (photograph by the author).

the coastal plain to the north and south (although not quite as good as the great towers later built at Chateau Pelerin). Within the tower a staircase (1.3 metres wide) constructed within the thickness of the northern wall led to the no longer surviving upper storey. Below the ground floor are two rock-cut cisterns. To the east are a row of mangers[11] and there are the remains of additional rock-cut rooms outside the tower on the north, which Johns suggests may have been used for a herd and the herdsmen.[12]

A very similar tower was constructed at Khirbat al-Manhata on the road from Castellum Regis to Montfort, less than one kilometre from Montfort (Figure 28).[13] As at le Destroit, there are remains of an extensive quarry at this site. This quarry supplied the building stones for the construction of the new Teutonic castle in 1226/27. The settlement of Trefile (or Tarphile/Tertille) existed in the twelfth century prior to the construction of Montfort.[14] The tower itself may have predated the larger castle, or may have been constructed to defend the workers at the quarry during the construction of Montfort. The surviving remains, as at Chateau Pelerin, consist almost only of the rock podium; it is possible that, as at Chateau Pelerin, the tower was dismantled when the large fortress was completed so that it could not be used by assailants as a defended position for attack. As at Chateau Pelerin, the new fortress is in view of and at a lower position than the tower. The podium at Khirbat al-Manhata measures 13 by 10 metres. A rock-cut staircase on the south rose to the constructed first-floor level, of which only part of the west wall survives.

The Templars occupied or constructed a tower on a slight rise above the road from Jaffa to Jerusalem in the village at Yazur, 6 km east of Jaffa. Known variously as Casel

Figure 28 Remains of the Teutonic tower at Tarphile near Montfort (photograph by the author).

des Pleins (Village of the Plains), Casale Balneorum (Village of the Baths) or Casellum de Templo, this tower has never been excavated but has recently been examined in a survey conducted by the British School of Archaeology in Jerusalem.[15] It too was a fairly typical Frankish tower. Casel des Plains measures 12.8 by 12.6 metres and its walls are 2.8–2.9 metres thick. The surviving ground floor is, once again, barrel-vaulted.[16] The entrance is in the north wall and there is a single, round-headed embrasure window in the east wall. A wooden staircase against the west wall, which has not survived, led to the first-floor level through a broad opening in the south-west corner of the vault. On the exterior of the south wall are springers for an adjoining vault that no longer exists. An enclosure wall that surrounded the tower can still be seen to the north-west; remains of Crusader vaults exist to the south.[17] As the walls of this tower are close to 3 metres thick, the interior of the tower was quite small (7 by 7.2 metres), leading Pringle to suggest that the structure was perhaps intended primarily as a refuge rather than a permanent residence.[18] Pringle notes that the first record of Templar involvement here was in October 1191, shortly after the town was destroyed by Saladin.[19]

A second castle protecting pilgrims on the Jaffa–Jerusalem road was constructed at Nicopolis (modern Latrun, identified by the Greeks as Emmaus) on a hill overlooking the road as it nears the pass into the Judean Mountains (Figure 29). There is a barrel-vaulted tower at this site, the surviving ground floor of which measures 14/15 by 14/15 metres. The walls are 3 to 4 metres thick. The tower, which probably represents the earliest stage of this castle, was later greatly expanded (apparently in a number of

Figure 29 Aerial photograph of Toron des Chevaliers (Latrun) (courtesy of Rafi Lewis).

stages) into the large fortress known as Toron des Chevaliers.[20] It covered an area in the region of 200 by 250 metres, making it one of the largest castles in the Kingdom of Jerusalem. Once again, the present lack of archaeological evidence makes it impossible to date the tower or to identify the stages of construction, or to determine when the outer lines of fortification were added.[21] However, it is safe to assume that the tower and perhaps the rectangular enclosure wall and talus surrounding it belonged to the earliest stage of development. This was probably the castle built between 1137 and 1141 which the *Chronica Aldefonsi imperatoris* attributed to Count Rodrigo Gonzalez of Toledo.[22] At this time the Jaffa–Jerusalem road was still threatened by intermittent incursions from Fatimid Ascalon and the tower was no doubt intended to serve a similar role to le Destroit at ʿAtlit. As Count Rodrigo was associated with the Templar Order, we can assign this early stage of Toron des Chevaliers to the Templars. This would make it the earliest of the Templar castles in the Kingdom of Jerusalem – as early as their Cilician castles, which were also built in *c.* 1137.

Another pilgrimage route which the Templars defended with towers is the road from Jerusalem to the Place of Baptism on the Jordan River. Here there are remains of two small towers overlooking the road. The first was at the place known as the Red Ascent (Maʿale Adumim), named for the red rock which can be seen as one ascends towards the castle. This is also the traditional site of the Inn of the Good Samaritan. Here the Templars built a tower with a rock-cut moat. They named it Maldoim, a Frankish version of the biblical name. It is also referred to in contemporary sources as the Red Cistern, Cisternam Rubea (a cistern is located in the east of the castle). Theoderich refers to this castle in 1169 as belonging to the Templar Order: 'ubi Templarii firmum castrum constituerunt'.[23] The tower, which stands at the centre of a dry-moated enclosure, is quite small, a mere 9.3 by 8.5 metres. The rock-cut moat surrounded the castle on all sides and additional structures were built within it. In the south-west corner of the enclosure is a barrel-vaulted 'L'-shaped undercroft, and foundations of additional structures can be seen on the western side of the keep and to its north. Even with these additions, the castle could have held only a very small garrison. As it was positioned on a prominent rise above the pilgrims' road, this small fort was ideally located to control traffic at the place where the road from Jerusalem to the Jordan River began its final descent towards the Jordan Valley. Below it stands the building known as the Inn of the Good Samaritan, which recent excavations have shown to have been occupied in the twelfth century as well.[24] A second small tower was built on the road to the Jordan further to the north-east.[25] At Bait Jubr at-Tahtani, 6.5 km east of Maldoim, are the remains of a small tower, also possibly built by the Templars in order to protect the pilgrims' road, this one measuring a mere 9.5 by 6.6–8.1 metres. A third castle on this route was located near the Place of Baptism itself on the bank of the Jordan River. This castle, the site of which is unknown, was possibly also a tower. Theoderich described it as a strong castle.[26]

In the twelfth and thirteenth centuries both the Templars and Hospitallers came into the possession of towers which they used as administrative centres for the management of their rural estates. At the Red Tower (al-Burj al-Ahmar) in the Sharon Plain,[27] the Templars and later the Hospitallers held a two-storey tower which served as a rural administrative centre.[28] Two large towers are located in the fertile region of the County of Tripoli: Chastel Blanc south-east of Tortosa and Chastel Rouge (Qal'at Yahmur) in the plains northeast of Tripoli. These are remarkable and well-preserved examples of Frankish stone towers. The keep of Chastel Blanc is located in the Nusairi Mountains dominating the region south-east of Tortosa in the County of Tripoli. It is situated about 380 metres above the plain. A castle was constructed here at an early date, possibly as early as 1112 when Safita was given by Tancred to the grandson of Raymond of St Gilles.[29] It was subsequently occupied and may perhaps have been destroyed by Nur al-Din, and was later devastated by an earthquake in 1170.[30] In 1171 Nur al-Din again briefly occupied the castle, and soon after this it was acquired by the Templars. They appear to have extensively rebuilt it; it was strong enough to resist Saladin in 1188. However, the vicissitudes of Chastel Blanc were not over; it was destroyed by yet another earthquake early in the thirteenth century.[31] The Templars rebuilt the castle (probably much as it survives today), and it may have been strengthened by Louis IX. At the time of its destruction by Baybars in 1271, Chastel Blanc had a garrison of 700. The keep is the finest surviving example of an *église-donjon* in the East. It measures externally 31 by 18 metres and is preserved to its original height of 25 metres, making it the tallest surviving keep in the Latin East. The barrel-vaulted chapel (23.6 by 10.5 metres, 13.5 metres high) is located on the ground floor. The first floor is a large groin-vaulted hall of eight bays supported on three free-standing cruciform piers. Below the chapel is a rock-cut cistern.

The tower was surrounded by two enceintes. The outer one, more or less oval in shape, has been largely obliterated by encroaching modern buildings. It measured *c.* 165 by 100 metres and had two towers. Like the inner enceinte, it is probably considerably later than the keep. On the inner polygonal enceinte were a number of vaulted structures, including a large building with a groin-vaulted ground floor and a

Gothic rib-vaulted hall above. Some of these structures may have served to house the brothers and as storerooms, barns and stables.[32]

Chastel Rouge (Qal'at Yahmur) occupies a hilltop in the County of Tripoli in the south of the Nusairi Mountains, 12 km south-east of Tortosa (Tartus) on the road to Rafaniyah. It was probably first built early in the twelfth century and was held by the Montolieu family. It was acquired by the Hospitallers in 1177/78. The castle consists of a large keep measuring 16.2 by 14.1 metres and stands 12 metres high (without the original battlements). Its walls are 1.8–2.2 metres thick. The main entrance to the keep was on the west side at the first-floor level, which is reached by an external staircase, an unusual arrangement in Crusader keeps which can however be seen at some other towers, such as Qalansuwa.[33] The ground-floor level had a small door on the east but no internal connection with the first-floor level. Corbels positioned high on the wall above the east door show that it was defended with box machicolation. The keep is surrounded by a rectangular enclosure (42 by 37 metres) defended by outworks, including a curtain wall 1.9 metres thick with two projecting corner towers, sufficient to supply defending fire along the walls of the enclosure. The tower in the south-east corner of the enclosure was a solid turret (3.65 metres square) which could have served as a fighting platform.

Large enclosure castles

Castles of the Military Orders generally contained a level enclosed courtyard. Although in some castles these were not particularly large, and in a number of cases they were drastically reduced in size by the construction of additional buildings, the courtyard played an important, indeed essential, role in these castles. Most of the castles built by the Orders were intended to fulfil at least three functions: (a) as a military base where soldiers could be housed and their supplies stored; (b) as a protected place for soldiers to train; and (c) as a fortified convent in which the brothers could carry out all the requirements of their communal conventual rule. The courtyard or enclosure castle best fulfilled these needs; the courtyard provided a protected training ground, the vaults surrounding it provided housing space for the garrison and storage for their food, weapons, livestock and other supplies. Monasteries had traditionally preferred the courtyard plan, which enabled them to withdraw from the outside world, with the church, chapter-house, dormitory, refectory, cellars and other elements located around an enclosed central cloister. Thus by adopting a courtyard plan for their castles the Military Orders were reflecting the very nature of their organisations, combining military and monastic functions.

At Yalu, on one of the roads to Jerusalem shortly before it enters the Judaean Mountains, are the fragmentary remains of an enclosure castle which has been identified with the Templar castle of Castellum Arnaldi (Chastel Hernaut) (Figure 30).[34] It is located about one kilometre south-west of Beit Nuba on the road to Jerusalem, north of the Valley of Ayalon. Here, where the road approached the mountains, as at le Destroit, the narrowing of the valley made it an ideal place for Muslim bandits to ambush pilgrims and travellers. This castle is first referred to as having been constructed by Baldwin I with the aim of defending the surrounding area and thus began its life as an early (pre-Templar) roadside fort. After being dismantled by the Fatimids (1106)[35] the castle was rebuilt in 1132/33 by Patriarch Warmund and the citizens of

Figure 30 Castellum Arnaldi (Yalu) (photograph by Ross Burns).

Jerusalem.[36] This was still early days for Templar involvement in castle building, and the first direct evidence for its being in Templar hands comes only in 1179 when the Hospitallers renounced their claims to certain Templar properties, including Castellum Arnaldi.[37] The castle had by then developed into a medium-sized enclosure castle, nearly rectangular in form. In its present condition, one can observe only parts of two curtain walls: the western wall about 80 metres in length, which has a tower projecting about 4 metres from the wall, and the southern wall with vaults and staircases. Benvenisti records traces of a vault which may be part of a north-west corner tower.[38] He suggests overall dimensions of 40 by 80 metres. There are also remains of a wall on the south-east. The gate was possibly located in the south.[39]

As their financial resources increased, the Military Orders were able to expand some of their smaller castles. The easiest way to do this was to add curtain walls around the existing structure with an external gatehouse and a few towers at the weak points in the defences. The new walls not only greatly increased the size of a castle but converted it into a much better defended one with concentric fortification. At Toron des Chevaliers and Belmont, both on the road to Jerusalem, and at Bethgibelin further to the south, small and medium-sized castles were thus expanded and improved.

Although archaeological examination is still required to determine the development of Toron des Chevaliers, it is likely that in the second half of the twelfth century the Templars greatly expanded the castle, which in its early phase probably consisted of nothing more than a keep, possibly with simple outworks of some sort (Figure 31).[40] At first they seem to have added a rectangular enclosure castle around it which measured 72 by 55 metres. This enceinte had no towers, although it did have a steep

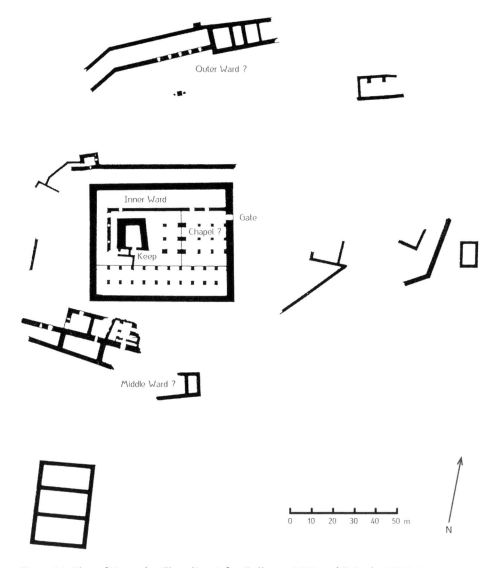

Figure 31 Plan of Toron des Chevaliers (after Bellamy, 1938 and Pringle, 1997a).

talus. Within these walls a complex of groin- and barrel-vaulted halls was constructed to house the garrison. An elaborately decorated chapel was constructed, possibly above the vaults to the east of the tower.[41] At a certain stage the castle was again greatly expanded by the addition of one or two outer polygonal lines of fortification which follow the contours of the hill.

Only excavations can reveal when these expansions took place and whether they were consecutive or contemporaneous. However, it is possible that the great expansion of the castle (the addition of the outer enceinte and perhaps the intermediate enceinte as well) coincided with similar expansions of other Frankish buildings such as Bethgibelin, Blanchegarde, Darom, Belmont and the Premonstratensian monastery of Montjoie

(Nebi Samwil) and dates from the period of Saladin's incursions into Frankish territories in the 1170s and 1180s.

Recent clearing of the vegetation and some of the topsoil on this site (August 2003) has exposed traces of all four faces of the inner enceinte with its steep talus. The northern face was exposed for almost its entire length. A portal in the south wall of the northern barrel vault, which does not appear in the plans published by Bellamy and later by Pringle, was uncovered.[42] Construction at Toron des Chevaliers is of good-quality masonry with various types of surface treatment including diagonal tooling, marginally drafted ashlar quoins and masons' marks (all hallmarks of Frankish construction). Sixteenth- and seventeenth-century illustrations give us only a vague idea of the appearance of the castle but show that considerably more of it was standing before it became a quarry for building stone and perhaps for lime kilns.[43] Today little survives above the basement levels.

Further along the road to Jerusalem, Hospitaller Belmont is an unusual castle in that it seems to have begun its existence not as a castle at all but rather as a large domestic courtyard building of a type generally known as a manor house or rural estate centre, a type of building which usually has little in the way of defences. However, when it was expanded by its Hospitaller owners, probably in the 1170s or 1180s when rural settlement in the region of Jerusalem was under the threat of Ayyubid raids, it was effectively converted into a castle by the additions of two polygonal lines of defence. These enceintes follow the contours of the hill and do not appear to have any projecting towers, although they do have a talus. The inner defensive line was barrel-vaulted. The gates of these two outer defences were located in the south.

Quadrangular enclosure castles with projecting towers (*quadriburgia*)

One of the most effective castle designs employed by the Military Orders was the quadrangular enclosure castle with projecting corner towers and, on the larger examples, with additional projecting towers at regular intervals along the walls. The use of projecting towers provided firing positions that overlooked the length of the side walls of the castle and thus enabled the defenders to control the entire approach to the castle. The regular quadrangular enclosure castle with projecting corner towers is a castle type found from quite early times and is particularly well represented in the Near East and North Africa. Examples are known from the Late Iron Age (for example the Middle Israelite fortress of Kadesh-Barnea dated to the eighth to seventh centuries BC) and from the Hellenistic, Roman Byzantine and Early Islamic periods; indeed, the Franks occupied and used two such castles of Islamic date.[44] Thus this castle type found popularity quite early in the Crusader period and the design was adopted for the group of castles constructed around Fatimid Ascalon in the late 1130s and 1140s (Bethgibelin, Blanchegarde, Ibelin and Gaza), which were intended to help put an end to raids coming from the city into the hinterland of the kingdom, and for the castle of Darom which was constructed some years later (shortly before 1170). Other *quadriburgia* were constructed at Castellum Regis (Mi'iliya), Coliath, Arima and Burj Bardawil.[45]

The inner fortress at Bethgibelin is an early example of such a castle, perhaps the earliest example built by the Franks themselves (Figure 32). However, only a small number of the *quadriburgia* were possessions of the Military Orders and it is not at all

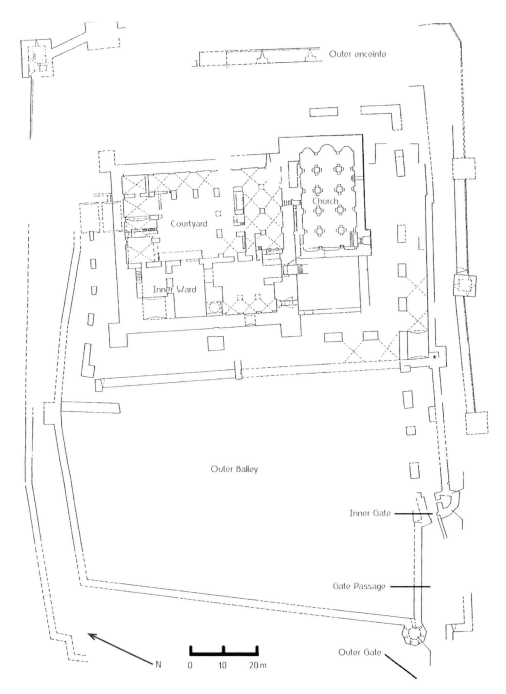

Outer enceinte

Church

Courtyard

Inner Ward

Outer Bailey

Inner Gate

Gate Passage

N   0   10   20 m

Outer Gate

Figure 32 Plan of Bethgibelin (after Kloner and Cohen, 2000).

certain that any of them were originally built by the Orders. Bethgibelin, which came into Hospitaller hands in 1136 shortly after it was constructed, originally consisted of an enclosure castle of average size (46 by 48 metres) which at a later stage became the inner ward of more expansive fortifications consisting of two parallel walls, several towers and a moat, which enclosed an area of c. 30,000 square metres, probably including the village (although, as noted, excavations have not revealed any evidence of the Frankish settlement).[46]

The inner castle had three corner towers; the fourth corner on the south-east was at some stage replaced by, or rather incorporated in, the chevet of a tri-apsidal church which was built against the south wall of the castle. The main entrance to the interior of the inner castle was to the west. Two-thirds of the interior were covered with groin-vaulted ranges around a central open area. According to the excavators, these vaults probably had been of two storeys and contained the dormitories and storerooms.[47] Stairs led from the central courtyard down into subterranean vaults which were apparently the remains of a Roman bathhouse; these were used by the Hospitallers for storage.[48] On the western side of the inner castle was an industrial area containing stores, pools, basins and furnaces. This was perhaps the castle forge and it would appear that the kitchen was located here as well. Water was stored in the south and a large groin-vaulted wing on the south of the eastern side of the castle has been identified by the excavators as the refectory.[49] At its western entrance a round construction was interpreted by the excavators as a fountain.[50]

At Mi'iliya (Mhalia), 10 km north-east of Acre in the western Galilee, the fortress of Castellum Regis is a fairly typical *quadriburgium* (Figure 33). Burchard of Mount Zion noted that it was situated in a valley belonging to the Teutonic Order which 'abounds with all good things, and with fruit which even in that land are rarely found elsewhere'.[51] Together with its appurtenances, the castle was purchased in May 1220 from Count Otto of Henneberg for 7,000 marks of silver and 2,000 bezants.[52] It occupies the summit of a hill within the town of Mi'iliya and measures 39.2 metres square. The curtain walls are about 3 metres thick and in each corner is a rectangular projecting tower, three of which have survived in reasonable condition (the fourth, in the south-east, is destroyed). The towers vary in size, the largest being that on the south-west corner. They each had at least four splayed arrow-slits, one in each of their walls. Two of these were placed flush with the curtain walls on both sides of the towers to enable the most effective defensive firing along the wall. On the east there was a vaulted range; on this side a wall 2.3 metres thick ran parallel with the eastern wall of the castle. Although the vaulting itself has not survived, the range was not too wide (less than 8 metres) to have been covered with a barrel vault. Construction of the castle is of roughly squared ashlars with marginal tooling on those used for the quoins. In the Crusader period the castle was surrounded by a walled village with a church. The polygonal outworks were described by Ellenblum as 8 to 10 metres high.[53] These walls are referred to in written sources as the *propugnaculum* or *barbicana*.[54]

Arima in the County of Tripoli was a complex of three adjacent enclosure castles extending laterally along a plateau 171 metres above sea level, overlooking the entrance to Nahr Abras (Figure 34). The castle overlooks Akkar to the south-west. It is north of the road from Tartus to Homs (the Homs Gap), but closer to the road than Crac des Chevaliers and Safita, and guarded the route between Tortosa and Tripoli. This plain was a rich agricultural area. The castle was probably originally built by the

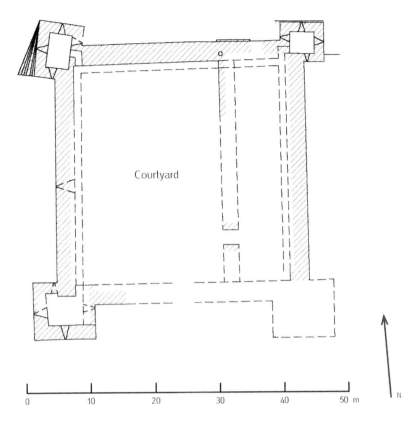

Figure 33 Plan of Castellum Regis (Mi'iliya) (drawn by Rabia Hamisa).

Count of Tripoli. After the Second Crusade Arima was seized by Bertrand of Toulouse, who suspected that the Count of Tripoli, Raymond II, had murdered his father Alfonso-Jordan, Count of Toulouse. Bertrand intended to oust Raymond as Count of Tripoli, but Raymond countered in September 1148 by calling upon the aid of Zengids and Damascus in order to remove Bertrand.[55] The castle fell to the Muslims, who killed or took prisoner most of the garrison;[56] Bertrand was imprisoned for eleven years. The Muslims did not hand Arima over to Raymond or occupy it themselves, but dismantled it instead. However, it would seem that the Franks subsequently rebuilt it, for in 1167 Nur al-Din is recorded as having taken the castle and dismantled it. By 1170, at the time of a major earthquake, Arab sources refer to it as being yet again in Frankish hands. In 1171 Nur al-Din again damaged Arima but did not retake it. It was possibly acquired by the Templars by 1177 and was strengthened with towers and other outworks. Arima fell to Saladin in 1188, but was returned shortly afterwards to the Templars, who held it until 1291.[57] It is referred to in this period in a treaty between the Templars and the Muslims in 1285.

The fortifications of Arima extend over an area *c.* 300 metres in length along the east–west ridge. Its maximum width is 80 metres (Figure 35). Plans of the ruins were published by Anus,[58] Müller-Wiener[59] and Deschamps.[60] Deschamps' plan shows the entire castle and appears to be reliable, whereas Anus's plan, which is only of the

Figure 34 Arima Castle: the eastern ward seen from the south (photograph by Ross Burns).

eastern ward, is disproportional and Müller-Wiener, who also drew only the eastern ward, has given erroneous directions (his north is actually east).[61] The three wards are divided by moats. Very little survives of the western and central wards, and only traces of walls and a single rectangular tower on the north-west corner of the central ward, set slightly askew from its walls, can be observed. The tower has a batter on its north and west sides.

Only the eastern enclosure is reasonably well preserved. It takes the form of a rectangular fortified *quadriburgium* (75 by 45 metres) with projecting corner towers surviving in the south-east, south-west and north-east. Entrance was through a gate on the west. On the plan of this castle published by Müller-Wiener it is defended by a ring wall on the south and west which has a gate flanked by two semicircular towers. If this is accurate, it would appear to be a later barbican and not part of the original design (it does not appear at all on Deschamps' plan.) On the north and south sides of this ward are barrel-vaulted halls. A keep to the right of the gate near the centre of the west wall measures 12.5 by 11 metres. It is massively constructed and has walls up to 4 metres thick. It is entered from within the enclosure and has an arrow embrasure facing west. The south-west corner tower of this ward has a batter, as do a tower in the central ward and a tower slightly north-east of the central ward on an outer wall which commanded the entrance to the entire complex. Construction varies, with rough basalt masonry in the earlier phases of the castle and well-cut limestone ashlars, some with marginal dressing, in later (late twelfth- and early thirteenth-century) additions such as the north-east and south-west towers of the eastern ward.

Chastel Rouge, although there are only two towers on its outer fortification, can

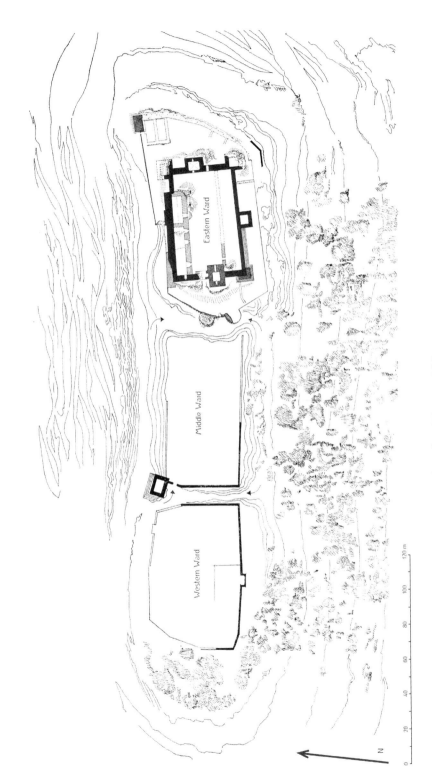

Eastern Ward

Middle Ward

Western Ward

N

0   20   40   60   80   100   120 m

Figure 35 Plan of Arima Castle (after Deschamps, 1973 and Müller-Wiener, 1966).

possibly also be included in this class of castles. Two corner towers on a castle of this size were sufficient to enable flanking fire to cover the entire length of the four walls. Thus if these towers, which both appear to be later additions to the outer fortifications, date from the period of Frankish rule, what we have here is essentially an example of a new type of castle consisting of a keep surrounded by a *quadriburgium*. In this design the outer walls and towers defend the keep and entirely shield its lower floor from attack, and the upper section of the keep defends the enclosure castle from above. This design may be considered an early and most basic form of the concentric castle.[62]

Most of the known *quadriburgia* date from the first half of the twelfth century. Coliath (al-Qulayat), located in the plain about 25 km north of Tripoli, was probably substantially built shortly after the Hospitallers had acquired it in 1127. This castle has an enclosure measuring 63 by 56 metres with corner and intermediate projecting towers. There are two gates, one on the south and the other between the intermediate tower on the western wall of the castle and the north-west corner tower. The latter is well protected by the two towers, whereas the southern gate has no protection from its sides. The curtains are well provided with arrow-slits at an average distance of 5 to 6 metres from one another. On the north there is a barrel-vaulted range and there are traces of another vaulted range on the south. The castle is surrounded by a rock-cut ditch.

Coliath is not an ideal *quadriburgium*, although it has been regarded as the classic example of this type of castle.[63] Though it has corner and intermediate towers, it seems that the Frankish builders did not yet entirely understand the principle of this long-established design. Only the north-west corner tower and the western intermediate tower project a substantial distance from the curtain. Two other towers had some ability to provide flanking fire along the walls: the intermediate tower on the north wall which, although it was barely salient, had arrow-slits flush with the curtain wall, and the north-east corner tower, which had an arrow-slit facing south on the east wall. All the other towers are practically flush with the curtain walls and consequently would have been incapable of protecting these walls from attack at close range. The outcome of these defects was that the northern and western sides of the castle were fairly well covered but the eastern and southern walls were unprotected by lateral fire.[64]

The Crusader *quadriburgia* all seem to date from the twelfth century, and Kennedy suggests that this design lost its relevance following the fall of numerous castles after the Battle of Hattin in 1187.[65] He suggests that the almost complete collapse of the Crusader defences alerted the Military Orders to the defects of this type of castle in light of the advances made by the Muslims in siege technology in the early thirteenth century.

However, this is a rather simplistic explanation and the truth is perhaps somewhat more complicated. If large enough, well positioned and embellished with concentric fortifications and other defensive fixtures, *quadriburgia* could be as successful as other castle types, perhaps more so than most. At Belvoir for example, the advantageous topography, concentric design, broad moat and complex gate system combined to turn this most basic of castle designs into a highly effective fortress which was able to withstand intermittent siege for a year and a half, a feat that would have been remarkable for even the most advanced and complex of thirteenth-century castles.

Belvoir was built by the Hospitallers after 1168, when the Order purchased land on the eastern edge of the Yissaschar Plateau 550 metres above the Jordan Valley, 13 km south of the Sea of Galilee and about 4 km west of the Jordan River (Figure 36).[66] Prior to excavations it was believed that this fortress consisted of an external enclosure castle

Figure 36 Belvoir Castle, facing east (photograph by Buki Boaz).

with a central keep, similar to the arrangement at Giblet, north of Beirut.[67] However, the excavations revealed that in the design of Belvoir Castle the Hospitallers made one of the most significant advances in the art of military architecture in the twelfth century. The plan is remarkably simple and compact (Figure 37). It consists of two enclosure castles, one within the other, the outer one considerably larger (*c.* 100/ *c.* 116 metres (n.–s.) by *c.* 110 metres (e.–w.) compared to the inner castle *c.* 46 by *c.* 46 metres) and about twice as large as the other known *quadriburgia*, but lower in height (one storey as opposed to the two-storey inner ward). It had some additional towers and entrance systems, but essentially it was of the same form as the inner ward.[68] Thus we have a concentric castle built at the time when such castles were coming into fashion. However, because of the almost exact repetition of the plan of the two wards, Belvoir has a superior arrangement to that of the other concentric castles which greatly enhanced its effectiveness under siege. The regular square form and the position of the inner towers exactly between the outer ones allowed the defenders on the towers a broad range of fire. They could observe the enemy across both lines of walls in two directions and they also had a wide field of vision within the fortress, improving communication between the defenders.

In western Cyprus (Paphos) there is a castle which, although much smaller and in a less impressive setting, is remarkably similar in form to Belvoir. Excavations of this

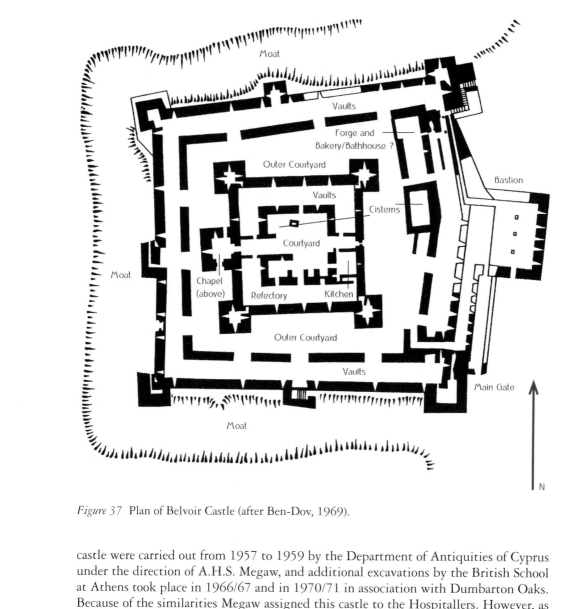

Figure 37 Plan of Belvoir Castle (after Ben-Dov, 1969).

castle were carried out from 1957 to 1959 by the Department of Antiquities of Cyprus under the direction of A.H.S. Megaw, and additional excavations by the British School at Athens took place in 1966/67 and in 1970/71 in association with Dumbarton Oaks. Because of the similarities Megaw assigned this castle to the Hospitallers. However, as no mention is made of it in Hospitaller sources this seems unlikely. Even if this is not a Hospitaller castle the similarity between it and Belvoir leaves no room for doubt that it was designed in imitation of the latter, and a brief description of it is warranted here.

Like Belvoir, this castle consisted of two similar enclosure castles with projecting towers, one inside the other. Though less well positioned topographically, it none the less made full use of this exceptional castle design. The inner ward of the castle measures 35 by 37 metres and, like that at Belvoir, it has quadrangular projecting corner towers and a central courtyard. However, it differs from Belvoir in a number of features. At Belvoir the towers at the corners of the inner castle are more or less square in shape and do not extend more than the thickness of their walls along the curtain walls or into the outer bailey. However, at Saranda Kolones the corner towers are rectangular and occupy a fairly large part of the outer bailey, particularly on the north and south.

The gate tower located on the east, like the inner gate tower at Belvoir, gave indirect access into the inner ward. However, it was apsidal rather than rectangular and probably contained a chapel. The vaulted chambers around the inner ward were groin-vaulted rather than barrel-vaulted and were supported on eight massive piers. As at Belvoir, the main living quarters were located in the inner ward, which was two storeys high, higher than the outer defences. However, this ward contained some elements which at Belvoir were relegated to the outer ward, such as the forge and bathhouse. Another feature which has no parallels at Belvoir is an impressive latrine system.

The outer defences, which measured *c.* 70 by 70 metres, were also similar to those of Belvoir, but again with certain important distinctions. As at Belvoir, they were surrounded by a ditch, but there were no natural topographical advantages such as the steep slope on the east of Belvoir overlooking the Jordan Valley. As at Belvoir there were projecting corner towers and intermediate towers, although the small size of Saranda Kolones meant that the latter were not truly necessary, as they were at Belvoir, in order to permit effective firing along the length of the curtain walls. The main outer gate was much simpler than that at Belvoir, nothing more elaborate than a bent-access tower, although there was probably a drawbridge and it may have been defended from above by machicolation.

Even the relationship between the inner and outer gateways shows none of the sophistication of Belvoir. On entering the outer gate the invader would find himself directly opposite the inner gateway, whereas at Belvoir he had to make his way around nearly half of the outer bailey, constantly exposed to the defenders' fire, before he reached the gate to the inner ward.

An additional distinction was the lack of large barrel-vaulted chambers around the outer bailey. At Saranda Kolones there were only lightly built, flat-roofed barracks, some of which had corner fireplaces and clearly had a domestic rather than a storage function. Another difference from Belvoir is the form of the towers on the outer defences: three of the corner towers were round, perhaps in keeping with advances made in Crusader castle building in the later twelfth century, while the fourth tower in the north-east corner was polygonal. Two of the intermediate towers, the gate tower to the east and the tower on the south wall, were rectangular. The other two were more or less triangular.

Improved siege weapons and the decline of the small enclosure castle

If the design used for these two castles was successful (and the extended siege of Belvoir would suggest that it was), why were the Military Orders so quick to dispense with it and to turn in the thirteenth century to an almost exclusive use of spur and hilltop castles? The answer would appear to lie in the improvement in Muslim siegecraft and specifically in the use during the Ayyubid period of ever-larger and more powerful artillery weapons, notably the counterweight trebuchet. This machine was known in Arabic as the 'big' trebuchet (*manjanîq kabîr*) or the 'frightful' trebuchet (*manjanîq hâ'il*).[69] Under the guidance of an Armenian artillery expert named Havedic, it was used effectively by the Crusaders as early as the second siege of Tyre in 1124, and counterweight trebuchets were used by Muslim armies throughout the twelfth century.[70] Towards the end of the twelfth century trebuchets were employed in increasing numbers. At the siege of Krak in August 1184 Saladin employed nine 'big' trebuchets; 11 were possibly deployed in the siege of Jerusalem in September 1187.[71] They were also used extensively and effectively by both sides in the siege of Acre (1189–91). The destructive capabilities of trebuchets when used in mass against men, and even against the solid, massively constructed medieval fortifications, were considerable. According to the *Itinerarium Peregrinorum*, a single stone fired from one of King Richard's machines killed 12 men; 'nothing could withstand their blows; everything was crushed or reduced to dust'.[72]

Large-scale use of these weapons coinciding with the loss of numerous Frankish castles to Saladin in the period 1187 to 1189 may have convinced the Military Orders to abandon the small enclosure castle design in the early thirteenth century. Even the larger and better-defended concentric enclosure castles were in danger, and only a combination of natural topographical defences and massive man-made fortifications were capable of withstanding bombardment by these new machines. Both of these means were now employed and the great spur and hilltop castles with their stronger and more complex concentric fortifications, exemplified at Crac des Chevaliers, Margat, Chateau Pelerin and Safed, were employed to counter the technological advances of siege weaponry.

Spur castles

One of the most effective castle designs, to which the Teutonic Knights turned when in 1228 they moved their headquarters from Castellum Regis to Montfort, was the spur castle, a castle which was constructed on the end of a mountain spur 180 metres above Wadi Keziv and a tributary wadi, 9 km east of the Mediterranean. The steep slopes on either side of the spur formed a natural defence and the unprotected side of the castle, on the shoulder of the mountain, was artificially protected by means of two moats and a massive tower (Figures 38, 39).

The adoption of the spur castle for many of their major fortresses was a logical outcome of the increasing defensive requirements of the Frankish states at the end of the twelfth century. The best way to defend a castle, in light of the improvement in siege machinery, was by building the castles in places where the siege machines could not be used. The end of a mountain spur, protected by steep cliffs on two of its three sides, was an excellent solution. The higher and steeper the cliffs, the less likely that siege weapons could be brought within range of the walls (even a comparatively gentle slope made the use of some siege machines difficult or impossible). The idea was not new, but it was used more effectively in the great Frankish castles than it had been before. The advantage of the spur castle design over simple castles like Blanchegarde or Yalu, which also occupied hilltops, was that this design enabled the defenders to concentrate their defence efforts in one direction – the one side of the castle not naturally defended by a steep decline but well defended by moats and fortifications. Spur and hilltop castles combined natural and artificial defences to create almost impregnable strongholds.

Montfort, or Starkenberg as the Teutons called it, was a much more formidable

Figure 38 Montfort Castle viewed from the north-east (photograph by Rabei Khamissy).

castle than the nearby Teutonic castle, Castellum Regis. It was located in a position better defended by nature, isolated on a steep mountain spur, whereas Castellum Regis was on a more easily approachable hill. It had concentric defences and two ditches, and a great keep cut it off from the only direction from which access was fairly easy, the shoulder of the mountain spur to the east. It was much larger than Castellum Regis and had sumptuous apartments, appropriate as the living quarters of a Master of the Order.

However, in some important aspects, most notably its location, Montfort is not a typical spur castle. The site was impressive but had a decided strategic disadvantage in that it occupies a hill which is lower than the range of hills which surround it. Consequently, only a very limited area immediately surrounding the castle could be observed from its walls. Moreover, it was far from any frontier and there were no important roads or passes below it. An additional disadvantage was that the hill to its south was not distant enough to prevent its being used as a position for siege machines such as mangonels, a fact supported by the discovery of some mangonel balls on the side of this hill.[73]

However, these disadvantages did not apparently deter the Teutonic Knights, who perhaps sought just such an isolated position for their new headquarters.[74] The site which had been held by Joscelin III de Courtenay in the twelfth century had subsequently come into the hands of Jacques de Mandelée, who sold it to the Teutonic Knights. They rebuilt it as a large spur castle and used it as their administrative

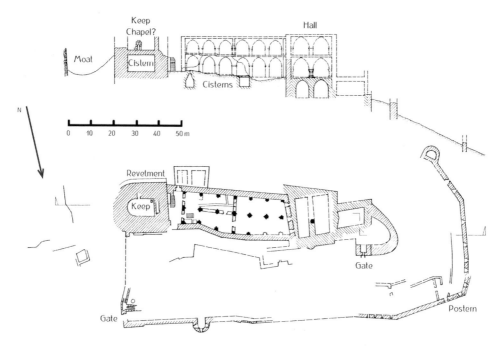

Figure 39 Plan of Montfort Castle (after Dean, [1927] 1982, Frankel and Gatzov, 1993 and Pringle, 1997a).

headquarters and residence of the Grand Master. The castle housed their archives and treasury. It was unsuccessfully besieged by Baybars in 1266, and in June 1271 the Muslims again besieged Montfort, mined the southern rampart, and occupied the outer bailey on 11 June. The knights sought refuge in the keep, but eventually surrendered on 18 June and were permitted to leave for Acre, leaving their arms and possessions behind. The Order's archives and treasury survived, having been returned to Acre after the siege in 1271. The castle was subsequently destroyed and abandoned, and in 1283 Burchard of Mount Zion described it as 'utterly ruined'.[75]

In 1926 an expedition from the Metropolitan Museum of Art, New York, was directed by W.L. Calver (in the field) and Bashford Dean. The excavations, which took place over a period of four weeks, exposed much of the castle (Figure 39). Montfort was cut off from the spur by its two moats and defended by the large keep at the highest point to the east. The moat at the keep is 20 metres wide, 11 metres long and 9 metres deep.[76] The second outer moat, located about 50 metres further to the east, appears to have been a natural chasm which was broadened to utilise as a moat. The keep occupies the width of the spur (c. 25 metres). Its east wall was apsidal, suggesting the possibility that the tower contained a chapel on one of its floors.[77] Below it is a large cistern, its roof being the floor of the storey above. A door on the south side wall of the keep gave access to small chambers located within the thickness of the walls, which have not survived. The keep was constructed of large, well-cut marginally dressed limestone ashlars.

A staircase leads down from the western side of the keep to the principal quarters of the castle, which were about 5 metres lower than the floor of the keep. The central part of the castle consisted of a two-storey building, 50 metres in length and about 20 metres wide, roofed with two parallel aisles of groin-vaulted bays supported on cruciform piers and columns, numbering 12 bays in all. The southern and western walls are 2 metres thick. Dean suggests that colourless and honey-coloured stained glass quarries found in the southern bays at the west end of the building came from a first-floor chapel. However, the stained glass could equally well have come from a reception hall, and, as noted, the chapel may have been located in the keep to the east. On a section of a rib from the vaulting is a polychrome rendering of a fleur-de-lis, a symbol which was adopted by the Teutonic Order as it was by the French royal house. This large building, the largest structure of the castle, would no doubt have contained the domestic apartments of the knights, the dormitory, refectory, kitchens and other conventual elements (Figure 40). The western wall was originally its external wall, but at some time a rib-vaulted hall, probably octagonal in form and possibly two storeys high, was constructed here, cancelling the existing arrow embrasures in this wall. These were blocked up and the new hall, which may have been the Grand Master's residence and a reception hall, was constructed over two large barrel vaults aligned north–south. These vaults were constructed because the hill drops away steeply to the west. The floor level of this hall was close to that of the main structure to its east. The hall had rib-vaulting supported on an octagonal central pillar. Though of far more massive construction, it

Figure 40 Montfort Castle: blocked doorway in the south wing (photograph by Rabei Khamissy).

may have been similar in form to the halls found in some of the later Teutonic castles in Prussia such as the summer refectory at Marienberg.

Below these buildings are the remains of outer fortifications. These consist of an outer wall with embrasures, three surviving towers and three gates and posterns (a gate in the north-east, a second gate adjacent to the keep and another gate or postern near the western end of the northern wall below an inner gate tower – Figure 63). These encircled the castle, about 25 metres below it on average, to the north, west and south. The curtain wall was less than 2 metres thick and some of the surviving sections, in the north and west, still stand to their original height. A passage running along the top of this wall was reached via a staircase located in the east on the section of the wall that ran north from the keep.

There were a number of cisterns and water reservoirs supplying the needs of the garrison. These included the large constructed cistern in the basement of the keep and an open pool north of the main moat outside the castle wall which drained the rainwater that collected in the moat.

Whatever its shortcomings with regard to strategic positioning (shortcomings only if we overlook its builders' apparent objective to create an isolated headquarters), Montfort is a remarkable example of a Crusader spur castle.

Even more remarkable is Crac des Chevaliers, which is generally considered the greatest of all Crusader castles (Figure 41). Lawrence went so far as to call it, with some justification, 'perhaps the best preserved and most wholly admirable castle in the world', and Boase called it 'one of the great buildings of all times' and enthusiastically compared it with the Parthenon and Chartres.[78] Magnificently sited on Djebel Kalakh

Figure 41 Crac des Chevaliers viewed from the south-west (photograph by Jonathan Phillips).

in the Djebel Anasarieh (Mount Lebanon range), it dominates the landscape at the Homs Gap. In the eleventh century a smaller castle with a Kurdish garrison had been stationed there. It was originally known as Hisn al-Akrad (Castle of the Kurds), and the Franks knew it as Le Crat and later as Le Crac.[79] In 1144 Raymond II of Tripoli granted the Hospitallers extensive tracts of land in the eastern part of the County of Tripoli, including towns and villages as well as the castle of Hisn al-Akrad and several other small castles. These holdings formed the base of a virtually independent principality.

The well-preserved remains of Crac des Chevaliers testify to the wealth of the Hospitaller Order and to the resourcefulness of Frankish military architecture. The intelligent choice of location, the ingenuity of its design and the incredible scale of the resources employed in its construction all attest to the castle-building capabilities of the Hospitaller Order. The castle was undeniably their masterpiece. Probably soon after it came into their possession, the Hospitallers rebuilt Crac des Chevaliers to serve as their chief headquarters in Syria and the base for their defence of the County of Tripoli against the Muslim threat from the direction of Homs. In 1170 a major earthquake damaged the castle, after which it was rebuilt. By May 1188, when Saladin marched through the region, the castle was again strong enough to deter him from attempting a raid. In the early thirteenth century Crac des Chevaliers was used as a base for Frankish raids on Hama and Montferrand, another Crusader castle which had fallen into Muslim hands. Around this time, possibly soon after the devastating earthquake of 1202, Crac des Chevaliers was greatly enhanced with a massive outer line of defensive works. Additional raids against the region of Hama took place in 1230 and 1233, but by the 1250s the Frankish position was in decline. In 1252 the region was raided by a horde of Turkmans who wreaked havoc on the countryside, causing serious losses to the castle's revenues. The garrison was reduced and the Hospitallers' hold on the region began to slip. By 1270 Baybars could taunt the Hospitallers by grazing his horses on their crops and fields without fear of reprisal. On 3 March 1271 Baybars returned and commenced his siege of the castle, breaching the outer defences by 29 March. The garrison surrendered on 8 April and was permitted to retreat to Tripoli.

Before it was expanded in the thirteenth century, the castle appears to have been an elongated enclosure castle similar in form to the Templar castle of Vadum Jacob, with perhaps originally a single tower on the south-west corner and a slightly curved northern end. Barrel vaults ran the entire circuit of the castle. It is possible that there were outworks of some kind which were later replaced by the thirteenth-century outer enceinte. The thirteenth-century additions around the inner ward and the forewall about 25 metres down the slope transformed Crac des Chevaliers into a huge concentric spur castle (Figure 42). The new forewall may have had machicolations, although what can be seen today, box and gallery machicolation used in a quantity and manner that is not found in other Near Eastern castles, is apparently Mamluk work.[80] There are semicircular towers on three sides (north, west and south) and on the east side is the remarkable gate complex. The defences on the south are particularly massive, since approach was possible from that direction along the shoulder of the hill. Here the outer castle was cut off from the spur by a rock-cut moat and horn-work, and the inner castle was made more secure by the excavation of a pool (*birqat*). The enormous, steep talus and high walls with three great towers provided almost impenetrable defences for the inner castle. A three-bayed chapel was built in the north-east of the inner bailey.

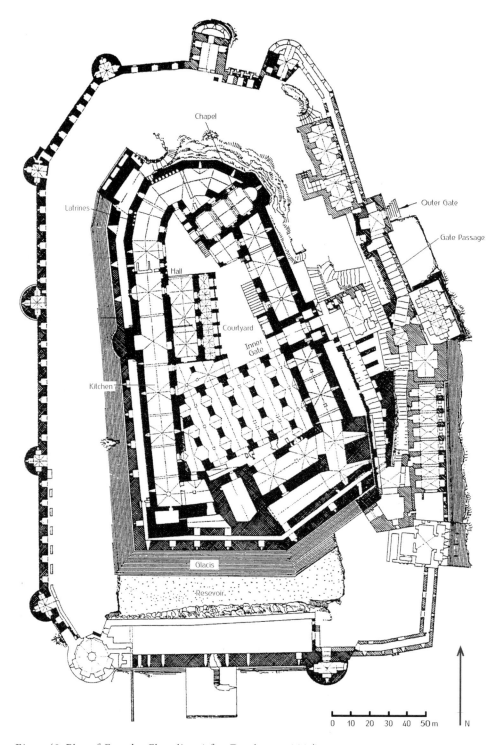

Chapel

Outer Gate

Gate Passage

Latrines

Hall

Courtyard

Inner
Gate

Kitchen

Glacis

Reservoir

0 10 20 30 40 50 m

N

Figure 42 Plan of Crac des Chevaliers (after Deschamps 1934).

The main (inner) gate, defended by two projecting square towers, is in the centre of the east wall at the end of the twisting passage leading from the outer gate. In the north of the inner ward is a postern tower and there are a round tower enclosing an earlier quadrangular tower on the west and three towers on the south. A large rib-vaulted Gothic hall was added on the west and a huge groin-vaulted magazine on the south.

Though Crac des Chevaliers is indisputably the greatest of the spur castles, there are other castles, smaller and less perfect but of no less interest as examples of the castle building-capabilities of the Military Orders. Such a castle is Beaufort, a large castle which, although it deviates somewhat from the principles of the spur-castle design, is best described here. It is located in a strategic position on a ridge high above the Litani River and the southern approaches of the Beq'a Valley on a site which was originally occupied by a fortified Muslim stronghold known as Qal'at al-Shaqif Arnun.[81] Beaufort was surveyed by Deschamps and described in detail in his 1939 volume of *La défense du royaume de Jerusalem*.[82] The small Muslim fort came into Frankish hands in 1139, when King Fulk granted it to the feudal lord of Sidon. The site was strengthened by the construction of a tower and outer wall. Beaufort withheld Muslim attacks after the Battle of Hattin and was again strengthened by the Franks, but finally fell to Saladin on 22 April 1190. While it was held by the Ayyubids a polygonal hall was added in the north and a large round tower in the south-west. The treaty between Richard of Cornwall and Sultan Salih Isma'il of Damascus in 1240 restored the castle to the Franks, although force was needed to expel the Muslim garrison. Once again held by the lords of Sidon, the castle was now enhanced with additional new buildings. It was sold by Julien de Sagette to the Templars in 1260.

Building under the Templars appears to have taken place in stages, commencing in or shortly after 1260. They augmented the fortifications, building outworks to the south. They also built the great hall to the east of the donjon. The latter is roofed with two groin-vaulted bays and has a fine Gothic portal which Rey illustrated in 1859. No doubt they added a chapel if one did not already exist, but no evidence has been found for its location. In any case the Templars did not hold the castle long, for in 1268 Beaufort fell to Baybars following a two-week siege. Baybars destroyed the Templar outworks,[83] but the castle was later strengthened by the Mamluks and later still by Amir Fakr ad-Din in the seventeenth century.

Beaufort is more or less triangular in shape, occupying an area of *c.* 150 by 100 metres. An inner ward occupies the higher part of the ridge, with a lower outer ward to the east. On the west side of the inner ward is a square keep (*c.* 12 by 12 metres), entered from the east. A staircase within the thickness of the wall leads from the entrance to the upper level. On the western wall of the keep, which is an external wall of the castle, are two arrow-slit embrasures. Where the topography is gentler, to the north, west and south, a rock-cut ditch severs the castle from the ridge; Beaufort differs in this from the ideal spur castle, which only had to be cut off from the hill in a single direction. The gate of the outer ward, on the south-east, gives access to the outer bailey and is defended by a round tower to the south. The curtain wall of this lower ward has a second round tower further to the west and the entire southern section of the wall and towers, opposite the faubourg, has a steep stone talus above the rock-cut ditch. Within the outer bailey it was necessary to follow a passage adjacent to the outer wall, turning first south, then west and finally north towards a gate on the inner fortification line. From this gate one passed through a vaulted passage into the inner ward.

There is one Templar castle which follows the principles of the spur castle (natural defences on all but one strongly defended side), although it was not actually built on a mountain spur. Chateau Pelerin ('Atlit Castle) is situated below Mount Carmel on the Mediterranean coast. There are larger and better-preserved castles, but the exceptional location, the unique design and the extraordinary strength of its eastern defences make this castle one of the most remarkable examples of Crusader fortification. It was built by the Templars on a small peninsula on the coast of the Kingdom of Jerusalem, south of Caifas (Haifa) and Acre (Figure 43). The main buildings of the castle consist of a series of vaulted halls that roughly follow the outline of the peninsula, with a second group of vaults and walls forming an inner bailey. However, the most remarkable feature of this castle is its imposing eastern fortification. The Templars, who built this castle in the winter of 1217/18, made use of the natural advantages of the site. It is surrounded on all sides but the east by the sea. It would be difficult if not impossible to bring ships into the shallow, rocky approaches of the castle in order to launch an attack or effect a landing and mining, a popular and often successful means of breaking through defences. In any case, the Italian fleets controlled the Eastern Mediterranean in the early thirteenth century and attack or siege from the sea were not major threats.[84] Consequently an attack on the castle could effectively be carried out only from the east, the one side of the site which had no natural defences. This single approachable side was made secure by the construction of massive parallel defensive works. This was basically the same principle as the spur castles: the peninsula was cut off from its approaches by the ditch, the forewall and the great inner wall. Both walls were enhanced with powerful projecting towers. So

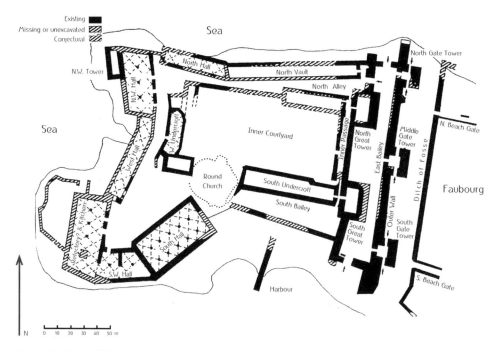

Figure 43 Plan of Chateau Pelerin (after Johns, 1997).

effective was the combination of natural and man-made defences at Chateau Pelerin that the castle was never taken and was abandoned only after the rest of the kingdom had collapsed in 1291.

The moat expanded from about 24 to 29 metres in width to the north (though it measured only 15 metres from the tower walls to the counterscarp) and was about 6 metres deep. It is possible that it could have been flooded with sea water when necessary for the defence of the castle, but it is doubtful that this was always the case. There is no evidence for bridges crossing the moat and it is most unlikely that any existed as they would have had to stretch from the north and south gates in the wall above the counterscarp of the moat to the gates in the sides of the gate towers.[85] The moat was none the less a formidable barrier, all the more effective because anyone approaching it would be within range of fire from both the outer bailey wall that rose above its scarp and the huge inner bailey wall, set back at a distance of nearly 30 metres and rising to a height of over 30 metres. On the eastern side of the ditch was the counterscarp with a revetment in the form of a smooth ashlar wall with a slight batter. To pass through the counterscarp and reach the ditch it was necessary to approach via one of two paths ending in narrow passageways 20 metres long and gates with draw-bars. The southern gate was wide enough for vehicular traffic, while the northern one was only passable on foot.

The outer bailey wall was nearly 16 metres high and had a batter at its base. Three projecting gate towers rose somewhat higher, provided firing positions facing east as well as north and south along the length of the defences. These tower gates gave access to the outer bailey and from there into the castle. Each tower had two outer gates on its sides (north and south) and a single inner gate giving indirect access into the outer bailey. The curtain wall included a firing gallery (*chemin de ronde*) about 10 metres above the level of the bailey and battlements at the top; there was probably a parapet walk which would provide an additional line of defence.

The outer bailey, together with the ditch, was excavated by the builders of the castle into the ancient tell.[86] From here one could approach the huge inner bailey wall, which was over 30 metres high and 12 metres thick. It had two enormous rectangular towers. Substantial remains survive only of the north tower, its eastern wall standing to 34 metres, nearly its full original height. The ground floor or basement level of this tower, which was connected with the south tower via a passage within the curtain wall, was barrel-vaulted. Above it rose a barrel-vaulted chamber on the first floor and above that a grand, rib-vaulted hall with two elegant Gothic bays rising from a circular central pier and 12 decorated corbels, three of which, carved with heads, survive on the inner face of the east wall.

The vaulted passage in the thickness of the curtain wall was entered at either end of the inner bailey wall behind the two towers. Because of the topography of the site, the entrances to this passage from the north and south baileys were at a considerably lower level than the central part of the passage.[87] The northern and southern sections of this passage consequently consist of broad staircases. From the outer bailey there was access to the shore beyond the outer side walls of the castle through two gates, on the north and the south. A third gate which gave access to an intermediate ward and to the inner ward was located to the north of the northern tower.

Chateau Pelerin is an exceptional castle, the only one of its type in the Latin East. Although it occupied a peninsula rather than a mountain spur, it shared with the spur castles the advantage of having natural defences on all but one side, making it possible for the defenders to concentrate their efforts in a single direction during a siege.

Hilltop (and island) castles

The final type of castle is one which occupies a hilltop (or alternatively an island) and in which the defensive works are built around the contours of the hill (or the shore of the island). The steep slope (or the sea) on all sides provided the castle with natural defences which, if steep (or deep) enough, could effectively prevent the approach of siege machines and even make approach on foot difficult and sometimes impossible. The only weak point in hilltop castles was the passage up to the gate, and this could be strengthened by the usual method with flanking towers, machicolation and other elements. A well-positioned hilltop castle constructed on an isolated hill with particularly steep slopes, such as the castle of Montreal (Shaubak) founded by Baldwin I in Oultrejourdan, could be even more easily defended than a spur castle. Of course, this is not to say that these castles were impregnable and could not be attacked from any position, but their success depended more on the difficulty of the approach than on the massiveness and complexity of their fortifications. If the hill was sufficiently steep, not only was it difficult for assailants to approach the walls but, no less important, it was almost impossible for siege machinery and sometimes even for missile-throwing machines to be used. The advantage of the hilltop castle over the spur castle lay in the fact that here there was not even one easy approach, unlike the shoulder of a spur which in spur castles had to be well defended with ditches, curtains and towers in order to prevent attack. On the shoulder of a spur it was always possible to set up mangonels and to bombard the castle from a distance. However, if the hill on which the castle was built was large enough, the distance at which mangonels and other stone-propelling machines had to be employed made them ineffective.

The castle builders chose hilltops that were large enough to provide sufficient space for all the required structures and a decent-sized courtyard. The hilltop castle dominated the entire top of a hill, its walls following the contours of the hill. Down to basics, it needed only curtain walls with a few projecting towers in order to turn the site into an almost impregnable stronghold. The Orders were responsible for the construction of a number of hilltop castles, some of them on a grand scale. A noteworthy example is Margat Castle (Marqab) located in the south of the Principality of Antioch (Figure 44). It stands on a triangular hill not far from the Mediterranean, 60 km north-west of Crac des Chevaliers. In the early twelfth century Margat, which was held by Roger of Antioch, came into the hands of the Manzoir family. The castle, which is in close proximity to the territory of the Assassins, became the centre of the Manzoirs' holdings from about 1140. Parts of the pre-Hospitaller fortifications, including stretches of curtain wall with square towers, can still be traced, notably on the western side of the fortress where they form the outer line of the concentric defences. Even before the massive additions of the Hospitaller Order, Margat must have been a formidable castle, for when Saladin approached after the Battle of Hattin in 1188 he bypassed Margat, recognising, according to Abu'l-Fida, that it was impregnable.[88] It had been purchased by the Hospitallers two years earlier in 1186, together with a fairly extensive tract of land, other castles and towns, including the nearby coastal town of Valenia (Banias), and lands further afield in the north of the Principality. Like Crac des Chevaliers,

Figure 44 Margat Castle from the south (photograph by Jonathan Phillips).

Margat served as a centre for attacks on the region of Hama. It was slightly damaged during Muslim raids in 1204/05 and underwent major rebuilding at various times throughout the thirteenth century. Margat came under attack between 1269 and 1271 at the time when Crac des Chevaliers fell to Baybars, though it held out and surrendered only 14 years later. In 1285 Qala'un besieged the castle and undermined the southern defences, causing the collapse of the outer southern tower, the Tour de l'Éperon (or Tour de l'Espérance). Margat was subsequently used by the Muslims.

The triangular fortification covers the entire top of a hill with a massive castle in the southern angle (Figure 45). The castle has parallel lines of defences on its eastern and western flanks which follow the natural escarpment and are protected by the steep slopes. The outer wall of the western flank dates from the twelfth century and has square towers. The towers on the east, like most of the towers on the fortifications as a whole, are semicircular. On the northern flank of the castle is a single line of vaults, cut off by a ditch from the rest of the fortified area (the faubourg). The castle has several barrel-vaulted halls around a central courtyard with a chapel of two groin-vaulted bays on the east. On the south, at a high position in the castle where the plateau joins a projection of the Djebel Anasarieh, is a huge round keep *c*. 20 metres in diameter with a rectangular inner chamber and walls up to 10 metres thick. Below the keep is the Tour l'Éperon which was destroyed in the siege of 1285 and rebuilt by Qala'un.

Despite a certain coarseness in the quality of the stonework due to the extensive use of local basalt (a hard stone, difficult to shape), the castle is remarkable in its size, strength and design, second only to Crac des Chevaliers. Lawrence described it as 'much more French even than Crac', and compared it to Carcassonne.[89]

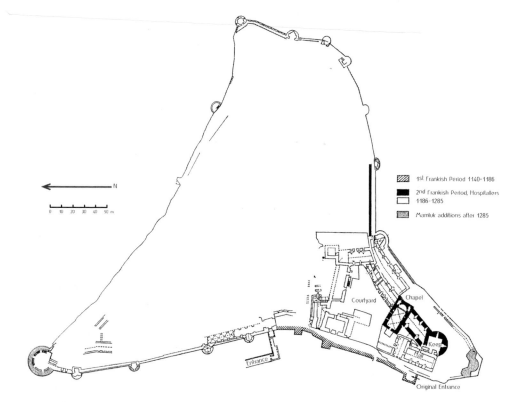

Figure 45 Plan of Margat Castle and faubourg (after Deschamps, 1973).

The huge Templar castle of Saphet is located in the mountains north of the Sea of Galilee, 12 km west of the Jordan River. A small fort was probably built here around 1102 by Hugh of St Omer, lord of Tiberias. It was refortified by King Fulk around 1138–40 as part of his general fortification work throughout the kingdom. In 1168, when the Hospitallers purchased Belvoir, Saphet was purchased by the Templars from King Amaury to serve as their headquarters in the eastern Galilee. In 1179 the faubourg was destroyed by the Ayyubids at the time of the destruction of the nearby Templar castle of Vadum Jacob (Jacob's Ford). However, the castle remained intact and the Templars occupied it until, a year and a half after the Battle of Hattin, it surrendered in December 1188 after a siege of two months. The castle was held by the Muslims until it was dismantled by al-Mu'azzam 'Isa in 1219, returning to Frankish hands only with the treaty of Richard of Cornwall in 1240. The Templars began to rebuild Saphet in December of that year as a much more grandiose project, employing Arab prisoners-of-war. Construction continued for two and a half years and is recorded in a detailed anonymous tract known as *De Constructione Castri Saphet*. Twenty-six years later, on 23 July 1266, the castle fell to Baybars after a siege lasting six weeks which ended when he deceived the Templars into surrendering, promising to allow them safe passage to Acre but subsequently massacring 917 of the defenders and two friars. Saphet was repaired by Baybars and used into Ottoman times as a local government headquarters until a major earthquake in 1837 left it in ruins. Since then even these ruins have largely disappeared.

A very large, now ruinous, oval hilltop castle, Saphet had a central ward and two concentric ranges of fortifications with two moats and covered a total area of *c.* 120 metres (e.–w.) by 280 metres (n.–s.). We know something of its dimensions from *De Constructione.* The fortifications of the inner ward, according to this source, were a remarkable 44 metres high, about 10 metres higher than the inner fortifications of Chateau Pelerin![90] The wall was 3.3 metres thick. The outer wall had at least seven round towers. The main gate appears to have been on the south-west. A subterranean tunnel south of the keep supplied water to the castle from a source beyond the walls.

Part of the Frankish construction in the south of the castle has been exposed in the past, including a small segment of a Frankish curtain wall uncovered in 1951.[91] Recent excavations (2004) have brought to light additional remains in this part of the castle (Figure 46).[92] These include segments of two concentric curtain walls and a passage cutting through them to the west. On one of the walls (W200) are the remains of four casemates and arrow-slits and on another (W109) there is an additional one. These arrow-slits have a parapet partly separating them from the casemates. A rib-vaulted chamber in the passage has corbels, on the base of one of which is a fleur-de-lis.

The much smaller castle of Vadum Jacob is located on a ford crossing the Jordan River 12 km north of the Sea of Galilee.[93] It was built by the Templars with the aid of King Baldwin IV and the Crusader army in 1178/79. Although the construction of the castle was never completed, excavations have been able to give us a good idea of how it was to have appeared. Its layout is remarkably similar to the twelfth-century stage of Crac des Chevaliers, although the topography of the two sites is very different. Both castles are more or less elongated rectangles, although Crac broadens out towards the north, and both castles have several angles in the northern wall. Crac des Chevaliers had barrel-vaulted galleries running around its circumference and Vadum Jacob, had it been completed, would also have had such galleries (they had been partly constructed at the time of its destruction). Vadum Jacob had only a single projecting tower on its south-west corner to defend its walls and could not have withstood serious opposition. However, it is possible that, if the Templars had had time to complete it, this castle would have had concentric defences like those built in the thirteenth century around the twelfth-century castle of Crac des Chevaliers. In such a case the lack of towers on the inner walls would have been of less importance.

Another large Templar hilltop castle, Gaston (Baghras), is located north of Antioch, just south of the eastern entrance to the Belen Pass (Syrian Gates) that cuts through the Amanus range (Figure 47). In 1211 Wilbrand of Oldenburg described the castle as very strong with three strong towered walls.[94] Imad ad-Din described the castle in his usual flamboyant style:

> We saw it towering on an impenetrable summit, rising on an impregnable rock, its foundations touching the sky . . .; penetrating the ravines, it climbed the mountains, it flaunted its walls in the clouds, shrouded in fog, inseparable from the clouds, suspended from the sun and the moon; . . . no-one could have aspired to climb up there; whoever coveted it had no means of getting there; whoever raised his eyes to it could not fix his gaze.[95]

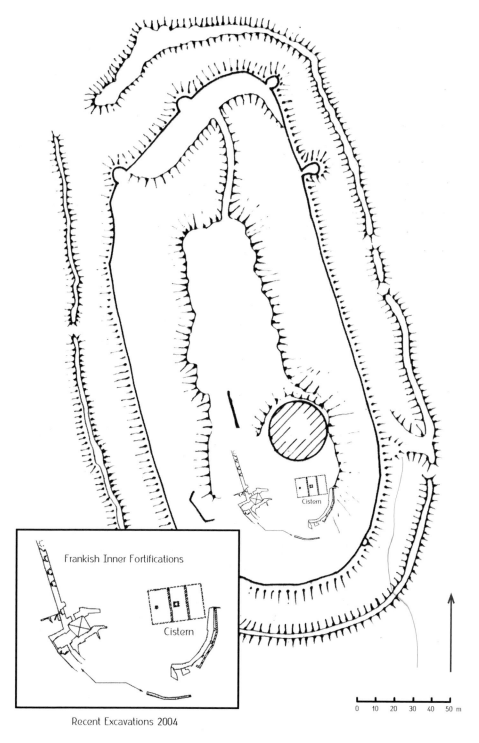

Frankish Inner Fortifications

Cistern

Cistern

Recent Excavations 2004

0 10 20 30 40 50 m

Figure 46 Plan of Safed Castle (after Conder and Kitchener, 1883; Pringle, 1998b and Barbé and Damatti, 2004).

Figure 47 Gaston Castle (Baghras) seen from the east (photograph by the author).

The castle was probably acquired by the Templars in 1153 and was held by them until 1188, when Saladin occupied it. In 1191, fearing the approach of Frederick Barbarossa's army during the Third Crusade, Saladin had the castle partly dismantled and abandoned. Gaston was later restored by the Armenian King Levon II and returned to the Templars in 1211 or shortly after. They held it until 1268, when it was taken by Baybars. It subsequently served as a local governor's residence into the Ottoman period.

Gaston was built on two levels covering the top of a steep rock (Figure 48). Most of the Templar work probably predates the occupation of the castle by Saladin. In the main the construction is rather poor, with wall facings of small, roughly shaped fieldstones. The plan consists of an outer, lower enceinte consisting of curtain walls and two round or semicircular towers. It defends the entire eastern and southern sides of the castle; on the other sides the steep slope of the rock prevented approach. Within this is an inner, upper ward containing several vaulted structures on two levels. On the east side of the lower level was a chamber with three doors, possibly a stable. The upper level of the upper ward has two large vaulted halls on either side of a courtyard, one of which was certainly a chapel and the other probably a refectory. An elongated hall aligned roughly north–south to the west of the south hall (chapel?) may have served as the dormitory; it has ventilation in the vaulting but little light enters it. The kitchen was probably located in the vault to the west of the north hall (refectory?). All of this is standard monastic layout. The main gate and entrance ramp are on the east.[96] An aqueduct (which today has almost entirely vanished but is visible in the aerial photograph published by Deschamps) approached the castle from the south-west, supplying water from an external source.[97]

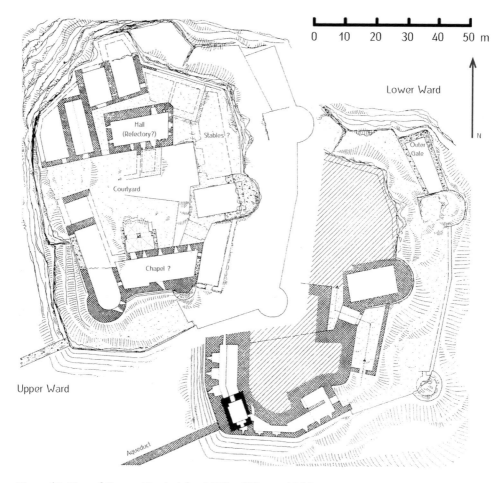

Figure 48 Plan of Gaston Castle (after Müller-Wiener, 1966).

The large Hospitaller castle of Silifke is located on the Mediterranean coast at the western extremity of Cilicia, at the delta of the Göksu (Calycadnus) River overlooking the ancient town of Seleucia (modern Silifke). It is another fine example of a Crusader hilltop castle (Figure 49). Silifke occupies a hill with fairly steep flanks rising to 86 metres above sea level, and its strategic importance lies in its command of the important coastal road. It was granted to the Hospitallers in 1210, a gift from Levon I, who himself had occupied the Byzantine fort here at least two decades earlier. Levon hoped to use the Hospitallers as a buffer against the encroachment of the Seljuks. Silifke was the principal castle in the Hospitaller march that he created, which included two other castles, Camardesium and Castellum Novum (Nobert). In return the Hospitallers were required to pay an annual tax and the service of a cavalry company of 400 lancers.

The Hospitallers completely rebuilt this castle, replacing the original Byzantine fort, of which there is little evidence today.[98] In the fourth decade of the thirteenth century additional expansion was carried out by Hetoum I, as is recorded in an inscription

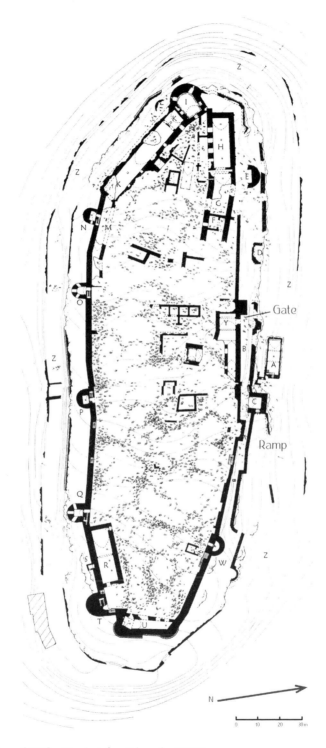

Figure 49 Plan of Silifke Castle (after Edwards, 1987).

dated to 1236 which was found in the castle.[99] The new castle is a large oval structure, its perimeter walls and towers skirting an area some 260 metres in length and *c.* 100 metres in width.[100] The perimeter wall has a number of prominent horseshoe-shaped towers placed at regular intervals of about 50 metres, a standard distance between towers in medieval fortifications.[101] Below it runs a broad ditch, up to 20 metres wide in places, lined with revetted walls and in parts by a talus which appears to be a later enhancement to these defences.

One of the important defensive features of this castle is the gate complex on the north[102] which includes an oblique approach wall crossing the moat towards a gate-house. To enter the gatehouse one had to pass along the wall and turn 90 degrees to the left into a corridor running along the north (outer) side of the main northern wall (this passage is marked B on the plan published by Edwards). No inner gate leading from this outer gate passage has been found.

Other than this gate complex, a large three-storey horseshoe-shaped tower (I on Edwards's plan) located at the west end is one of the most remarkable defensive elements of the castle, dominating the defences. It is much larger than the other towers and probably served as the donjon.[103] A narrow talus skirts the base of this tower. Because of the topography, the entrance to the tower from within the castle leads into its first-floor level. As is always the case with a donjon, the lower level is a cistern. The interior of the first floor has a niche on the north-west, with jambs that may have framed shutters. There are two other niches, one on the south-east wall without jambs and a smaller one in the east corner which has an opening in its sill into the cistern below. A shelf or bench formed by a protrusion of the first course of stone by about 29 cm extends around the entire interior of the chamber. On the south-east is a narrow elbow-shaped chamber in the thickness of the wall; this would probably have been a latrine.[104] The other chief feature of this tower is a pair of huge arrow-slits with casemates, one facing south and the other slightly north-west. Though the upper level of the tower is poorly preserved, there are remnants of the battlements on the west. A square drain opening on the east carried rainwater that collected on the roof via a pipe in the thickness of the wall to the cistern below.

Among other horseshoe-shaped towers in the castle are two (Edwards's towers O and Q) which, unlike the donjon, have broad rectangular windows rather than arrow-slits. However, like the donjon the position of these openings is somewhat unusual. In both towers there are three windows, the central one facing directly forward (south in the case of these towers) and the others at oblique angles like those of the donjon. Consequently, none of these three towers offered the possibility of effective defence of the adjacent curtain walls with flanking fire. Moreover, the large windows in two of them would have provided no protection to archers. Edwards suggests that they were probably intended to accommodate torsion catapults.[105] The limited effectiveness of the towers in defending the walls may have been counteracted by the presence of wooden hoarding or of machicolation as at Crac des Chevaliers, but no evidence survives for this. The whole arrangement is rather strange, especially when we consider that at this time the Hospitallers had rebuilt Crac des Chevaliers in a much more intelligent manner, employing well-positioned arrow-slits and extensive use of machicolation.

Other features at Silifke include a completely solid tower (Edwards's tower T) containing nothing but an internal staircase, a tower with a postern (tower N) and a small apsidal building located just west of the gate complex (D) which may have been a chapel, although its location is outside the main inner ward. Barrel-vaulted chambers, undercrofts and cisterns skirt the circumference of the bailey and at the centre are several structures including what looks as if it may have been a two-storey rectangular keep built over a cistern (X on Edwards's plan).

The dating of this castle remains something of a puzzle. A Byzantine fort was constructed on the hill at some time between the seventh and eleventh centuries. Prior to 1190 the castle was in the hands of the Armenians; in 1210 it was handed over to the Hospitallers, who abandoned it in 1226. After 1226 the castle was again held by the Armenians and may have been enlarged in 1236.[106] Although it had a Frankish castellan in 1248, there is no evidence of a return of the castle to the Hospitallers after 1226. It is difficult to know how much of this large castle should be assigned to the 16 years of Hospitaller ownership, but its scale and the ingenious entrance complex suggest that at least a fair part of it was built by them.

On a much smaller scale is the Templar castle of La Fève, of which little remains today. It may have been a hilltop castle, although it has been suggested that it may have been a *quadriburgium*.[107] The remains of this castle have entirely vanished today under the trees and houses of Kibbutz Merhavia. However, aerial photographs taken prior to the establishment of the kibbutz show a large courtyard complex with long barrel-vaulted galleries.[108]

The castle of Harunia, located in the foothills of the Amanus Mountains in the north-east of Cilicia, was occupied by the Teutonic Knights in 1236 and apparently rebuilt by them (Figure 50).[109] It occupies the summit of a hill commanding a broad expanse of the Cilician Plain to the south-west and across the foothills of the Amanus

Figure 50 Harunia Castle from the south (photograph by the author).

Mountains to the east. Harunia is an unusual castle with a simple design of an almond shape, its walls following the contours of the hill, narrowing at either end towards the gates (Figure 51). Edwards's description of it as 'an elongated keep' is certainly a misuse of that term.[110]

A single large horseshoe-shaped tower guards the gate on the north-east and there is a second gate on the south-west. The tower has an apsidal interior facing east and probably contained the castle chapel. The wall running along the north and west sides of the castle between the two gates is nearly 5 metres thick and has a series of casemates with arrow embrasures. A pointed barrel-vaulted gallery runs the length of this wall.

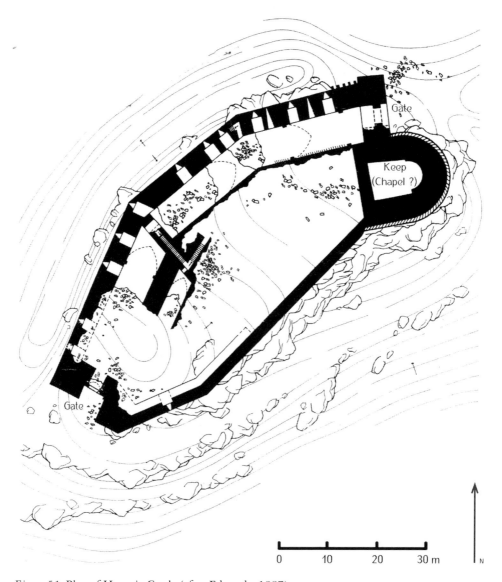

Figure 51 Plan of Harunia Castle (after Edwards, 1987).

The presence of two large gates, one either side of the castle, has no parallels. The lack of projecting towers except for the round tower on the left side of the north-east gate is also unusual. However, the elongated design with a great apsidal tower guarding the most approachable end and a second gate at the other end is somewhat comparable with the main castle of the Teutonic Order, the castle of Montfort, which was built a decade before Harunia came into their hands.[111] It also has similarities with Judin (Figure 52).

Another castle in Cilicia which makes admirable use of its natural setting is the Templar castle of La Roche de Roissol (Chivlan), which was built to control the secondary Hajar Shuglan Pass through the Amanus Mountains (Figure 53). Had Imad ad-Din visited here he certainly would have had much to say about its dramatic setting. Chivlan stands 1,200 metres above sea level above steep cliffs overlooking the pass and is almost impregnable.[112] It occupied the whole of a sloping plateau, and the somewhat scanty surviving remains of the castle consist of fragments of circuit walls around the periphery of the plateau, some ruined vaults and a chapel in the upper bailey on the east. In the same region, but further south on the eastern edge of the mountain range, is the small hilltop castle of Trapesac. It was built by the Templars on a small mound

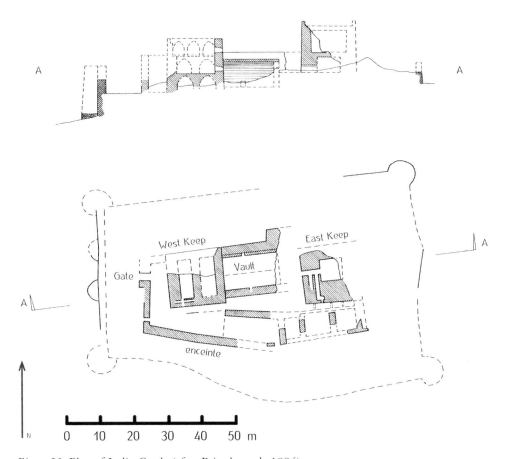

Figure 52 Plan of Judin Castle (after Pringle *et al.*, 1994).

Figure 53 La Roche de Roissol (photograph by the author).

slightly north-east of the Belen Pass through the Amanus Mountains. The hill has a good command of the plain to the east and south and the north-eastern approaches to the pass and contributes to the defence of the pass's eastern entrance.

Others

The exceptional small castle known as the Cave de Tyron, about 20 km east of Tyre, was occupied on and off by the Franks between *c.* 1134 and 1265.[113] It was held by the Teutonic Order from 1257 until it fell in 1260. The castle, like al-Habis Jaldak in the Yarmuk Valley, was built on a cliff site, half way up the cliff. It was accessed by a narrow path up the cliff face and consisted of chambers cut into the cliff, some serving for accommodation, others for storage or as cisterns. It overlooks the principal route from the Beqa Valley to the coast and probably served principally as a lookout post.

10

NON-DEFENSIVE COMPONENTS
OF A CASTLE

In basic terms, a castle need consist only of four thick walls with a door, some arrow-slits and a battlement. Indeed, some castles were little more than this. A water supply was vital, however, and there had to be space for the basic domestic requirements of the garrison and storage of essential supplies. However, castles of the Military Orders had to include additional elements that would allow their occupants to carry out a daily routine based on their monastic rule. Furthermore, the larger the castle and garrison and the more significant its strategic role, the greater the need for additional space for living quarters, protected training grounds, etc. It is not always easy to identify the use of a structure within a castle, although its location sometimes hints at the function, particularly so in castles which have a monastery-like layout. For example, a large hall located adjacent to a kitchen is most likely to have been the refectory and the presence of a latrine near a large room makes it probable that the latter served as the dormitory.

Chapels

Chapels were essential components of the castles of the Military Orders, playing a dominant role in the monastic life of both the brother knights and the associated clergy. Not surprisingly, the Rules of the Temple and of the Hospital go into consider-able detail on the subject of prayer, liturgical requirements and the conduct of the brothers. According to statute no. 146 of the Rule of the Temple:

> When the bell sounds or the call is given to say the hours or for the brothers to assemble, all the brothers should go to chapel, if they are not ill, do not have their hands in pastry, or the fire is not burning in the furnace to forge hot iron, or they are not preparing the horses' feet for shoeing (or they are not washing their hair); and for these aforementioned things the brothers may absent them-selves from nones and vespers. And when they have done what is listed above, they should go to the chapel to say the hours or to hear them, or go where the other brothers have gone. But they may not be absent from the other hours without permission unless they are ill.[1]

A castle chapel could be quite small and simple or large and elaborate, its size and the quality of its decoration depending on who built it, how much effort and money they were prepared to invest in it, how large was the garrison that used it and how important was the castle as an expression of the Order's wealth and might. Of the larger chapels were those at Chastel Blanc, which measured 23.6 metres long (internally) and 10.5 metres wide (13.5 metres high), and that of Margat, which was 23 metres long and 10 metres wide. Even when we lack the form and dimensions we can sometimes get an idea of the importance of a chapel from the quality of surviving architectural remains. If, as is quite likely, the very fine capitals found at Toron des Chevaliers came from the castle chapel, it was a splendidly decorated structure. The polygonal chapel at Chateau Pelerin was a remarkable and unusual structure, as can be seen from the reconstructions of Johns and Pringle (Figure 55).[2]

Single-aisle chapels

Three very similar chapels were located in the Templar castle of Chastel Blanc and the two Hospitaller castles of Crac des Chevaliers and Margat. The ground-floor chapel of the *église-donjon* at Chastel Blanc was dedicated to St Michael the Archangel. It was one of the largest castle chapels in the East. The roof is a high barrel vault supported on two transverse arches, a third arch dividing the eastern bay from the apse. The inscribed apse in the east has a large lancet window and is flanked on either side by square sacristies built in the thickness of the 4-metre-thick chevet, also illuminated by lancet windows. There are four additional lancet windows in the chapel, two in the north wall and two in the south. A staircase in the south-west corner leads up through the thickness of the wall to the upper storey, where there is a large groin-vaulted hall (dormitory).[3]

In the twelfth century the Hospitallers built a barrel-vaulted chapel against the north-eastern interior wall of the castle of Crac des Chevaliers. Deschamps identified three phases of building in the chapel. The first stage was constructed between 1142, when the Hospitallers received the castle, and June 1170, when much of it was destroyed by a major earthquake. The second stage consists of the repairs and additions carried out soon after the earthquake. The third stage took place in the first half of the thirteenth century, during the general expansion of the castle. As it survives, the chapel largely reflects the construction after 1170 when the massive barrel-vaulted structure was built. It measures 21.5 by 8.5 metres and is constructed from marginally drafted flat ashlars. It has no decoration other than frescoes (the lack of architectural sculpture is exceptional).[4] The interior is lit chiefly by deeply splayed lancet windows on the east, in the apse and on the west above the door, although additional light came from windows, some of which were later blocked, on the north and south sides, at the base of the vault. It was divided by two transverse arches into three bays, with a deep apse and thick *chevet* constructed into what was then the outer wall of the castle.

In Margat Castle the Hospitallers built a similar chapel near the great keep in the south. The chapel is more elaborate than the earlier chapel at Crac des Chevaliers. The construction is of flat squared basalt that contrasts impressively with the white limestone used to frame the doors and windows. The hood-arched west portal is flanked by two pairs of crocket capitals which originally surmounted four columns that have not survived. Above the portal is a large lancet window. On the north side of the chapel is a second door, almost identical in form to the west portal and with the four columns intact. A lancet window to the west of this door and a second small window below at ground level are also framed by limestone ashlars; the smaller window is within a limestone structural arch. The single-aisle chapel is constructed of two groin-vaulted bays together and, as noted, is only slightly smaller than the chapel at Chastel Blanc. The bays are divided by a transverse arch supported on columns on either side with groups of three engaged capitals. In the east, the chevet is set on line with the outer wall of the inner ward. In the inscribed apse is a large lancet window and on either side is a small quadrangular room with lancet windows/arrow-slits entered through small doors in the apse.

Very little survives of the chapel of Belvoir Castle, which was located in the upper storey of the inner castle above the gatehouse. When he occupied the castle in January 1189, Saladin destroyed the chapel and, as can be seen today, made a very thorough job of it. Other than a few fragments of sculpture, all that remains is a small section of well-cut limestone ashlars, five courses of the south-east corner of the structure, located above the west wing of the inner ward. The chapel possibly had a belfry, an unusual feature in castle chapels.[5]

The Templars built a large chapel at Gaston (Baghras) probably opposite the hall, on the south side of the courtyard of the upper level. Although the east end of the structure has collapsed and there is no surviving evidence for an apse, its identity as a chapel is fairly certain. Like the great hall opposite, it is aligned east–west. It measures 9 by 20 metres but would originally have been longer.

At the highest position in the castle of Saphet, the Templars constructed a tower that was later rebuilt or expanded by Baybars and his successors into a massive round keep, remains of which can still be seen today. The Templar keep was possibly an *église-donjon*. Late sources refer to a large octagonal room with a dome which occupied the interior of this tower, and one eighteenth-century source records niches in the walls in which statues could have been placed and some small side chambers.[6]

As noted, to judge from the quality of architectural sculpture found on the site, Toron des Chevaliers must have possessed a remarkably fine chapel. While the capitals[7] could have come from a ceremonial hall or some other building, the chapel would have been the most likely origin for them.[8] If so, it is clear that this was a fine structure. Bellamy, in his unpublished plans which were amended and published by Pringle, located the chapel on the first-floor level of the vaulted structure on the north side of the central ward. He gives no explanation for the choice of this position, and it might seem an odd choice as this structure was not oriented east–west. However, as the chapel would probably have taken up only part of the upper level (which covers over 20 by 20 metres), and as the north is often (although not always) the location of a chapel in a cloistral setting, this is a reasonable identification. Francesco Quaresmi stated that in 1626 a large ruined church was to be seen at the centre of the castle, and other writers of the seventeenth and eighteenth centuries also refer to the church.[9] In the nineteenth century the church was described as 'three-quarters destroyed'.[10]

At the Teutonic castle of Amuda in Cilicia a small vault located to the north-east of the *donjon* possibly served as the castle chapel; there is no apparent reason to support Edwards's dismissal of this identification simply because the east end is three-sided rather than rounded.[11]

Chapels in towers

Fortified towers containing chapels are found in several castles of the Military Orders. The chapel in the Sea Castle at Sidon, located in the upper storey of the south-eastern tower of the inner ward, was on a modest scale (Figure 54).[12] It consisted of two rib-vaulted bays measuring in its entirety 16.25 by 8.25 metres (internally).[13] It was entered via an external staircase in the south-west and there may have been a second door on the north wall of the west bay giving access to the residence of the knights. Kalayan shows a curving staircase leading up from this level and a door in the north wall of the eastern bay, giving onto a sacristy/portcullis chamber. In the middle of the west wall is a window (partly surviving) and there is a three-sided apse to the east.[14]

The best-preserved example of an *église-donjon* is at Chastel Blanc, where the ground-floor level consists of a large single-aisled chapel. The chapel is roofed with a barrel vault strengthened by three transverse arches. Two small rooms are located in the thickness of the wall either side of the apse (perhaps serving as sacristies) and the hall is lit by five lancet windows (two on each of the side walls and one in the chevet).

At the Teutonic castle of Harunia in Armenian Cilicia, the chapel was probably located in the tower adjacent to the gate to the east. In their principal castle in the Kingdom of Jerusalem, Montfort, the excavators believed that the chapel was located in the upper storey of the vaulted range, on its south side (based on finds of stained

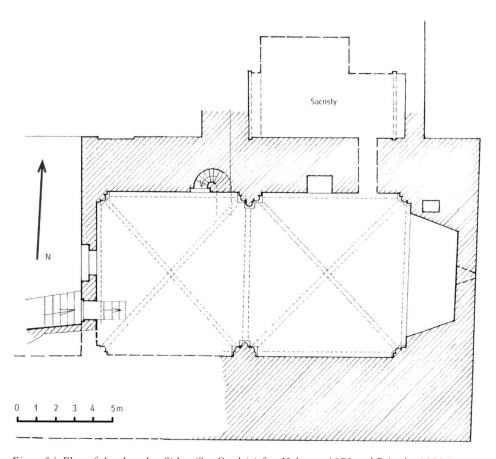

Figure 54 Plan of the chapel at Sidon (Sea Castle) (after Kalayan, 1973 and Pringle, 1998a).

glass). However, elsewhere I have suggested that here as well the Teutonic Knights may have built their chapel in the apsidal keep.[15]

There was another *église-donjon* at Saranda Kolones in the apsidal gate tower in the middle of the east wall of the inner ward. The chapel occupied the upper storey of the tower. From fallen voussoirs it is evident that the chapel was rib-vaulted, and a rather simple foliate limestone capital found in the excavations gives an idea of its decoration. It is possible that a similar use was made by the Hospitallers of one of the apsidal towers on either side of the main gate at Arsuf Castle. These towers were aligned roughly east–west. As the tower to the south of the gate contained various installations, it is likely that if one of these towers served as the chapel it would be that to the north.[16]

Tri-apsidal church

The only example of a tri-apsidal castle church attached to a Military Order castle is that of the church at Bethgibelin, which was constructed on the southern side of the castle. It was surveyed by the BSAJ in 1981 and excavated by the IAA in 1982 and more extensively in the 1990s.[17] Only the north aisle has survived. Pringle estimates the original internal measurements of the entire church as *c.* 30 by 16.5 metres.[18] A barrel-vaulted sacristy was built within the church's north wall, which is shared with the castle. The nave would have been 6.5 metres wide and the aisles 5 metres. Judging from the surviving remains, both aisles and nave were roofed with five groin-vaulted bays (a total of 15 bays) supported by eight free-standing square columns (1.66 metres square), each with four engaged marble *spolia* columns, and twelve pilasters, each with a single column. The columns had reused marble fifth- or sixth-century Corinthian capitals supporting dentillated Romanesque *abaci* and the well-cut transverse arches that separated the bays. Pringle notes that the main door to the church appears to have been on the south. This church is large, whereas in much more important and larger castles such as Belvoir, Margat and Crac des Chevaliers the chapels are much smaller.[19] In the light of this, it seems more appropriate to regard this church as the parish church of the Frankish village which happened to be built up against the castle, rather than as a castle chapel intended only for the use of the garrison.[20]

Polygonal chapels

Perhaps the most remarkable of castle chapels was the Templars' chapel at Chateau Pelerin (Figure 55). This was the second of the two chapels at ʿAtlit, the other being located outside the castle walls in the faubourg to the south-east.[21] The castle chapel is located in the south wing of the inner ward at a point where the vaults of the inner and outer wards converge. It is a 12-sided structure, 26 metres across (internally), and it was reconstructed by Johns as having had a central round pier which, together with 12 pilasters formed by triple colonettes, supported the rib-vaulted roof. Half of the chapel had small chambers attached to it, a central seven-sided sanctuary in the east flanked by two barrel-vaulted chambers (sacristies?) to which were attached five-sided chapels. An additional small antechamber attached to the southernmost chapel served as the southern door of the church. The main door, 3 metres wide and flanked by two double

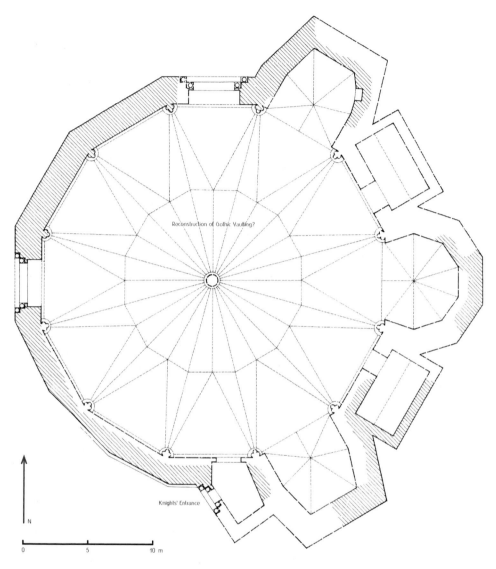

Figure 55 Plan of the chapel at Chateau Pelerin (after Johns, 1947; Pringle, 1993).

pilasters, was in the west and there was another large door in the north. Both the northern and southern doors were also decorated with double pilasters. It was probably in this chapel that the Templars kept their important relics (the heart and body of the virgin martyr St Euphemia of Chalcedon). These attracted many pilgrims travelling along the road south from Acre.[22] At Bethgibelin there is a tri-apsidal church attached to the south-east corner of the castle. Only the northern aisle survives; it is exceptional to find a three-aisled church in a castle.

Chapter houses

Another basic element in monastic establishments, the chapter house, is not always easy to identify. The presence of tiered seats around three sides of the room would be a means of identification, but generally we have to rely on location rather than the presence of any identifying architectural feature to suggest its function. In medieval monasteries the chapter house, where daily chapters were held, was usually located beside the church. At Tortosa the chapter house may have been located in the north of the castle. Johns has suggested that the chapter house of Chateau Pelerin was located in one of the two great towers on the east face of the inner ward.[23] At Crac des Chevaliers the great hall in the upper ward served as the chapter house. At Margat the chapter house appears to have stood at the north-west corner of the castle. Only its vaulted substructure has survived.[24]

Halls

Kennedy referred to the vaulted hall at Beaufort as 'so characteristic of the architecture of the Military Orders'.[25] In fact, virtually every castle, great or small, had a hall, and some of these would have been quite remarkable structures. The hall was used primarily for important assemblies, chapters and court hearings rather than for everyday use. In some castles the hall may have had a dual function, serving also as a refectory. This may have been the case with the northern hall at Gaston. The great Gothic vaulted hall in the north tower at Chateau Pelerin would have been a remarkable building, its rib-vaulted bays supported on consoles carved with heads and no doubt with high lancet windows decorated with stained glass or opening onto the vast expanse of land to the north and south. The hall at Montfort was possibly octagonal in form, also built in the Gothic style, its rib-vaulting supported on a central pier as in the castle chapel at Chateau Pelerin and in the later Teutonic castles of Prussia. At Crac des Chevaliers the hall added to the west side of the inner courtyard had three rib-vaulted bays and a beautiful rib-vaulted porch rather like one arm of a cloister. It is built in the finest mid-thirteenth-century French Gothic style, similar to that of the Île-de-France and Champagne. Its outer wall has two doors and five pairs of double windows divided by slender columns and supporting finely carved tracery.

At Margat the castle hall was probably the rather elegant vault at the southern apex of the castle, just north of the Tour de l'Éperon and adjacent to the castle keep, on its west. At Beaufort the Templars apparently added the Gothic groin-vaulted hall to the castle.[26] It had two groin-vaulted bays and an elaborate gate on its west face. At Sidon (Sea Castle) a large Gothic-style elongated hall traversed the entire castle from east to west.[27] It was *c.* 60 metres long (internally) and *c.* 15 metres wide, somewhat irregular in form, with a row of seven free-standing columns supporting 16 rib-vaulted bays divided by transverse arches. The large size of the hall suggests that it may have served as a dormitory. According to the excavator, the hall at Belvoir was located adjoining the chapel at first-floor level on the northern side of the inner ward.[28] He noted that it had columns with basalt capitals. One of these is still to be seen outside the castle to the west.

Dormitories

For very practical reasons communal sleeping was the rule in monastic houses; it made it easier to call the brothers to prayer at regular intervals. In castles with a large garrison communal sleeping was essential, and this was particularly true of the castles of the Military Orders, where a monastic regime was followed. A number of halls identified as dormitories survive in the castles of the Orders. At Chastel Blanc the upper storey of the tower above the chapel has sometimes been identified as the dormitory of the garrison. It was a large hall (about 24 metres long) with three large cruciform piers supporting eight groin-vaulted bays divided by transverse arches. It was reached by a staircase built in the thickness of the wall; an internal staircase gave access to the roof. However, Pringle points out that as there were no latrines in the tower this may be considered a doubtful identification.[29] At Chateau Pelerin the dormitory may have occupied the largest of the vaulted halls located on the south side of the central range, south-west of the church and to the east of what may have been the castle refectory (and kitchens). This three-aisled hall, which measured approximately 27 by 53 metres, was appropriately located in relation to the other buildings to be convenient for the brothers' activities, amongst these being attendance at night services. A staircase in the east wall led to a point near the church doors on the west and south.[30]

Although archaeology has not shed any light on the arrangements for sleeping within the dormitories, the Rules can fill in some of the missing details. According to the Rule of the Templars, each brother received bed linen (two sheets), a mattress (a bag filled with straw), a bolster and a blanket, or at the least a rug and soft linen blanket.[31] The dormitory was to be lit throughout the night and the brothers were required to sleep dressed in a shirt, breeches, a belt and shoes.[32] A brother who slept naked in the dormitory was liable to punishment.[33]

Water systems

A substantial water supply was essential for every castle to supply the daily needs of the garrison and, more importantly, to enable it to withstand siege. It was crucial that the occupants of a castle have enough water to enable them to survive a siege. The Crusaders may have learned this lesson during the First Crusade in the ill-fated siege of the castle of Xerigordon, not far from Nicaea. In that case the water supply of the castle was located outside the walls and the defenders were forced to drink urine and the blood of their horses, surrendering after only eight days. The importance of water in the planning of a castle can be seen in the inclusion of a paragraph on this topic in the well-known thirteenth-century tract *De Constructione Castri Saphet*.[34] In this text the author records that when the castle was constructed, an attempt was made to locate a source of fresh water within its area. Water had previously been brought from a distance by pack animals, which was both expensive and labour-intensive. A local Arab showed Benoît d'Alignan, bishop of Marseilles, who was the instigator of the castle's construction, the location of a well which had probably served the previous castle on this site.[35] This water system, which apparently consisted of a well or several wells and conduits which supplied the large garrison with sufficient water for their needs, is referred to in Arab sources as one of the wonders of the world.[36]

When possible the castle-builders took advantage of existing cisterns. At Belmont

Castle the central ward was built over a series of cisterns which apparently date from the Byzantine period (fourth to seventh centuries). They were fed by a system of rock-cut and stone-lined drains, some of which were also part of the earlier system. Castle architects planned the construction of new cisterns in locations that enabled the collection of the maximum amount of rainwater. At Silifke there is a good example of this. The principal cistern here is located at the lowest point of the dry moat in the north so that it could catch all the rainwater that collected in the moat during winter storms. The water collected in a conduit, entering the cistern at its western end.

In the Crusader period the *antilliyah* well employing a large wheel to draw water from a well, was a common device. The *antilliyah*, which is recorded elsewhere in the Crusader period (in the Hospitaller compound in Jerusalem at Bir Ayyub to the south of the city), was a machine consisting of a vertical wheel rotated by a horizontal wheel turned by draught animals. On the vertical wheel was a rope with jars tied to it; these were lowered empty into the well and raised full of water. There is evidence for the use of these devices in two castles. Theoderich records that at La Fève the Templars constructed a large cistern with a 'rotalem machinam ad deducendam aquam'.[37] In another Templar castle, Vadum Jacob, numerous fragments of *antiliyyah* jars were found in the ruins of the vault in the south-east of the castle. These jars have distinctive long necks and long oval bodies, rounded bases and no handles – the typical form of *antilliyah* jars.

A well in the western vault of the inner ward at Crac des Chevaliers was 27 metres deep. Several cisterns were also recorded in this castle in addition to the great reservoir and the aqueduct. Aqueducts were used to supply several castles with water from a more distant source. The aqueduct represented an obvious disadvantage, as it was outside the castle and therefore could easily be cut off by a besieger. None the less, it was useful as a supplementary source, and water from an external source was supplied via aqueduct not only to Crac des Chevaliers, where the aqueduct fed the great reservoir, but also to several other castles including Gaston, Trapesac, Belvoir and Bethgibelin. A large open reservoir (*berquilla*) at Crac des Chevaliers served the double purpose of supplying water to the garrison and forming a barrier against an enemy who, having scaled the outer fortress, wished to attack the southern wall of the inner castle. At Belvoir a deep section of the moat in the south-west may have been used to collect rainwater. At Castellum Beleismum (Khirbat Bal'ama) beside the Janin–Nablus road, a staircase and passages linked the ancient spring (Bir as-Sinjib) to the chapel of St Job and the castle above.[38]

Latrines and waste disposal

As a rule, in monasteries the latrine was located at one end of the dormitory and near the kitchen for the practical reason that both latrines and kitchens frequently used the same stream or channel for water supply and waste disposal (the kitchen preferably being upstream). A stone-lined drain running from the inner ward of Belmont to the south-west probably carried waste from the kitchens or latrines. At Crac des Chevaliers latrines were located in niches in the great western vaulted hall of the inner ward and these were probably replaced by latrines in tower P (which was built as a latrine tower with latrines at two levels) when, with the construction of the talus along the inner wall, the old latrines probably went out of use.[39]

At Toprak in Cilicia, latrines were rather precariously positioned on the exterior of the curtain walls in the angle between the curtain wall and towers. At the

Ayyubid/Mamluk castle of Qal'at Nimrod (Subeibe), two latrines were located in Tower 11.[40] Latrines have also been identified in some of the castles of the Military Orders. A possible latrine was located in the *donjon* of the Hospitaller castle of Silifke in a small chamber on the south-east side of the first floor.[41] At the Teutonic castle of Judin (Qal'at Jiddin), latrines were located in the two keeps. According to the surveyors, they were located in the thickness of the southern wall on the ground and first-floor levels of the eastern keep and on the second floor of the western keep.[42] One of the latrines in the eastern keep was described thus:

> Two doorways originally opened on the south side of the entrance passage. Both seem originally to have been closed by timber doors, but virtually all trace of the jambs and lintels has now disappeared. The door nearest the basement led into a long-lintelled passage, 70 cm. wide and dog-legged towards the end, where it opened out into an irregular space lit by a slit window (10 cm. wide) in the tower's south wall. Although choked by rubble, this may be identified as a latrine, which would formerly have emptied down a chute inside the wall into the wadi below.[43]

At Montfort there appears to have been a latrine on the southern side of the large western hall where a chute carried the waste down the slope (Figure 56).[44]

Figure 56 Latrine chute at Montfort; the excavated area to the left is believed to be from Muslim sapping (photograph by Rabei Khamissy).

Bathhouses

Though not every castle had a bathhouse, examples can be seen in some of the larger castles. In some cases the bathhouses had an economical system for saving fuel, sharing a heat source with other installations such as bakeries or forges. Archaeologists have identified a small bathhouse beside the forge on the east side of the outer range at Belvoir.[45] It received its water supply from a large cistern to its south which was fed with water from the spring to the south of the castle via an aqueduct. It was heated by the small brick-built furnace just behind the eastern wall adjacent to the forge, which was possibly shared with the blacksmith. At Saranda Kolones, in the north wing of the inner ward, a small circular chamber on a mezzanine floor above the bakery was tentatively identified by the excavators as a bathhouse which would have been heated by the bakery oven.[46] This may also have been the case in the bathhouse and adjacent bakery located in the faubourg of Chateau Pelerin.[47]

Refectories

Another central element in the monastery, the refectory, demonstrates the presence of a community living according to a monastic order. The requirement of communal eating was clearly set out in the Rules. According to statute 8 of the Rule of the Hospital (Statutes of Margat, 1203–06):

> The table of the Convent should be held in common in this manner: all the brethren, both Bailiffs and others, should come to the table of the Convent. No brother in good health, whether Bailiff or otherwise, should eat in his chamber, without permission to do so.[48]

And in the Rule of the Temple:

> In the palace, or what should rather be called the refectory, they should eat together.[49]

Although they ate together, the brothers were not all seated at the same table. Sergeants and crossbowmen were required to sit at different tables from brother knights, but doctors of medicine and surgeons, as well as certain other important persons, could sit with the brothers.[50]

The refectory referred to as 'palace' in the Rule of the Temple[51] was generally a large and spacious hall. The location of refectories in castles (as in some of the urban quarters) was similar to that of regular convents; that is, on the cloister opposite the chapel, adjacent to the dormitory and next to the kitchens. At Chateau Pelerin a rib-vaulted hall on the south-west of the castle seems to have been the castle refectory. It is an appropriately large hall, and the kitchen appears to have been located at its northern end.[52] At Belvoir Castle the refectory was probably located in a long, barrel-vaulted ground-floor hall on the south side of the inner courtyard beside the kitchen. At Bethgibelin, in the eastern side of the south wing of the castle, there is a hall which has been identified by the excavators as the refectory.[53] It was a large hall of eight groin-vaulted bays supported on three square columns, with entrances in the west and north and a staircase in the south wall giving access to the church. The identification of this hall as the refectory is partly based on the discovery of some large stone columns which had been cut laterally and mounted on stone supports to be used as tables. This rather odd and clumsy arrangement suggests that there was a difficulty obtaining wood.[54] On one of these tables a Nine-Men's Morris board has been incised in the stone.[55]

Kitchens

As in medieval monasteries, castle kitchens were generally located in the heart of a castle near the refectory and dormitory. At Gaston the kitchen was possibly located in a vault to the west of the northern hall that probably served as the refectory. At Chateau Pelerin the kitchen appears to have occupied the north end of the south-west hall (refectory?) and the area outside it to the east. Just north of the two doorways on the eastern wall of this hall, excavations have uncovered the remains of two large, round stone-built ovens constructed partly within the wall of the hall. One of these ovens was lined with brick and the other was entirely of stone.[56] Water for use in the kitchen came from a cistern to the north, which had a capacity of over 800 cubic metres, or alternatively from a well dug in the sand on the nearby shore.[57]

At Montfort, archaeologists have identified a chamber west of the keep (C) as the kitchen in view of the discovery of ceramic storage containers, a stone mortar, a stone trough and several small flasks.[58] In the south corner of the inner ward of Belvoir there is a small kitchen containing three ovens or perhaps hobs for cooking in metal cauldrons, with flues on its north side (Figure 57). There is a large bin, possibly used to store grain, and a stone mortar was found here. Ash collected during the cleaning of the oven was stored in an adjacent room, perhaps for use in the preparation of plaster.[59] Here a staircase within the thickness of the wall gave onto the upper floor. Water for use in the kitchen came from the nearby cistern in the north-west corner of the courtyard, which had a capacity of 100 cubic metres.[60] The kitchen of the castle of Arsuf was located in the north-west corner of the courtyard between the keep and the northern hall (Figure 58).[61] It was originally a vaulted room with some other function, measuring 7 by 10 metres, with a plaster floor and a door in the east wall. It was possibly when the Hospitallers occupied the castle that this room was converted to serve as the kitchen. It was paved with stone flags, and five hearths or hobs were constructed on its north. They had openings on the north in a narrow passage; the passage has a plaster floor sealing a thick layer of ash from the hearths and ovens. At the end of the passage in its western wall is a chute (80 cm wide by 90 cm deep) which may have ventilated the passage or fulfilled some other function (the excavators suggest that it perhaps gave access to the upper floor via a wooden ladder).[62] Against the east wall of the kitchen, to the north of the door leading from the courtyard, are two plastered pools and ceramic pipes. Under the floor to the south-west is a sewage channel. There is a small (3.5 by 6 metres) service room to the west. The location of the kitchen suggests that the northern hall may have served as the refectory.[63]

Mills, presses, bakery ovens and forges

At Crac des Chevaliers there is evidence for a windmill having stood on the platform of Tower I.[64] We might think the use of wind power exceptional, and it is rarely recorded

Figure 57 Ovens in the kitchen at Belvoir (photograph by the author).

Figure 58 Ovens in the kitchen at Arsuf (photograph by the author).

in the Latin East, but windmills alongside animal-powered mills and 12 water mills are recorded around the castle of Saphet.[65] At Saranda Kolones two donkey mills were discovered in the area inside the inner ward, adjacent to the north-east corner tower.[66] Nearby were mangers, a small storeroom, and a well located in the corner pier, possibly connected to the upper storey. The millstones were surrounded by paved paths for the donkey to perambulate. Related finds included a pestle and mortar, the upper stone of a hand mill, and a jar (possibly a sugar jar). The excavator suggests that these two mills may indeed have been sugar mills.

At Belmont, a wine press was located in a groin-vaulted chamber on the east side of the inner ward. Excavations uncovered a pressing floor (3.3 by 2 metres), constructed of plaster-coated masonry on a bedrock shelf, and a collecting tank (2 by 1.4 metres), partly constructed and partly hewn out of the bedrock and lined with plaster.

Bakeries were important in a castle and are almost always present. At Saranda Kolones there was an oven in the north wing of the inner ward. Together with the mill found to the east, it comprises the *furnum et molendinum* that so often appear in documents. At Crac des Chevaliers a large bread oven was discovered after clearance work carried out in 1927/28 in the long barrel-vaulted hall on the west wing of the inner ward.[67] It was built against the west wall of the hall opposite the entrance from the inner courtyard located between the knights' hall and the large groin-vaulted structure which occupies the entire southern third of the courtyard. The oven measures *c.* 6.5 by 7 metres and is largely constructed of rubble with ashlars used for the chimney flue and the arched openings on the north face. The lower part of the oven was constructed of well-made bricks of a deep pink colour measuring 22 by 12 by 4 cm. It has a diameter of 4.95 metres. The upper part of the oven was domed and had a maximum diameter of 5.30 metres. The chimney flue, which measures 1.45 by 45 metres in section, is located at the centre of the north side of the oven. It was built of limestone ashlars 30 to 40 cm high. It carried the smoke from the oven out through the vault above.

At Chateau Pelerin two ovens were found in an annexe adjacent to the bathhouse. Recent excavations in the Templar castle of Vadum Jacob have uncovered a large bread oven in the south-east corner of the castle within the barrel-vaulted gallery (Figure 59). The oven appears to have been almost identical to the oven at Crac des Chevaliers. It was square, 5 by 5 metres, with a dome constructed of brick and on the west side a small opening through which the bread would have been passed. There would certainly have been a chimney to remove the smoke from the vault. At the base of the oven was a hard cement floor covered by a thin layer of ash, showing that the oven was in use during the construction of the unfinished castle. A group of installations on the north-east side of the courtyard of Arsuf Castle may have functioned as a bakery. One of these, which the excavators suggest was later converted for use as a silo,[68] was polygonal in its external form and round within (3.3 metres in diameter). It was built of stone and lined with brick and had a concrete dome. The floor of the installation (a secondary floor) is constructed of broken basalt mill-stones. Though the original use of this installation has yet to be established, it is similar in design to other bread ovens. A second adjacent installation, 3.4 metres diameter on its interior, is built of limestone. It has an arched opening on the south, where it is approached by descending five steps from the courtyard floor. The floor of the installation was paved with limestone with a large mill-stone inset at its centre.[69]

The forge was an important institution in any castle, and essential in one with a

Figure 59 Bakery oven at Vadum Jacob (photograph by Buki Boaz, courtesy of Ronnie Ellenblum).

large garrison. In the forge the smiths manufactured and repaired tools, weapons and armour. They were responsible for the shoeing of horses and for numerous other basic functions. A forge was excavated in the east range of the outer ward at Belvoir. Amongst the finds were tools and unfinished horseshoes. At Saranda Kolones a forge was located in the south range of the inner bailey.[70] At Montfort a forge was possibly located in an annexe between the kitchen (chamber C) and chamber F.[71] This identification was based on the discovery of several metal objects, including hammers, chisels, fragments of chain mail and armour scales (jazerans), possible fragments of a basinet and a pothelm, arrow, dart and lance heads, spikes and various other items.[72]

Storage and stables

Virtually every castle, from the smallest isolated tower to the greatest of the spur castles, had storage space. In towers the ground floor was used for storage, while in larger castles the vaulted ranges that surrounded courtyards served this purpose. In large castles the amount of covered storage space was often vast. At Crac des Chevaliers the vaulted range of the western side of the inner ward alone is some 120 metres in length and averages 7 metres in width. This vault was not only used for storage but contained a bread oven and latrines as well. The other vaulted ranges on this ward give an overall covered area somewhere in the range of 1,800 square metres. On the south side of the outer ward another barrel-vaulted hall 60 metres in length (8–9 metres wide) was added in the thirteenth century.

Stables were another essential part of any castle, just as a horse was an essential possession of a knight. In many small castles the stables could simply be located in a ground-floor vault and there is often no surviving archaeological evidence for them. In castles with large garrisons the stables would necessarily be large and consequently are much more likely to be located and identified. In some castles there was stabling not only for the knights and for work animals but also for the pack animals of travellers and visitors. At Chateau Pelerin Johns excavated the large stable (referred to on pp. 36–7) which was located against the southern wall of the faubourg. This large courtyard structure had stabling for more than two hundred animals. Additional stables were located in the north-west corner of the yard of the adjacent fort. To the north there was a large walled area surrounded by a low boundary wall, which was used as a cattle enclosure. At nearby le Destroit stables were located in the quarried yard to the east of the tower. Some 18 mangers cut in the rock scarp can be seen here and Johns suggests that there may have been standing room for about two dozen horses.[73] At Saranda Kolones stables occupied the east and the south-west ranges in the inner ward. At Bethgibelin the Hospitallers probably used the vaulted service corridors in the Roman amphitheatre as stables, utilising the existing troughs made from dismantled stones.[74] Although there is little archaeological evidence to confirm this, the area was conveniently located within the outer fortified compound on the western side; it had first been converted into stables by the Hospitallers' predecessors in the Early Islamic period.

11

ELEMENTS OF FORTIFICATION

The varied and often complex elements of fortification employed by the castle-builders of the Military Orders were adapted and developed in response to the growing complexity of medieval siege warfare and the advances made in both siege machines and siege techniques in this period. Alongside castle design, it was in the development of elements of fortification that the Military Orders were most innovative. They borrowed and adapted without hesitation from the technical achievements of the West, the Byzantine Empire and the Muslim East. Although the Military Orders did not adopt the irregular plans found in Armenian castles, they did borrow heavily from the range of defensive elements found in the castles of Cilician Armenia.

Gate complexes

In most of the castles of the Military Orders, as elsewhere in Crusader fortifications, bent-access gates were employed. The idea was not new; bent-access gates were used at Tiryns and Mycenae in the Late Helladic period, and in the Roman period Vitruvius recommended the use of indirect approaches from right to left. The aim was to force the assailant, once he had passed through the outer portal, to turn to the left, thus exposing the right side of his body, unprotected by the shield, to attack from defended positions to the right as he entered the *intervallum*. According to Creswell, the use of the bent-access entrance in a tower first appears in pre-Islamic Central Asia, becoming popular in Islam during the Abbasid period.[1] By the Crusader period it had become a common practice in urban fortifications to place the gate in a tower with the outer portal on one of the sides of the tower (although not always on the right-hand side), thereby forcing the person entering to turn at a right angle; in many cases a second turn was required to exit the gatehouse into the city. As castles became larger and more complex, this type of entrance was adopted in many of them as well. This occurred fairly early on, before the Military Orders became seriously involved in castle building; indirect entrances were used before 1132 in the southern gate towers of Saone Castle and early in the 1140s in the northern gate of Karak.[2] The contribution of the Military Orders to the design of castle gates was not in inventing the bent-access gate and gate tower, or in introducing them into the defensive architecture of the Crusader states. Rather, it was in improving and embellishing them and in developing castle entrances into far more complex and effective structures. They made use of virtually all the defensive features used in gates in Muslim and Byzantine fortifications: drawbridges, adjacent external towers, machicolation above the outer gate, one or more portcullises, gates protected with iron plating and strengthened with massive bolt-posts, long dark passages beyond the gate which often bent 180 degrees back upon themselves, murder holes in the passage vaulting, arrow-slits on either side of the gatehouse or passage, and dead-end corridors.

The most innovative and advanced gates seem to have been built by the Hospitallers. They developed elaborate gate complexes at Bethgibelin and Belvoir in the twelfth century and at Margat, Silifke and possibly at Crac des Chevaliers in the thirteenth century. The entrance arrangements which evolved with the expansion of the castle of Bethgibelin illustrate the quality of their work (Figure 32). Here, as recent excavations have shown, the castle had a system which required the assailant to pass through an outer gateway in the external wall (only parts of which, not including the gate, have been found) into and through a second gatehouse in the second or inner enceinte, which included a portcullis and an irregular-shaped tower on its south. This inner gate gave into a covered passageway running along the southern perimeter of the second enceinte. At a distance of about 40 metres it became necessary to turn 90 degrees to the north (left). The assailant then had to pass along a north–south wall which divided the fortified area in two until he reached a ramp leading to a third gate, where he had to turn 180 degrees to the other side of the north–south wall. From there he continued south between this wall and the western wall of the inner castle to the entrance of the latter, where once again a turn of 90 degrees to the left was necessary.

The date of construction of this complex is uncertain. The archaeologists noted a difference between the masonry of the inner castle and that of the outer fortifications, and have suggested that the outworks belong to a second phase which was not very much later than the first.[3] Whereas the original fortifications were built in an attempt to put an end to incursions from Fatimid Ascalon, the outer fortifications here, and in other castles in the region, may have been constructed in the 1170s to face the new threat from Egypt under Saladin.[4]

At Belvoir the Hospitallers built a compact but effective gate system comprising an outer gate without a portcullis which was reached by crossing the moat, perhaps on a bridge which has not survived. Passing through the outer gate, one entered a narrow passage. In the wall to the left were a number of arrow-slits, albeit placed rather high on the wall, through which the defenders would have been able to fire on attackers. After about 40 metres, the passage entered the great eastern tower and turned back 180 degrees. The passage was once again defended on the west, the attackers' right (unprotected) side. After about 33 metres the passage turned 90 degrees to the west and brought the attacker to a double-leaf gate with arrow-slits on both sides and a slit machicolation above. A bolt-beam sealed the door. The gate opened into a vaulted gatehouse from which one had yet again to turn 90 degrees to the right to enter the outer courtyard. Passing through to the courtyard, the attacker had to cross to the west side of the inner ward and enter through an inner gatehouse which also had indirect access and was defended with machicolation and bolted gates.

At Silifke in Western Cilicia, the gate complex began at the base of the moat in the north.[5] A gatehouse was located at the western end of the approach ramp, a square tower which formed a bent-access entrance to the area below the main curtain wall. There is a box machicolation above the tower gate. The gate to the inner ward must have been located to the west of this tower, although no trace of it can be seen today.

The Templar Sea Castle at Sidon had a complex gate system which consisted of an outer gate on the south side of the castle facing the shore and an inner gate on the east side of the inner ward, with a covered passage between them. The outer gate was reached by a drawbridge at the end of the gangway from the shore. It was defended by a box machicolation and had a portcullis. In order to reach the inner bailey after entering the gate, it was probably necessary to turn right along a groin-vaulted passageway to the south-east corner of the castle, where it became necessary to turn left and continue about 15 metres to the gate into the inner ward on the left. This inner gate was defended with a slot machicolation and two portcullises.

At Gaston the outer gate tower was located at the northern end of the lower, outer eastern wall. A two-storey gate tower was constructed on a rock platform projecting over the abyss. It had a round-arched portal occupying the entire east wall. From here a 90-degree turn led to an inner round-arched portal which gave access to a ramp ascending gently to the south along the eastern wall. At the top of the ramp is a large horseshoe-shaped tower constructed of marginally drafted ashlars with pronounced bosses, the only such stones used in the castle. The northern end of the ramp was roofed with groin vaults, ensuring that anyone entering from the sunlight would be momentarily blinded by the dark and the defenders could attack them with impunity, firing from the door and window of the tower. The southern end of the ramp was apparently not vaulted. A staircase, which has not survived, may have led to the roof of the vaults and was perhaps used by the defenders to reach murder holes in the vault. A narrow pointed-arched doorway with a draw-bar led into the inner tower. Behind it a narrow passage in the thickness of the wall gave onto an embrasure which faced the ramp, enabling it to be controlled from the inner tower. The room in the tower was groin-vaulted and had an arched recess in the northern end of its east wall giving onto an embrasure facing the ramp at the centre of the tower's south face. This recess had a doorway with draw-bar holes on the inner side. Large pointed arches gave access from the tower to rooms on the south and west. From here one turned again 90 degrees, through an inner room, into the outer lower bailey of the castle. Another gate gave access from the lower bailey to the upper inner bailey.

The principal entrance at Margat included an outer gatehouse, which was added to the earlier fortifications after 1200. It is on the west side of the fortifications just north of the castle. It was approached via a stepped ramp from the north which turns 90 degrees to the east. Above the portal on the western side of the gatehouse is a large box machicolation flanked by arrow-slits. The inner portal of gatehouse is on the south wall, thus requiring a second 90 degree turn. It gives onto the outer courtyard, where there is an inner gate that gives access via vaulted chambers into the inner courtyard.

The finest and most complex of castle gates is that at Crac des Chevaliers. Whereas this may have been of Mamluk construction,[6] there can be little doubt that it was influenced by the increasingly complex gate designs in such Frankish examples as Bethgibelin and Belvoir. At Crac the entrance of the castle begins at the outer gate in the northern part of the eastern outer wall. One enters the gatehouse and turns 90 degrees to the south (left) to begin the long passage ascending towards the interior of the castle. A vaulted passage leads south for about 90 metres, at which point it comes to a dead end. It then becomes necessary to turn right and right again through nearly 180 degrees. From here another long vaulted passage rises fairly steeply to the north for about 60 metres until it reaches the twelfth-century gatehouse of the inner ward. The vaulted ceiling of the passage has murder holes at regular intervals, enabling the defenders to attack invaders from above as they advanced along the dark passage. Arriving at the northern end of the passage, one has to turn 90 degrees to the left and pass through the two flanking projecting towers of the gatehouse in order to enter into an inner vestibule and, from here, finally, into the bailey of the inner castle. Like so much else at Crac des Chevaliers this was the art of defensive architecture taken to its peak of development (albeit, in this case, perhaps not by the Franks but by the Mamluk inheritors of the castle). The vulnerability of the gate, the weakest point in a castle, is diminished to such an extent that an assailant would possibly be better off attacking the castle wall.

Posterns (sally-ports)

Posterns – small gates hidden away in towers or in isolated parts of the walls leading out of the fortifications, sometimes into the moat – were intended to enable the defenders to sally out and attack the unsuspecting enemy, to serve as escape routes in times of danger or to permit reinforcements to enter a besieged castle. They were typical of most large castles and of urban fortifications. From around the late third century AD siege machinery had been covered by 'cats', wooden constructions with vinegar-soaked leather coverings which were intended to protect besiegers from bombardment, including incendiary missiles, coming from the walls. However, the cat had a disadvantage: it allowed protection only for a limited number of men and it isolated them from the main force of the besiegers. From posterns in various parts of the walls the besieged could carry out surprise sorties against these men, emerging rapidly to attack them and in large numbers.[7]

Posterns were opened in some of the towers of the outer ward at Belvoir (Figure 60).[8] Staircases descended within the towers, exiting on side walls at the base of the moat. They were partly but not entirely hidden from the view of the enemy beyond the moat. At Bethgibelin one of the towers on the outer southern wall (tower 650) had a staircase which led down to two posterns at the base of the moat, one facing east and the other facing west. One of these was later sealed off and the lower part of the tower filled with rubble. This is perhaps an indication of the disadvantage of a postern: during a siege it could sometimes be a hazard, a means by which the castle could be entered. This would always be the quandary with posterns; the advantage of a door from a castle into the moat had to be weighed against the possibility of its being used by an invader.

Portcullises

The portcullis, a wooden or iron grille which was mechanically lowered in front of a gate, is known from at least as early as the Roman period. Creswell notes that the Herculaneum Gate at Pompeii (built before 78 BC) had a portcullis, as did the Roman gate of Qasr ash-Sham' in Old Cairo.[9] The portcullis was lowered before a castle or city gate to make it more difficult for an invader to reach or damage it. In addition, as can be seen in the descriptions of Polybius and Vegetius, it could suddenly be lowered on the attackers as they stood before the gate. Polybius, referring to an attack on Salapia, wrote: 'But the portcullis, which they had raised somewhat higher by machinery, they

Figure 60 Stairs to a sally port in a tower at Belvoir (photograph by Buki Boas).

suddenly let down.'[10] This would trap the attackers in the space before the door, where they could be neatly disposed of through well-placed arrow-slits or machicolation. Vegetius describes its use in greater detail:

> But more useful is the ancient device of adding in front of the gate, a projecting tower, in the entrance to which is placed a portcullis, suspended from iron rings, in such a fashion that, if the enemy gets in, it could be dropped behind them and they, so imprisoned, be dispatched.[11]

For some reason the portcullis seems to have lost its attraction after the Roman period, for it virtually disappears from Byzantine and Early Muslim fortification and it appears probable that the Crusaders were responsible for its reintroduction in the twelfth century. Evidence for the presence of portcullises (slots and tracks located within gates outside the portals) can be seen in many Crusader castles. Amongst those of the Military Orders, they can be seen at Crac des Chevaliers in the postern between towers 12 and 13 of the northern side of the outer defences, in the south-west (second) gate of Bethgibelin, in the western gate of the inner ward of Toron des Chevaliers, in the main south gate of Vadum Jacob (Figure 61), in the gate of the castle of Arsuf (Figure 62), in the Sea Castle of Sidon, in the west entrance tower of Margat Castle, in

Figure 61 Portcullis channel at Vadum Jacob (photograph by the author).

the entrance passage of Crac des Chevalliers, and in the northern and southern gates of the south outer tower of Chateau Pelerin where there are also murder-holes (*meurtrières*) above, just before the portcullis and machicoulis.

Machicolation, murder-holes (*meurtrières*) and hoardings

Machicolation was developed as a means of protecting the weak points in defensive works such as gates, by enabling the defender to harass assailants located directly below at the base of the walls. Arrow-slits and positions between the merlons at the top of the walls were not effective against an enemy once he had reached the wall. The term 'machicolation' generally refers to a small balcony (box) or projecting gallery (the equivalent of wooden hoarding) placed high on a wall which has openings in its floor through which liquids or objects could be dropped on the enemy.[12] The floor itself was

Figure 62 Portcullis channel at Arsuf (photograph by the author).

often formed by a row of parallel corbels placed slightly apart from one another. Another form of machicolation known as slot (or slit) machicolation was formed by leaving an open slot above and before a gate.

Box machicolation, which Kennedy refers to as 'true machicolation', appears in Early Islamic fortifications.[13] The direct source is quite clearly Islamic, although box machicolation is also present on pre-Islamic Syrian tower houses.[14] Frankish examples can be seen at Montfort Castle on the north-west gates (Figure 63).

Slot machicolation, slot-shaped openings above and before a gate, may have been an Armenian introduction; Edwards considers it so.[15] It is found in Armenian castles such as Yilan, over the outer portal of the castle's main gate which gives access to the upper ward, and at Anavarza, over the external portal of the eastern gate to the lower (south) bailey. While Yilan cannot be dated at present, the eastern gate of Anavarza (G on Edwards's plan) is dated to the rule of Thoros I (*c.* 1102–1129).[16]

In Frankish castles slot machicolation can be seen in several castles, including Saone, Belvoir (the inner gate) and the Frankish keeps of Baisan (Beit She'an) and al-Burj (Horvat Tittura, located in the modern town of Modi'in, west of Jerusalem). However, Belvoir dates to some time after 1168 and, although the other examples probably date to the first half of the twelfth century, it is unlikely that they are as early as Anavarza. In any case, as Edwards points out, slot machicolation is found in Armenian work as early as the seventh century.[17] Later (thirteenth-century) use of slot machicolation can be seen in the gate on the east of the Sea Castle at Sidon (Kalayan's D4) and in the outer fortification gates of Chateau Pelerin.[18]

171

Figure 63 Machicolation on the north-west gates of Montfort (photograph by Rabei Khamissy).

What appears to be another type of machicolation at Crac des Chevaliers is found on the northern latrine tower of the inner enceinte. Here four buttresses were attached to the face of the tower, joined above by three pointed arches. Above these arches the tower ascends flush with the outer face of the buttresses. It is constructed with two rows of relieving arches, a feature which Lawrence described as 'peculiar', as they are apparently 'relieving nothing'![19]

Machicolation was exceptional in twelfth-century Crusader castles, notwithstanding the examples mentioned. Other than these examples, the different types of machicolation are known in Saone and Bourzey, which were not Military Order castles, on the keep of the Teutonic castle of Amuda and in the Templar castle of Beaufort in the south gate into the inner ward.

In the thirteenth century machicolation became more common in Frankish fortifications. It was used by the Hospitallers at Margat on the outer southern enceinte and on the entrance tower on the west. As for the Templars, Lawrence believed that they did not make use of machicolation at all.[20] However, box machicolation is in fact to be found at Sidon (Sea Castle) over the southern, outer gate; at Beaufort; and at Chateau Pelerin, at the east end of the southern side of the inner ward, above the gate next to the great tower and possibly on the south gate tower of the outer enceinte, above its outer north and south gates.[21] It was possibly also in use in other Templar castles where it has not survived or been identified. Written sources suggest that it may have been present in Saphet.[22] In contemporary Arab work box machicolation is found in the thirteenth-century Muslim fortifications in the citadels of Damascus and Aleppo, at 'Ajlun and, as noted, at Crac des Chevaliers after it fell to the Mamluks.[23]

Like machicolation, murder-holes (*meurtrières*) were openings left in a vault, usually in a gatehouse or entry passage, through which rocks could be cast down or liquid poured on the unsuspecting intruder. The entrance passage at Crac des Chevaliers contains an excellent example of the use of this feature. In a dark passage the assailants would not be aware of the danger above them.

Related to machicolation were wooden hoardings (*bretêche*). Common in the West, where there was often a plentiful supply of wood, in the East these were generally replaced with stone machicolation. However, there is evidence for some examples of hoarding. At Chateau Pelerin, for example, a series of slots and grooves can be seen in the stonework adjacent to the machicolation. A reference of Ibn al-Furat to *sata'ir*, apparently wooden projections, burned by the Franks during the siege of Saphet Castle in 1266, has been interpreted as hoardings.[24]

Curtain walls, battlements (wall-head defences), arrow-slits, embrasures and the *chemin de ronde*

The major part of a castle's defence was the curtain wall itself, which surrounded and protected the other buildings of a castle. In its basic form a castle really only needed to have a curtain wall and a gate to become a castle, although of course it was never actually so limited. Few castles other than tower keeps lacked mural towers, many castles had moats and additional defensive elements, and most castles had additional buildings in the interior. The curtain wall generally functioned as the outer support wall for barrel vaults which surrounded the interior of the castle and served as living space, storage and various other functions.

Curtain walls were built in the same manner as other types of Frankish construction; that is, walls were constructed of three layers, the outer and inner layers consisting of ashlars or fieldstones and the space between them filled with a very solid mortar and rubble fill.

The top of the curtain wall was an excellent position from which to fire upon an enemy attacking the walls. It was defended by battlements composed of merlons and open embrasures which provided the defenders with numerous protected firing positions. In most cases a wall-walk ran along the top of the wall, providing access to the embrasures and enabling the defenders to move easily from one position on the wall to another as the need arose. The wall-walk was reached via stone staircases within the thickness of the wall or towers, or by stone or wooden staircases on the inner side of the curtain wall. It was generally possible to gain access to the wall-walk through the towers and to pass along large areas of the castle defences via these passages.[25] If the curtain wall was high enough it could have a *chemin de ronde* at a lower level than the battlements, giving access to additional firing positions in the wall. This was the case in many of the larger castles, such as in the outer defences of Chateau Pelerin, where there was a *chemin de ronde* 5.6 metres below the top of the battlements. This passage, about 2 metres wide, gave access to 3-metre wide casemates (wide enough for four men, two at the arrow-slit and two for relief) with the arrow-slits 5 metres apart.[26] At Margat the defences are preserved almost intact on the north-east tower of the citadel, where there are large casemates at a lower level with a wall-walk above that gave access to the battlements. The latter were well-protected firing positions for the archers.

The arrow-slit or loop was intended to provide a protected position from which a defender could fire arrows at the assailants (Figures 64, 65). The opening had to be narrow enough to afford maximum protection, while the interior had to be wide enough to allow the archer to stand or crouch in reasonable comfort to position, load, aim and fire his bow. Originally nothing more than a vertical gap left between two ashlars, the arrow-slit became longer in the twelfth and thirteenth centuries. Its principal disadvantage, the inability of the archer to fire at the base of the wall, was somewhat overcome by the development of the splayed or stirrup-shaped base of the arrow-slit, which enabled the archer to direct his fire at least somewhat nearer to the base of the wall. The ideal solution was to build a talus, preferably at the same angle as the sloping base of the arrow-slit, which removed the assailant from the base of the wall and into the field of fire.[27]

The arrow-slit was usually expanded into a triangular compartment which was high enough to allow a convenient approach to the firing position and, ideally, broad enough to enable two men to take up position within it, one to use the slit and the second to stand by as a replacement. However, this was often not the case, and at Belvoir the arrow-slits had room for only one archer, sometimes in a crouching position and sometimes only lying down. The top of the casemate was generally vaulted with a small barrel vault. Though the use of arrow-slits was limited in early Crusader castles, they greatly increased in number and improved in design towards the end of the twelfth century and particularly in the thirteenth century as the use of archery increased and developed.

Figure 64 Arrow-slit at Safed (from within) (photograph courtesy of Herve Barbé, IAA).

Figure 65 Stirrup-shaped arrow-slit at Doc (photograph by the author).

The best location for arrow-slits in defending the length of a castle wall was in the side walls of a projecting tower adjacent to the curtain walls.[28] However, they are not always ideally located. In some towers at Silifke they are placed in a position that would allow no flanking fire at all and were of use only for firing upon an approaching enemy who had not yet reached the blind areas at the foot of the walls. In this castle many of these openings are broad windows probably intended for the use of small torsion mangonels; these are useful features, but it is none the less odd that no measures were taken to enable flanking fire.

Forewalls (*antemuralia*) and barbicans (*barbicana*)

The forewall was a defensive element with which the Crusaders came into contact during the First Crusade, when they encountered the walls of Constantinople, Nicaea,

175

Antioch and Jerusalem. As they developed more advanced castle architecture during the twelfth century, they adopted the use of forewalls and introduced concentric defences in their castles. *De Constructione Castri Saphet* refers to the *antemuralia* of Templar Saphet.[29] This tract also refers to casemates (*fortie cooperte*) which were: 'above the ditches and underneath the outer wall, where there can be crossbowmen with great balistas which defend the ditches'.[30] This sounds like another reference to forewalls or barbicans (*barbicana*).

Projecting wall towers

The positioning of projecting towers along the curtain walls was of supreme importance in the defence of a castle. Their presence turned a castle from a purely passive refuge, with almost no possibility of defending itself beyond relying on the strength of its walls, to one which could actively defend itself through the use of lateral arrow fire along its walls and towers from positions in the towers.

In order to cover the entire area of the curtain between two towers, it was necessary to place them at a distance that would allow arrow fire from embrasures in a tower to cover at least half of the distance between one tower and the next. However, to be able to fire upon an enemy attacking at the base of the next tower it was desirable for arrow fire to reach all the way to the next tower. In most Crusader castles the maximum distance between towers is on average around 50 metres, a distance that the medieval archer was well able to cover as the range of a standard bow was about 100 metres with accuracy and up to 200 metres with less accuracy; a crossbow or arbalest had a considerably greater range.

Throughout the history of fortification the tower has played a dominant role. In the Crusader period, despite the appearance of towers in a wide variety of shapes, the rectangular or square tower remained the most common form. This was partly because a quadrangular tower is the easiest to construct. As in other Crusader fortifications, in the castles of the Military Orders quadrangular towers were used almost exclusively in the twelfth century. Exceptions include the triangular, pentagonal, hexagonal and octagonal towers at Saranda Kolones and the octagonal tower in the outer enceinte of Bethgibelin. In Crusader castles the move to semicircular, horseshoe- or D-shaped and round towers came with the construction of the great castles of the Military Orders in the early thirteenth century (Figure 66). The rounded form was much more difficult to construct, as it required stones cut to a specific shape. The alternative use of very small stones resulted in construction that was less solid and was more vulnerable to damage during siege. Round towers could have round or square interiors.[31] On the whole the round tower was advantageous for four reasons. Firstly, having no corners, a round tower was less vulnerable to attempts at dismantling it by knocking out the quoins.[32] Secondly, unless very small stones were used, trapezoid-shaped ashlars with a curved face, like the voussoirs of an arch, were employed; these formed a more compact and tighter construction than regular ashlars. Thirdly, windows or arrow-slits in a round tower could cover a more extensive area. Fourthly, the round shape left only the minimum of blind space before the tower which could not be covered by firing positions in the adjacent curtain walls, whereas it was impossible to defend the area in front of a quadrangular tower completely.

Round towers were favoured in Hellenistic, Roman and Byzantine fortifications and

Figure 66 Round tower at Silifke (photograph by Denys Pringle).

were extensively used in Muslim defensive works. However, in Crusader fortifications they rarely appear prior to the thirteenth century. Amongst the few exceptions are Saone, Tripoli, Beaufort and the Cilician castles. In the latter, the D-shaped tower was the most popular form and was adopted in the castles of the Military Orders in Cilicia – for example in the twelfth century at Templar Gaston and in the thirteenth at Hospitaller Silifke. In the Crusader states round towers were adopted by the Hospitallers in the late twelfth and early thirteenth centuries at Crac des Chevaliers and are found at Margat, Arima, Chastel Blanc and in the south at Arsuf (although it is not certain if the round towers here were built by the Hospitallers). At Crac des Chevaliers one round and three D-shaped towers replaced the rectangular twelfth-century towers on the inner ward and at least six semi-circular towers were constructed on the outer ward. At Saranda Kolones in western Cyprus there are round towers on the corners of the outer ward (one is polygonal) and a D-shaped gate tower on the inner ward. The

Templars adopted round towers at Sidon (the Sea Castle) and at Saphet. The Teutonic Knights built a horseshoe-shaped keep and semicircular towers on the outer wall at Montfort.

No less significant than the use of the round or angular form of the tower was the extent of its projection from the curtain wall. Fedden and Thomson note: 'Towers have a variety of uses, but their *raison d'être* is to provide flanking fire. Whatever method of attack is used, the besieger must approach close to the castle walls. Towers of bold projection enable the defenders to enfilade from advantageous positions with slings, arrows, and other missiles.'[33] The height of the tower was another factor which might be significant in its effectiveness in a castle's defences. As towers rarely survive to their full original height, in most cases we have to rely on estimation. The most exceptional example with regard to its height is Saphet: the seven towers at Saphet, according to *De Constructione Castri Saphet*, were 22 cannas (48.8 metres) high. If this report is reliable, Saphet was exceptional even amongst the greatest of the Military Orders' castles. At Chateau Pelerin, the great north tower was over 34 metres high, while at Margat the great round keep was a comparatively low 27 metres high (including the battlements).

The talus (glacis)

This element, common in fortifications from ancient times, was a standard feature in Byzantine defensive works and can be seen, for example, in the fortifications at Nicaea and Antioch. The talus was intended to fulfil a number of functions. It made scaling of the walls more difficult by necessitating the use of longer ladders and preventing the enemy from achieving a stable footing for the ladders close to the base of the wall (Figure 67). It increased the width of the fortification, making it more difficult to damage the wall using a ram or by sapping. The heavy boulders sometimes inserted into the foundations of the talus added to the difficulty of sapping the walls, as they increased the likelihood of collapse of the mine before it reached the desired position beneath the wall. The talus distanced the assailant several metres from the blind area at the base of the wall, thereby exposing him to attack from positions above. It also served as a buttress to strengthen the wall against damage caused by missiles or by earthquakes. Finally, if the defenders dropped heavy stones from the walls onto the talus, they would shatter and the fragments would ricochet off with a shrapnel-like effect.

At Crac des Chevaliers an enormous, steep talus over 20 metres high was constructed to protect the entire south and west sides of the inner enceinte. Here the principal function was clearly to buttress the wall against damage by mining, siege engines and earthquakes.[34] The talus was occasionally created simply as a stone facing on an existing natural slope. In such examples it was intended to make it more difficult for assailants to scale the slope by removing any natural handholds or footholds in the native rock. The talus was cut in the bedrock (Belmont) or constructed of fieldstones or ashlars (Belvoir, Crac des Chevaliers). It was usually on a more modest scale than that of Crac des Chevaliers, sometimes no more than a batter at the base of the walls. Examples of the use of batters or a talus are to be seen at most castles. At Arima batters are found on the well-constructed limestone towers in the central and eastern wards. At Belvoir and Beaufort sections of the rock-cut scarp of the moat to the north, west and south were faced with a stone talus. At Belmont the outer fortification had a rock-cut batter

Figure 67 Talus at Toron des Chevaliers (Latrun) on the middle ward (photograph by the author).

and at Toron des Chevaliers the walls of the inner rectangular enclosure, as well as the outer bailey walls, had a steep talus (Figure 67).

The moat (ditch)

The moat was one of the most effective means of cutting off the castle from its surroundings; in combination with the other elements of fortification, including fore-walls and barbicans, it made the use of siege machines much more difficult (Figures 68, 69). In the East, it also served as a quarry to provide the building stones from which the defences were constructed. The dimensions of the moat could vary considerably. According to *De Constructione Castri Saphet*, the ditches at Saphet were cut in the rock and measured 7 cannas (15.4 metres) deep and 6 metres wide.[35] At Belvoir the ditch

179

Figure 68 Moat at Belvoir (photograph by the author).

Figure 69 Moat at Maldoim (photograph by the author).

was 20 metres wide and 12 metres deep. At Montfort the inner ditch was approximately the same (20 metres wide and 11 deep). While the castle ditch at Chateau Pelerin varied from 15 to 29 metres in width, it was only 6 metres deep. However, as noted, it may have been occasionally filled with seawater, which would have increased its effectiveness as a barrier.

Other than its use as an obstacle in siege warfare, the ditch on occasion had a secondary function. Part of it, as at Belvoir,[36] could serve as a reservoir collecting rainwater that could be used by the defenders.[37] Karak and Margat had pools which both supplied water and played a defensive role in cutting the castles off from an extension of the mountain ridge. At Crac des Chevaliers the open reservoir was located below the great talus of the inner fortification on the south. A vaulted cistern was built into a low point in the floor of the moat at Silifke to catch rainwater that collected in the moat.[38]

12

STONEMASONRY AND CONSTRUCTION TECHNIQUES

To what extent were the Military Orders innovative in the technical side of construction? This is a question that can be satisfactorily answered only by a serious and comprehensive study of medieval building methods in the Latin East. As no such study has yet been carried out, we are obliged at present to limit our observations, relying on a restricted number of discussions of construction techniques carried out at certain sites. One of the few such studies is found in the excavation report on the castle of Crac des Chevaliers by Paul Deschamps.[1] Deschamps describes different methods of stone tooling, the use of masons' marks, and the techniques used in the construction of vaults, arches, windows, gates, towers, firing embrasures, machicolations and various non-defensive features including water installations and the baking furnace. An examination of stonemasonry in Armenian castles was published by Edwards in his major study of the Cilician castles.[2] Edwards identified nine distinct types of masonry. He also noted that the Armenians built their walls using the 'poured-wall technique'; that is, they constructed outer and inner facings and poured a mortar and rubble fill into the space between them. This was the technique employed by the Franks in almost all their buildings.

The choice of stone

The type of stone employed in castle construction naturally depended on what was available in the immediate vicinity of the castle construction site. In the Kingdom of Jerusalem limestone of various qualities was the dominant stone used in castles built in the central highlands and parts of the inland plain. Basalt was employed in volcanic regions such as those around the Sea of Galilee. Easily quarried but less resilient sandstone was used consistently in coastal sites. A supply of building stone was always available in the East, although the quality varied considerably from region to region. As a result, stone for certain elements was sometimes brought from distant quarries to supplement the local supply. For example, where the local stone was basalt, a hard stone that is difficult to cut, limestone was often brought from afar to be used for special architectural elements such as voussoirs and decorative pieces. This was the case at Belvoir, where much of the building stone was basalt from the excavation of the ditch surrounding the castle, but for arrow-embrasure vaults, arches and window frames and for large parts of the upper level of the inner ward a softer limestone was brought from distant quarries, possibly in the nearby Gilboa range. An additional type of limestone was employed in the construction of the chapel. A similar use of basalt and limestone is found at Margat. Some castle-building sites were fortunate enough to have more than one type of stone available. At the quarry site adjacent to Vadum Jacob, a layer of basalt is overlain by a layer of soft limestone. The builders peeled off the upper limestone layer and used it to make ashlars for use in the main walls of the castle. Basalt chips and roughly shaped fieldstones from the lower layer or from the building site itself were used in the mortar fill and in the construction of the barrel-vaulting.

The type of stone used in the construction of a castle could have a significant visual impact. This is particularly the case with castles built of basalt, which have a decidedly ominous appearance. Taking this into account, one might ask whether this factor played any part in the choice of building material for a castle. Certainly the designers of castles took into account the psychological effect on the assailant of a dramatic and foreboding (one might even say theatrical) manifestation. Beyond their physical advantages, high walls and massively constructed towers undoubtedly made a strong impression on an approaching enemy. It seems quite likely that when Saladin chose to bypass Crac des Chevaliers and Margat in the summer of 1188 his decision was influenced not only by the obvious tactical issues but also by the physical appearance of these imposing structures.[3] Clearly, however, the type of stone used was primarily dictated by what was available on the site or at nearby quarries: sandstone on the coast, limestone in the uplands and basalt in volcanic regions. Where there were ancient ruins, *spolia* of marble, granite and porphyry were used (Figure 70).

Foundations

The Franks were aware of the need to construct deep foundations, preferably extending down to the bedrock. By the time the Military Orders were constructing their great castles in the early thirteenth century there had been enough instances of mining of fortifications to demonstrate to them the importance of founding a wall on a solid base.[4] Unfortunately, there are few examples where foundations have been exposed and examined. One negative example is at Vadum Jacob where sections of the foundations were exposed in 1994. Three types of wall foundation were recorded. In the south the castle walls were constructed in a deep foundation trench cut into the stratigraphic deposits of the tell, and on the east (the inner facing) the wall is set on an ancient wall, possibly of Hellenistic date. However, on the north (the north-west corner) the foundation consists of nothing more than a poor basalt rubble construction only about half a metre deep. Here, no doubt, it was the ever-present threat of an attack by Saladin before the fortifications were completed (a threat which was indeed fulfilled) that led the builders to construct the wall hastily on such feeble foundations. And it was here, on the north, that Saladin dug the mine which brought down the wall and captured the castle from the Templars.

Wall construction

The structural walls of Frankish buildings consisted of inner and outer facings with a rubble and mortar fill, either poured from above after the facings were raised or constructed in levels.[5] This technique was used consistently in their buildings, whether they were castles, urban public or domestic buildings, or rural structures. The same

Figure 70 Spolia at Arsuf (photograph by the author).

building technique with stone facings and a poured core was employed in Armenian castles.[6] In the latter, Edwards noted that the core appears to be layered at the level of each course.[7] This technique would have involved raising the inner and outer facings by a single course, filling the space between them with mortar and rubble and then repeating the process. A similar technique may have been used in Crusader castles, although this was not always the case, and it seems likely that more often several courses were raised before the core was poured in. The strength of the mortar used in Crusader fortification construction is not only evident in that of the Military Orders but is well attested in sites such as the walls of Ascalon, where the sandstone facings have eroded but the core has survived comparatively well. In the Templar castle of Vadum Jacob, the facings were robbed several hundred years ago but the core still stands in places up to 7 or 8 metres in height. Where the stone robbers levered the limestone ashlars free, the strength of the mortar was such that large fragments of the stone remain adhering to the core.

Types of masonry

As in Frankish building in general, wall facings vary in the castles of the Military Orders, consisting either entirely of ashlar construction or of ashlar quoins with field-stone facings between them. Ashlars are sometimes flat-tooled stones with or without marginal drafting, at other times rusticated stones with marginal drafting. Different types of ashlars are occasionally found together in the construction of a single wall. The sources of these traditions are European, Armenian and probably local as well. The marginally drafted ashlars, either flat-tooled or rusticated, that were frequently used in Frankish construction may have been imitated from the numerous examples of such masonry from earlier periods in the East. Diagonally tooled stones (Figure 71), frequently with masons' marks, were in common use in Western medieval architecture; the Armenians occasionally employed the same techniques.[8]

According to Edwards, in Armenian castles rusticated masonry was used 'on the exterior of circuit walls, towers and gatehouses, and in all places where an enemy could inflict damage with siege weapons'.[9] Edwards noted that these stones had pointed sides to bind them firmly with the core. This is fundamentally true of Crusader construction as well, although rusticated masonry is found in unexposed places as well. On the exterior walls of castles it is often limited to the quoins of the walls and towers. The margin enabled the stones to be set accurately, particularly important in the forming of corners. Leaving the rough bosses saved time in the preparation of stones and, perhaps more important, had a defensive value. The corners were the points of the structure most threatened by siege machines. Rusticated stones with pronounced bosses are sometimes able to deflect a missile, or at least to lessen the force of impact. If they are firmly set in the core, the exterior face is better able to absorb the shock.

Marginally drafted ashlars with pronounced bosses were used long before the Crusader period. By the Crusader period these stones appear in most cases to have been used primarily for their aesthetic quality rather than for any defensive advantage they might provide. Thus they are sometimes found in use in the interior of castles, within courtyards and even within vaulted halls, where they could only have had a decorative value.

Figure 71 Masonry (diagonal tooling) (photograph by the author).

Ashlars of superior limestone dressed with a fine diagonal-tooled finish are a common feature in all types of Crusader construction. The entire surface of the stone which was to be exposed was worked with a comb-shaped chisel, leaving fine diagonal striations. This type of masonry, often found in contemporary European structures, has long been identified in the East as a uniquely Frankish technique, a hallmark of building of the Crusader period.[10] It is never found in buildings constructed prior to the twelfth century and is found only in secondary use after the Crusader period. Drafted margins were sometimes added to diagonally tooled stones. This was done purely for the sake of appearance, usually in large elaborate castles. It can be seen, for example, in extensive use in tower M and other towers at Crac des Chevaliers and, in combination with rusticated ashlars, in the great towers of the inner defences at Chateau Pelerin. It is found in limited use in many other castles, for example in the gate to the upper bailey at Beaufort and in parts of Belvoir.

In castles, as in other forms of Crusader construction, walls were often constructed of roughly shaped fieldstones with mortar and chip fillings. This technique saved a great deal of time and required less expertise in its construction. However, in almost all cases where it was used, the quoins of the building and the frames of doors, windows and firing embrasures were constructed of well-cut ashlars. The use of this type of masonry is particularly common in Cilician castles.

The decorative technique which involves the alternate use of different coloured stones, well represented in Islamic architecture (in particular that of the Mamluk period) where it is known as *ablaq*, is occasionally found in Frankish buildings. The use of different coloured stones at Belvoir and Margat are examples in which the application is partly in order to achieve decorative effect but mainly motivated by the fact that the locally available stone in these two castles was basalt. Clearly decorative is the limited use of different types of stone in the keep of Montfort Castle. Closer to the true *ablaq*, the use of sandstone with limestone can be seen in the Sea Castle at Sidon, notably in the east gate and in the chapel.[11]

The tendency of the Franks to choose sites of ancient ruins on which to build their castles is frequently evident.[12] Indeed, it is exceptional to find a castle or other major building which does not incorporate the reuse of ancient building materials. Such *spolia* were used in the construction of Belvoir Castle. These pieces came from the ancient Jewish village of Kohava, located about 700 metres to the south of the castle. They included fragments from a synagogue, amongst them a basalt lintel with representations of the Ark of the Law and a seven-branched menorah (candelabrum). An example can be seen at the base of the entrance passage into the inner ward, where a piece of basalt carved with a vine-leaf pattern can be seen.

One common example of *spolia* is the use of antique columns to tie the core and facings of a wall together. This was a widespread technique in Frankish and contemporary Muslim architecture and can be seen extensively in the walls of Ascalon and Caesarea and the Sea Castle at Sidon.[13] The early phase of the castle of Bethgibelin was constructed using a large number of *spolia*, including seats from the adjacent Roman amphitheatre.[14] Here the large spaces left in the walls as a result of joining regular masonry to *spolia* of various shapes were filled with white lime impressed with a trowel to form a herringbone pattern.

Masons' marks

The use of masons' marks in Frankish building is well known (Figure 72).[15] These marks, which are common in all types of construction, were used as a means of paying the mason for his work. In Military Order work they are found in most castles, from the finer structures like Crac des Chevaliers and Chateau Pelerin through castles of the middle range like Vadum Jacob and Toron des Chevaliers and down to the smallest and simplest of all, such as the tiny keep at Maldoim on the pilgrims' road from Jerusalem to the Jordan Valley. Masons' marks are a valuable tool for the identification of a building as being of Frankish construction. In some cases they have an additional value, making it possible to determine whether a building was constructed in several stages or a single structural stage.

Property ownership and ownership marks

Property lists similar to those of the Genoese and Venetian communes in Acre and Tyre do not exist to enlighten us on the extent of the urban possessions held by the Military Orders. However, other types of documentary evidence, such as the numerous references to properties in the Hospitaller cartulary and the archives of the Teutonic Order, go a long way towards filling the gap, as does the evidence found in pilgrimage itineraries. There is also some archaeological evidence for the ownership of large public buildings in the form of inscriptions, heraldic devices and other remains.

Figure 72 Mason's mark (photograph by the author).

Do we have a means of identifying minor buildings for which there are no historical records as the property of one or other of the Military Orders? Property ownership marks may be one means of doing this. A number of marks have been found that may possibly have been ownership marks. Three types of incised marks have been recorded on buildings of Crusader date in Jerusalem. They all take the form of lapidary shields cut on the walls of buildings, usually at eye level. In the central market street of the Triple Market on the northern part of the ancient Cardo, on a building of twelfth-century date built by Queen Melisende, a large 'T' is incised on one of the shop fronts. On houses in Temple Street and in the Armenian Quarter are circles each containing an inverted 'T'. At the end of Temple Street in Bab al-Silsilah (Crusader Porta Speciosa) north of the Triple Market and on the southern extension of the eastern street on the Cardo south of David Street are marks in the form of isosceles triangles each containing an inverted 'T' (Figure 73).[16] The same mark was found in Acre.[17] Similar marks have been found elsewhere in contexts which relate them to the Military Orders. An isosceles triangle containing an inverted 'T' was found on a lead *jeton* from the Templar castle of Chateau Pelerin.[18] The same design was found in what were apparently masons' marks at another Templar castle (Beaufort) and in Templar Sidon.[19] This suggests that if indeed the larger marks are ownership marks they identify the buildings on which they appear as Templar property.[20] Michael Burgoyne suggests that these marks must have dated to after 1187 and before 1260. If they are indeed Templar marks, this would limit their dating to between 1229 and 1244, when the Crusaders held Jerusalem. At this time the Templars did not return to the Temple Mount, which according to the terms of the treaty of 1229 remained in Muslim hands, but they may have held other properties in Jerusalem. This dating is supported by the fact that the

Figure 73 Ownership mark of the Templars, Jerusalem (photograph by the author).

Figure 74 Possible mark of the Teutonic Order from Mi'iliya (photograph by Rabei Khamissy).

example of this mark on a building south of David Street mentioned above is on an outer wall of a covered bazaar which appears to have been built at that time.

If indeed these marks date to the thirteenth century it is possible that some of them belong to the Teutonic Order, which was present in Jerusalem in this period. We can perhaps assign to them the round marks. Such marks are found elsewhere in buildings belonging to them. In the village around the castle of Castellum Regis, which was in Teutonic hands from 1220, two such marks can still be seen. On the wall of one of the village houses is a stone, now in secondary use, on which a circle enclosing a 'T' is contained within a triangular shield (Figure 74). It is exceptional in the combination of the triangular shield and the circle and in the fact that it is carved in the stone rather than incised. In a field near Mi'iliya there is a rather coarse incised circle with a 'T' or a cross. It could possibly be a boundary stone.[21]

13

WEAPONS, ARMS AND ARMOUR

In 1926 the New York Metropolitan Museum of Art sent an expedition to Palestine with the aim of excavating suits of thirteenth-century armour to fill a gap in the museum's collection.[1] The Department of Antiquities of the British Mandatory government assigned them the Teutonic spur castle of Montfort. The archaeologists were, perhaps not surprisingly, to be disappointed in their hope of obtaining Crusader armour from an excavation. Their only finds of this nature were several lumps of rusted iron chain mail and some other fragments.[2] None the less, even these finds are not without significance. Other archaeological finds of arms and armour come from Chateau Pelerin and Vadum Jacob. This limited corpus is augmented by information from a number of written and illustrated sources, giving us an idea of the weapons and armour used by the brothers of the Military Orders (Figure 75). Amongst the most useful written sources in this regard are the Rules and Statutes of the two Military Orders.

Siege weapons

As siege machines were largely constructed from perishable materials, archaeology rarely provides information about them and we chiefly have to fall back on written sources. The surviving physical evidence is limited to constructions (platforms or openings) on castle or city walls and the missiles that they fired, such as stone mangonel balls and ceramic incendiary vessels containing the combustible Greek Fire, which are often found in excavations. Several mangonel balls have been recovered in excavations in the Hospitaller Quarter of Acre and are now displayed in the fortress grounds. These are cut from the local sandstone and average about 40 cm in diameter. The largest of these has a diameter of about 50 cm and weighs approximately 165 kg.[3] Additional mangonel balls are seen in the Protestant cemetery to the east of the walls of Turkish Akko, adjacent to the probable location of the Quarter of the Teutonic Order. At Arsuf over 600 mangonel balls were found during the excavations in the area of the castle.[4] These were made of the local sandstone and sometimes from other stone, including reused marble *spolia*. They are mostly very roughly shaped, have diameters ranging between 20 to 40 cm and weigh between 8 to 48 kg.[5] Several roughly shaped mangonel balls have been found at Montfort. They are of varying diameter, from *c.* 25 to 43 cm.

Figure 75 Knight of the Military Orders (designated as St George) from a medieval map of Jerusalem.

Arms

The Rule of the Temple includes a number of references to swords. The high regard for this weapon, the principal weapon of a knight, is reflected in the statute where the sword is listed amongst the basic equipment of a knight.[6] It is specifically mentioned as a piece of equipment which could not be given by the master as collateral for a loan.[7] Nor could it be risked in a wager by knights.[8] Damage or loss of a sword was a major offence; damage could be punished by the loss of the habit[9] or by expulsion.[10] A brother forced to leave the house could not take his sword with him.[11] Repair of a sword could only be carried out after the brother had received permission.[12]

In the waters off Chateau Pelerin two badly corroded swords of Crusader date were found by the underwater survey conducted in 1978 by Avraham Ronen and Yacov Olami.[13] One of these had a disc-shaped pommel and the hilt turns towards the blade in the fashion of Saxon swords. Another sword was found offshore at Dor (Merle).[14]

Various types of knives are referred to in the Rule of the Temple as another basic element in the equipment of a knight. Though not all of these are weapons, the dagger is specifically referred to.[15] Daggers were made in Antioch and England.[16]

Both longbows and crossbows are referred to in the Rule of the Temple.[17] They were used not only in warfare but also in lion hunting.[18] The bow, not a knightly weapon,

191

was not held in the same esteem as a sword. None the less, we read in the Rule of the Temple that the loss of a longbow could result in expulsion.[19] When not employed in the battlefield crossbows were used primarily for target practice.[20] Most parts of a bow were perishable, being made of wood, and consequently few remains of these extremely common weapons are preserved. However, the nut, a small part of the locking mechanism of the arbalest (crossbow), was made of bone and thus occasionally survives. In a small chamber at the east end of Montfort Castle below the keep (C on Dean's plan) a large number of arbalest nuts were found, suggesting, along with other finds, that this room may have been used as an armoury. The nut is a disc divided nearly in two with a semicircular piece cut out of it. Its task was to catch and hold the bow cord, releasing it by being turned.

The brothers of the Military Orders apparently used both Western and Eastern types of arrows, probably adopting the Eastern arrows when they came into their hands as spoils or booty (Figure 76). The socket-type arrowhead, popular in the medieval West, was round in section and slightly thicker than the shaft, becoming flatter and broad towards the end and then narrowing to a point. The tang-type arrowhead shaped like an elongated pyramid, square in section, had a narrow tang sometimes nearly as long as the head itself. Dean published examples of both of these arrowhead types from Montfort, as well as a large arbalest bolt head or javelin head which has a spine and two flat wings.[21] Johns published a spearhead from Chateau Pelerin and some Western socket-type and Eastern tang-type arrowheads from the stables of the faubourg.[22] The spearhead was c. 30 cm long, of the flat winged type with a central spine and a short socket. A smaller spearhead from Montfort was c. 10.5 cm long and squatter in shape with a proportionately much longer socket, nearly half its length.

However, the most extensive finds come from the Templar castle of Vadum Jacob.[23] The archaeological record left by the Ayyubid siege of Vadum Jacob and the subsequent abandonment of the castle includes a large number of weapon fragments,

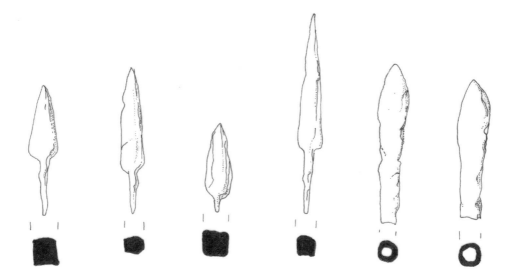

Figure 76 Arrowheads from Military Order sites.

some of them unique. Hundreds of arrowheads were found on all medieval surfaces at this site. They vary from short, squat arbalest heads and small darts to elongated arrowheads which were specifically used to kill horses. Arrow shafts, remarkable in having survived in the ruins of Montfort, were made of cypress wood and were painted in bands of pale blue and red.[24] Archers' finger guards, which protected the archer's fingers while he fired his bow, have been found at Chateau Pelerin and at Montfort.[25] These were of thin beaten copper decorated with rows of tiny impressions.[26]

Armour

Although the search for Crusader armour was the incentive for the excavations by the New York Metropolitan Museum at Montfort carried out in 1926, the finds from that site were very insubstantial. None the less there were some interesting and unique fragments. Amongst these were pieces of chain and scale armour and fragments of helmets, possibly including a pothelm. At Montfort fragments of two types of helmets, a possible part of the ventail of a pothelm (the only example found in the East to date[27]) and various fragments of a round helmet with a sloping rim were found. Two Templar knights illustrated riding a single horse on the Templar seal, appear to be wearing conical helmets with rims.[28]

Examples of scales, roughly square or round, with rounded corners and a single small hole, were found at Montfort.[29] The largest example is 8 cm long. According to Nicolle, these came from an early form of a jack or scale cuirass; he suggests that they are of Byzantine origin. Several corroded lumps of chain mail were found at Montfort in room C. They consisted of large rings (1.8 cm in diameter), round or nearly round in section, rather than flattened as is typical of Western chain mail.[30]

Part IV

ADDITIONAL ARCHAEOLOGICAL EVIDENCE

14

DAILY LIFE OF THE
MILITARY ORDERS

The unique relationship between the military and monastic aspects of the daily lives of members of Military Orders was reflected in their architecture. A castle or urban headquarters of the Military Orders possessed, in addition to its defensive components of curtain walls, towers and fortified gates, many of the regular components of a monastery such as chapels, communal refectories, dormitories and chapter houses. Within their castles the brothers combined the activities of warrior and monk. The Rules and Statutes of the two great Orders are most enlightening on this, as are the related archaeological finds. We have already looked at some of the architectural components typical of a house or castle of the Military Orders.[1] We will now re-examine these in conjunction with the information supplied by the written sources about living conditions, work, prayer, military training and duties of the brothers, and archaeological remains.

The conventual life of a brother living in a castle of one of the Military Orders was determined by monastic *regulae* or Rules. These compilations of regulations included the 'Primitive Rule' of the Templar Order, drawn up by the great supporter of the Templar cause, Bernard of Clairvaux, and the 'Rule of Raymond du Puy', drawn up by the second leader of the Hospitallers under whose rule they became a Military Order. The Rule of the Temple was influenced by the Benedictine and Cistercian Rules, and the Hospitaller Rule was inspired by the Augustinian Rule and also by that of the Cistercians, although to a lesser degree than was the Templar Rule.[2] Under these regulations the brother was expected to rise between two and three in the morning, make his way to the latrines and then to chapel to attend the first of the night offices. The remainder of the day was divided by the other monastic offices interspersed with lessons and prayer, meals, work, care of equipment and horses and military exercises and practice.

In establishments of the Military Orders, with the exception of very small castles, the living quarters and associated institutions, including the chapel and chapter house, the dormitory and latrines, the refectory and kitchens, would be located around the central courtyard or cloister. This arrangement, long established in Western monasteries, was the most convenient design for communal activities. In a castle it was also the safest layout, with the brothers being located in the inner ward protected by the outer defences. As was generally typical of the Middle Ages in all types of buildings, the domestic quarters were whenever possible located above ground-floor level.

At the table

For convenience, refectories were located near the brothers' dormitories and obviously near the kitchens.[3] Silence was strictly observed by the brothers during meals, when a clerk would read the holy lesson.[4] With some exceptions, all members of the convents were to receive the same food. According to the Hospitaller Statutes of Margat (1203–06):

> The food of the Convent should be in common, and the drink likewise. Neither Bailiff nor any other should have better food nor different than the others at the table of the Convent . . .[5]

The quality of the food served probably differed from convent to convent. A rather amusing clause in the Statutes of Margat states that:

> The food and drink should be sufficiently good, according to the ability of the House, so that the brethren can and should tolerate and endure it.[6]

The eating of meat was restricted because it was believed that 'eating flesh corrupts the body'.[7] Thus, meat was not eaten except at feast times, Christmas, All Saints, the Feast of the Assumption and the Feast of the Twelve Apostles. Livestock were raised in castle baileys and were kept in the cattle yards and piggeries in the city quarters. At Vadum Jacob, alongside horses which would not normally have been used for food, pig bones were prevalent amongst the faunal remains uncovered, together with some cattle bones. Finds from the Red Tower, which was held at times by both of the great Orders, are informative with regard to the preferences of the brothers.[8] Forty-nine out of a total of 53 pig-bone fragments (probably domestic pigs as they were all very young) came from phase C, the period following the Third Crusade when the castle was first in the hands of the Templars (up to 1248 and then held by the Hospitallers until the time of its destruction in *c.* 1265).[9] They form 86 per cent of the mammal bones of this phase, the remaining 14 per cent being of caprines (goats and sheep).[10] There were no finds of cattle bones in this phase, and Judith Cartledge suggests that this composition reflects the Templar dietary rules or preferences. This phase also contained a disproportionately large number of bird bones – 118 out of a total of 168. These were mainly domestic geese (50 per cent), the remainder being almost totally made up of other domestic fowl.

At Hospitaller Belmont Castle most of the bones were from caprines (37.9 per cent), followed by 34.8 per cent pig and 27.3 per cent cattle.[11] Here most of the fowl bones (1,457) were from chickens. There were few (only two) fragments of probably domestic geese, and several pigeons of various species and a partridge (possibly hunted).[12]

Some fish bones were also recovered, though they have not yet been studied.[13] Fish bones and crab shells have been found at Vadum Jacob (in the firing chamber of the bakery oven). Fish is mentioned in the Rule of the Temple as one item of food with which brothers were permitted to supplement what they received at meals. Rule 369 notes:

> And let it be known that the brothers should not search for any other food except what is given communally, except green vegetables from the fields, or

fish if they know how to catch them themselves, or wild animals if they know how to take them without hunting, in such a way that they do not transgress the commandments of the house.[14]

Possibly, poorly cooked fish in the Hospitaller compound in Acre resulted in some of the residents suffering from parasites.[15]

As regards vegetables and grains, the Templar Rule mentions lentils, broad beans, cabbage and green vegetables.[16] At the Red Tower, carbonised plant remains probably dating to the Hospitaller phase included broad beans, chick peas, lentils, grass peas, barley, wheat and olives.[17]

Grain collected from the Orders' rural possessions was stored in warehouses in the large urban centres before being sent off for use in the castles and smaller houses. The granary of the Hospital in Jerusalem is mentioned in the Statutes of Fr. Jobert,[18] and that of the Templars is referred to in various statutes.[19] The Templar granary, possibly at Acre or at Chateau Pelerin, had a nearby drying floor to be used when grain became damp during marine transport.[20]

As was the custom in the West and in the Crusader states, mills and ovens (bakeries) were monopolistic rights (*bannum*); this also applied to the urban and rural possessions of the Military Orders. As previously noted, the Hospitallers had mills on the Na'aman River (Flum d'Acre) at Recordane south of Acre, as well as the Molendina Trium Pontium and, further upstream, the Molendina desubter Mirabellum (al-Mirr) on the Yarqon River.[21] They seem to have had a windmill at Crac des Chevaliers.[22] The Templars had mills downstream from Recordane at Doc. Outside David's Gate in Jerusalem the Knights of St Lazarus set up a mill to serve their needs, which, however, obstructed traffic into the city and was considered a public nuisance until Queen Melisende had it removed in 1151.[23] The Teutonic Order had a mill house in the valley below Montfort.[24] In 1227/28 Bohemond IV Prince of Antioch and Count of Tripoli granted the Teutonic Order a mill near Antioch.[25]

The Hospitaller Rule refers to the provision of white bread for the poor and sick in the hospital.[26] Bread was probably baked in large ovens in every large and medium-sized castle and house.[27] The bakery was an important installation, necessary even before the completion of the castle to supply bread for the builders and defenders of the construction site. Thus we find a bread oven in use at Vadum Jacob during its construction. Although the castle was far from complete, the large workforce on the site had to be supplied with bread and, as noted, the presence of a layer of ash found within the oven shows that it was already in use. The Orders probably possessed bakeries in most of the towns as well.

The Hospitaller statutes specify the required weight of a loaf of bread as 2 marks, a measure generally applied in the West to gold and silver and being the equivalent of 8 ounces, though it varied considerably throughout the Middle Ages.[28] A loaf given to the poor was to be shared by two persons.

Tableware and eating utensils

Tableware consisted primarily of jugs and bowls (*escueles*), the latter far outnumbering other vessels. The Primitive Rule of the Temple refers to a shortage of bowls which necessitated the sharing of a bowl between two brothers.[29] This shortage in the early years of the twelfth century (the Rule postdates the Council of Troyes in 1129) would be unthinkable in the thirteenth century, when vast quantities of imported vessels were supplementing the locally manufactured wares. This perhaps throws light on the financial situation of the Templar Order in its first years, suggesting that the Templars found it difficult to supply themselves with even the most basic needs.

All the types of pottery, including locally manufactured storage and cooking vessels and local and imported tableware, are found in excavations of sites of the Military Orders (Figure 77). Large numbers of ceramics were found in excavations at Chateau Pelerin, though Johns published only a small selection of these.[30] The rich yield of pottery from the Hospitaller Quarter in Acre is one of the most extensive ceramic assemblages from a Military Order site. Reports on these finds are in preparation, but to date only a limited number of the finds have been published.[31] Alongside local wares, consisting of the usual storage, industrial and cooking vessels and oil lamps, all the finer types of imported tableware, including high-quality luxury wares, are present. While it is possible that some of these vessels were intended for trade, they are found in all of the sites belonging to the Hospitaller Order in Acre, including the section of the northern wall that they defended. It seems probable that there were no restrictions on the use of fine ceramic wares, despite the disapproval of luxury items expressed in the Rule.[32] However, many of these fine vessels which appear to us today to be luxury items may not have been considered as such in the Middle Ages. Indeed, such ceramics are found in many minor sites, including rural locations elsewhere in the Latin East.

Coarse undecorated ceramic vessels, probably mass-produced, including bowls which have been labelled 'Acre Bowls' in recent publications, have come to light in various sites of the Military Orders (Figure 78). Many examples were found in the excavations of the Hospitaller complex in Acre, and similar bowls were found in the excavation of the so-called 'Courthouse Site', north of the present town walls, at the site to the east of the Turkish walls which has been tentatively identified as the

Figure 77 Glazed imported ceramics from Acre (courtesy of Edna Stern, IAA).

Figure 78 Ceramic vessels used by the brothers or pilgrim inmates at the Hospitaller complex, Acre (courtesy of Edna Stern, IAA).

quarter of the Teutonic Order, and in the ruins of the sugar refinery at Manueth (Horbat Manot), north-east of Acre.[33] These are small hemispherical bowls with short ledge rims and string-cut bases. They are made of coarse local fabric with many gritty inclusions and have a whitish self-slip covering their entire surface. Kiln wasters have been found in the Hospitaller complex at Acre. Petrographic analysis has shown that they were manufactured both in Acre and in southern Lebanon.[34] Stern has offered the plausible explanation that these bowls were generally used by the sick and pilgrims residing in the Hospitaller complex when they ate in the soup kitchens.[35] It is equally possible that they were used by the brothers of the Order. She notes occasional traces of soot on these bowls and suggests that they may sometimes have been used as lamps.[36]

The Rule informs us that after meals the bowls were washed in the kitchen. This, together with peeling garlic, cutting chives and making a fire, was considered one of the basest tasks in the house and was sometimes imposed as a penance on brothers who had sinned.[37]

In use alongside ceramic vessels were vessels of glass. The Templar Rule mentions glass goblets and flasks.[38] Glass finds come from many Military Order sites, and a glass factory excavated at Somelaria (es-Samariya), adjacent to the Templar courtyard estate centre about 6 km north of Acre, was probably a Templar property. A brick furnace with two firing chambers, a glass melting tank and an adjacent work area were used to reprocess blue and greenish-blue glass, which was blown to form such vessels as the beakers commonly found in many Crusader sites. Beakers with prunted decoration (pronounced glass protrusions on the exterior of the vessel) have been found at Acre at the Courthouse Site and in the possible Quarter of the Teutonic Knights in the east of the city. The finds of this type of vessel at Somelaria point to a local source of manufacture for these vessels.[39] Glass finds have come to light at other Military Order sites. Items found at Montfort included fragments of stained glass, parts of a hanging lamp (the handles), bottles and phials and a prunted beaker.[40] At Chateau Pelerin glass finds included stained glass fragments from the parish church and bowls and flasks from the stables.[41] Other sites such as Belmont and the Red Tower have produced comparatively meagre finds.

Eating utensils are also mentioned in the Rules. According to the Rule of the Temple, each brother knight received a bread knife.[42] Knives have been found at several sites, including Vadum Jacob.[43] Each brother also received a spoon amongst his personal equipment.[44] At Montfort two wooden spoons have somehow been preserved. One of these survives to a length of 14 cm, its bowl being 5 cm long. These spoons had rat-tail-type handles.[45]

Sleeping quarters

The gates of frontier castles were closed after Compline when the monastic day ended and the brothers took to their beds. Dormitories are not easy to identify or to distinguish from other apartments in a castle, as they are today simply represented by large vaulted chambers which could easily have served some other purpose. The best that we can do is to attempt to identify them by location. We can assume that large halls connected to latrines, and located not far from the chapel (to which the brothers had to make their way without too much difficulty to attend the night offices) and the refectory, functioned as dormitories.[46] At Chastel Blanc the large groin-vaulted upper-floor hall has been identified as probably serving this function, but as there is no evidence for latrines this identification is uncertain at best. If however it did serve as the dormitory, the brothers would have descended to the chapel via the staircase built in the thickness of the wall at the south-west corner, the equivalent of the night stairs that led from the dormitory of a monastery directly into the church. At Belvoir the dormitory may have been located in the vaults to the north or south of the cloister/courtyard, adjacent to the chapel on the west. The knights' dormitory in thirteenth-century Acre was the *auberge*, located far from the main compound, in the suburb of Montmusard.[47]

Bathing and hygiene

It appears that in general the Military Orders frowned upon the practice of bathing, considering it a form of recreation rather than a necessity. This is suggested in the Customs (*usances*) of the Hospitallers, in which the baths are mentioned in conjunction with other places of recreation (*leuc desdure*).[48] Consequently we find in their Rules and Statutes attempts to curtail bathing. At the Teutonic Order the sick in the infirmary were allowed to bathe, but others had to obtain special permission from their superiors.[49] In a Hospitaller statute dating to shortly after the fall of Acre, it was quite simply stated that brothers should not go to the baths 'except of necessity'.[50] One can imagine that the necessity for bathing none the less arose fairly often when knights were in training or returning from the field. These restrictions on bathing were no doubt a reaction to the fact that it had become popular amongst the lay community in the Latin East to go to the bathhouse for recreational reasons.[51] Indeed, the custom of the Franks to bathe was the subject of harsh condemnation by Bishop James of Vitry, who referred to their tendencies towards orientalisation, noting that they were 'more used to baths than battles'.[52] The Hospitaller statute goes on to require that the brothers not go to the bathhouse without being accompanied by others and that they should not eat or sleep there.

None the less, as bathing was required on occasion, bathhouses were located in the urban centres as well as in some of the castles of the Military Orders. The Templars had bathhouses at Chateau Pelerin and in their quarters on the Temple Mount in Jerusalem,[53] and the Hospitallers had bathhouses at Belvoir castle and in their urban compounds at Jerusalem and Acre.[54] Considering the remains exposed by Johns at Chateau Pelerin, these bathhouses were similar in layout to the Eastern hammam, the principal room being the changing room which had benches around the walls and a central pool or tank. The bathing rooms were located in an adjacent row ending in the furnace.

Here, perhaps, shaving took place when necessary. Amongst the finds at Belvoir Castle were two iron razors with elongated tangs that would have attached the blades to wooden or bone handles.[55] In form they are not unlike traditional straight razors. At Montfort a well-preserved razor was recovered in the excavations of 1926.[56] The blade is 17 cm long with a maximum width of 3 cm.

Games and other forms of recreation

Various types of board games (Nine-Men's Morris, chess), as well as games of dice, were played by members of the Orders, despite the limitations or prohibitions in the Rules.[57] It appears that the brothers also on occasion read works which were not of a religious nature. Assuming that a rule forbidding a particular activity is evidence of a tendency towards that activity which requires regulation, a statute of the Hospitallers forbidding inmates of the infirmary to take advantage of their confinement by playing chess, reading romances and eating forbidden foods suggests that these were activities that sometimes took place and that the brothers occasionally saw the infirmary as a means of escape from the austerity and inconvenience of conventual life.[58]

A number of game boards and game pieces have been found in Military Order castles. Bone dice were found at Chateau Pelerin (Figure 79).[59] Game boards have been found at Vadum Jacob and at Arsuf. Some boards were found in places which suggest rather cunning attempts to hide this apparently illicit pastime; at Chateau Pelerin, for example, one board was scratched in the plaster surface of the roof of the stables.[60] One of two boards found in the kitchen of Belvoir Castle was incised into the underside of a large stone mortar which if necessary could easily be hidden by turning it over. However, on some occasions they appear to have been located in places where they could not be hidden from view. This may, for example, be the case at Bethgibelin, where a game board was scratched onto one of the pillars which had been cut lengthways and used as tables in the refectory.[61] This can only lead us to conclude that these games were not always frowned upon.

Cast lead or lead–tin alloy tokens or *jetons*, possibly also used in games, or alternatively a type of local currency of restricted use, have been found in Military Order

Figure 79 Bone dice from Chateau Pelerin (courtesy of IAA).

sites at Chateau Pelerin, Vadum Jacob and Belmont.[62] Of the three *jetons* from Chateau Pelerin published by Johns, one shows a Templar emblem, a shield containing an inverted 'T', another has a five-petalled flower on one side and a cross on the other, and the third has a rounded swastika on one side and a complex cross pattern on the other. At Vadum Jacob four of these *jetons* were found in excavations; these had on the obverse partial inscriptions surrounding a cross *patée* which proved to be the name of the castle: VADI: IACOB ('of(?) Jacob's Ford'). On the reverse they displayed a blazon-type shield surrounded by nine small anullets. At Belmont 436 tokens were recovered in a drain in the central courtyard, all with the same design: on one side the word PON with the N reversed and on the other a three-arched bridge with battlements and below it a fish. Like the other *jetons*, these are 190–200 mm in diameter, with a weight of *c.* 3.5 to 4 g. Another token found at Belmont had a cross with pellets in each angle on the obverse and the letter T on the reverse.

Seals and bullae

The right of using seals (i.e. of sealing documents) was, like the right of minting coins, restricted to the king and certain nobles, and the Assises de Jérusalem contained a list of baronies which held that right. Other than lords, royal officials and certain members of the Church hierarchy, this right was also held by the Masters of the Military Orders. The Templar seal displayed on the obverse a depiction of the Templum Domini (Dome of the Rock) with the inscription DE TEMPLO : CRISTI + and on the reverse the well-known design of a horse bearing two knights, symbolic of the poverty of the brothers, and the words SIGILLVM : MILITVM + (Figure 80).[63] It is not in fact a representation that should be taken literally: the Templar Rule forbade the sharing of a horse by two brothers.[64] The seal of the Order of the Hospitallers displayed a cross on the obverse with the inscription HOSPITALIS IHR[VSA]L[E]M + and the agnus dei

Seal of the Templar Order

Seal of the Jerusalem Hospital

Seal of the Teutonic Order

Seal of the Leper Knights

Seal of the Order of St Thomas
Guildhall Museum, London

Figure 80 Seals of the Military Orders (seal of the Order of St Thomas is courtesy of the National Archives, Kew).

(image of the divine lamb) on the reverse with the words SIGILLVM SIOHANNIS +.[65]
A thirteenth-century seal of the Teutonic Order in the Israel Museum in Jerusalem
shows the seated reading figure of Master Jacob de Laghini.[66] Others of the Order
show the Virgin and Child. A lead bulla of the Leper Order was found, probably in
Jerusalem, in the late nineteenth century and came into the hands of the Franciscan
Father Paul de S. Aignan, who gave a copy of it to Clermont-Ganneau for publication.[67] It displays on one side the figure of a bishop or a mitred abbot holding a crozier
in his left hand, his right hand raised in blessing. Around him is the inscription
S[ANCTI] LAZARI DE IERUSALEM +.[68] On the other side is a bust of a leper,
identified by the rattle held in his right hand and his disfigured face. His left hand
is placed inside his shirt and he appears to be wearing a sort of bonnet. The inscription
on this side reads SIGILLVM D.(OMUS)LEPROSORVM +.

Horse equipment: shoes, bridles, spurs and saddle fittings

An important component amongst the few possessions of the knight of the Military
Order was the equipment for their horses (Figure 81). Consequently it is discussed in
some detail in the Rules and is represented amongst the finds from archaeological
excavations of Military Order sites. The Rule of the Temple refers to bridles, stirrups
and spurs, specifically mentioning that these were to have no gold or silver on them.[69]
The Hospitaller Rule, equally opposed to embellishments, forbids gilding or silken
embroidery on saddles and peytrals (horse armour).[70] Turkish saddles could only be
used if covered with white or back leather.[71]

Two types of horseshoes are found in the Crusader period; the thick iron shoe with
an open form, well known in the West, and the closed Eastern type made of thin iron
plate with a small hole at the centre. According to Johns, those of the Western type

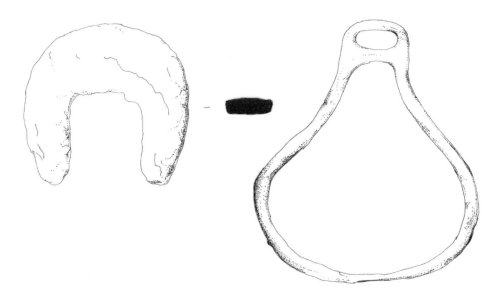

Figure 81 Examples of horse equipment from Military Order sites.

that were found at Chateau Pelerin were broader in the web and exceptionally long at the tips, possibly in order to bend them to give a better grip. Johns suggests that as these were comparatively small (13.3 by 12.5 cm maximum) they were probably for saddle horses (the *chevaucheheures* of the knights) rather than pack horses (*somiers*), although not for war horses.[72] Horseshoes of the open Western type have been found at several medieval sites, amongst these on a thirteenth-century floor at the possible site of the Teutonic headquarters at Acre in the 1291 destruction level[73] and in the forge and stables at Belvoir, where a number of examples were found as well as a well-preserved stirrup.[74] At Chateau Pelerin, Johns also recovered harness rings and buckles and what may have been a saddler's needle.[75] At Belmont an Eastern-type iron horse-shoe with a central hole was recovered from a possibly twelfth-century context.[76] It measures 11.5 by 8 cm (maximum). Eastern-type horseshoes have also been found at Abu Ghosh[77] and Chateau Pelerin.[78] These are iron plates with a slightly pointed oval shape, flattened at either end and with a small hole (*c.* 2 cm in diameter) in the centre.

15

WORKS OF ART IN URBAN
SITES AND CASTLES OF THE
MILITARY ORDERS

A large number of decorative works are found in or came from the urban centres and castles of the Military Orders. Several useful studies by art historians have dealt with them in considerable depth.[1] Though these are by and large examples of architectural sculpture, there are also a few examples of wall painting. In addition to these works, which may be considered examples of the fine arts, there survive a small number of items found in Military Order sites which fall into the category of minor objects but which are worthy of discussion in the context of a general study of this type.

Sculpture

Sculptural works, mainly decorative pieces from buildings, were carved in marble and limestone and occasionally in other types of stone in various workshops in the twelfth and thirteenth centuries. Buildings of the Military Orders have yielded no free-standing pieces sculptured in the round, like those of the Church of the Annunciation in Nazareth. The surviving pieces are by and large decorated with non-figurative foliate forms, primarily acanthus leaves. Many of the finest examples of these works come from buildings of the Military Orders, since the Orders more than any others had the ability to finance large-scale building projects and to employ the finest Western and local artists in decorating them.

Architectural sculpture possibly from the 'Templar Atelier' in Jerusalem

Of the many examples of sculptural work of the Latin East, the largest body of examples, including some of the finest pieces of sculptural work, may have originated in what has become known as the Templar Atelier, a workshop producing sculptural pieces mainly intended to decorate the buildings of the Templar Quarter constructed on the southern part of the Temple Mount in the twelfth century.[2] Works from this atelier include capitals, abaci, arch stones, panels, altars, pulpits and canopies which decorated the Templar buildings and other buildings in Jerusalem and elsewhere. The style that developed here is known as the 'Wet-Leaf Acanthus Style', the basic feature of which is 'a spiky, fleshy acanthus leaf of broad palmette-like shape; often twisted and convex, it sometimes curls inwards at the tips'.[3] Additional features include pine cones and rosettes formed by acanthus leaves.

There are a large number of frieze panels of similar design to friezes found on the exterior of Provençal churches like St Gilles. These were most likely intended for the external decoration of both new and existing buildings. The workshop not only produced decorative pieces but was directly involved in the actual construction of buildings, preparing architectural features such as portals. The presence amongst the works of many double and triple capitals point to the probability that it also supplied decorative pieces for cloisters, including no doubt the cloisters recorded by John of Würzburg and Theoderich in the Templar compound and possibly the cloisters of the Augustinian monastery north of the Templum Domini, mentioned by Muhammad al-Idrisi.[4]

Amongst the many examples of such work which survive on the Temple Mount are panels and capitals reused in the *Mihrab* of Zakariyya and the *dikka* (prayer platform) of the al-Aqsa Mosque. Above the *Mihrab* of Zakariyya is a panel which is tightly decorated with vine-scrolls of acanthus leaves, containing large flowers formed by curled acanthus leaves. The *dikka*, which is located in front of the *qibla*, is almost entirely constructed from Crusader *spolia* but so well placed that the work appears almost original; in the words of Folda, it consists of 'numerous fragments carefully joined to give the impression of wholeness'.[5] Clusters of slender columns and capitals at the corners and single columns and capitals at the midpoints support the platform, which is enclosed by a low balustrade carved with spiralling vine-scroll acanthus design. The capitals and abaci are similarly decorated with acanthus leaves. Interspersed in these pieces are occasional representations of humans, animals and birds. The design on the panel is less crowded than that on the *Mihrab* of Zakariyya and is more varied, with the scrolls spreading out on either side of a central stalk, each scroll containing a distinct flower.

On the upper platform of the Temple Mount, to the south of the Dome of the Rock, is the *Minbar* of Qadi Burhân which is largely made up of *spolia*, including acanthus panels and voussoirs. In the Dome of the Rock the Ibrahim *Mihrab* has a trefoil arch surrounded by panels decorated with two large flowers formed by radiating curled acanthus leaves. The arch of the *mihrab* is supported by two groups of twin braided columns supporting Corinthian capitals similar to the braided columns used on the Tomb of Baldwin V. A piece of similar design, but with two conchoid niches, was originally also located in the Dome of the Rock and is now located in the Islamic Museum on the Temple Mount.[6] A simple wheel window of six columns is located in the eastern wing of the al-Aqsa Mosque. It has a hexagonal centre supporting six small radiating columns with bases and capitals. The remaining space is occupied by six large teardrop-shaped spaces and small chevron and triangular spaces.

Outside the Temple Mount compound, opposite the principal western gate (Bab al-Silsilah), is a small, elaborately carved wheel window in secondary use in the tympanum of an Ottoman public fountain (the Sabil Bab al-Silsilah).[7] At its centre is a rosette formed by three concentric rows of curled acanthus leaves. Radiating out from this are 12 small columns supported on bases with diminutive Romanesque capitals supporting 12 arches (the bottom four are cut off to fit the tympanum). It is unclear in its present condition whether this was the entire window or only the centre of it. In the West such windows, of which only one other survives in the Kingdom of Jerusalem (that in the al-Aqsa Mosque), often carried additional rows of pillars and arches. It would most probably have originally been positioned above the main portal on the western façade of one of the churches in the vicinity.

There are additional possibly Templar *spolia* in another Ottoman fountain (Sabil Bab al-Nazir). The extrados of the archivolt of this fountain are decorated, the outer ones with tendrils carrying acanthus leaves and flower-heads and the inner one with rosettes formed by acanthus leaves. Elsewhere in Jerusalem there are collections of fragments of similar work. Amongst several fine pieces kept in a storeroom on the south side of the Church of the Holy Sepulchre is a panel with a double row of acanthus scrolls. In the Greek Orthodox Patriarchate museum in Jerusalem there is a marble corbel (21 cm high, 19 cm wide and 35 cm in diameter) displaying a haloed winged bull holding a book between its hooves. This is the symbol of St Luke. Jacoby notes that the realistic rendering of the bull and the flat tendrils on the sides of the piece are typical of the work of the 'Templar Atelier'.[8] Some pieces in the museum have been used to reconstruct the Tomb of Baldwin V, the most elaborate of the royal tombs that stood around the Chapel of Adam until they were dismantled and destroyed in the early nineteenth century. The pieces carved in greyish marble which were used in this reconstruction include foliated panels, a conchoid niche with a bird, heads, capitals and bases, braided columns and a foliated frieze decorated with leaves and cones.[9]

Another piece in the museum's collection, also possibly an example of the same workshop, is a fragment of a marble panel (30 cm high, 52 cm wide) bearing an acanthus scroll enclosing a scene of animals in combat. There are other acanthus-decorated panels, including a very fine piece with pointed arches and large single flowers. Several pieces found in the Church of the Holy Sepulchre are now located in the museum of the Studium Biblicum Franciscanum on the Via Dolorosa. Among other pieces that appear to be from the same atelier is a Corinthian capital from Bethany. It is of local limestone, measures 20 by 20 cm, and is decorated with small heads and spiky acanthus leaves. There are several pieces from friezes, abaci and panels with animals and human figures in acanthus scrolls.

The northern and southern portals leading to the crypt in the Church of the Nativity in Bethlehem are decorated with capitals from the same atelier. The tympanum of the south portal is decorated with shoots of acanthus leaves spreading from a point at the centre of the base and above rise three globe thistles. In design it is similar to a rectangular panel in the al-Aqsa Mosque, although the rendering of the leaves is rather flatter.[10] A similar design on a much smaller panel was found in secondary use near the cathedral of St George at Lydda.[11] A triple abacus and capital from Toron des Chevaliers, removed to Istanbul in 1917 and now located in the Archaeological Museum there, is a remarkably good example of the achievements of artists working in the East (Figure 82). Above the finely worked Romanesque Corinthian capitals, the abaci display heads, various animals and birds and acanthus leaves. This group must originally have been located in the chapel or one of the halls of the castle.

A marble fragment (44 cm wide) from Mount Tabor, probably part of a canopy surmounting an altar, depicts a gabled structure with two towers, one of which is now missing. The floral motifs on the gable clearly identify it as a product of the same workshop. It is now located in the Studium Biblicum Franciscanum museum in Jerusalem.[12] Another piece is an unfinished frieze in the Archaeological Museum at Tiberias.[13]

A recent sculptural find from the excavations of Saphet is a larger-than-life head of a bearded man carved in limestone (48 cm high) (Figure 83).[14] The head has a tonsure, a deeply lined forehead and straight hair with neat, round curls lining the face. The nose and the lower right side of the face have been destroyed.

Figure 82 Capitals from Toron des Chevaliers (photograph by Claudine Delacroix-Besnier).

Architectural sculpture from the Hospitaller Quarter in Acre

A large number of fragments of architectural sculpture, mostly of little interest, have been found in the excavations of the Hospitaller complex in Acre. Amongst them is a rather fine marble capital found at the site of the Church of St John the Baptist.[15] Other examples *in situ* include a sandstone console with three busts and a second console decorated with a double row of leaves, both badly worn, located in the remains of the interior of the west wing of the compound. The other well-known pieces found *in situ* are the two consoles carved with fleur-de-lis supporting ribs of the vaulting in the north-east and south-east corners of the refectory, found in excavations in 1954. Goldmann suggests that these were carved in honour of the visit of Louis VII in 1148 during the Second Crusade (1148), but there is no hard evidence for this. The symbol is a common one in the East,[16] and among Military Order sites appears in the thirteenth century at Montfort.[17]

Sculptural works from Hospitaller castles

On the south-eastern tower of the inner enceinte at Crac des Chevaliers are carvings of two large seated lions. This tower, which Deschamps assigned to the last stage of Frankish construction in the thirteenth century, is entirely constructed with marginally drafted ashlars with smooth bosses, a type of masonry not typical of this fortress.[18]

211

Figure 83 Sculpted head from Safed (photograph by Clara Amit, courtesy of IAA).

The lions are placed high on the western wall of the tower on either side above a pointed-arched portal. They are rather unsophisticated works; the ribs for example are incised in a crude manner and the manes are stylised and not at all realistic. None the less they are quite impressive heraldic monuments. The heads have not survived.

At Belvoir Castle a few surviving fragments of limestone sculpture came from the chapel on the first floor of the inner ward which Saladin destroyed in 1189, or alternatively from the chapter house or refectory. These include three figurative pieces. One is the larger-than-life head of a smiling youth, carved in marble-like limestone and bearing traces of paint. The second piece is a bearded head carved on an engaged capital. The third figurative piece is a representation of a rather disproportionate winged figure holding a book.[19] It was carved on a bevelled block of stone measuring 115 cm high, 58 cm wide and 31 cm deep.[20] It may represent an apocalyptic angel, or St Matthew as he appears in renditions of Christ in glory.[21] Each of these three pieces is carved on the light yellowish marble-like limestone of the region, though some of the non-figurative pieces from this site were carved in the local basalt. Jacoby suggests that the winged figure may have originated in the entrance porch of the chapel.[22]

Sculptural works from Teutonic castles

A limestone corbel carved with a helmeted head (14.5 cm high) was recovered from the excavations at Montfort. Dated to the mid-thirteenth century, its realistic rendition is in the French Gothic style typical of examples in Reims Cathedral (1225–41) and in the southern portal of Notre Dame de Paris (1260–65).[23] Non-figurative works from Montfort include a leaf-decorated limestone rosette measuring 49 cm high by 48 cm wide.

Sculptural works from Templar castles

Three fine but rather badly eroded corbels carved with heads are still to be seen in the rib-vaulted hall of the great northern tower of Chateau Pelerin. Two of these corbels bear single heads, one of which is bearded, while the central corbel bears three crowned heads.[24]

Frescoes and painted decoration

Fresco painting in the Crusader states is much more limited in quantity than sculptural works, and only three works of any importance and a handful of decorative fragments of minor artistic value can be assigned to the Military Orders. Thus a meaningful discussion of artistic sources and stylistic development is not possible. The most important discussion of the frescoes in the Kingdom of Jerusalem is that of Gustav Kühnel.[25] Of the four sites discussed by him, the recently restored frescoes in the Church of the Resurrection at Emmaus (Abu Ghosh) were carried out under Hospitaller patronage. Recent restorations of the surviving frescoes in the church have made it much easier to appreciate the quality of this group of works (Figure 84). These include renderings in the three apses of the Deësis (the falling asleep of Mary), the Anastasis (the descent to Limbo) and Paradise (represented as the Three Patriarchs with the souls of the just in their laps). On the south aisle wall is the Crucifixion and on the north aisle wall the Koimesis (the Dormition representing the death of the Virgin). The style and iconography of this work is Byzantine, the early 'dynamic' phase of the Comnenian style dated to around 1170 (the Deësis scene, for example, came into Western iconography only in the thirteenth century), although the inscriptions are in Latin.

The Deësis in the northern apse shows the enthroned Christ with his right hand raised in blessing, with Mary and John as intercessors for mankind on either side. Kühnel notes that the work differs from other renderings of the Deësis in the Kingdom of Jerusalem (Bethlehem, Queen Melisende's Psalter) in the inclusion of new motifs, suggesting that a different atelier produced this work.[26] The Anastasis scene in the central apse shows the figure of Christ with groups of figures, including Adam, Eve, Abel, Isaiah, David and Solomon. Another fragment, located lower down, represents a standing bishop and a row of standing saints. Many of these representations are now lost and their form is known only from the drawings made by A. de Piellat of 1901.

Figure 84 Fresco from church at Abu Ghosh (photograph by the author).

In the southern apse the Paradise scene shows the seated Abraham, Isaac and Jacob, Abraham in the centre, with the souls of the just in their laps represented as children. Angels on either side of Abraham hold additional children, captive souls about to be released. In the Koimesis scene on the north wall the apostles are on clouds and the death of Mary on Mount Zion is shown below; Jesus is behind her holding her soul. The Crucifixion on the south wall is badly preserved but still includes fragments of the figures, including Mary, John the Evangelist, the three women, a centurion, the spear and sponge-bearers, and the two thieves on their crosses. Above are two angels and on either side of Christ are the figures of Ecclesia and Synagoga. The walls and piers include additional representations such as icons of saints.

Fragments of fresco painting are located in the chapel of Crac des Chevaliers. Remnants of a fresco depicting the Presentation of Christ in the Temple are located on the exterior north wall of the chapel, and fragments showing the Virgin and Child enthroned (Hodegretria), St Pantaleon and St George mounted on a horse, rescuing the cup-bearing youth from Mitylene, are located in a separate external baptismal chapel near the castle gate. These works were carried out by various artists and display a marked Byzantine style. Folda notes that these works are better compared with twelfth-century frescoes in Maronite and Orthodox churches in Lebanon and Syria than with contemporary examples of fresco work in Bethlehem and Abu Ghosh.[27]

In 1979 fragmentary remains of frescoes were discovered in the apse of the chapel at Margat and more substantial remains of frescoes were found in the north-east sacristy adjacent to the apse.[28] The latter consists of a Pentecost scene with the 12 seated apostles (six on each side of the vault) and additional figures representing saints (possibly also numbering 12) on the north and south side walls below the vault. A badly damaged Nativity scene occupies the west wall; no recognisable remains can be made out on the east wall.

Some minor fragments of painted designs were recovered in Calver's excavations of Montfort Castle in 1926. These were polychrome painted vault ribs with designs including black and yellow stripes and a faded yellow fleur-de-lis. In a paper by Helmut Nickel they were restored as part of a heraldic device representing the arms of the Grand Master of the Teutonic Order. As restored it consisted of a large shield within which was a smaller shield with an eagle on the boss, out of which branched four arms on the four ribs attached to the boss, each ending in a fleur-de-lis design.[29] The fleur-de-lis design found is also incised on a leather mould from Montfort, together with another Teutonic heraldic device (Figure 85).

The reliquary of the Church of St John the Baptist

A remarkable mitre-shaped reliquary from the Hospitaller Church of St John the Baptist in Jerusalem has been described by Clermont-Ganneau, Vincent and Abel, Enlart, and recently by Folda (Figure 86).[30] The reliquary, originally located in the crypt of the Church of St John the Baptist in the Hospitaller Quarter and now in the museum of the Greek Orthodox Patriarchate, was probably commissioned for the church by a Hospitaller, possibly an Englishman.[31] Folda suggests that it is the work of local goldsmiths. The Syrian and Latin goldsmiths in Jerusalem to whom this work

Figure 85 Teutonic Order insignia on stone from Montfort (courtesy of IAA).

Figure 86 Reliquary from the Hospitaller Church of St John, Jerusalem.

may well be assigned were located around or perhaps even within the Hospitaller Quarter. Folda dates this reliquary to the 1150s.

The reliquary consists of two parts. A mitre-shaped piece of rock crystal bordered with gold sheets is encrusted with jewels and hollowed out to contain the second part, a wooden plaque, also encased in gold and jewels, with inscribed hollows on both sides. Those on one side are in the form of two crosses (a simple cross and below it a two-armed Cross of Lorraine, which probably contained fragments of the True Cross) and have rectangular openings for relics of St John the Baptist and St Peter. On the other side are 15 small niches which once contained various other tiny relics.

CONCLUSION

After the expulsion of the Crusaders from the Holy Land in 1291, the castles, urban centres and other possessions of the Military Orders shared the fate of most other Crusader buildings, being destroyed or badly damaged by the Mamluks. The subsequent 800 years of neglect, earthquakes, stone robbing and the expansion of modern settlements over the past century have left a very uneven record of the architectural achievements of the Military Orders in the Frankish East. It not always clear why some buildings have fared so much better than others. It is, for instance, perhaps a quirk of history that the castles and urban headquarters of the Templar Order have suffered much more than the buildings of the Hospitallers and, in some cases, like the Templar Order itself, have entirely disappeared. The Templar headquarters in Jerusalem was almost completely dismantled by Saladin after he occupied the city in 1187. Of all the extensive construction work carried out around the al-Aqsa Mosque, only fragments and a large quantity of *spolia* survive. The Templar palace in Acre, one of the greatest buildings in that city, was entirely dismantled by 1752. Only in the town of Tortosa do fairly substantial Templar remains survive. Nothing is known of the Templar houses and castles in Tripoli, Giblet, Tyre, Caifas, Gaza and Jaffa. In addition, although remains of several Templar castles survive, the number of substantial ruins is small in comparison to those of the Hospitallers. The castle of Chateau Pelerin is an exception. Having remained intact till the very end of the Frankish presence in the kingdom, it was damaged by earthquakes and used as a quarry for the building of Turkish Akko in the seventeenth and eighteenth centuries. However, fairly extensive remains still exist and have been exposed and recorded by archaeological work carried out in the 1930s. The tower of Chastel Blanc also survives in comparatively good condition, although little can be seen of its once considerable outworks which are built over by the modern town. Gaston (Baghras), guarding the eastern approach to the Belen Pass north of Antioch, is comparatively well preserved. But other Templar castles have almost entirely vanished. La Fève has vanished under trees and houses of Kibbutz Merhavia and, were it not for an early aerial photograph taken of the site before reforestation and building, we would have no idea at all of the appearance of this castle.[1] The current excavations of the thirteenth-century castle of Saphet have so far revealed mainly the Mamluk additions; this great fortress seems to have almost vanished, once again the result of stone robbing and earthquakes. Similarly little survives above ground level of the once large Templar castle at Toron des Chevaliers.

The Hospitaller houses and castles have survived somewhat better. The extensive remains of the Hospitaller headquarters in Acre have been exposed by excavations carried out over the past decade and, although little can be seen today of the headquarters in Jerusalem, enough of it survived into the early twentieth century to allow a detailed survey to be carried out. Two major Syrian castles, Margat and the great castle of Crac des Chevaliers, remain in remarkably good condition. Excavations have uncovered the important castles of Belvoir, Saranda Kolones, Belmont and Bethgibelin. Others like Chastel Rouge, Coliath and the large castle of Silifke in Cilician Armenia, to name only a few, await archaeological investigation.

Two centuries of archaeological research have barely scratched the surface of this field of study. In all likelihood future excavations and surveys will require a new analysis of the architecture of the Military Orders, and it is likely that questions with which we cannot deal today because of a lack of archaeological evidence may be more easily dealt with in the future. Such questions might include the extent of the influence of the Armenian and Byzantine castles on the military architecture of the Hospitallers, the distinction (if one actually existed) between the architecture of the Hospitallers and that of the Templars, and the evidence for an influence of German fortifications on the castles built in the East by the Teutonic Order. Increased archaeological research could greatly change the picture that we have at present. It is enough to look at the plans made for castles like Chateau Pelerin and Belvoir before their excavation to realise how very greatly a site can differ from a conception based only on the surface evidence. The potential for expanding our knowledge is great. For instance, the ongoing examination of the Hospitaller Quarter in Acre is constantly providing new information on the nature of that compound and consequently of Hospitaller conventual life. The remains of the Hospitaller church have only recently been uncovered, and a vaulted building which may have served as the *domus infirmorum* still awaits examination. Many important castles have never been excavated at all and others have only been superficially examined.

This survey has covered the two centuries during which the Military Orders were invented, established and evolved into prosperous and important institutions, vital to the survival of the Crusader states. Although these two centuries were the Golden Age of the Orders, the idea of the Military Order did not die with the Crusader states. In the second half of the thirteenth century the Crusader states were in an advanced state of disintegration which accelerated with the Mamluk invasions and conquests of Baybars and his followers, culminating in the fall of Acre in May 1291. The last Franks to depart the Crusader mainland left from two Templar strongholds: the castle of Chateau Pelerin was evacuated in August 1291 and the small island of Arwad off the coast near Tartus, also a Templar stronghold, held out for another decade, though this was no more than a swan song. The Templar Order was soon to be dissolved. Following the Templar Trial of 1307 and the abolition of the Order in 1312, their vast wealth passed to the Hospitallers. The other Orders fared better but were obliged to replace their lost holdings in the Holy Land. The Hospitallers occupied Rhodes from 1306 to 1309 and later, after the Ottoman conquest of the island in 1523, moved to Malta (1530). The Teutonic Order retained possessions in Apulia, Sicily, Germany and briefly in Hungary, and in 1309 moved its central headquarters from Venice to Marienburg in northern Poland, where in Prussia and Livonia it fulfilled the long-cherished territorial aspiration of the establishment of a Teutonic state. In 1410 the Teutonic army suffered a major defeat at the hands of the Poles and their allies at Tannenberg, and they were expelled from Poland by 1525. By the mid-sixteenth century, of the five Military Orders only the Hospitallers, now known as the Order of Malta, retained a genuine military role. The Teutonic Order continued some minor military functions but by 1699 numbered only 94 knights. Today, it has evolved into the Deutscher Orden, an organisation which carries out social work amongst poor communities in various parts of the world.

Appendix I

CHRONOLOGY OF CASTLES

Order		Commencement of date(s) of possession
Hospitaller		
1	Arsuf	1261
2	Belmont	mid-12th century
3	Belveer (Qastel)	by 1168
4	Belvoir	1168
5	Bethasaphace (Bait Safafa)	by 1110
6	Bethgibelin	1136 (restored to Hosp. in 1240)
7	Bethsura	1136
8	Caferlet	1213
9	Calansue (Qalansuwa)	1128
10	Camardesium	1210
11	Castellum Beleismum	12th century
12	Castellum Bochee	1144
13	Castellum Novum	1210
14	Chastel Rouge	1177–78
15	Cola (Qula)	1181
16	Coliath	1127
17	Crac des Chevaliers	1142, 1169–70, 1202
18	Exerc (Eixserc)	1163
19	Felicium	1144
20	Forbelet	poss. 1168
21	Gibelcar	1170 (restored to Hosp. in 1192)
22	Govasse	1233
23	Jabala	by 1188
24	Karak de Moab	1152
25	Khirokitia	?
26	Kolossi	by 1210 (present donjon – 1450)
27	Lacum	1144
28	Manueth (Le Manuet)	1212 (restored to Hosp. in 1270)
29	Mardabech	1144
30	Margat (Marqab)	1186
31	Silifke	1210–26 (completely rebuilt)
32	Mount Tabor	1255
33	Tour Rouge	1248
34	La Tor de l'Ospital	mid-12th century
35	Tuban	1180
36	Turris Salinarum (Burj al-Malih)	by 1168 (confirmed 1182)
37	Varan	1214

Templar

1	Alexandretta	1155
2	Arima	13th century
3	Aradus	?
4	Bait Jubr at-Tahtani	by 1169/72
5	Beaufort	from 1260
6	Caco (Qaqun)	prob. Templar by 1169/72, certainly before 1187
7	Cafarlet	Templar by 1255
8	Caifes (St Margaret's Castle)	by 1169
9	Casel des Pleins	by 1191
10	Castellum Arnaldi	by 1179
11	Caymont	by 1262
12	Chastel Blanc	by 1152 (restored to Templars after 1202)
13	Chateau Pelerin	1217–18
14	Coliath	by 1243
15	Districtum (Le Destroit)	12th century until 1218–20
16	Doc/Docum (Tell Da'uk)	13th century
17	Docus (Castellum Abrahami)	by 1169
18	Famagusta	?
19	La Fève	by 1172
20	Gastria	by 1210
21	Gaston (Baghras)	1137 or 1153 (refortified by the Templars 1156)
22	Gaza (Gadres)	c. 1149/50 (restored to Templars in 1191)
23	Giblet	?
24	Iezrael (Jezreel)	by 1180s until 1187
25	Maldoim	by 1169
26	Merle	by 1187
27	Port Bonnel	c. 1137
28	Jordan River (Place of Baptism)	by 1169
29	La Roche Guillaume	c. 1137?
30	La Roche de Roissol	c. 1137?
31	Le Saffran	by 1172
32	Saphet	1168 (restored to Templars, c. 1240)
33	Sari Seki	early 12th century, 1154–1266
34	Sidon (Sea Castle)	acquired 1260
35	Toron des Chevaliers	possibly between 1137 and 1141, between 1150 and 1170
36	Tortosa	c. 1152–58
37	Tour Rouge	12th century
38	Trapesac	probably c. 1137
39	Tyre	12th century
40	Vadum Jacob	1178–79

Teutonic

1	Amuda	1211
2	Casale Imbert	1256
3	Castellum Novum Regis	1220
4	Cave of Tyron	1257
5	Cumbethfort	from 1209
6	Harunia	1236
7	Jaffa	after 1206
8	Judin	after 1220
9	Manueth (Le Manuet)	1270
10	Montfort	1227–29
11	Raheb	1220
12	Tarphile	1227–29

Appendix II

GAZETTEER OF SITES OF THE MILITARY ORDERS

The following catalogue includes urban and rural settlements and castles of the Military Orders of known location for which there are archaeological remains. Regarding the site names, I have given the Frankish name where known, otherwise the most commonly used site name. The historical summaries relate only to the Crusader period, the lists of excavations and surveys and site descriptions are restricted to buildings of the Military Order rather than general descriptions of the sites, and bibliographical references are limited to the principal descriptions of Military Order buildings. Grid references for sites in Israel and some sites in Lebanon are given according to the Israel (Palestine) grid (IG). Otherwise the geographical coordinates system (GCS) has been used.

1 Acre (Akko/Akka) (IG map ref. 1568E–2586N)

Location. Port town located on the coast in the northern extension of Haifa Bay.

History in the Crusader period. Acre was captured by the Crusader army aided by the Genoese fleet in 1104. After their establishment in Jerusalem, the Templars and the Hospitallers established quarters in Acre, as possibly did the Order of St Lazarus. Following the fall of Jerusalem in 1187 and the reoccupation of Acre in 1191, this coastal port city became the administrative capital of the kingdom and consequently the location of the principal headquarters of all of the Military Orders. The Order of the Teutonic Knights had its beginnings in Acre at the end of the twelfth century, beginning as a German hospital, which was established in Acre during the Third Crusade, and by 1198 becoming a fully fledged Military Order. The Order of St Thomas, a house of regular canons which was founded in Acre, had by the late 1220s also developed into a Military Order. These Orders were present in Acre until its fall in May 1291.

Excavations and surveys. During the British Mandate of Palestine a survey of the historical buildings and archaeological sites of Acre was carried out and published as the Winter Report. Small-scale archaeological excavations in the Hospitallers' Quarter directed by Z. Yeivin and Z. Goldmann were carried out in the 1950s. These exposed and subsequently cleared the refectory (then known as the 'Crypt'). A short discussion of the complex was published by Goldmann. Since 1990 large-scale excavations of the entire Hospitaller complex and of the so-called 'Templar Tunnel' have been carried out by the IAA under the direction of archaeologist Eliezer Stern.

The Templars' Quarter. The Templars' Quarter was located in the south-west of the city. The Templars acquired the palace of al-Afdal, the Fatimid governor, in the south-west of the town and subsequently built their palace and conventual buildings on that site. Saladin occupied the palace after he captured Acre in 1187, but with the recovery of the city by the Third Crusade in 1192 the Templars regained their Quarter and held it until the Mamluk conquest in 1291. Due to the extensive destruction of the late thirteenth, eighteenth and nineteenth centuries, as well as a subsequent rise in the sea level, the fragmentary remnants of these buildings are at present submerged off the western shore. A recently discovered subterranean vaulted passage connected the quarter to the port.

The Hospitallers' Quarter. The Hospitaller Quarter was located against the northern wall of the city prior to its expansion further north in the second half of the twelfth century. Ongoing excavations over the past decade have exposed almost the entire complex, which consisted of several large buildings, including the palace, stores, the refectory, a communal latrine and its sewage system, and remains of the Church of St John the Baptist. Various structures, including the possible remains of the hospital to the south, have not yet been excavated.

The Quarter of the Teutonic Knights. The Quarter of the Teutonic Knights was located in the east of the city. Its location outside the area enclosed by the Turkish walls resulted in all surface remains being removed at the time of the latter's construction.

The Quarters of the Leper Knights of St Lazarus and of the Order of St Thomas Becket. The Quarter of the Leper Knights of St Lazarus, originally located well beyond the northern wall of the city, came within the city walls as it expanded in the late twelfth and early thirteenth centuries. The Quarter of the English Order of St Thomas Becket was located near the Quarter of St Lazarus in the northern part of Montmusard. No definite remains of either of these quarters have yet been uncovered.

Bibliography. Benvenisti, 1970, pp. 84, 87, 89, 91, 92, 93, 95, 104–113; Boas and Melloni, forthcoming; Goldmann, 1962a, 1962b, 1967, 1974, 1987, 1993, Hartal, 1997, Pringle, 1993, p. 111; 1997a, 15–17; Shavit and Galili, 2002; E. Stern, 2000; Stern and Avissar, 1994, 1996; Winter, 1944.

2 Amuda (GCS map ref. 3605E–3714N)

Location. This small castle is located on a low (80 metres high) hill on the western flank of the northern extension of the Amanas mountain range.

History in the Crusader period. The hill was probably fortified prior to the mid-twelfth century, but nothing is known of its history prior to sometime between 1146 and 1148 when it was occupied by Thorus II. In 1212, during a visit of the Grand Master of the Teutonic Order, Herman von Salza, it was granted to the Order by Levon I. The castle may have been abandoned when Baybars took the surrounding region in 1266, and it was certainly in Mamluk hands by the end of the century.

Excavations and surveys. A survey was carried out by R. Edwards in 1973 and 1981.

Description. This is a castle on a small hill with a curtain wall, a ramp, gatehouse, various ruined vaults (one possibly a chapel), and a keep. The four-storey keep has an underground cistern which was fed by rainwater via pipes in the thickness of the wall. Above the door is a box machicolation.

Bibliography. Edwards, 1987, pp. 58–62, pls. 3–5.

3 Aqua Bella (Ain Hemed/Dayr al-Banat/Khirbat ʾIqbala) (IG map ref. 1621E–1337W)

Location. This courtyard building is situated on the Tel Aviv–Jerusalem road in Hospitaller lands opposite Abu Ghosh. This is a fertile, well-watered area, under intensive agriculture and densely settled in the twelfth century.

History in the Crusader period. A reference to this site dating to between 1163 and 1169 records that its income was temporarily offered to the Hungarian Duke Bella, who planned to come to the Holy Land, in exchange for 10,000 bezants (*Cart. des Hosp.*, no. 309). This arrangement fell through and Aqua Bella fell to Saladin in September 1187. It is not known whether the Hospitallers reoccupied the site when the area was restored to the Franks between 1229 and 1244.

Excavations and surveys. The ruin known as Dayr al-Banat has been examined several times in the nineteenth and twentieth centuries by Guérin, C.R. Conder and H.H. Kitchener, E. Hoade, C. Enlart, M. Benvenisti, and most recently by D. Pringle. No excavations are recorded, although some clearance work and restoration has been carried out by the INPA (no date recorded). Pringle (BSAJ) surveyed the building (1979, 1982, 1984, 1986) and published the most detailed account of it to date.

Description. This is a well-preserved and somewhat exceptional example of a Frankish rural estate centre. It consists of a rectangular, two-storey courtyard building constructed into the side of a hill. The ground-floor level has large barrel vaults on three sides, one containing an olive press. The east side is closed with a wall in which there is a gate. A staircase in the courtyard leads to the first-floor level. A second entrance to the upper level is via a turret chamber on the west. The south range of the upper storey is a hall of three groin-vaulted bays, including a small chapel on the east. Pringle suggests that this building was perhaps a *maison forte* converted after the Hospitallers acquired it (*c.* 1140) into an infirmary. In the north-west corner of the building is a small tower from which the nearby Hospitaller fortress of Belmont could have been seen.

Bibliography. Benvenisti, 1970, pp. 19, 229, 233, 236, 241–44, 257, 258, 349; Boas, 1999, p. 74; Clermont-Ganneau, 1896, vol. I, p. 57; Enlart, vol. II, 1928, pp. 103–06, pl. 78; Guérin, 1868, vol. I, pp. 278–79; Pringle, 1992; 1993, pp. 239–50; *SWP*, vol. III, 1883, pp. 114–15.

4 Arima (al-Ariymah) (GCS map ref. 3606E–3474N)

Location. This castle occupies a steep isolated ridge overlooking the entrance to Nahr Abras in the County of Tripoli.

History in the Crusader period. Held by Bertrand of Toulouse in 1148 when he attempted to oust Count Raymond II of Tripoli; with Raymond's compliance it was taken by Nur al-Din who then dismantled it. The castle appears to have been rebuilt and in 1167 it was again taken by Nur al-Din and dismantled. It was damaged by earthquake in 1170, and additional sacking in 1171 suggests that it had again been rebuilt. Arima was acquired by the Templars possibly by 1177 or in the thirteenth century. Almost nothing is known of its subsequent history, but it was apparently held by the Templars until 1291.

Excavations and surveys. No excavations have been carried out. Surveys resulting in very different plans were carried out by T.E. Lawrence, P. Deschamps and H. Müller-Wiener. Müller-Wiener's plan is only of the eastern ward (and the orientation is erroneous).

Description. This complex consists of three enclosures extending one next to the other from west to east along a plateau 171 metres above sea level. The length of the complex is *c.* 300 metres and the maximum width 80 metres. Moats separated the wards. Of the three wards, less is visible of the westernmost and central fortifications. Lawrence shows the western ward as horn-work and considered all but the eastern, inner ward to be mostly Byzantine work and not very effective: 'One might wish only for some curtain towers in an attack. Parts of the wall are a little bare against unexpected escalade, above all as they are mostly of very poor height. The horn-work too is not intended seriously' (Lawrence, 1988, p. 73). However, a well-constructed tower can be seen at the north-west corner of the central ward. It has a batter on its north and west sides. The eastern enclosure is certainly the best preserved. It is a regular quadrangular enclosure castle design with projecting corner towers in the south-east and south-west and possibly on the north-east. It has a gate in the western wall, to the south of which is a massive keep (12.5 by 11 metres). There are barrel-vaulted halls on the north, south and east. The south-west corner tower of the castle has a talus, as does an additional tower on the north-east which commands the entrance to the complex.

Bibliography. Deschamps, 1973, pp. 313–16; Kennedy, 1994, pp. 68–73, 138, 141, fig. 8, pls. 25–26; Müller-Wiener, 1966, pp. 53, 98, pls. 42–43.

5 Arsuf/Arsur/Apollonia (IG map ref. 1329E–1781N)

Location. Coastal town between Caesarea and Jaffa about 17 km north of Jaffa within the modern town of Herzliyya.

History in the Crusader Period. This ancient settlement was a small fortified fishing port when it was captured by Baldwin I in 1101. It fell to Saladin in 1187 and was recaptured by the Franks following the Battle of Arsuf in 1191. In 1261 it was sold to the Hospitallers, but four years later in 1265 it fell to Baybars and was subsequently demolished.

Excavations and surveys. Soundings were carried out by I. Roll and E. Ayalon of Tel Aviv University in 1977 and 1981, excavations by Roll in the city and fortress since 1982.

Description. Excavations have exposed parts of the walls and moat of the town, including the east gate, and have concentrated in the castle which is located in the north-west above the small harbour. How much of these defensive works date to the few years of Hospitaller occupation is uncertain. The castle is separated from the town by its own moat. It has a barrel-vaulted gatehouse, set between two D-shaped towers in the south-east, which was reached by a drawbridge across the moat. The northern of these towers, of apsidal form and facing due east, may have contained the castle chapel on the upper storey. On the west of the courtyard is a polygonal donjon. To its south a broad staircase gave access to an upper level which has not survived. North of the donjon was the kitchen.

Bibliography. Benvenisti, 1970, pp. 130–35; Pringle, 1993, pp. 59–61; 1997a, pp. 20–21; Roll, 1996; Roll and Ayalon, 1982, 1989, 1993; Roll and Tal, 1999; *SWP*, vol. II, 1882, pp. 135, 137–40.

6 Aradus/Ruad (Arwad) (GCS map ref. 3552E–3450N)

Location. Aradus, modern Arwad, is a small island 2.5 km off the coast of Syria to the south of Tortosa (Tartus).

History in the Crusader period. Held by the Templars, Aradus was the site of the last stand of the Crusaders in Syria. The attraction of establishing a long-term base on this island after the loss of the mainland was offset by its small size and the disadvantage of its proximity to the Mamluk-occupied mainland. In any case, in October 1302 or 1303, more than a decade after the fall of the mainland, the island was taken, the Frankish occupants were slaughtered, and the Templar knights were taken into captivity.

Excavations and surveys. No published studies.

Description. There are only fragmentary remains of the Templar castle located on the centre of the island. Above the gate can be seen the coat of arms of the Lusignan family.

Bibliography. Burns, 1992, pp. 51–52; Hanna, 1994, pp. 19–26; Jacquot, 1929, pp. 89–96.

7 Ascalon (IG map ref. 1071E–1191N)

Location. Coastal town 20 km north of Gaza.

History in the Crusader period. The town of Ascalon was the last of the coastal cities to come into Crusader hands, remaining a Fatimid enclave within Frankish territory for the entire first half of the twelfth century. Because of its proximity to Fatimid territory and its strong defences, which included massive walls constructed on a Middle Bronze Age ramp several metres high, the Franks were unable to occupy the city until 1153, decades after they had gained possession of the entire region and all the other fortified towns. Saladin occupied the town in September 1187, and in 1191 he dismantled its defences and destroyed the buildings. Ascalon was reoccupied and refortified by the Crusaders in 1192, but later in the same year was again dismantled and abandoned following an agreement between Richard I and Saladin. In 1239 it was reoccupied by the Crusaders and in 1247 fell again to the Egyptians. However, it came into Hospitaller possession between 1261 and 1265 before it was finally destroyed by Baybars in 1270.

Excavations and surveys. Excavations have been carried out over the years but have exposed little that relates to the Middle Ages or the brief period of Frankish rule in the town.

Description. At present the limited evidence of a Frankish presence in Ascalon comprises primarily the ruins of three churches and of the town's fortifications, not all of which are of Crusader origin. There is nothing which can be specifically identified as work of the Military Orders, although one of the town's towers may have been known as the Turris Hospitalis (Beha ad-Din, 1897, p. 299). Although Benvenisti has suggested that it was located together with the Maidens' Tower (Turris Puellarum) in the south (Benvenisti, 1970, p. 125), Beha ad-Din describes it as 'a building that commanded the sea and was as strong as a castle' and refers to its destruction by fire taking 'two days and two nights'. This suggests that it was possibly a fortress rather than a mural tower. Another record of the presence of the Military Orders in Ascalon is the tombstone of the Templar marshal, Hugh de Quiliugo. Now in the Ustinow Collection in Oslo, its inscription records that the marshal had been killed by being struck by a mangonel stone (de Sandoli, 1974, p. 256–57).

Bibliography. Benvenisti, 1970, pp.114–30; Pringle, 1993, pp. 61–69; 1997a, p. 21; Rey, 1871, pp. 205–10, fig. 52, pl. XIX; *SWP*, vol. III, 1883, pp. 237–48.

8 Bait Jubr at-Tahtani (IG map ref. 1905E–1396N)

Location. This tower is located on the road from Jerusalem to the Jordan River on a rocky protuberance not far from Cisterna Rubea, 6.5 km further east.

History in the Crusader period. Nothing is known of the history of this castle, but it was probably similar to that of Cisterna Rubea (see pp. 237–8).

Excavations and surveys. A survey was carried out by D. Pringle (BSAJ) in 1988/89.

Description. This small tower measuring 9.5 by 6.6–8.1 metres was constructed on a scarped rock spur. The barrel-vaulted ground floor survives. The door is to the east, and on the south, in an arched recess, is a staircase which originally led to the first-floor level. Although there is no direct evidence for Templar ownership, Pringle notes that the probable identity is supported by the similarity of this castle to nearby Templar Maldoim (Cisterna Rubea/Qal'at ad-Damm) and to its similar location on the pilgrim road from Jerusalem to the Jordan River (Pringle, 1994b, p. 165).

Bibliography. Benvenisti, 1970, p. 325; Pringle, 1993, pp. 101–102; 1994b; 1997a, p. 27.

9 Beaufort/Belfort/Belliforte (Qal'at al-Shaqif Arnun) (IG map ref. 1999E–3032N)

Location. Beaufort Castle is located 300 metres above the Litani River on the narrow rocky shoulder of a hill with a steep drop to the east. To the west the slope is steep for a short distance and then there is a gentler slope towards the village of Arnun. On the ridge to the south is an artificially levelled area where the faubourg of Beaufort was probably located.

History in the Crusader period. A small Muslim fort on this site came into Frankish hands in 1139, when King Fulk granted it to the feudal lord of Sidon. The fort was subsequently enhanced by the construction of a tower and outer wall. Beaufort withstood Muslim attacks after the Battle of Hattin and was strengthened by the Franks, but finally fell in 1190. The Ayyubids added a polygonal hall in the north and a large round tower in the south-west. The treaty between Richard of Cornwall and Sultan Salih Isma'il of Damascus in 1240 returned the castle to the Franks and it was again in the hands of the lords of Sidon, who enhanced it with additional building including a chapel in the upper fortress. In 1260 it was sold by Julien de Sagette to the Templars. They augmented the fortifications, building the outworks to the south. However, in 1268 Beaufort fell to Baybars, who destroyed the Templar outworks. The castle was later strengthened by the Mamluks and by Amir Fakr ad-Din in the seventeenth century.

Excavations and surveys. Beaufort was surveyed by V. Guérin (1880), C.R. Conder and H.H. Kitchener for the SWP (1881), C. Enlart (1925) and P. Deschamps (1934).

Description. The roughly triangular castle covers an area of *c.* 150 by 100 metres. An inner ward occupies the higher part of the ridge, with a lower fortress to the east. A massive square keep (*c.* 12 metres square) is located on the west side of the inner ward, entered from the east and with a staircase from the entrance running up within the wall to the upper level. There are two arrow-slit embrasures on the west wall, which is the external wall of the castle. A rock-cut ditch severs the castle from the ridge where the topography is gentler, to the north, west and south. The outer gate was on the south-east. It gave onto the outer bailey protected on the south by two round towers, a stone talus and rock-cut ditch opposite the faubourg. Within the outer bailey it was necessary to follow a passage adjacent to the outer wall, bending first to the south, then west and finally north towards an inner gate on the inner fortification line. This gave access via a vaulted passage into the inner ward.

Bibliography. Bessac and Yasmine, 2001, pp. 241–320; Boase, 1967, pp. 66–67; Deschamps, 1934, 29–30, 82, 92–93, 97, 136 n. 2, 196 n. 2, 228–29, 276; 1939, pp. 176–208, pls. LIII–LXXV; Enlart, vol. II, 1925, pp. 42–43; Kennedy, 1994, pp. 41–44, fig. 3, pls. 13, 14; Lawrence, 1988, pp. xxx, 46, 58, 126, figs. 42–43a; Müller-Wiener, 1966, pp. 62–63, plan 15, pl. 84; Pringle, 1993, vol. I, p. 110; 1997a, p. 31, fig. 14; Rey, 1871, pp. 127–39, fig. 40, pl. XIII; Smail, 1956, pp. 218, 221–23, 226, 227, fig. 2, pl. IIIa, b; *SWP*, vol. I, 1881, pp. 128–33.

10 Belmont/Bellum Montem Belveer (Sova/Suba) (IG map ref. 1620E–1324N)

Location. Belmont Castle is located on a small hill above the Tel-Aviv–Jerusalem road, *c.* 10 km west of Jerusalem.

History in the Crusader period. According to Theoderich (1169), the name Belmont referred to the mountainous region west of Jerusalem. The Hospitallers' courtyard building here was subsequently fortified, probably in the 1170s or 1180s. It was abandoned in 1187 and subsequently destroyed by the Ayyubids.

Excavations and surveys. Excavations from 1986 to 1988 by R. Harper and D. Pringle (BSAJ).

Description. This castle is formed of three wards, an inner courtyard structure and two external wards. The two parallel lines of outer fortifications of this castle are irregularly polygonal (probably octagonal) with gates to the south. The outer one measures 100 metres (e.–w.) by 115 metres (n.–s.). It has a partly rock-cut, partly constructed sloping talus. The inner line, parallel to the outer one, consists of barrel-vaulted chambers. At the highest point of the site is the inner ward, the original rectangular two-storey courtyard building (33 by 39–41 metres), which in design is remarkably similar to the nearby building at Aqua Bella and probably fulfilled a similar function as a rural administrative centre. It lacks fortifications but has turrets near the centre of two walls (north and east), barrel vaults around the courtyard on the south, west and north, and two groin vaults on the east. The main gate was on the east (1.69 metres wide) and a second, narrower gate was on the north.

Bibliography. Harper, 1988, 1989a, 1989b, 1990; Harper and Pringle, 1988, 1989, 2000; Kennedy, 1994, pp. 58–59, 113.

11 Belvoir/Belvear/Coquet (Kohav Ha-Yarden/Kaukab al-Hawa) (IG map ref. 1992E–2224N)

Location. Belvoir Castle stands on the eastern edge of the Yissachar Plateau, 500 metres above the Jordan Valley and overlooking two fords across the Jordan River south of the Sea of Galilee.

History in the Crusader period. A castle was possibly originally erected here by King Fulk in 1138–40 as part of a fortification programme aimed at strengthening the outer defences of the Kingdom of Jerusalem. By 1168 it was held by one Ivo Velos, who sold it to the Hospitallers (*Cart. des Hosp.*, no. 398; *RRH*, no. 448). They subsequently rebuilt the castle with concentric defences in the form of two enclosure castles (*castra* or *quadriburgia*). After the collapse of the Frankish army at the Battle of Hattin in July 1187, the castle, although now in Muslim-held territory, managed to withstand the Ayyubid threat for a year and a half until falling to Saladin on 5 January 1189. Saladin allowed the defenders to leave for Tyre and then destroyed the chapel, but he probably repaired the castle walls and a Muslim garrison occupied the castle. In 1219, al-Mu'azzam 'Isa destroyed Belvoir, along with other fortifications in the Holy Land. By 1228 the destruction was completed and, although the treaty of 1240 returned Belvoir to Crusader hands, it is not known whether they reoccupied or refortified the site. In any case, by 1263 Baybars had control over the region.

Excavations and surveys. A survey was carried out by N. Tzor (INPA) in the early 1960s and excavations by M. Ben-Dov (INPA) in 1966.

Description. One of the finest castle designs produced by the Franks in the East, Belvoir consists essentially of two *quadriburgia*, one enclosed within the other. A rock-cut ditch, *c.* 12 metres deep and 20 metres wide, surrounds the castle on three sides (south, west and north), the eastern side defended by the natural slope and a massive bastion. The moat was cut into the basalt, serving as a quarry for building stone. The outer ward measures about 100 metres square. It is entered via the main gate of the castle, located in the south-east, or a secondary gate across the moat on the west which was reached by a suspended bridge. Four towers project from the corners and additional towers were located at mid-points on the north, west and south walls. In the outer ward are a large cistern, a bathhouse, a forge and a vast covered storage and stabling area (the external vaults). The inner ward measures about 40 metres square. It was two storeys high and had four corner towers, as well as a large gate tower in the middle of the west wall. The ground-floor level contained a kitchen, refectory and other service vaults. On the upper floor were additional vaults, including a chapel on the west and possibly the knights' dormitory. In the courtyard are a cistern and what the excavators identified as a laundry area.

Bibliography. Ben-Dov, 1969, 1972, 1975, 1993a; Benvenisti, 1970, pp. 294–300; Biller, 1989; Boas, 1999, pp. 106–08; Kennedy, 1994, pp. 59–61; Prawer, 1967, 1972, pp. 300–307; Pringle, 1993, pp. 120–22.

12 Bethgibelin (Bet Guvrin/Bait Jibrin) (IG map ref. 1400E–1129N)

Location. This town and castle are located 34 km south-east of Ascalon, 22 km north-west of Hebron.

History in the Crusader period. In *c.* 1134 King Fulk built a castle here in order to stave off Muslim sorties from Fatimid-held Ascalon into the hinterland of the kingdom. It passed to the Hospitallers in 1136 and a settlement of Frankish settlers was established here. The castle and settlement fell to the Muslims in 1187, but were in Frankish hands again between 1240 and 1244.

Excavations and surveys. Extensive excavations of the castle and church (1992–99) were directed by A. Kloner and others on behalf of the IAA.

Description. The castle in its entirety covered an area of approximately 150 by 190 metres. The settlement of Bethgibelin may have been situated to the west of the enclosure castle, within the recently exposed double line of outer fortifications, in the area of the Roman amphitheatre. However, the excavations did not uncover evidence for domestic (or other) twelfth-century buildings in this area and the excavators believe that the settlement was elsewhere, possibly on the hill to the south-east. The inner castle is a typical enclosure castle, measuring 46 by 48 metres, with corner turrets, that to the south-east being incorporated in the *chevet* of the attached three-aisled church. Two-thirds of the interior of the castle were covered with groin-vaulted ranges around a central open area. The outworks of the castle consist of two defensive lines of curtain walls and projecting towers with an outer gate to the south-west and an inner gate east of the amphitheatre on the inner northern wall. The outermost line of walls was surrounded by a moat.

Bibliography. Kloner, 1983; Kloner and Chen 1983; Kloner and Assaf, 1996; Kloner and Cohen, 1996a; Kloner 1996b, *et al.*, 2001; Pringle, 1993, pp. 95–101; 1997a, p. 27.

13 Bethasaphace (Bait Safafa) (IG map ref. 1690E–1281N)

Location. Bethasaphace is situated south of Jerusalem near the road to Bethlehem.

History in the Crusader period. This village was granted to the Hospitallers by Baldwin I before September 1110.

Excavations and surveys. Surveyed by C.N. Johns in 1937, D.C. Baramki in 1941 and D. Pringle (BSAJ) in 1994.

Description. A three-storey tower and adjacent vaults form a rectangular enclosure fortified on three sides with a talus.

Bibliography. Pringle, 1997a, pp. 28–29, pl. XVI.

14 Burj as-Sabî (GCS map ref. 3558E–3512N)

Location. This tower is situated near the Mediterranean shore below Margat Castle in the south of the Principality of Antioch.

History in the Crusader period. This tower was built to form part of the defences of Margat Castle and to protect its harbour, as well as to serve as a toll post on the coastal road.

Excavations and surveys. This building was surveyed by P. Deschamps and H. Müller-Wiener.

Description. This is a three-storey tower constructed of roughly shaped basalt fieldstones with ashlar quoins and door and window frames. Large stepped corbels around the top of the tower originally supported machicolation.

Bibliography. Deschamps, 1973, text, pp. 284–85, album, pls. XXXVI, XXXVIII, LV; Müller-Wiener, 1966, p. 100, pl. 60.

15 Caco/Cacho/Tor de Quaquo (Qaqun) (IG map ref. 1497E–1962N)

Location. This site is in the lordship of Caesarea 19 km south-east of Caesarea.

History in the Crusader period. Referred to by Fulcher of Chartres in 1123; by 1131 the Hospitallers held property here, including a house. The Templars may have held the castle here in the 1180s.

Excavations and surveys. D. Pringle (BSAJ) carried out a survey at this site in 1983.

Description. A Frankish tower (17.6 by 14.5 metres) with two barrel vaults on the ground floor and a groin-vaulted first floor.

Bibliography. Pringle, 1997a, pp. 83–84, fig. 45, pl. LXXXV; 1998a, pp. 164–65.

16 Caesarea/Cesaire (IG map ref. 1401E–2120N)

Location. Caesarea was a port town located on the coast *c.* 50 km north of Jaffa.

History in the Crusader period. What had been the principal port city of Roman Palestine had by the Crusader period declined into a medium-sized settlement with a small and shallow harbour. The town walls enclosed an area of approximately 450 metres (n.–s.) by *c.* 240 metres (e.–w.), and the population was probably no more than a few thousand. The Teutonic Order held some houses in the town and properties outside the walls granted to them by Juliana of Caesarea in February 1206. This grant included two towers on the town walls. The Leper Knights of St Lazarus also possessed two houses and a garden in the town (Pringle, 1993, p. 180). Caesarea was the centre of a lordship and both of the major Military Orders were active in the region, possessing several castles and rural properties.

Excavations and surveys. Excavations have been carried out sporadically within the Crusader walls of Caesarea since the 1960s. Nothing directly related to the Military Orders has been identified to date.

Bibliography. Benvenisti, 1970, pp. 135–46; Boas, 1999, pp. 46–48; Hazard, 1975, pp. 79–114; Pringle, 1993, pp. 166–83; 1997a, pp. 43–45.

17 Cafarlet/Capharleth/Kafarletum (Habonim/Kafr Lam) (IG map ref. 1440E–2269N)

Location. This castle is situated on the sandstone ridge just off the Mediterranean coast, 8 km south of ῾Atlit.

History in the Crusader period. Built in the Umayyad period, this *quadriburgium* was still standing in the Crusader period and together with Castellum Beroart (Ashdod Yam) probably had a direct influence on the choice of this design by Frankish castle builders. It came into Hospitaller hands in 1213, purchased from the lord of Caesarea. By 1255 they had sold the castle to the Templars for the sum of 16,000 bezants. The Templars held Cafarlet until 1265 when it was captured by the Mamluks.

Excavations and surveys. The castle was surveyed by D. Pringle (the BSAJ) in 1989 and was excavated by the IAA in 1999 under the direction of H. Barbé and Y. Lehrer.

Description. A trapezoid enclosure castle with round corner towers and gate towers on the south. There are buttresses on the exterior of the curtain. A few barrel vaults are located on the interior at the south-east corner and halfway along the western wall. Excavators Barbé *et al.* found little evidence for the Crusader occupation and believe that in the Crusader period the castle was neglected and most activity was outside the fortifications, including the construction of a small church.

Bibliography. Barbé *et al.*, 2002; Benvenisti, 1970, pp. 329–31; Petersen, 2001, pp. 193–94; Pringle, 1997a, pp. 58–59, fig. 31; 1991a, p. 89; *SWP*, vol. II, 1882, pp. 29–30.

18 Calansue/Calanson/Calanzon/Kalensue/Calumzum (Qalansuwa) (IG map ref. 1485E–1878N)

Location. 18.5 km north-east of Arsuf.

History in the Crusader period. On 8 April 1128 the Hospitallers received this village from Godfrey of Flujeac (*RRH Add.*, no. 121a). They held it (except between 1187 and 1191) until it fell to Baybars in 1265. This tower may have been the first castle of the Hospitallers.

Excavations and surveys. A survey was carried out by D. Pringle (BSAJ) in 1983.

Description. Various buildings, including three vaulted structures, a tower (12.05 metres square) and a first-floor hall-house (16.5 by 28/30 metres) roofed with eight groin-vaulted bays.

Bibliography. Pringle, 1986a, pp. 41–58, figs. 10–14, pls. X–XXII; 1997a, pp. 77–78, fig. 40, pl. LXXVIII.

19 Casale Doc (Khirbat Da'uk) (IG map ref. 1616E–2530N)

Location. This site is located about 3 km north of the Templar mill of Doc at Khirbat Kurdana on the Na'aman River.

History in the Crusader period. There is no informative historical evidence for this site.

Excavations and Surveys. This site was surveyed by R. Ellenblum and D. Pringle.

Description. The medieval remains on the summit of Khirbat Da'uk are of a rectangular courtyard building (70 by 40 metres), which probably served as the administrative depot for Templar possessions in the region. They consist of three long barrel vaults enclosing three sides, the vault on the north being 6 metres wide and 35 metres long.

Bibliography. Ellenblum, 1998, pp. 205–09, fig. 18, pl. 11; Pringle, 1997a, p. 47.

20 Casale Montdidier/Casale Latinae (Khirbat Madd ad-Dair) (IG map ref. 1412E–1966N)

Location. This ruined tower is located 16 km south-south-east of Caesarea.

History in the Crusader period. Passing from the lord of Caesarea, Eustace Garnier, to the abbey of St Mary Latin in 1105, it later, together with the Red Tower (Burj al-Ahmar), became a Hospitaller and subsequently Templar possession.

Excavations and surveys. Surveys were conducted by C.R. Conder and H.H. Kitchener (SWP); J. Ory (PAM) in 1937 and D. Pringle (BSAJ) in 1983.

Description. Fragmentary remains of a tower measuring *c.* 16 metres (n.–s.) by *c.* 12.5 metres (e.–w.) with walls 1.7–2 metres thick.

Bibliography. Dar and Mintzker, 1987, pp. 210–13, pl. 52a; Kennedy, 1994, pp. 33, 36; Pringle, 1986a, pp. 37–39, figs. 2–3, 9, pl. VIII; 1997a, p. 67; *SWP*, vol. II, 1881, p. 140.

21 Casel des Pleins/Casellum Balneorum/Casellum de Templo (Azor/Yazur) (IG map ref. 1317E–1592N)

Location. This small castle was located on the road to Ramla 5.5 km east of Jaffa.

History in the Crusader period. In Crusader hands from the beginning of the twelfth century, Casel des Plains was briefly reoccupied by the Fatimids in 1102, but subsequently remained in Frankish hands until it was destroyed by Saladin after the Battle of Arsuf in September 1191. Later that year in October it was retaken and refortified by the Templars, but was subsequently destroyed by Saladin in 1192 together with other fortresses in the plain before being returned to the Franks according to the terms of the treaty between Richard and Saladin. The castle was again restored early in the thirteenth century.

Excavations and surveys. A survey was carried out by D. Pringle (BSAJ) in 1981.

Description. This is a nearly square two-storey keep (12.8 by 12.6 metres), barrel-vaulted on the ground floor; the upper level has not survived. Remnants of the enclosure wall survive.

Bibliography. Benvenisti, 1970, pp. 168, 259, 276, 313; 1982, p. 144, figs. 12–13; Petersen, 2001, pp. 312–13; Pringle, 1989b, pp. 16–17; 1997a, p. 108, fig. 62, pl. CX; 1998a, pp. 377–78; 1998b, pp. 92–94, figs. 9.2–9.3.

22 Castellum Arnaldi/Chastel Arnoul (Yalu) (IG map ref. 1525E–1388N)

Location. Remains of this castle, rediscovered in 1967, can be seen 4.5 km north-east of Latrun on a hill which is an extension of the Deir Ayyub-Latrun ridge.

History in the Crusader period. This was a royal castle which was destroyed by the Muslims in 1106, rebuilt in 1132/33 and in Templar hands by 1179. It fell to Saladin in 1187.

Excavations and surveys. This site has not been excavated; it was surveyed by D. Pringle in 1988.

Description. This was a medium-sized, more or less rectangular enclosure castle. Traces survive of the western wall with a centrally located tower which projects *c.* 4 metres from the line of the wall, and a southern wall with vaults and staircases. The western wall was apparently 80 metres in length. Benvenisti noted traces of a vault which may be part of a north-west corner tower. There are also some remains of a wall on the south-east which probably originally measured *c.* 40 metres. The gate was located in the south, flanked by a vaulted hall; adjacent to it was a spiral staircase.

Bibliography. Benvenisti, 1970, pp. 314–16; Kochavi, 1972, p. 236; Pringle, 1989b, p. 17; 1991a, pp. 90–91; 1997a, pp. 106–07, fig. 61.

23 Castellum Beleismum (IG map ref. 1782E–2061N)

Location. Castellum Beleismum is located on a hilltop 3 km south of Jenin on the road to Nablus.

History in the Crusader period. The site was first recorded in 1156 (*RRH*, no. 321) and identified by Ernoul as St Job; by 1187 it was held by the Hospitallers (Ernoul, 1871, p. 153).

Excavations and surveys. The tunnel to the spring was partly excavated by Z. Yeivin, and recent excavations were carried out by H. Taha (PDA).

Description. This is a rectangular enclosure (*c.* 40 metres n.–s. by *c.* 60 metres e.–w.) within which is a two-storey tower measuring 8 metres square with vaulted ranges lining the east and west sides. A vaulted tunnel led some 30 to 40 metres to a spring at the foot of the hill. A cist grave and a tombstone incised with a Latin cross were found in excavations at the mouth of the tunnel.

Bibliography. Pringle, 1993, pp. 106–07; 1997a, pp. 29–30; 2004, p. 29; Taha, 2000; Yeivin, 1973, p. 150, pl. 19.1, 2, p. XIX.

24 Castellum Novum/Chateau Neuf/(Margaliot/Hunin/ Qal'at Hunin) (IG map ref. 2011E–2917N)

Location. This castle is situated on a steep scarp 600 metres above the fertile Hula Valley on the eastern frontier of the Kingdom of Jerusalem facing Mount Hermon.

History in the Crusader period. The castle was built by Hugh of St Omer, Prince of the Galilee, who was probably responsible for the original castle at Saphet.

Excavations and surveys. The castle was surveyed by C.R. Conder and H.H. Kitchener and by R. Frankel, N. Gatzov, M. Aviam and A. Dagani in 1975 and 1986–90; excavated by I. Shaked (IAA) in 1994.

Description. This is a rectangular enclosure castle with round corner towers which do not project from the line of the curtain and thus could not have been effectively used for flanking fire. In 1994 archaeologists uncovered within the Ottoman gatehouse an earlier phase: two square towers with a curtain wall between them, possibly part of a small enclosure castle.

Bibliography. Deschamps, 1934, p. 29; 1939, pp. 14, 17, 119, 126, 128, 130, 134, 146–59, 178, 236, pls. XXXIVA–C; Frankel *et al.*, 2001, p. 45, no. 386; Kennedy, 1994, pp. 42–43; Pringle, 1997a, p. 79, pl. LXXX; Shaked, 1997; *SWP*, vol. I, 1881, pp. 87, 123–25.

25 Castellum Regis/Chasteau dou Rei/Castellum Novum/ Castellum Novum Regis/Mhalia (Mi'iliya) (IG map ref. 1746E–2699N)

Location. This enclosure castle is located on a hilltop in the Western Galilee, 22 km north-east of Akko.

History in the Crusader period. Castellum Regis was possibly built by King Fulk, hence the name. This castle was held by Henri de Milly in the 1160s and in the 1170s by Joscelin de Courtenay. In 1187 Castellum Regis fell to Saladin. It was later returned to the de Courtenay family until it was finally acquired by the Teutonic Order in 1220. The castle fell to Baybars in 1265.

Excavations and surveys. Surveyed by R. Frankel, N. Gatzov, M. Aviam and A. Dagani in 1975 and 1986–90; R. Khamissy in 2004.

Description. A standard enclosure castle (*quadriburgium*) measuring *c.* 40 by 40 metres with four projecting corner towers and some form of inner vaulted ranges. Benvenisti erroneously refers to a moat.

Bibliography. Benvenisti, 1970, p. 196–98; Ellenblum, 1996a, 104–22; 1998, pp. 41–45; Frankel *et al.*, 2001, p. 25, no. 161; Kennedy, 1994, pp. 37–38, 129, 132; Pringle, 1986b, pp. 52, 76 n. 3; 1997a, p. 71, fig. 36, pls. LXIX–LXX.

26 Cave le Tyron (Qal'at an-Niha) (IG map ref. 2070E–3310N)

Location. This castle is located on a cliff face about 20 km east of Tyre above the principal road from the Beqa Valley to the coastal towns of Tyre and Sidon.

History in the Crusader period. In the Crusader period the cave was occupied and probably fortified some time before 1133, when it fell to the Muslims. The Franks subsequently reoccupied it until 1165, when it was taken by Saladin's uncle, Shirkuh. In 1257 the castle was back in Frankish hands and Julien de Sagette granted it to the Teutonic Order, who apparently occupied it for only three years.

Excavations and surveys. Commandant Bigeaud examined the site in 1936.

Description. This small castle was built on a cliff site, half way up the cliff. A number of chambers serving as living quarters, storage and a water supply were cut in the cliff face and reached by a narrow path up the cliff.

Bibliography. Deschamps, 1939, pp. 217–20; Kennedy, 1994, p. 54.

27 Caymont/Caimum/Mons Cain, (Yoqne'am, al-Qaymun) (IG map ref. 1604E–2289N)

Location. This town is located at the eastern end of the Wadi Milh Pass through the Carmel Range at the entrance to the Jezreel Valley.

History in the Crusader period. Early in the twelfth century (1103) Caymont is recorded as a village in the possession of the monastery of Mount Tabor. According to Kedar it first became a royal castle and, some time before 1182 (when a charter refers to *territorio de Caimont*) it was the centre of a small lordship (Kedar, 1996, p. 4). It fell to Saladin after the Battle of Hattin (1187). Regained by the Franks (Balian of Ibelin received it from Saladin) in 1192. In 1262 a dispute between the Hospitallers and Templars over ownership of the town and lordship was settled in favour of the Templars. By 1283 Caymont was in Mamluk hands.

Excavations and surveys. Caymont was surveyed by C. Conder and H.H. Kitchener from 1881 to 1883 and A. Raban in the 1970s. Excavations were carried out by A. Ben-Tor in 1977/78 and by M. Avissar in 1995.

Description. A fortress (*quadriburgium?*), church, houses and town fortifications have been exposed on the top of the tell.

Bibliography. Avissar, 1995; Ben-Tor, *et al.*, 1996; Kedar, 1996; Pringle, 1998a, pp. 159–61.

28 Chastel Blanc (Safita) (GCS map ref. 3607E–3480N)

Location. This is a remarkably well-preserved keep, dominating the landscape some 380 metres above sea level, not far from Arima and *c.* 30 km south-east of Tortosa in the County of Tripoli.

History in the Crusader period. A castle was probably constructed on this hill around 1112. It may have been destroyed by the earthquake of 1170 and by incursions by Nur a-din, one of these having taken place in 1171. Around this time it came into Templar hands and was reconstructed. When Saladin passed through the region in 1188 he failed to take the castle, a fact which suggests that it was already a strong fortress. However, an earthquake occurring near the end of the twelfth century or early in the thirteenth century, possibly the well-documented one of 1202, left the castle '*prostrate*'. It was subsequently rebuilt, probably at this time taking on its present form. It was strengthened by Louis IX in 1251, but in February 1271 the failure of resistance by the 700-strong garrison was followed by the destruction of Chastel Blanc by Baybars.

Excavations and surveys. Surveys were conducted by E.G. Rey, C. Enlart and P. Deschamps.

Description. The castle consisted of a large keep surrounded by two enceintes. Of the latter little can be seen today. The outer enceinte was polygonal, almost oval, in form (it is today mostly buried under the village houses that have spread all the way up to the keep) and measured about 165 by 100 metres. The inner enceinte was rectangular or polygonal. The keep is 25 metres high, making it the tallest keep extant in the Latin East. A barrel-vaulted chapel is on the ground floor. The first floor is a groin-vaulted hall divided into eight bays supported on three free-standing piers. Below the chapel is a rock-cut cistern.

Bibliography. Burns, 1999, pp. 213–14; Deschamps, 1973, pp. 249–58; Kennedy, 1994, pp. 138–41; Müller-Wiener, 1966, pp. 51–52, 98, pls. 36–39; Rey, 1871, pp. 85–92, pl. IX.

29 Chastel Rouge/Castrum Rubrum (Qal'at Yahmour/Hisn Yahmour) (GCS map ref. 3590E–3480N)

Location. This fortified keep is situated in the County of Tripoli in the foothills of the Nusairi Mountains, 10 km west of Chastel Blanc and 12 km south-east of Tortosa (Tartus) on the road to Rafaniyah.

History in the Crusader period. Probably built early in the twelfth century and held by the Montolieu family, Chastel Rouge was given to the Hospitallers by Raymond III of Tripoli in 1177/78, the Montolieu family being compensated with 400 bezants.

Excavations and surveys. Surveys were conducted by P. Deschamps and by D. Pringle (1985).

Description. A large keep (16.2 by 14.1 metres) is surrounded by a rectangular enclosure (42 by 37 metres) defended with two projecting corner towers (probably later additions), that on the south-east corner being a solid turret (3.65 metres square). The forewall was surrounded by a moat. The keep had an external staircase leading to the main entrance at the first-floor level. The walls of the keep are 2 metres thick.

Bibliography. Deschamps, 1973, pp. 317–19; Kennedy, 1994, pp. 72–75; Lawrence,

1988, p. 128, figs. 30–33; Müller-Wiener, 1966, pp. 52, 98, pls. 40–41; Pringle, 1986a, pp. 16–18, fig. 4, pls. I–II.

30 Chateau Pelerin/Castellum Peregrinorum ('Atlit) (IG map ref. 1434–50E–2327–28N)

Location. Chateau Pelerin is situated on a small peninsula on the Mediterranean coast, *c*. 21 km south of the site of medieval Haifa (Caifas).

History in the Crusader period. The castle was erected in 1217/18 by the Templars, together with knights of the Teutonic Order and pilgrims from Acre, with the financial aid of a Flemish knight, Walter of Avesnes. It replaced the small Templar tower of le Destroit (Districtum) (see p. 240) on the sandstone ridge to the east, which was dismantled during its construction so that it could not be used by an enemy during a siege. This enormous project was aimed at redressing the imbalance caused by the Muslim fortification of Mount Tabor. In 1219/20 the castle came under attack from Malik al-Muazzam 'Isa, but withstood the siege successfully. Frederick II attempted to take over the castle in 1229 but was successfully resisted by the Templar garrison. The castle remained in Templar hands until 1291. A faubourg developed under the castle to its east and south and was enclosed by its own walls and moat. In August 1291 the castle was the last place on the mainland to be abandoned by the Franks, who departed from there to Cyprus.

Excavations and surveys. Excavations directed by C.N. Johns (PDA), 1930–34.

Description. The castle consists of a range of large vaulted halls around a central courtyard, including a 12-sided church, a groin-vaulted refectory and other installations. In the east were the castle's main defensive works, the other sides having the natural protection of the sea. The eastern defences consisted of two massive curtains; the inner one was 12 metres thick and over 30 metres high with two huge towers, and the outer curtain was 6.5 metres thick and 16 metres high with three gate towers and a broad moat to its east. These three elements effectively cut the castle off from the mainland in the same manner in which the defences of a spur castle cut it off from the hill on which it stood.

Bibliography. Benvenisti, 1970, pp. 175–85, 259–60, 283, 287, 289–90; Boas, 1999, pp. 110–12; Conder, 1874, p. 13; Deschamps, 1934, pp. 45, 71–72, 79, 84–85, 88, 91, 94–95, 131, 138, 226–27, 229, 279; 1939, pp. 16, 23 n. 5, 24–33, 137, 140, 196, 215, 237, 239; Johns, 1997; 1975, pp. 130–40; 1993, pp. 112–17; Kennedy, 1994, pp. 124–27; Lawrence, 1988, pp. XXXI–XXXIII, XXXIX, 71, 74n., 131, fig. 49; Müller-Wiener, 1966, pp. 71–72, 102, plan 22, pl. 98; Pringle, 1997a, pp. 22–24; *SWP*, vol. I, 1881, pp. 281, 293–301.

31 Cisterna Rubea/Turris Rubea/Le Rouge Cisterne/ Maldoim/Castrum Dumi (Qal'at ad-Dam) (IG map ref. 1841E–1361N)

Location. This is a small fortified tower located on a hill opposite the Inn of the Good Samaritan on the road from Jerusalem to the Place of Baptism on the Jordan River.

History in the Crusader period. The site was probably fortified in the first half of the twelfth century and was in Templar hands until they abandoned it around the time of the Battle of Hattin.

Excavations and surveys. The site was surveyed by D. Pringle and M. Pease (BSAJ) in 1988. Cleaning of this site in preparation for an excavation took place in 2005 by Y. Magen.

Description. A rectangular courtyard (*c.* 60 by 50 metres) is surrounded by a rock-cut moat with some barrel vaults along the periphery and a small, two-storey keep, 9.5 by 6.6–8.1 metres, at the centre. The keep was barrel-vaulted, with a staircase in the wall on the right-hand side of the door leading to the upper level which has not survived. Like the other vaults in the complex, it was constructed of locally quarried roughly shaped ashlars excavated from the rock-cut ditch which surrounds the entire castle. There is no evidence for a perimeter wall or additional towers.

Bibliography. Benvenisti, 1970, pp. 324–25, pl. on p. 327; Pringle, 1994b, pp. 153–62, figs. 16.2–16.10; 1997a, pp. 78–79, fig. 42, pl. LXXIX.

32 Cola (Qula) (IG map ref. 1459E–1605N)

Location. The ruins of this Frankish estate are located 19 km east of Jaffa.

History in the Crusader period. A privately held estate which was purchased by the Hospitallers from Hugh of Flanders in 1181.

Excavations and surveys. A survey was carried out by Pringle (BSAJ) in 1983.

Description. On this site are the remains of a barrel-vaulted tower (*c.* 17 by 12.8 metres) and nearby an elongated barrel-vaulted hall with an adjacent cistern.

Bibliography. Benvenisti, 1970, pp. 227–29; Deschamps, 1939, p. 22; Guérin, vol. II, 1874, pp. 390–91; Pringle, 1986a, pp. 21–22, fig. 7; 1997a, p. 87, fig. 47; *SWP*, vol. II, 1882, pp. 297, 358.

33 Coliath/La Colée (GCS map ref. 3602E–3455N)

Location. This castle is located in the plain about 23 km north of Tripoli.

History in the Crusader period. The castle was given to the Hospitallers by Count Pons of Tripoli in 1127. It was attacked and damaged by al-Malik al-Adil in 1207/08 during his campaign against Tripoli, after which it remained in ruins and finally fell to Baybars in 1266.

Excavations and surveys. Surveys were carried out by M. van Berchem and P. Deschamps.

Description. An enclosure castle (63 by 56 metres), with corner and intermediate projecting towers, surrounded on all sides by a rock-cut ditch (now filled in on the south). Gates are on the north and east. On the south is a barrel-vaulted range and there are traces of another ruined range on the north.

Bibliography. Deschamps, 1973, pp. 311–12; Kennedy, 1994, pp. 78–79, fig. 11; Van Berchem and Fatio, 1914, pp. 131–35.

34 Crac des Chevaliers/Crac de l'Ospital/Crat/Cratum/Crati (Hisn al-Akrad/Qal'at al-Hisn) (GCS map ref. 3618E–3444N)

Location. Crac des Chevaliers is located on a spur of the Nusairi Mountains dominating the Homs Gap.

History in the Crusader period. A small Kurdish castle known as Hisn al-Akrad (Castle of the Kurds) came into Hospitaller hands in 1142 as part of a gift from Raymond II, Count of Tripoli, of an extensive tract of land, towns, villages and a number of small castles in the eastern part of the County of Tripoli. Probably soon after occupying the castle, the Hospitallers expanded it. Certainly it was repaired or rebuilt following a major earthquake in 1170. By May 1188, when Saladin marched through the region, the castle was strong enough to deter an attack. In the early thirteenth century the castle was used as a base for Frankish raids on Hama and Montferrand. About this time, following the earthquake of 1202, Crac was expanded by the addition of extensive outworks. In March 1271 Baybars besieged the castle, and after the outer defences were breached the castle fell on 8 April. The Hospitaller garrison was allowed to retreat to Tripoli. Baybars subsequently repaired the damage he had done to the outer defences through bombardment and sapping. In the south, where most of the damage had occurred, he built a huge square tower.

Excavations and surveys. Surveys, clearance work and restoration were carried out by P. Deschamps and F. Anus from 1927.

Description. This is a large, well-preserved spur castle with concentric defences, strongest on the south where the outer defences of the castle are cut off from the hill by a rock-cut ditch; an open reservoir (*birqat*) and steep glacis protect the inner castle. The inner, twelfth-century castle is almost triangular in shape, the northern end forming an angular curve. It consists of lateral barrel vaults running the entire circuit of the castle. A three-bayed chapel is located on the north-east, the main (inner) gate defended by two projecting square towers on the east, a tower on the north and three towers on the south. Within the inner ward are various structures, including a large chapel on the north-east, a Gothic-style vaulted hall on the west and a huge groin-vaulted magazine on the south. In the thirteenth century the castle was greatly expanded by the addition of a wall with a steep glacis along the entire west and south. Lower on the slope, at a distance of about 20 to 30 metres, a new forewall was added, surrounding the entire castle. This wall has semicircular towers and an elaborate outer gate complex on the east.

Bibliography. Deschamps, 1934; Kennedy, 1994, pp. 145–66; Lawrence, 1988, pp. 77–88, figs. 55–65; Müller-Wiener, 1966, pp. 59–62, 100–01, pls. 66–83.

35 Crac de Moab/le Crac de Montreal/Cracum Montis regalis, Petra Deserti (Karak) (IG map ref. 2170E–0660N)

Location. This castle is located on the eastern frontier of the Kingdom of Jerusalem, about 5 km east of the Dead Sea.

History in the Crusader period. The castle was built by Payen the Butler, lord of Montreal, in 1142. A tower and barbican in this castle were granted to the Hospitallers by Maurice of Montreal in 1152. The castle later came into the hands of Reynauld de Chatillon through marriage and he used it as a base to attack the nearby caravan and pilgrimage route from Syria to Mecca.

Excavations and surveys. This castle was surveyed by P. Deschamps and H. Müller-Wiener.

Description. The spur castle occupies the narrow ridge extending to the south of the walled town of Karak. The location of the tower and barbican belonging to the Hospitallers is not known.

Bibliography. Deschamps, 1939, pp. 35–98; Kennedy, 1994, pp. 45–52, fig. 4, pls. 15–19; Müller-Wiener, 1966, pp. 47–48, 97, plan 4, pls. 23–27; Pringle, 1993, pp. 286–93; 1997a, pp. 59–60, figs. 32, pls. XLVIII–LI; Riley-Smith, 1967, p. 56.

36 Le Destroit/Casel Destreiz/Districtum/Petra Incisa (Horvot Karta/Khirbat Dustray) (IG map ref. 1452E–2348N)

Location. This tower is located on the inner sandstone ridge that runs adjacent to the Mediterranean, 21 km south of the medieval site of Haifa at the place where the medieval road passes through a narrow defile in the ridge.

History in the Crusader period. Though the date of its construction is not known, presumably it was in the first half of the twelfth century. With the construction of Chateau Pelerin in 1217/18 it ceased to serve a purpose and was subsequently dismantled (1220) so that it could not be used by an assailant in support of a siege of the new castle and its faubourg.

Excavations and surveys. The tower was surveyed by C.R. Conder and H.H. Kitchener and was examined and published by C.N. Johns in 1932.

Description. Rock-cut foundations and some fragmentary construction survive of a square tower, *c.* 15.5 metres (e.–w.) by 11 metres (n.–s.) with walls 2.4 metres thick, a rock-cut staircase and two cisterns. Around the tower is a rock-cut courtyard with remains of stables containing mangers.

Bibliography. Benvenisti, 1970, pp. 176–78; Johns, 1932, pp. 111–13; 1947, pp. 15–17, 94–98, figs. 6, 38; Pringle, 1997a, p. 47; *SWP*, vol. I, 1881, pp. 288, 309–10.

37 Doc/Doke/Dochum (Khirbat Kurdana) (IG map ref. 1606E–2501N)

Location. This mill is located downstream from the source of the Na'aman River, 12 km south of Akko. Until recently (and for some time, as the Arabic name suggests), the complex at Khirbat Kurdana has been identified with the Hospitaller mills of Recordane. However, recent work (see Shaked, 2000) has shown that this site should in fact be identified with the Templar mills of Doc and that the Hospitaller mills were located upstream at the source of the Na'aman.

History in the Crusader period. Probably in the thirteenth century, the Templars established a flour mill here powered by water from the Na'aman River.

Excavations and surveys. The site was surveyed by M. Benvenisti, and by D. Pringle and M. Pease (BSAJ) in 1989.

Description. On Tel Afeq there is a courtyard building (70 by 40 metres), including a barrel vault (35 by 6 metres), Below, on the Na'aman River, is a complex comprising of a mill and dam with a two-storey keep (*c.* 11 by 9.9 metres). The keep had a timber floor between the two levels supported on stone corbels. On the west of the tower there was a machicolation above the doorway. A door in the south wall of the tower gave access above one of the mill rooms on the south. A second mill room was located on the north side of the tower.

Bibliography. Benvenisti, 1970, pp. 249–52; Frankel, 1980, pp. 200–01; 1988,

p. 261; Petersen, 2001, pp. 290–91; Pringle, 1997a, p. 47; Rey, 1883, p. 481; Riley-Smith, 1967, pp. 446, 450; Shaked, 2000.

38 Docus/Duk/Castellum Abrahami (Jabal Quruntul) (IG map ref. 1909E–1422N)

Location. The ruins are located on the summit of Jabal Quruntul overlooking Jericho.

History in the Crusader period. Theoderich (XXIX) refers to caves located here which were used by the Templars to store food and arms.

Excavations and surveys. The site was surveyed by C.R. Conder and H.H. Kitchener.

Description. Conder and Kitchener suggest that the ruin of a medieval structure with rusticated masonry was the Templar castle of Duk (Docus)

Bibliography. Pringle, 1993, p. 253; *SWP*, vol. III, 1883, pp. 201–05.

39 Famagusta (GCS map ref. 3357E–3506N)

Location. This important medieval port city is located on the east coast of Cyprus.

History in the Crusader period. Famagusta replaced Acre as the principal port in the region after the latter city fell to the Mamluks in May 1291.

Excavations and surveys. The site was examined by C. Enlart.

Description. Two churches in the town were identified by Enlart as having belonged to the Templars and the Hospitallers. However, the evidence for this is slight.

Bibliography. Enlart, [1899] 1987, pp. 290–93.

40 La Fève/Castrum Fabe (Kibbutz Merhavya) (IG map ref. 1789E–2243N)

Location. This castle is located on a low tell on the northern side of the Jezreel Valley on the south-west side of the Little Hermon (Givʿat Ha-Moreh).

History in the Crusader period. First recorded in 1169 by Theoderich as 'a castle of no small size' (XLIV), La Fève was probably built by the Templars some decades earlier, to serve, amongst other things, as a supply depot. It was twice used as an assembly point for the royal army during Saladin's campaign in 1183, when the Frankish army under Guy de Lusignan camped here on 30 September and returned again later. On 30 April, just over two months before the Battle of Hattin, the Masters of the Temple and the Hospital, together with the Archbishop of Tyre and Reginald of Sidon, came to La Fève as envoys of the king and patriarch, followed by knights of the Orders and of the king. On the following day these forces found its gates open and the castle unoccupied except for two sick men. The garrison of Templars, together with Hospitaller and secular knights, had suffered a major defeat at the nearby Springs of Cresson, north-east of Nazareth. Imad al-Din described the castle as 'the best castle and most fortified, the fullest of men and munitions and the best provided'. After the defeat of the Crusaders at Hattin the castle was dismantled by the Muslims.

Excavations and surveys. The castle was examined on the basis of an aerial photograph by B.Z. Kedar (HUJ) and D. Pringle (BSAJ).

Description. Too fragmentary to define, this was apparently an enclosure castle estimated at 80–90 metres (n.–s.) by 110–120 metres (e.–w.) surrounded by a broad ditch (*c.* 30–35 metres wide). According to Theoderich it had an *antilliyah* well (Huygens, 1994; p. 189; *PPTS*, p. 64), as did another Templar castle, Vadum Jacob.

Bibliography. Benvenisti, 1970, p. 323; Kedar and Pringle, 1985; Kennedy, 1994, pp. 55–56, 61, 124; Pringle, 1997a, p. 49; Rey, 1883, p. 439.

41 Forbelet (Umm at-Taiyiba) (IG map ref. 1965E–2638N)

Location. This castle is located in the centre of the Arab village of Umm at-Taiyiba 7 km west of Belvoir.

History in the Crusader period. Forbelet was apparently a Hospitaller castle. It was damaged by Saladin in 1183 but subsequently restored by the Hospitallers. It was used by Sayf al-Din Mahmud as a base to besiege Belvoir in 1187/88.

Excavations and surveys. This building was surveyed by D. Pringle.

Description. A well-built tower-keep, measuring 26.3 metres square with four groin-vaulted bays supported on a massive 2.1 metres square central pier and walls over 4 metres thick.

Bibliography. Pringle, 1991a, p. 90; 1997a, p. 104.

42 Gaston/Gastin/Gastun (Baghras) (GCS map ref. 3617E–3620N)

Location. Gaston was a major Templar castle in the vicinity of Antioch. It controlled the eastern end of the important Belen Pass (the Syrian Gates) through the Amanus Range and the northern approach to Antioch.

History in the Crusader period. A castle was constructed here, supposedly by the Umayyad Caliph Hisham, in the first half of the eighth century. It had a garrison of 50 men. In the late tenth century the Byzantine emperor Nicephorus Phocas built a larger castle with a garrison of 1,000. After the Byzantine defeat at Manzikert (1071) it came into Seljuk hands and in 1097 was occupied by the Crusaders during the siege of Antioch. Later the castle was garrisoned by Franks and Armenians. In 1142/43 it was again held by the Byzantine emperor before returning to Frankish hands on the emperor's death. It was held by the Templars from 1153, but in 1169 they were expelled by Mleh, brother of Thoros II. However, in 1175 he was overthrown and the Templars returned to Gaston until 1188, when Saladin occupied it along with several other castles. Fearing the approach of the German contingent of the Third Crusade led by Frederick Barbarossa, Saladin subsequently partially dismantled the castle. Levon II occupied and refortified Gaston but refused to hand it back to the Templars until 1211 or 1212, after he had been excommunicated for his refusal to return it and for his attempts to usurp the Principality of Antioch. The castle remained in Templar hands until it fell to Baybars in May 1268.

Excavations and surveys. This castle was surveyed by P. Brown in collaboration with A.W. Lawrence (see Boase, 1978), by H. Müller-Wiener and by R. Edwards.

Description. Most of the castle of Gaston as it appears today is Templar work predating the occupation of Saladin. Above an outer lower ward is the inner or upper ward which contains several vaulted structures on two levels, including two large vaulted halls on either side of the central courtyard, one of which served as a chapel, the other probably as the refectory. An aqueduct (of which little survives) supplied water from an external source.

Bibliography. Edwards, 1983; Kennedy, 1994, pp. 142–43; Lawrence, 1978; Müller-Wiener, 1966, pp. 48–49, pls. 28–31; Sinclair, 1990, pp. 266–71; Upton-Ward, 1994.

43 Gastria/la Castrie (GCS map ref. 3400E–3520N)

Location. Scanty remains of this castle are located on the Bay of Famagusta in eastern Cyprus, visible from Famagusta.

History in the Crusader period. One of the oldest castles in Cyprus, Gastria was built by the Templars some time before 1210 (*Cart. des Hosp.*, no. 1354). With the suppression of the Templars in 1307 the castle was handed over to the Hospitallers. It may have been demolished in 1310, or around 1425, and was later completely levelled (Enlart, [1899] 1987, p. 474).

Excavations and surveys. C. Enlart carried out survey of the remains of this castle.

Description. Little survives apart from the rock-cut ditch. Of apparently minor military importance, this castle, like the Hospitaller tower at Kolossi, should be regarded chiefly as an estate administrative centre. Enlart notes somewhat vaguely that this castle 'seems to have been one of those castles that had no flanking works and was defended only by its ditches, a type which according to Baron Rey was the normal one for the Templars in Syria'. Remnants of the walls show that they were only about 1 metre thick.

Bibliography. Enlart, [1899] 1987, pp. 473–75.

44 Harunia/Haruniye/Haroun (GCS map ref. 3629E–3717N)

Location. Harunia occupies the fairly flat crest of a prominent hill in the foothills of the Amanus Mountains *c*. 3 km north of the village of the same name. The approach to the castle is from the south towards the main north-east gate. The castle has an excellent view across the Cilician Plain as the land drops away steeply to the north and west.

History in the Crusader period. A castle was built here by Harun ar-Rashid in 785/86 to protect the road between Marad and the Cilician Plain. In the Crusader period the castle was in the hands of the Armenian Baron Levon and later was held by Baron Godfrey. The Armenian king Hetoum I and his wife Zapel bestowed the castle on the knights of the Teutonic Order in 1236. After the departure of the Franks at the end of the thirteenth century, the castle was held by the Mamluks.

Excavations and surveys. The castle was surveyed by R. Edwards in 1973 and 1979.

Description. A medium-sized hilltop castle of fairly simple design, Harunia is roughly almond-shaped with a gate at either end (north-east and south-west). It has a single, massive, horseshoe-shaped tower which protects the main gate. Between the two gates is a pointed barrel-vaulted gallery. Firing embrasures line the thick (*c*. 5 metres) external wall of the gallery. South of the gallery are an open courtyard and minor additional buildings.

Bibliography. Edwards, 1987, pp. 143–46, fig. 38, pls. 96–100; Sinclair, 1990, p. 328.

45 Iezrael/Parvum Gerinum/Petit Gerin (Tel Yizra'el/Zir'in) (IG map ref. 1811E–2182N)

Location. A town in the Jezreel Valley, 17 km north-west of Bait Shean.

History in the Crusader period. The town was held by the Templars in the 1180s until 1187.

Excavations and surveys. Excavations were carried out by D. Ussishkin and J. Woodhead.

Description. This site has remains of a town with a church and some form of fortifications.

Bibliography. Petersen, 2001, pp. 322–23; Pringle, 1993, pp. 276–79; 1997a, p. 56; *SWP*, vol. II, 1882, pp. 88–89, 130–31; Ussishkin and Woodhead, 1992, 1994.

46 Jaffa/Jafis/Japhe/Joppe (Yafo/Joppa) (IG map ref. 1265E–1624N)

Location. Jaffa is a port city located on a hill on the Mediterranean coast (within modern Tel Aviv).

History in the Crusader period. Jaffa was the first city occupied by the Crusaders in the Holy Land, having been abandoned by its inhabitants as the armies of the First Crusade approached in 1099. During the Crusader period it was a minor port, overshadowed by Acre and Tyre.

Excavations and surveys. Excavations were carried out by J. Kaplan in the 1960s and 1970s, and there are ongoing excavations directed by M. Pielstöcker (IAA).

Description. At present there are no identifiable remains of the Military Orders.

Bibliography. Pringle, 1993, pp. 264–73; 1997a, p. 52.

47 Jerusalem/Ierusalem/Hierusalem (Yerushalayim/ al-Quds) (IG map ref. 1720E–1316N)

Location. Located on the watershed of the Judaean Hills, 58 km from Jaffa on the Mediterranean coast.

History in the Crusader period. Jerusalem was occupied by the armies of the First Crusade on 15 July 1099, bringing the Crusade to a successful end. In the twelfth century the two major Military Orders were established here, as was the smaller Order of the Leper Knights of St Lazarus.

Excavations and surveys. Surveys in the Hospitaller Quarter were carried out by Schick in the 1890s (published in 1901, 1902). Excavations and surveys of the Templar complex were carried out by Clermont-Ganneau (published in 1899), Warren and Conder (published in 1884). Hamilton recorded the work carried out in the al-Aqsa Mosque from 1938 to 1942 (published 1949) and described the Templar structures that still existed at that time.

Hospitaller Quarter. The Hospitaller Quarter was located between the Street of the Patriarch (modern Christian Street) on the west and the Triple Market on the ancient Cardo to the east, and between the Church of the Holy Sepulchre and its conventual buildings on the north and David Street on the south. The quarter included three churches, St Mary Latin, St Mary Major and St John the Baptist, two hospitals, a bathhouse, stores, magazines and various other remains. In the early twentieth century most of the surviving remains were destroyed and the quarter was rebuilt.

Templar Quarter. An extensive building project took place on the southern part of the Temple Mount around the middle of the twelfth century. The Templars converted al-Aqsa Mosque into their headquarters and added several other structures, including a new palace, warehouses, bathhouses, cloisters and a new church (which was still under construction in 1169). They used the underground vaults as their stables and added outworks to the south of the southern wall of the Temple Mount. Almost all of these structures were demolished by Saladin in 1187.

Quarter of St Lazarus. No remains of this quarter, which included a hospital and a church, have been identified with certainty. Remains of the gate in the city wall between the quarter and the city and a gate on the forewall have been found in excavations. A burial chamber to the east could possibly have belonged to the brothers of St Lazarus. The open reservoir known as the Pool of St Ladare can still be seen to the north, although it is largely built over.

Bibliography. Benvenisti, 1970, pp. 56–58; Boas, 2001; Clermont-Ganneau, 1899; Patrich, 1984; Pringle, 1991b; 1997a, pp. 53–56; Schick, 1873, 1889, 1901, 1902; *SWP* (Jerusalem volume), 1884.

48 Judin/Iudyn (Mezudat Gadin/Yehi'am/Qal'at Jiddin)
(IG map ref. 1710E–2665N)

Location. Judin is located on a ridge on the north of Nahal Yehi'am (Wadi Jiddin), 16 km north-east of Acre and 5 km south of Montfort.

History in the Crusader period. This castle is not recorded before *c.* 1283, when it is mentioned by Burchard of Mount Sion, a Dominican friar, as being destroyed and as having belonged to the Teutonic Order (*Descriptio*, IV.I, ed. Laurent, p. 34).

Excavations and surveys. The site was surveyed by C. Conder and H.H. Kitchener in 1877, Masterman in 1919, Johns in 1941; by R. Frankel, N. Gatzov, M. Aviam and A. Dagani in 1975 and 1986–90 and more extensively by D. Pringle, A. Peterson, M. Dow and C. Singer (BSAJ) in 1992.

Description. The castle consists of upper and lower wards, possibly with an intermediate wall between them. In the upper ward are two massive keeps and an enclosure wall with a gate to the west. The eastern keep, designated (A) by Pringle, is a three-storey structure measuring *c.* 15.5 metres (n.–s.) by 16 metres (e.–w.) with walls 3.3 to 5.4 metres thick. The western keep or residence (B) is 16.4 metres square, consisting of two barrel vaults on the ground- and first-floor levels and possibly six groin-vaulted bays on the upper (second-floor) level. It has walls 2.3 metres thick. The design, with its two keeps enclosed within a curtain wall, has been compared to German castles like Munzenburg.

Bibliography. Frankel, *et al.*, 2001, p. 23, no. 145; Masterman, 1919, pp. 71–75; Pringle, 1997a, pp. 80–82, fig. 44, pls. LXXXI–LXXXIV; Pringle, *et al.*, 1994.

49 Kolossi/Le Colos (GCS map ref. 3251E–3440N)

Location. Ruins of a large keep and sugar refinery are located in a fertile area a few km west of Limassol in southern Cyprus, on the Paphos road.

History in the Crusader period. There was probably a small Byzantine stronghold here until Richard I captured the island in 1191. Hugh I handed over Kolossi to the Hospitallers by 1210 and compensated its owner, Garinus de Colos. The original castle, traces of which were incorporated in the east and west sides of the surviving keep, may have been built at this time. In the early thirteenth century after the loss of Acre Kolossi briefly served as the Hospitallers' headquarters. In 1310 the Hospitallers transferred their headquarters to Rhodes and Kolossi remained the seat of the Grand Commander of Cyprus. The castle was damaged during the numerous raids of the Genoese and Mamluks in the late fourteenth and fifteenth centuries, and the keep was subsequently rebuilt. The present structure is largely of this later date.

Excavations and surveys. The keep was surveyed by C. Enlart in 1896.

Description. This is a superb example of a Frankish rectangular keep, although the present structure is rebuilt, possibly along similar lines to the early thirteenth-century keep.

Bibliography. Aristidou, 1983; Enlart, [1899] 1987, pp. 494–502; Megaw, 1964.

50 Manueth (Horvat Manot/Khirbat Manawat) (IG map ref. 1644E–2716N)

Location. This site is located *c.* 14 km north-east of Acre some 5 km from the Mediterranean coast.

History in the Crusader period. The village of Manueth was held by Geoffrey le Tor in the twelfth century until 1187. By 1191 it was again in Frankish hands, and in 1212 was sold to the Hospitallers by John of Brienne for 2,000 bezants.

Excavations and surveys. Surveys were conducted by C.R. Conder and H.H. Kitchener, and by R. Frankel, N. Gatzov, M. Aviam and A. Dagani in 1975 and from 1986 to 1990. In 1995 part of the sugar mill was excavated by the IAA under the direction of E.J. Stern.

Description. Ruins here are of a village, tower and sugar refinery. The refinery consists of two barrel-vaulted structures, the larger being a two-storey building containing on the ground floor the ovens used in the refining process. There is also a subterranean vault on the south. On the east are the remains of the aqueduct, a water-driven mill and a sugar press.

Bibliography. Deschamps, 1939, p. 120; Ellenblum, 1998, pp. 198–204; Frankel, 1988, 257–58, 260, fig. 1; Frankel and Stern, 1996; Frankel, *et al.*, 2001, p. 18, no. 86; Guérin, vol. II, 1880, pp. 37–38; Pringle, 1997a, pp. 69–70; Stern, 2001; *SWP*, vol. I, 1881, p. 173.

51 Margat (Marqab) (GCS map ref. 3558E–3512N)

Location. This large castle is located in the south of the Principality of Antioch on a triangular hill in Djebel Anasarieh, just inland from the Mediterranean coast and 360 metres above sea level.

History in the Crusader period. A castle and its walled faubourg in close proximity to the territory of the Assassins, Margat was held by the Manzoir family from about 1140, when they made it the centre of their holdings. However, earthquake damage made it difficult for the Manzoir family to maintain it and in 1186 Margat was sold to the Hospitaller Order, together with a fairly extensive tract of land including other castles and towns, amongst these the nearby coastal town of Valenia (Baniyas) and lands in the north of the principality. Margat became an important Hospitaller administrative centre, and in the thirteenth century general chapters were held here and the archives of the Order were kept in the castle. Like Crac des Chevaliers, Margat was strong enough to deter Saladin from attempting to besiege it in 1188 and, also like Crac, it served as a centre for counter-attack on the region of Hama. The castle was slightly damaged during Muslim raids in 1204/05 and underwent major rebuilding in the thirteenth century. In 1285 the castle was besieged by Sultan Qala'un; after it was successfully mined in the south, the Hospitaller garrison agreed to surrender in exchange for safe conduct to Tripoli and Tortosa. Under the Mamluks the castle retained its importance as a major stronghold.

Excavations and surveys. The castle was surveyed by P. Deschamps.

Description. A triangular fortification covering the entire top of a hill surrounds a faubourg and the massive castle to its south. The castle has concentric defences on the east and west sides, which are also defended by the steep slopes of the spur. The outer wall of the western flank dates to the twelfth century and has square towers. The towers on the east and most of the towers of the faubourg fortifications are semicircular. The northern flank of the castle has a single line of vaults and a ditch cutting it off from the rest of the faubourg. Within the castle are several barrel-vaulted halls surrounding a central courtyard. On the east is a large chapel with two groin-vaulted bays and on the south is a huge round keep, 20 metres in diameter, with a rectangular inner chamber and walls up to 10 metres thick. Below the keep is a second round tower which was destroyed in the siege of 1285 and rebuilt by Qala'un.

Bibliography. Boase, 1977, pp. 151–52; Burns, 1992, pp. 184–87; Deschamps, 1964, pp. 138–49, pls. 43–48; 1973, pp. 259–85; Folda, 1982b; Kennedy, 1994, pp. 163–79; Müller-Wiener, 1966, pp. 57–58, 99–100, pls. 52–61.

52 Merle/Merla Templi (IG map ref. 1422E–2246N)

Location. Ruins of a castle with a keep are located on the western edge of an ancient tell (Tel Dor) on the Mediterranean coast, 13 km north of Caesarea.

History in the Crusader period. Virtually nothing is known of the history of this castle.

Excavations and surveys. Extensive excavations of the tell have been carried out by the Hebrew University of Jerusalem and by Berkeley University, but the remains of Crusader tower have not yet been excavated.

Description. A poorly preserved ruin which appears to have covered a total area of *c.* 74 metres (e.–w.) by *c.* 30 metres (n.–s.). A small square tower (*c.* 6.1 metres square) was recorded by Conder and Kitchener (1881, p. 7), but it collapsed in 1895; Pringle points out that it may in any case have been a later addition (Pringle, 1997a, p. 99). It was naturally defended on three sides by the sea and on the east by a deep moat.

Bibliography. Benvenisti, 1970, p. 189; Deschamps, 1939, p. 23; Guérin, vol. II, 1874, pp. 314–15; Pringle, 1997a, p. 99; Stern, *et al.*, 1993; *SWP*, vol. II, 1882, pp. 7–11.

53 Molendina Trium Pontium (Haddar/Hadra) (IG map ref. 1340E–1680N)

Location. This ruin is located on a bend in the Yarkon River 9 km north-east of Jaffa.

History in the Crusader period. The mill was granted to the Hospitallers in 1133.

Excavations and surveys. The site was examined by C.N. Johns and A. Petersen.

Description. This poorly preserved ruin consists of a dam, embankment walls and three mills.

Bibliography. Benvenisti, 1970, p. 252; Johns, PAM, 19.3.41; Petersen, 2001, pp. 141–43; Pringle, 1997a, p. 49; *SWP*, vol. II, 1882, pp. 251, 265.

54 Montfort/Starkenberg (Qal'at al-Qurain) (IG map ref. 1715E–2722N)

Location. A spur castle occupies the western end of a steep east-west spur, 180 metres above Nahal Keziv (Wadi Kurn) to the north and a second tributary to the south.

History in the Crusader period. In the twelfth century, the castle came into the hands of Joscelin III de Courtenay. In 1228 it was sold by Jacques de Mandelée to the Teutonic Order. It was rebuilt by them and served as the headquarters of the Grand Master, where the archives and treasury were located. In 1266 Baybars unsuccessfully laid siege to Montfort. In June 1271 the Muslims reopened siege on the castle and after a week managed to mine the southern rampart and occupy the inner bailey. The knights sought refuge in the keep but eventually surrendered and were permitted to leave for Acre.

Excavations and surveys. Excavations of the Metropolitan Museum of New York were directed by W.L. Calver (in the field) and B. Dean in 1926. A survey was conducted R. Frankel and N. Gatzov of the IAA.

Description. A classic spur castle, exceptional principally in its location near neither border nor important road and occupying a hill which is lower than the surrounding hills and thus entirely lacking strategic advantages. It was also unusual among Military Order castle in lacking a level courtyard. The castle was protected on the north, south and west by the steep slopes of the valleys and was cut off from the spur to the east by two moats and defended by a large keep. The keep occupied the highest part of the castle and took up the entire width of the spur (*c.* 25 metres). It overlooked the other buildings to the west, as well as the ridge of the spur to the east, and provided a lookout position over the two dry-river valleys to the north and west. Below the keep to the west were two-storey groin-vaulted halls which contained the living quarters of the knights. Further west, beyond a massive wall, are two barrel vaults that once supported a large Gothic rib-vaulted hall, its vaulting supported on an octagonal central pillar. Around the castle are the remains of outer fortifications. Below the castle at the foot of the valley to the north are remains of a two-storey building which Pringle suggests was a mill which in the thirteenth century was converted into a first-floor hall, possibly used as a guest house.

Bibliography. Benvenisti, 1970, pp. 331–37, 345; Boase, 1971, p. 181, pls. 121–22; Dean, 1982; Deschamps, 1934, pp. 81–82, 99; 1939, p. 17, 120, 138–39, 225, 237, fig. 11; Frankel, 1988, pp. 265–67; Frankel and Gatzov, 1986; Frankel, *et al.*, 2001, p. 27, no. 191; Guérin, 1880, vol. II, pp. 52–58; Kennedy, 1994, pp. 38, 124, 129–31, fig. 17; Lawrence, 1988, pp. xxx, 130n; Marshall, 1992, pp. 108–11, fig. 7, pls. 8, 9; Müller-Wiener, 1966, pp. 24, 28, 74–75, pls. 104–105; Prawer, 1972, 308–12; Pringle, 1986b; 1997a, pp. 73–75, figs. 38–39, pls. LXXII–LXXV; Rcy, 1871, 143–51, pl. XV; *SWP*, vol. I, 1881, pp. 152, 154, 186–90.

55 Mount Tabor (Har Tavor/Jabal at-Tur) (IG map ref. 1871E–2325N)

Location. This isolated, oval mountain is situated on the north-east side of the Jezreel Valley.

History in the Crusader period. Mount Tabor was given to the Hospitallers by Pope Alexander IV on 1 April 1255, together with extensive possessions and privileges, on condition that they would fortify the hill with a castle garrisoned by 40 knights. Thus properties possessed by the Benedictine monastery of Mount Tabor (estates in the plains below the monastery, including several villages and properties near Tripoli and Jerusalem and also in Transjordan) passed to the Order, as did fishing rights in Antioch. Within four years the Hospitallers had installed a castellan. However, Hospitaller possession of this large property was to be short-lived. In April 1263 it fell to Baybars, who destroyed the church. There is no evidence for Hospitaller building on the hill, if indeed any took place.

Excavations and surveys. Sporadic excavations were carried out by the Franciscans between the 1850s and 1900. These exposed remains of the Crusader church.

Bibliography. Benvenisti, 1970, pp. 358–62; Friedman, 1982; Pringle, 1998a, pp. 63–85.

56 Naples/Neapolis (Shekem/Nablus) (IG map ref. 1750E–1815N)

Location. Nablus is located some 50 km north of Jerusalem on the principal internal route from Jerusalem to Acre.

History in the Crusader period. A charter of 1159 (*Cart. des Hosp.*, I, 209, no. 279) records that a hospital was founded here by Baldwin II (1118–31). An inscription on a block of marble which was recorded in *c*. 1592 by a Portuguese Franciscan, Pantaleone d'Aveiro, stated that in 1180 the master of the Hospital established a hospice, 'habitation of pilgrims', in Nablus.

Excavations and surveys. Surveys in this town were carried out by C. Clermont-Ganneau, C.R. Conder and H.H. Kitchener, V. Guérin, and, more recently, by D. Pringle (see 1998a).

Description. From remains on the site (on modern Shariʿ al-ʿAnbiya, Street of the Prophets, previously known as Shariʿ al-Masakin, Street of the Paupers, a name possibly originating in this institution), the hospital (or hospice?) was, according to Benvenisti (1970, p. 165), a courtyard building, 80 metres long (n.–s.). According to Pringle (1998a, p. 106), what remained of the structure early in the last century was an elongated building measuring 50 to 55 by 15.8 metres. Two-thirds of this structure was destroyed in 1946, but photographs from 1919 give us an idea of this building. Originally it was probably a huge building, facing a courtyard with large open arches. Today the surviving vault is the western part of the structure.

Bibliography. Benvenisti, 1970, pp. 161–65; Pringle, 1998a, pp. 104–107.

57 Raheb (Metzad Rahav/Qal'at Rahib) (IG map ref. 1800E–2755N)

Location. Remains of this possible keep are located 8.5 km east-north-east of Montfort Castle.

History in the Crusader period. A village dependent on Chateau de Roi (Mi'iliya) was purchased by the Teutonic Order in 1220.

Excavations, and surveys. This site was surveyed by C.R. Conder and H.H. Kitchener, and by R. Frankel, N. Gatzov, M. Aviam and A. Dagani in 1975 and from 1986 to 1990.

Description. There are ruins of what may have been a small keep, as well as additional vaults.

Bibliography. Frankel, *et al.*, 2001, p. 35, no. 279; Pringle, 1997a, pp. 82–83.

58 Rama/Ramatha/Ramelie/Rames/Ramola/Ramula (IG map ref. 1379/81E–1479/81N)

Location. This town is located 19 km south-east of Jaffa on the road between Jaffa and Jerusalem.

History in the Crusader period. Ramla was an important town on the road between Jaffa and Jerusalem and on the *via maris*. The Military Orders held various properties here, the Hospitallers already coming into possession of properties in the town before 1126. Later, in 1180, they received lands outside the town. By 1196 the Teutonic Knights also held some houses in Ramla. The town fell to Saladin in 1187.

Excavations and surveys. There have been no surveys or excavations of buildings identified as having belonged to one of the Military Orders.

Description. Few remains have been assigned to the Crusader period. The parish church, possibly the Church of St John (now the great mosque), is the only substantial Frankish building surviving today. Fragments of another Crusader church survive in the present church of St George.

Bibliography. Pringle, 1998a, pp. 181–99.

59 Recordana/Recordane/De Recordaine (IG map ref. 1606E–2501N)

Location. The ruins of this recently discovered Hospitaller mill (Shaked, 2000) are located at the spring which is the source of the Naaman River, about 12 km south-east of Acre and *c*. 370 metres east of the Templar Mill of Doc – Khirbat Kurdana (no. 37, see p. 240).

History in the Crusader period. Mills run by the Hospitallers which, together with the nearby Templar mills downstream, served as a source of conflict between the two Orders in the thirteenth century.

Excavations and surveys. The site was surveyed by Shaked, and excavations carried out by the IAPN and INPA in 1999.

Description. Excavations at this site exposed the foundations of a mill, pentagonal in plan, constructed of ashlars dressed with the typical Frankish diagonal tooling. To the east is a well-constructed dam, *c*. 135 metres in length. In the south of the mill structure excavators found the ashlar base of one of the mill chutes.

Bibliography. Shaked, 2000.

60 La Roche de Roissol (Çalan/Chivlan/Sivlan) (GCS map ref. 3619E–3638N)

Location. This name is sometimes identified with a castle located on the Nur Daglari, overlooking the Hajar Shuglan Pass, 15 km north of the Belen Pass through the Amanus Mountains. It occupies a remarkable setting on a plateau-like, steeply inclined ledge above a precipice 1,200 metres above sea level.

History in the Crusader period. There is some dispute over the identification of the castle now known as Çalan Kalesi. Deschamps identified it with Templar La Roche Guillaume. Cahen and Edwards ('somewhat reluctantly') identify it with another Templar castle, La Roche de Roissol. This site was occupied and fortified by the Templars some time in the twelfth century.

Excavations and surveys. The castle was surveyed by R. Edwards in 1981.

Description. There were two wards here, an upper and a lower bailey. More fragmentary structures survive on the upper bailey to the east. Only fragments of the circuit walls survive. These appear to have originally surrounded the entire edges of the plateau. A mass of rock outcropping separates the southern part of the upper bailey from the lower bailey and fragments of a wall. In the south-east of the upper bailey is a chapel, the best-preserved structure in the castle.

Bibliography. Cahen, 1940, pp. 141–44, 512, 539; Edwards, 1987, pp. 99–102, pls. 47–52; Rey, 1883, p. 350; Sinclair, 1990, pp. 314–16.

61 Saphet (Zefat/Safad) (IG map ref. 1965E–2638N)

Location. This large hilltop castle is located in the mountains north of the Sea of Galilee, 12 km west of the Jordan River.

History in the Crusader period. Saphet Castle was probably originally a small castle, possibly a keep, built around 1102 by Hugh of St Omer. It was reconstructed and expanded in *c.* 1140, and in 1168 was purchased from King Amaury by the Templar Order who intended to use it as their headquarters in the eastern Galilee. In 1179, when Saladin destroyed the Templar castle at Jacob's Ford (Vadum Jacob), he also destroyed the faubourg of Saphet. Following the Battle of Hattin the castle remained in Frankish hands until December 1188, when it surrendered after a siege of two months. It was dismantled by al-Mu'azzam 'Isa in 1219. With the treaty of Richard of Cornwall in 1240 Saphet was returned to the Templars, who in December of that year began to rebuild it employing Arab prisoners-of-war; construction continued for two and a half years. This work was recorded in a detailed anonymous tract known as *De Constructione Castri Saphet*. Twenty-six years later, on 23 July 1266, the castle fell to Baybars after a siege lasting six weeks, which ended when he persuaded the Templars to surrender. Baybars promised to allow them safe retreat to Acre but subsequently massacred 917 defenders and two friars. He later repaired the castle and it served into Ottoman times as a local government headquarters until in 1837 a major earthquake left it in ruins.

Excavations and surveys. The castle was surveyed by C.R. Conder and H.H. Kitchener for the *SWP* in the 1870s and by R. Frankel, N. Gatzov, M. Aviam and A. Dagani in 1975 and from 1986 to 1990. Ongoing excavations since 2003 are conducted by Hervé Barbé and Emanuel Damati for the IAA.

Description. A very large, now ruinous, oval hilltop castle with a central ward and two concentric ranges of fortifications with two moats covering a total area of *c.* 120 metres (e.–w.) by 280 metres (n.–s.). We know something of its dimensions from the *De Constructione Castri Saphet,* according to which the inner walls were a remarkable 44 metres high (compared to 34 metres at Chateau Pelerin). The outer wall had at least seven round towers. Ruins of a large polygonal keep (possibly Mamluk) occupy the highest part of the hill to the south and the main gate appears to have been on the south-west. Part of the Frankish defensive works in this area has now been exposed. A subterranean tunnel south of the keep supplied water to the castle from a source beyond the walls.

Bibliography. Barbé and Damati, 2004; Benvenisti, 1970, 199–204; Frankel, *et al.,* 2001, p. 39, no. 322; Kennedy, 1994, pp. 128–29; Pringle, 1985; 1997a, pp. 91–92; *SWP,* vol. I, 1881, pp. 248–50, 255–56.

62 Sari Seki (map ref. 3614E–3639N)

Location. This site is on a hill overlooking the road leading north to the Cilician plain, 11 km north of Iskenderun, 1 km north of the Pillar of Jonah and less than 1 km inland.

History in the Crusader period. Edwards (1987, p. 215) notes that it was probably first built by the Templars in order to help secure the Nur Daglari (the lesser pass through the Amanus Mountains, 15 km north of the Belen Pass). Later, between 1135 and 1150, it was alternately in Armenian and Byzantine hands. In *c.* 1154 Reginald of Antioch took control of the forts in the region, returning Sari Seki to the Templars. They retained control of it until 1266 when it was taken by al-Malik al-Mansûr, who massacred the Templar occupants.

Surveys and excavations. This site was surveyed by R. Edwards in 1981.

Description. This was apparently an enclosure castle. It was largely reconstructed in the Ottoman period.

Bibliography. Cahen, 1940, p. 149; Edwards, 1987, pp. 215–16.

63 Le Saffran/Sapharanum/Castrum Zafetanum/Cafram (Shefar'am/Shafa 'Amr) (IG map ref. 1663E–2457N)

Location. There are possible remains of the castle in the town of Shefar'am *c.* 12 km east of Haifa on the road to Nazareth, apparently located within the Ottoman castle built by Dahr al-Umar in 1761.

History in the Crusader period. Le Saffran was a predominantly Christian village in which the Templars built a castle which Theoderich (1896, p. 69) described as 'very strong'.

Surveys and excavations. A brief excavation was carried out by the IAA under the direction of D. Syon in 2002/03 within the Ottoman building constructed by Dahr al-Umar in the eighteenth century.

Description. The only possible evidence at present for the Templar castle is a massive medieval wall within the Ottoman complex incorporating ashlars with diagonal tooling. However, the identification of this as Frankish is tentative at best.

Bibliography. Petersen, 2000; Pringle, 1997a, p. 115. New discoveries not yet published.

64 Sidon/Saida/Sagitta/Saget/Saiete/Sayette/Seete (Sayda) (IG map ref. 1844E–3282N)

Location. Sidon is located on the Mediterranean coast 70 km north of Acre and 35 km south of Beirut. The Templar Sea Castle is at the entrance to the northern bay of Sidon.

History in the Crusader period. Sidon was captured by the Baldwin I on 4 December 1110 following a siege of 47 days. It was subsequently held by Eustace Garnier. Saladin took the town on 29 July 1187, and in 1190 the walls were destroyed and the population removed to Beirut. Saladin shortly thereafter granted half of the town and its revenues to Reginald of Sidon (ratified by the Treaty of Jaffa in 1192), but he does not seem to have taken advantage of the grant and it is recorded as still in Muslim hands in 1217 (James de Vitry, *Lettres* II, 314–22). In November 1227 a group of French and English Crusaders waiting the arrival of Frederick II occupied the town and began the construction of the Sea Castle; the treaty signed between Frederick and al-Malik al-Nasir Da'ud authorised the return of the town to the possession of the Franks. Between 1249 and 1250 it was briefly taken by Damascus, but was then returned to Frankish hands; in 1253/54 Louis IX strengthened its fortifications. In 1256 part of the lordship was sold to the Teutonic Knights, and in 1260 – after a raid on the town by the Mongols – Julien de Sagette sold the entire lordship to the Templars. After the fall of Acre the Templars abandoned Sidon in 1291.

Excavations and surveys. From 1946 to 1950 repairs and restoration of the Sea Castle were carried out by the LAD.

Description. Houses and property of the Order of St John, the Templars and the Teutonic Order are recorded in Sidon but nothing is known of their whereabouts. Apart from their house, the Hospitallers had a gate in the town wall and possibly substantial sections of the forewall. The Templars had the Sea Castle on the northern harbour. The Sea Castle appears to have developed in various stages. Kalayan has distinguished four stages on the basis of varying types of stonework, although, as Kennedy notes, the builders came from different countries and may have used different types of stonework in contemporary construction work. In any case it is clear that the castle developed and expanded on the island, and it would seem that in the early stage it had square towers. These were later encased in massive walls, apparently the work of Simon de Montceliart (master of crossbowmen for Louis IX) in 1253. The elongated rib-vaulted hall, possibly including the dormitory and refectory, could date to this phase or to the final Templar phase. This great hall had 16 bays supported on seven free-standing octagonal piers and measured 60 by 15 metres (internally), with walls *c.* 3 metres thick. There was an upper storey reached by staircases in the thickness of the southern wall.

Bibliography. Ben-Dov, 1986; Deschamps, 1939, pp. 224–33; Kalayan, 1973; Kennedy, 1994, pp. 122–24; Müller-Wiener, 1966, pp. 69–70, 102; Pringle, 1997a, pp. 94–95, fig. 52; 1998a, pp. 317–29; Rey, 1871, pp. 153–59.

65 Silifke (Seleucia) (map ref. 3354E–3623N)

Location. This hilltop castle is located on the summit of a large elongated hill overlooking the Göksu River (Calycadnus), 86 metres above sea level.

History in the Crusader period. Occupied by the army of the First Crusade in 1098,

Silifke became part of the Principality of Antioch. It was taken by the Byzantines in 1104. Parts of the present defences no doubt date to this period. Silifke passed several times between Byzantine and Armenian control. In the last decade of the twelfth century it was held by the Armenians. With the decline in the military situation on the western frontier of Cilicia, King Levon II ceded the town and fortress to the Hospitallers in 1210, together with the nearby castles of Camardesium and Castellum Novum (Norberd) in exchange for the services of 400 heavily armed knights and an annual tax. Edwards (1987, p. 228) believes that, in spite of Armenian influences such as the entrance and rounded towers, most of the work is probably Frankish (i.e. Hospitaller). In 1226 the knights abandoned the castle and it was reoccupied by the Armenians. Improvements were made and it appears to have remained in their hands.

Excavations and surveys. Edwards surveyed this castle in 1973 and 1979.

Description. Well-preserved curtain walls, towers and a ditch. Barrel-vaulted galleries run around the entire circumference of the castle, surrounding a large courtyard containing a number of ruined structures.

Bibliography. Edwards, 1987, pp. 221–29, pls. 200–204, 299–300; Müller-Wiener, 1966, pp. 80–81.

66 St Johan de Tire/Tyr (Tirat Ha-Karmel/at-Tira) (IG 1480E–2410N)

Location. This site is located opposite Chateau Pelerin on the lower south-western slope of Mount Carmel.

History in the Crusader period. This was possibly a Templar possession in the thirteenth century (Johns, 1997, I, p. 26; Pringle, 1998a, p. 371).

Excavations and surveys. The ruins were examined in the nineteenth century by Rey and Guérin and in the twentieth by Makhouli, who sketched a plan of one of the churches which had been converted into a mosque. In 2002 excavations uncovered fragmentary building remains which possibly belonged to the larger of the two churches. These consisted mainly of ribs from Gothic rib vaults.

Description. Two churches and a fortified building with two towers and some barrel vaults were located here.

Bibliography. Benvenisti, 1970, p. 344; Guérin, vol. II, 1874, pp. 282–83; Pringle, 1997a, pp. 102–03, pl. CII; 1998a, pp. 369–72; Rey, 1883, p. 432.

67 St Margaret's Castle (Cava Templi, castrum) (IG map ref. 1474E–2482N)

Location. This castle was located in the area of the modern town of Haifa, towards the northern end of the Carmel Mountains, overlooking the Bay of Acre.

History in the Crusader period. Theoderich refers to a Templar castle here (1169).

Excavations and surveys. None.

Description. This was apparently a roughly square enclosure castle. It was destroyed in 1821 and the lighthouse was built over the remains. A fragment of a tombstone with the name Hugh, which was found in the vicinity, was possibly from the tomb of a Templar from the castle.

Bibliography. Pringle, 1997a, p. 93; 1998a, pp. 248–49.

68 Tarphile/Tharthilla/Trefile/Tertille (H. Nahat/Kh. al-Manhata) (IG map. ref. 1721E–2715N)

Location. This site is located about 1 km on the road above the castle of Montfort leading to Castellum Regis (Mi'iliya).

History in the Crusader period. Tarphile was a Teutonic *casale*; in the thirteenth century a quarry and guard tower served in the construction of Montfort.

Excavations and surveys. Surveyed by N. Makhouli in 1946 and by R. Frankel, N. Gatzov, M. Aviam and A. Dagani in 1975 and from 1986 to 1990.

Description. Remains survive of a fortified courtyard with a broad gate, a tower and the quarry which supplied building stones for Montfort. The quarry was linked by two ramps to the road leading to Montfort. The quarry itself covers an area of about 70 metres (n.–s.) by 90 metres (e.–w.), and a considerable area around it also contains medieval remains. A solid rock podium near the centre of the quarried area, which measures 13 by 10 metres, formed the base of the tower, smaller but similar in form to the podium of Le Destroit. A cistern was cut into the rock and on its south side there is a rock-cut staircase rising to the constructed first-floor level, of which only part of the west wall survives. Stairs were also cut in the rock sides of the quarry area.

Bibliography. Frankel, *et al.*, 2001, p. 28, no. 197; Masterman, 1919, p. 73; Pringle, 1997a, p. 70.

69 Toron des Chevaliers/Toron Militum/Toron de los Caballeros (IG map ref. 1485E–1375N)

Location. This castle is located on a low hill above the road between Jaffa and Jerusalem near the site of Nicopolis – Emmaus according to Greek tradition.

History in the Crusader period. A Castilian chronicle informs us that this important roadside castle was built by Count Rodrigo Gonzalez of Toledo between 1137 and 1141 when he was in the East fighting the Muslims (Pringle, 1998b, pp. 94–95). He garrisoned and equipped the castle and then handed it over to the Templars. They probably expanded it after 1150. The keep may possibly represent the first stage of the castle prior to its Templar ownership. Subsequent Templar construction at this site appears to be extensive, but only with excavation will it be possible to date the different stages of this castle. In September 1187, al-Adil occupied the castle. On 25 December 1191 Richard I and the army of the Third Crusade camped here during his first attempt to reach Jerusalem. By this time the castle had already been destroyed by Saladin. He camped here again during his second attempt to reach the Holy City in the summer of 1192. After the signing of the Treaty of Jaffa in 1229 Toron des Chevaliers was returned to the Templars, although it is not known whether they restored the castle. It was finally lost to them in 1244.

Excavations and surveys. No systematic excavations have been carried out here. An unpublished survey was carried out by D. Bellamy in 1938 and a later survey was published by Ben-Dov in 1974. The most recent surveys were carried out by Denys Pringle (BSAJ) in 1989 and by Adrian Boas (Haifa University) and Rafi Lewis (IAA) in 2003/04.

Description. The castle includes a keep (14 metres square). The basement of the keep is a barrel vault, with walls 3–4 metres thick. It is contained within a large rectangular enclosure castle measuring 72 by 55 metres with no projecting towers, in which there are barrel-vaulted ranges, those to the east probably forming the ground-floor base of the castle chapel. The gate of the rectangular enclosure, which had a portcullis, was located to the east. The outer wall has a talus, as do the outer ranges of the castle, traces of two of which survive, including mural towers, a *chemin de ronde* and an outer gate to the south.

Bibliography. Ben-Dov, 1974, pp. 117–20; 1993b, pp. 911–13; Boas and Lewis, forthcoming; Guérin, vol. I, 1868, p. 257; Pringle, 1997a, pp. 64–65, fig. 34, pls. LX–LXIII; 1998a, pp. 5–9; 1998b, pp. 94–102, figs. 9.4–9.8.

70 Tortosa/Tortouse (Tartus) (GCS map ref. 3553E–3453N)

Location. This town is located on the Syrian coast, half way between Latakia and Tripoli.

History in the Crusader period. The Crusaders occupied Tartus in the early years of the twelfth century during the campaign of Raymond of Toulouse to occupy Tripoli and expand his control towards the Orontes and Homs in the East. In 1152 Tartus was briefly occupied and destroyed by Nur ad-Din and subsequently, in order to strengthen the Crusader hold on the region, William, Bishop of Tortosa, granted the Templars land in Tortosa on which to build a new castle (Barber, 1995, p. 81). This was situated: 'from the entrance to the port to the house of William of Tiberias and reaching on all sides to the Gate of St Helen', apparently in the north-west corner of the city. Here they constructed a large castle which included two parallel defensive lines on all sides but the west. At the centre stood the great keep which had two flanking towers, one on its north-west corner and one on the south-east corner. A postern gave access to a landing point on the shore. In the north-east was a chapel. The Templars turned the city into their principal fortress in the north, and refortified the castle, town and harbour. In July 1188 Saladin briefly occupied most of the city but failed to take the donjon, and although he did much damage, including destruction of the cathedral, the Templars regained their control. Tartus fell on 3 August 1291, a week before the fall of Chateau Pelerin.

Excavations and surveys. The medieval remains were examined by G.E. Rey, C. Enlart and P. Deschamps. Recent surveys were carried out by M. Braune (published 1985).

Description. Remnants survive of the city walls and the fortress, as well as the cathedral.

Bibliography. Braune, 1985; Burns, 1992, pp. 229–32; Deschamps, 1973, pp. 287–92, pls. LVII–LIX; Enlart, text, vol. II, 1927, pp. 395–430; Kennedy, 1994, pp. 132–38, figs. 18, 19, pls. 46–49; Müller-Wiener, 1966, pp. 50–51, 98, pls. 33–35; Rey, 1871, pp. 64–83, 211–214, pls. VIII–XX.

71 Tour Rouge/Turris Rubea (Burj al-Ahmar) (IG map ref. 1455E–1917N)

Location. The Red Tower is located in the Plain of Sharon 23 km south-east of Caesarea on the road to Tulkarm.

History in the Crusader period. The castle is first recorded as held by the Abbey of St Mary Latina (*c.* 1158). It was obtained by the Hospitallers in *c.* 1187/91 and later (by 1236) it was in the hands of the Templars. Subsequently, by 1248 it had returned to the Hospitallers. It was destroyed by the Mamluks around 1265.

Excavations and surveys. Excavations here were directed by D. Pringle on behalf of the BSAJ in 1983.

Description. Remains survive of a two-storey rectangular keep surrounded by an enclosure wall. Of the keep only the south wall stands to nearly its full height. The keep measured 19.7 metres (n.–s.) by 15.5 metres (e.–w.). The ground floor consisted of two joining barrel vaults. A staircase on the north-east led up to the second-floor level, which had six groin-vaulted bays supported on two square piers. The tower was surrounded by an enclosure wall.

Bibliography. Pringle, 1986a; 1997a, pp. 38–39, fig. 21, pl. XXVII.

72 Trapesac (Darbsak) (GCS map ref. 3622E–3634N)

Location. A small Templar castle occupies a low hill 4 km to the north of the town of Kirikhan, north of the Belen Pass. It guards the road from the north to Antioch and the northern approaches of the Belen Pass.

History in the Crusader period. This castle was apparently originally constructed by the Templars in order to serve as part of the defences of the Syrian Gates (Belen Pass). Together with Gaston to the south, it remained in Templar hands except for a brief interlude when it was occupied between 1171 and 1175 by the rebel Armenian Baron Mleh. It fell to Saladin after a two-week siege on 16 September 1188. It was subsequently returned to Templar hands, survived an attempted siege by Levon I in 1205 and was soon reoccupied by the Muslims. A Crusader attack in 1237 failed to retake the castle. In 1261 Darbsak was returned to Armenian hands as a gift from the Mongol Khan Hulagu. In 1268 it fell to the Mamluks and was badly damaged in a Mongol attack in 1280.

Excavations and surveys. The site was surveyed by R. Edwards in 1979.

Description. This castle is largely built over by a modern village and, although many medieval remains can be seen amongst the village houses, the only part of the hill on which substantial remains can be observed is the south. Remains of an aqueduct which supplied water to the castle can be seen to the west. It was far better preserved in recent times; see the aerial photograph in Deschamps, 1973 (album), pl. 85b.

Bibliography. Edwards, 1987, p. 253, pls. 246–48; Sinclair, 1990, p. 297.

73 Tripoli (GCS map ref. 3552E–3426N)

Location. This town and castle are located on the Mediterranean coast, 68 km north of Beirut.

History in the Crusader period. In 1103 the Church of St Mary of the Latins in Jerusalem was granted property on Mount Pelerin (Mons Peregrinus) near Tripoli by Raymond of Toulouse. Bishop Pons of Tripoli made a grant to the Hospitallers, of a church dedicated to St John the Baptist, also on Mount Pelerin. This grant, which apparently dates to some time in the first decade and a half of the twelfth century, received papal confirmation in 1119, and in 1126 the Hospitallers were also granted a *hospitale pauperum*.

Excavations and surveys. A survey and excavations were carried out by H. Salamé-Sarkis.

Description. A chapel and crypt excavated by Salamé-Sarkis may possibly be remains of the church of the Hospitallers. The chapel consisted of a three-bay barrel-vaulted nave. Remains of an octagonal crypt (funeral chapel) are located below the apse.

Bibliography. Salamé-Sarkis, 1980, pp. 57–94; Pringle, 2004, pp. 36–38.

74 Tyr/Tyrus (Tyre) (IG map ref. 1685E–2975N)

Location. The port town is situated on a promontory on the Mediterranean coast 40 km north of Acre.

History in the Crusader period. Tyre held out against Crusader attacks until July 1124, but was subsequently held by them until May 1291, being the only Crusader city to resist Saladin successfully after the Battle of Hattin.

Excavations and surveys. Surveys were carried out by D. Roberts, C.R. Conder and H.H. Kitchener and G.E. Rey.

Description. No remains of buildings of the Military Orders are known.

Bibliography. Chéhab, 1975; 1979; Guérin, Galilée, vol. II, 1880, pp. 180–95; Rey, 1871, pp. 167–69, fig. 42; *SWP*, vol. I, 1881, pp. 72–81.

75 Vadum Jacob/Le Chastelez (IG map ref. 1433E–1052N)

Location. The fortress of Vadum Jacob is located above and to the west of the Jordan River, north of the ford across the river and south of the present bridge (Gesher Benot Ya'acov), 12 km north of the Sea of Galilee. The castle is on a low hill, an ancient tell with remains dating from the Middle Bronze Age to the Hellenistic period.

History in the Crusader period. In 1178 the Templars began to fortify the ford across the Jordan River north of the Sea of Galilee. The area of the ford was claimed by the Muslims as being in their territory and Saladin demanded that the Templars cease construction, even offering them the sum of 60,000 gold dinars. Vadum Jacob was never completed; it was far from completion when in the last week of August 1179 Saladin opened siege. Within days, following a partially successful mining operation in the north, the castle fell and the entire Templar garrison was slain or taken into captivity. The Ayyubid army then set about systematically dismantling the castle. However, they had not completed their task when plague broke out amongst the troops and they were forced to abandon the site.

Excavations and surveys. Ongoing excavations are headed by R. Ellenblum (HUJ) (with IAA 1993–97 co-directed with M. Hartal 1993 and A. Boas 1994–1997).

Description. The castle would have been an elongated rectangle in form but for the fact that, as in the twelfth-century castle of Crac des Chevaliers, the northern end of the castle has several angles forming an angular, curved wall. Indeed, despite the far less impressive topography, the poor state of preservation and the fact that considerable parts of this castle were never completed, Vadum Jacob would appear to be very similar to the early phase of the great Hospitaller castle. The circumference wall of the castle was possibly completed (fallen arrow-slits suggest that at least it had reached a fair height), but the parallel inner wall and the barrel vault between the two had only been partly constructed by the time the castle was destroyed. This was in the south and south-east of the castle between the main south gate and the small postern near the centre of the eastern wall. In the south-east corner of the castle, within the vault, the Templars built a large stone baking oven (5 by 5 metres). Nothing else has been found so far of additional contemporary buildings within the castle wall. The castle's outer wall has three small gates (posterns?) which could have been intended to serve as doors to towers which were to be constructed onto the exterior of the wall but were never completed. Alternatively, and perhaps more likely, these could have been intended to serve as gates between the internal courtyard and an outer bailey, and the outer curtain which had not been built.

Bibliography. Boas, 1999, pp. 118–20; Ellenblum and Boas, 1999; Ellenblum, *et al.*, forthcoming.

NOTES

BACKGROUND

1 Prawer, 1972, p. 252. The development of Prawer's other 'original' contribution, warfare and fortification, was closely tied to the activities of the Military Orders.

2 References in contemporary sources to Muslim raiders on the roads are frequent. See for example Fulcher of Chartres, II.IV.3 and Saewulf, (quoted on p. 3, this volume). William of Tyre's description (William of Tyre, 9.19) is perhaps the most detailed account of the situation in the early years of settlement: 'The cities which had come under our power were but few, and these were so situated in the midst of the enemy that the Christians could not pass from one to another, when necessity required, without great danger. The entire country surrounding their possessions was inhabited by infidel Saracens, who were most cruel enemies of our people. These were all the more dangerous because they were close at hand, for no pest can more effectively do harm than an enemy at one's very doors. Any Christian who walked along the highway without taking due precaution was liable to be killed by the Saracens, or seized and handed over as a slave to the enemy.' His account goes on to describe the dangers even within the cities, where there were too few defenders to prevent the Muslims from climbing the walls and attacking the Franks in their houses.

3 Albert of Aachen, 12.33. The identity of these pre-Templar castles is unknown.

4 On the date of the foundation of the Templar Order, see Barber, 1995, pp. 8–9; Forey, 1985, pp. 175–76, n. 2; Richard, 1999, p. 119.

5 Simon de St Bertin, vol. 13, p. 649.

6 Forey, 1994, I, pp. 175–76.

7 William of Tyre, 12.7.

8 Saewulf, pp. 8–9.

9 Daniel, XXVII.

10 Walter Map, p. 29.

11 William of Tyre, 12.7.

12 Upton-Ward, 1992, no. 121.

13 Fulcher of Chartres, II.VI.9. Prawer refers to the difficulty of establishing a stable knightly class due to the continual state of war. Prawer, 1980a, p. 23.

14 Upton-Ward, 1992, p. 6.

15 Ibid.

16 William of Tyre, 12.7.

17 On the rule of the Templars, see Upton-Ward, 1992; Barber, 1995, pp. 14–18, 182–83.

18 Ibid., pp. 42–50.

19 Not January 1128 as often appears. See Barber, 1995, p. 14.

20 Riley-Smith, 1967, p. 36, n. 5.

21 William of Tyre, 18.5.

22 Nicholson (2001, pp. 2–3) notes that the cathedral of Amalfi was dedicated to the Virgin Mary and St John the Baptist.

23 On Gerard's possible origins, see King, 1931, pp. 20–21.

24 Albert of Aachen, no. 70.

25 *Cart. des Hosp.* nos. 25, 29. Subsequent papal privileges even freed the hospital from the jurisdiction of the patriarch of Jerusalem and other Church authorities, archbishops and bishops in the East and West.

26 Several of these hospices were located in port cities which were embarkation points for traders and pilgrims travelling to the East.

27 For the Rule, see King, [1934] 1980. For the Augustinian Rule, see Canning, 1984. Some clauses in the Rule of Raymond du Puy were adopted in their entirety from the Rule of Saint Augustine. These include clause 4 which deals with behaviour of the brothers when travelling, clause 8 regarding the manner in which they should act when going out of the convent to preach, clause 13 on the punishment due to a brother who retains and conceals private property, and clause 17 regarding the manner in which a brother may correct a fellow brother who has gone astray.

28 For a discussion of the origins of the Teutonic Order, see Sterns, 1985, pp. 315–56.

29 Ibid., p. 320.

30 Ibid., p. 321, n. 14.

31 It appears that by 1250 the Teutonic Order had drawn up its own Rule and Customs. See ibid., pp. 323–26.

32 The motivation for the move from Acre to Montfort was, at least in part, due to fear of the young Order's rivals in Acre; thus the choice of an isolated castle, far, but not too far from the city, for their new headquarters. How complete was this move? The constitution of the Teutonic Order required that the high officials of the Order, including the Master, reside in the main convent at Acre where, according to the statutes, the chapters were to be held. The central archive would normally have been located there as well. However, as for the residence of the Master, Hermon von Salza who headed the Order between 1210 and 1239 spent much of his time in Montfort or outside the boundaries of the Kingdom of Jerusalem (mostly in Italy). As regards the archives, it appears that archive material was divided between several of the Order's houses. The treasury of the Order, according to the constitution, could have been located in either Montfort or Acre. On these matters see the introduction by Mayer to the photographic reprint of Strehlke, [1869] 1975, pp. 75–77. The hospital, not surprisingly, was not transferred to Montfort; the isolated castle would have been ill suited to this function.

33 Lee, 1996, pp. 19, 66.

34 Clermont-Ganneau, 1901, p. 110.

35 King Fulk and Queen Melisende granted gifts to the Order. King Amaury, whose son Baldwin (later Baldwin IV) was leprous, was a strong supporter of the Knights of St Lazarus. In 1164 he promised them one slave for every ten Muslim captives, and he granted 72 bezants to the Order annually from the tolls taken at Porta David (Jerusalem) and 40 bezants from the customs of Acre. See Marcombe, 2003, p. 10 and n. 48. Support for the Order came from the count of Tripoli, the lords of Beirut and Caesarea, and others. Raymond of Tripoli was a *confrère*; Walter, lord of Beirut, considered entering the Order; and Eustace, brother of Hugh, lord of Caesarea, did so, although possibly for reason of piety rather than having contracted the disease. See Barber, 1994b, pp. 442–43.

36 Dichter, 1979, p. 118.

37 On the former see Strehlke, [1869] 1975, no. 128; *RRH*, no. 510 (item 13). Ellenblum's study of this source has shown that the first 21 transactions referred to in this document were located in or near Castellum Regis. The *domus leprosorium* is amongst these. See Ellenblum, 1998, pp. 42–43.

38 Upton-Ward, 1992, p. 115

39 This claim, based on medieval sources, has been challenged by some writers, but Alan Forey has convincingly refuted the claims for an earlier foundation. On this matter see Forey, 1977, pp. 481–503.

40 Ibid., pp. 487–88.

41 Dichter, 1979, pp. 111–12.

42 Riley-Smith, 1967, p. 425. See Prawer and Benvenisti, 1970, Sheet IX/10.

43 Riley-Smith, 1967, pp. 480–91.

44 Guy established a dynasty that ruled Cyprus until the Venetians took over in 1474.
45 Edbury, 1991, pp. 77–78.
46 The fortress at Paphos (Saranda Kolones) has been referred to as Hospitaller, but this identification is based on the similarity of the design of the castle to Hospitaller Belvoir rather than on any textual evidence. This claim, like the equally unsupported suggestion that it is Templar (see Cadei, 1999, pp. 131–42), must be regarded as unlikely. I am grateful to Denys Pringle for pointing this out to me.
47 Cane sugar was a field of agriculture and industry in which the Hospitallers were actively involved on the mainland too. See pp. 93–4.
48 Edbury, 1991, p. 78.
49 Ibid., pp. 78–79; Dichter, 1979, p. 113.
50 Boase, 1978, pp. 94–95.
51 Edwards, 1987, p. 224.
52 Sirarpie Der Nersessian (in Setton, vol. II), 1969, p. 650.
53 Strehlke, [1869] 1975, no. 298.
54 Ibid; also Sirarpie Der Nersessian (in Setton, vol. II), p. 650, n. 30.
55 Upton-Ward, 1992, p. 178.
56 An *Auberger* is referred to from 1239. See Riley-Smith, 1967, pp. 309–10.
57 Ibid., pp. 317–19.
58 Sterns, 1985, p. 328.
59 Probably the latter was required of sergeants and not of knights, as the latter did not normally engage in archery. Archery was not considered a noble occupation and was not a practical one for a knight, as it required the use of two hands, whereas a knight with his shield in one hand had only one hand free to hold a weapon.
60 King, [1934] 1980, p. 145.
61 Wilkinson *et al.*, 1988, p. 225. This is from the second-hand account by the Muslim geographer from Sicily, who, it appears, did not himself visit Jerusalem.
62 For the archaeological evidence on these, see pp. 190–3.
63 Upton-Ward, 1992, pp. 53–54.
64 King, [1934–] 1980.
65 De Curzon, [1886] 1977; Wojtowicz, 1991; Upton-Ward, 1992; Dailliez, 1996.
66 Strehlke, 1869, republished in Toronto, 1975.
67 Perlbach, 1890; Sterns, 1969.
68 Many of these were translated into English and published by the Palestine Pilgrims' Text Society (PPTS) in the last decades of the nineteenth century.
69 The text, published with an introduction by Huygens, 1965, pp. 355–87, was published in an English translation by Kennedy, 1994, pp. 190–98.
70 Rey, 1871.
71 Conder and Kitchener, 1881–83.
72 Schick, 1902, pp. 42–56.
73 Dean, 1982 (facsimile of 1927 edition).
74 This survey was carried out by Rafael Frankel and Nimrod Gatzov. See Frankel and Gatzov, 1986 (Hebrew).
75 Deschamps, 1934. For Kennedy's comments, see Kennedy, 1994, p. 208, n. 4.
76 See Deschamps, 1939, pp. 177–208, pls. LIII–LXXV.
77 See Johns, 1997.
78 A survey was conducted by N. Tzori in 1963, and from 1966 to 1968 the entire castle was excavated and partly restored by Meir Ben-Dov on behalf of the Israel Parks Authority. See *NEAEHL*, vol. 1, 1993, pp. 182–86.
79 Compare the pre-excavation plan of the castle published by Conder and Kitchener, 1882, p. 117, which was still used by Smail a decade before the excavations. Unfortunately this excavation has never been published in detail.
80 In 1957 Peter Megaw commenced a series of seasons of excavation at Saranda Kolones; they continued over a 30-year period. See Megaw, 1994. As already noted (see p. 262, n. 46), there is no sound basis for his suggestion that this is a Hospitaller castle – but its design was certainly influenced by Hospitaller Belvoir.

81 The excavations were carried out by a team from Bar-Ilan University and the IAA under the direction of Amos Kloner, together with Michael Cohen.
82 Kloner and Cohen, 2000 (Hebrew). See also Kloner and Cohen, 1996a, 1996b.
83 Ellenblum and Boas, 1999; Ellenblum *et al.*, forthcoming.
84 The excavations were carried out by the British School of Archaeology in Jerusalem and were directed by Richard Harper and Denys Pringle They were published in two preliminary reports and subsequently in a detailed final report. See Harper and Pringle, 1988, 1989, 2000.
85 For the best study of this site see Pringle, 1993, pp. 239–50; 1992, pp. 147–67.
86 Pringle, 1986a, pp. 41–58, figs. 10–14, pls. X–XXII.
87 Ibid.
88 Pringle, Petersen *et al.*, 1994.
89 See Figure 8.
90 Hamilton, 1949.
91 Buschhausen, 1978; Folda, 1995, pp. 441–56, 467–69; Jacoby, 1979, pp. 3–14; 1982, pp. 325–94; 1985, pp. 442–50.
92 This section of wall, 20 metres long and 2.8 metres thick, was dismantled after being exposed and was unfortunately never properly recorded. It can, however, be seen on aerial photographs. See for example Kedar, 1999, p. 132 (foldout).
93 This survey was named after the architect Percy H. Winter who headed the team. It was published in four volumes: Winter, 1944. A summary is published in Dichter, 1973, pp. 181–88.
94 These excavations were carried out on behalf of the Israel National Parks Authority and the Department of Antiqities of Israel by archaeologists Ze'ev Goldmann in 1956 and Ze'ev Yeivin in 1960. See Goldmann, 1994.
95 The renewed excavations and restoration are being carried out by the Israel Antiquities Authority and the Old Akko Development Company under the direction of archaeologist Eliezer Stern. See Stern and Avissar, 1994, 1996, and E. Stern, 2000 (Hebrew).
96 This excavation was directed by Adrian Boas of Haifa University and Georg Philipp Melloni of the Deutscher Orden. Preliminary publication is in press. See pp. 61–3.
97 The excavations in 1977 and 1980–81 were headed by Israel Roll and Eitan Ayalon on behalf of the Department of Antiquities of Israel and Tel Aviv University. Since 1982 Israel Roll headed the excavations on behalf of Tel Aviv University and in 1998 they continued as a joint project of the Department of Archaeology of Tel Aviv University and the Federal University of Porta Alegre in Brazil.
98 Enlart, [1899] 1987.
99 Megaw, 1977, p. 206.
100 As noted on p. 5, Megaw's own identification of Saranda Kolones at Paphos as a Hospitaller castle has been brought into doubt.
101 Edwards, 1987.

PART I URBAN ADMINISTRATIVE CENTRES

1 The Hospitaller property in Jerusalem goes back to the century prior to the Crusader period, when Amalfitan merchants set up an establishment for Latin pilgrims (see p. 5). In Acre they were granted property near the cathedral of the Holy Cross by Baldwin I shortly after the city was captured by the Crusaders in 1104. These grants were confirmed in 1110. See *Cart. des Hosp.*, no. 20; *RRH* no. 57.
2 One example of a role played by the Military Orders in urban life was the responsibility of the Hospitaller and Templar Masters, together with the patriarch, as holders of the keys of the crown jewels. See *Chronique d'Ernoul et de Bernard le Trésorier*, p. 133; Eracles, vol. II, p. 28. In 1186, on the death of Baldwin V, Sibylla, the sister of Baldwin IV, claimed the throne. The Hospitaller Master, Roger de Moulins, who supported Raymond of Tripoli in opposition to Sibylla and her husband Guy, refused to hand over the key to the crown jewels needed for the coronation. When pressure mounted he threw the key out of the window.

3 Not all cities had an appeal for the Military Orders. John of Ibelin allegedly told Emperor Frederick II that when he had taken possession of Beirut it 'was all destroyed, so much so that the Templars and Hospitallers and all the barons of Syria refused it' (Edbury, 1997, pp. 28–29, n. 21). The Teutonic Order seems to have played down its urban role in Acre after 1227 in favour of its isolated headquarters at Montfort Castle.

4 Riley-Smith, 1967, p. 130; Pringle, 1993, p. 181.

5 Riley-Smith, 1967, pp. 127–28.

6 These connections were often directed towards their own interests, not always in accordance with the interests of the Frankish states. In 1248 St Louis had to order the Templars to cease negotiations with Egypt and in 1252 with Damascus. Ibid.

7 Ibid., p. 147.

8 Ibid., p. 79.

9 Richard, 1982, p. 90 and n. 3.

10 Ibid.

11 On this, see for example Kedar, 1998, p. 7.

12 *Cart. des Hosp.*, no. 79.

13 On the defences of 1218, see James de Vitry, III. 35–41, p. 99; Oliver of Paderborn, 1894, p. 168. On 1251–52 see Matthew Paris, *Chronica maiora*, ed. H.R. Luard (*RS* 57), vol. V, p. 257; *Cart des Hosp.*, no. 2605; John of Joinville, 1963, pp. 289–95, 318.

14 Pringle, 1995, p. 99.

1 THE URBAN QUARTERS OF THE TEMPLARS

1 It is interesting and equally ironic to note the similar fate of many of the Templars' castles, which seem in general to have survived the passage of time far less successfully than those of the Hospitaller Order.

2 In comparison, the Hospitaller Quarter in Jerusalem, although in a ruined state, survived until the beginning of the twentieth century and was recorded in detailed plans and photographs before it, too, largely disappeared in 1905. In Acre, the main Hospitaller Quarter was partly preserved under the Turkish citadel, and its monumental remains are now largely exposed following a decade of intensive archaeological excavation.

3 William of Tyre 12.7; Babcock and Krey, 1943, vol. I, p. 525.

4 See Boas, 2001, p. 79. His predecessor, Baldwin I, had probably made it more uncomfortable by selling lead tiles that he had stripped from the roof. See Fulcher of Chartres, 1.26.

5 William of Tyre, 12.7.

6 Boas, 2001, pp. 79–82.

7 Kühnel, 1994, p. 42.

8 John of Würzburg (English translation), p. 21.

9 Theoderich, p. 31; Huygens, 1994, pp. 164–65.

10 Benjamin of Tudela, 1907, p. 22.

11 William of Tyre, 12.7. William of Tyre was working on his history from *c.* 1170 until 1184. See Edbury and Rowe, 1988, p. 26. Benjamin of Tudela is perhaps a less-than-reliable source regarding such information. He gives an equally implausible number of 400 Hospitaller knights in Jerusalem (see p. 43, n. 5).

12 Imad ad-Din, in Gabrieli, [1969] 1989, p. 164.

13 This church may have been intended to replace the small church, once a mosque, adjacent to the Templum Salomonis which was referred to by Usamah Ibn-Munqidh, pp. 163–64.

14 Huygens, 1994, pp. 165.

15 See pp. 208–10; also Jacoby, 1979, pp. 3–14; 1982, pp. 325–94; 1985, pp. 442–50.

16 Hamilton, 1949.

17 Ibid., p. 23, pl. XVI: 2 and 3.

18 Ibid., p. 25.

19 Ibid., p. 27, fig. 13.

20 Ibid., fig. 14a.

21 Ibid., p. 27.

22 See pp. 24–5.

23 Enlart 1927, pl. 357.
24 Ibid., pl. 355.
25 Ibid, p. 44.
26 See p. 208.
27 Le Strange, 1887, pp. 90–103.
28 Pierotti called it the Abu Bekr Mosque and noted (Pierotti, 1864, vol. 1, p. 81) that his guide identified it as the armoury of the Crusaders. Le Strange, 1887, p. 91 repeats this identification.
29 Clermont-Ganneau, 1899, vol. I, p. 143.
30 Charles Wilson noted that the foundations of its apse were still visible in 1896 on the east side of the al-Aqsa Mosque. Though these cannot be seen today, the location of Wilson's apse is supported by the description of Imad ad-Din, who refers to a church built by the Templars 'east of the *qibla*'. See Gabrieli, [1969] 1989, p. 164.
31 Huygens, 1994, p. 165.
32 Gabrieli, [1969] 1989, p. 144.
33 Huygens, 1994, p. 165.
34 Ibid., p. 31.
35 Hamilton describes these in detail. See Hamilton, 1949, pp. 48–53, pls. 27–30. This complex of vaults, although not very appropriate for such use, served in the past as a *madrasa* (see Schick, 1887, p. 91 – *Madrassah al-Farsiyyah*)
36 Hamilton, 1949, p. 53.
37 For an illustration of this, see Pierotti, 1864, vol. 2, pl. XXIII (3).
38 Huygens, 1994, p. 165.
39 King, [1934] 1980, p. 107.
40 See the copy of the Cambrai Map in Röhricht, 1891, p. 138.
41 Gibson and Jacobson, 1996, p. 277.
42 Benjamin of Tudela, 1907, p. 23.
43 See p. 20.
44 John of Würzburg, p. 134; Huygens, 1994, p. 165. Malcolm Barber suggests that, assuming that the building also housed squires, grooms and possibly pilgrims as well, it could probably not have held more than 500 horses. See Barber, 1995, p. 94.
45 Pierotti, 1864, vol. 1, pp. 77–78.
46 This was perhaps the pool at Mamilla to the west of the city, which a thirteenth-century text refers to as being used to water horses; *La Citez* (PPTS 6), 1896, p. 21.
47 Walter Map, 1983, pp. 29–30.
48 The use of camels for the transport of goods is illustrated on one of the versions of Matthew Paris's map of the Holy Land (*C.* Cambridge, Corpus Christi ms 26), where just east of Acre a camel is shown carrying what it has been suggested may have been a bundle of sugar cane. See Dichter, 1973, p. 11.
49 Schick, 1891, p. 201.
50 Barber, 1995, p. 93.
51 Wilkinson, 1988, pp. 225–26.
52 Theoderich, p. 33; Huygens, 1994, p. 166.
53 See Kedar, 1999, foldout following p. 130. See also a photograph of 1918 in Dalman, 1925, pl. 16. For a photograph of the section of the wall that was exposed during the excavations, see Meir Ben-Dov, 1985, pp. fly-leaf, 10, 58–59, 275, 292 (back to front), 313, 331.
54 Possibly much of what can be seen in the photographs is a later terrace wall.
55 As it appears that the Fatimid south city wall at this point was constructed on the ruins of the southern and eastern walls of one of the ruined Umayyad palaces (see Wightman, 1993, p. 238) it is possible that the origins of this tower were Fatimid as well. It would have defended the recently reconstructed (Umayyad period) Double Gate.
56 See Schick's description and plan in Schick, 1892a, p. 20.
57 Ben-Dov has given a different interpretation of this complex. See Ben-Dov, 1983 (Hebrew), pp. 79–81. In his version the gate complex has two stages of construction. In the Fatimid period the three parallel chambers, each consisting of three groin-vaulted bays, were constructed against the Double Gate. The complex could be accessed on either side (west

and east) via gates against the Temple Mount wall. However, according to Ben-Dov, the Crusaders added a large fortified structure on the west and apparently blocked access on the east, replacing it with three arrow embrasures. If Schick's reconstruction is correct, the tower would have been an important element in the Templar foreworks. The Templar wall could have extended west to the tower or to the wall to its south, ensuring that the only access to the Quarter in this direction was through the tower, turning north through the Double Gate into the Templum Salomonis or through the east gates of the tower into the approach between the two walls leading up to the Single Gate and from there into the Stabuli Salomonis. The latter option would not be possible in Ben-Dov's interpretation.

58 Consequently, the tunnel built under Solomon's Stables, which was discovered in the nineteenth century by Charles Warren and which exits in two rectangular cuttings in the Herodian masonry several metres below the gate, is almost certainly not a Crusader postern, as Ben-Dov has suggested (Ben-Dov, 1985, p. 347). Its presence at the time would have prevented use of the Single Gate. The arched postern which appears on the Cambrai Map (*poterna*) represents the Single Gate. Without taking the illustrations of buildings on this map too literally, it is tempting to suggest that the drawing of this gate is additional evidence for the existence of the Templar bastion. It is shown not in the city wall itself as all the other gates are, and with no road exiting from it as is the case in the other gates, but rather above (behind) the wall – that is, perhaps behind the bastion.

59 Pierotti, 1864, vol. 1, p. 78.

60 See Jacoby, 1979, 1982, 1985.

61 On its output, see pp. 208–10.

62 See Buschausen, 1978; Burgoyne and Folda, 1981, pp. 321–22.

63 Pringle, 1991b, p. 111.

64 De Sandoli, 1979, pp. 19–20; Pringle, 1989a, pp. 197–201.

65 An additional epigraphic find relating to Templar activity on the Temple Mount is a fragment known as the Templar Letter, which was found in the roof of the al-Aqsa Mosque in the 1920s and was originally published by Abel. See Abel, 1926, pp. 288–95.

66 Glüksmann and Kool, 1995, pp. 87–104.

67 There is no evidence for the use of these palaces in the twelfth century, and they were certainly in a ruined state by that time.

68 Dichter, 1973, pp. 17–18, 20–24, 26–27, 29–30.

69 The use of ashlar construction for the entire vault is not typical of Crusader work, in which vaults are usually constructed of roughly shaped stones or rubble covered with plaster. It is more similar to Ayyubid or Mamluk work like the vaults at Subeibeh. However, as this is clearly a Frankish structure, this type of vault construction may suggest a late date, possibly after the War of St Sabas (1256–58). A late date would perhaps explain how it was possible to construct this remarkable complex of large tunnels running several hundred metres under houses of two or three storeys in a densely built-up area. During the war many of the houses in the area, which is located close to the boundary between the Genoese and Pisan Quarters, may have been damaged or destroyed. It would be easier to understand this engineering feat in the light of such destruction, which would have enabled the construction of the passages before the houses were rebuilt.

70 The Military Orders had large numbers of ships in their possession in the thirteenth century. In 1216 the Templars and Hospitallers had to negotiate with Marseilles on their right to build ships and transport pilgrims and merchants, and attempts were made to limit the number of ships they possessed. See Pryor, 1988, p. 135; Richard, 1999, pp. 402–03.

71 *Les Gestes des Chiprois*, p. 253.

72 Shavit and Galili, 2002, pp. 10–12 (Hebrew).

73 See, for example, in the south-west faubourg tower at Chateau Pelerin, p. 34.

74 Mayr, 1782, p. 56.

75 *Les Gestes des Chiprois*, p. 253. The combined value of these lions was given as 1,500 Saracen bezants.

76 Ludolf, *PPTS*, 12, 1895, p. 59.

77 According to Ludolf they held out for two months. Ibid.

78 *Cronica S. Petri Erfordiensis moderna*, vol. 30, pp. 424–25.

79 Ibid.
80 Barber, 1995, p. 199. Presumably the relic had some calming power over the elements.
81 *Gestes des Chiprois*, p. 245.
82 Prawer, 1977, p. 182.
83 Johns, 1997, II, pp. 110–29, pls. XL–L.
84 Ibid., p. 120
85 Ibid., pp. 99–118, 120–24.
86 Ibid., p. 120
87 Raban, 1986, p. 185.
88 Johns, 1997, II, pp. 123–24.
89 Ibid., p. 124.
90 Ibid., pl. XLVII, figs. 1 and 2.
91 Ibid., V, pp. 122–37, pls. LXXI–LXXV; Pringle, 1993, no. 27, pp. 75–80.
92 Pringle, 1993, p. 75.
93 Metcalf, *et al.*, 1999, pp. 102–03.
94 Johns, 1997, II, pp. 124–29, pls. LI–LII, figs. 22–24.
95 Metcalf, *et al.*, 1999, pp. 103–04.
96 Johns, 1997, II, p. 128.
97 Ibid., I, p. 67.
98 Ibid., VI, p. 35.
99 Ibid., p. 32.
100 Johns prefers the former: ibid., p. 34.
101 Ibid., II, pp. 118–20.
102 Ibid., p. 118.
103 Ibid., VI, pp. 47–54.
104 On this, see p. 188.
105 Metcalf, *et al.*, 1999, p. 94.
106 Johns, 1997, VI, p. 56.
107 Ibid., IV, p. 147, fig. 3.
108 For houses at Caesarea see Boas, 1996b, pp. 77–79. For Yoqne'am see Ben-Tor, *et al.*, 1996, pp. 20–23. For Arsuf (Apollonia) see Roll and Ayalon, 1989 (Hebrew), pp. 75–76 and for Jaffa, Peilstöcker, 2000, p. 48.
109 An aerial photograph of the cemetery is published in *NEAEHL*, vol. 1, p. 115.
110 In Acre their access to the port depended on others and on maintaining the subterranean passage mentioned on pp. 29, 31.
111 Huygens, 1994, p. 185.
112 Le Bruyn, 1698, between pp. 306–07; Friedman, 1971, pp. 295–348. According to Elias Friedman it was located on the present site of the Stella Maris monastery, but the scanty archaeological evidence from that site is not at all enlightening. Friedman, 1979, pp. 90–91.
113 William of Tyre, 20.20.
114 Ibid.
115 Edbury, 1996, pp. 119, 121.
116 Pringle, 1993, pp. 208–20.
117 *Itin. Ric.* vi, 15 (*RS* 38.1, 409).
118 Pringle, 1998a, p. 323.
119 It was probably from this house that in 1173 King Amaury forcibly removed to prison the Templar knight who killed an Assassin envoy (William of Tyre, 20.30). The grant to the Hospitallers was made as part of an exchange of possessions between the two Orders carried out in 1260, whereby the Hospitallers handed over all of their possessions in the Lordship of Sidon (Pringle, 1998a, p. 323).
120 Riley-Smith, 1969, p. 283.
121 Raynouard is mentioned in *Cart. des Hosp.*, no. 199; *RRH*, no. 270.
122 This connection is reflected in the Frankish name 'Tortosa', derived from the Arabic name Tartus which itself derived from the classical name Antaradus (*anti-Aradus, the town facing Aradus or Arwad*). Burns, 1999, p. 229.
123 Riley-Smith, 1969, p. 283.

124 Kennedy, 1994, p. 136.
125 Boase, 1977, p. 157.
126 Wilbrandus de Oldenborg, 1864, p. 169. The strength of the castle is revealed by the fact that the Templars held onto it until 3 August 1291, two months after the fall of Acre and only just before another strong Templar castle, Chateau Pelerin, served as the setting for the departure of the last Franks from the Crusader mainland on 14 August.
127 For illustrations of the guardhouse see Enlart, 1927, atlas vol. 2, pl. 166 (558); also Deschamps, Album, Paris, 1973, pl. LVII, a and b, and plan in Deschamps, Texte, 1973, p. 290.
128 On the Grand Hall see Enlart, 1928, text vol. 2, pp. 427–30, and illustrations in Enlart, 1927, atlas vol. 2, pls. 175–83 (549–57). Decorative consoles are illustrated in Enlart, 1928, fig. 558 and atlas vol. 1, pl. 26.85.
129 Folda, 1995, p. 302. For details see Braune, 1985, pp. 45–54. For illustrations of the portal and vaulting see Enlart, 1927, atlas vol. 2, pl. 174 (547–48).
130 Enlart, [1899] 1987, pp. 291 suggests that this refers to a hall or a bridge. However, the reference here is probably to warehouses. According to Riley-Smith, in the Hospitaller Order the 'vault' was a collective term for the warehouses, and the Hospitallers in thirteenth-century Acre had a 'Commander of the Vault'. See Riley-Smith, 1967, p. 308.
131 Enlart, [1899] 1987, pp. 214, 290–93.
132 Ibid., p. 292.
133 Ibid., p. 77.
134 Ibid.
135 *Gestes des Chiprois*, p. 207; Edbury, 1991, pp. 95–96; 1994, p. 193.
136 Enlart, 1987, p. 488.

2 THE URBAN QUARTERS OF THE HOSPITALLERS

1 See p. 5.
2 William of Tyre, 18.3; Riley-Smith, 1967, p. 247; Folda, 1995, p. 275.
3 Boas, 1999, pp. 85–88.
4 For photographs see, for example, Schiller, 1979, p. 202 (a); Perez, 1988, pp. 92–93. See also Schick, 1902.
5 Benjamin of Tudela, 1907, p. 22.
6 See p. 264, n. 11.
7 Schick, 1902.
8 Ernoul, pp. 31–52.
9 Ibid., p. 34.
10 Ibid., p. 35.
11 Schick, 1902, p. 50.
12 Kedar, 1998, p. 8.
13 Boas, 2001, pp. 159–60.
14 See Schick, 1902, plan facing p. 48; Pringle, 1997b, pp. 201–15.
15 On the Church of St John the Baptist see Dickie, 1899, pp. 43–45; Pringle, 1982b, p. 11.
16 The Pool of the Patriarch, modern Hezekiah's Pool, itself received its water from a pool outside the city walls to the west, the Mamilla Pool. In the Crusader period this was also known as the Pool of the Patriarch and supplied water to a cistern under one of the towers of the citadel.
17 De Vogüé, [1860] 1973, p. 253, n. 3; Bresc-Baurtier, 1984, no. 68.
18 Warren and Conder, 1884, p. 256; Pringle, 1991b, p. 110.
19 Pringle, 1991b, p. 110, has suggested that the row of corbels above the arched entrances on David Street probably supported a timber balcony.
20 Ernoul, p. 34; See Prawer 1991, p. 148; Bahat, 1991, p. 91. However, see Boas, 2001, p. 144–45.
21 Schick, 1902, plan and pp. 50–51.
22 Ibid.
23 Bresc-Bautier, 1984, no. 68; *RRH*, no. 223. For bakeries and flour mills see also *Cart. des Hosp.*, nos. 20, 100, 225.

24 The term refers to a stable used for asses.

25 *Cart. des Hosp.*, nos. 312, 469; vol. IV, no. 372.

26 English translation from *PPTS* 6, 1896, p. 16.

27 A forthcoming paper by Misgav Har-Peled will describe remains in the grounds of the Garden Tomb.

28 On the Garden Tomb see Vincent, 1925, pp. 401–31, pls. XIV–XVIII.

29 Conder, 1882, p. 117; Warren and Conder, 1884, pp. 387–93.

30 Unfortunately the quality of this photograph is very poor but the massively constructed pointed barrel vaults appear decidedly Frankish.

31 *Cart. des Hosp.*, nos. 154, 155.

32 For a plan of this complex see Boas, 2001, fig. 10.2.

33 Warren and Conder, 1884, p. 272.

34 See Ovadiah, 1973, pp. 208–12.

35 Ben-Dov, 1993c, pp. 140–42. These two buildings subsequently became a small archaeological garden and sadly of late have fallen into neglect.

36 Schick, 1902, plan facing p. 48.

37 Warren and Conder, 1884, p. 255.

38 John of Würzburg, p. 131.

39 Had there been any truth to Ludolph of Suchem's extraordinary claim that the bodies decomposed within three days, the value of this burial site would have been even greater. An entertaining attempt to ascertain the miraculous quality of the soil of Akeldama is recorded in Pierotti: 'I was anxious to test the truth of the belief, and so buried at a depth of four feet the body, not indeed of a human being, but of a lamb. After eight days I disinterred it, and unfortunately for my sense of smell, found that although I had carefully selected a piece of natural ground free from rubbish, the experiment was unsuccessful; I am therefore driven to conclude that the soil has lost its former virtue. I also filled a box with the soil, and placed therein birds, small quadrupeds, and reptiles; but in all cases the flesh was consumed slowly. I also planted flowers in some of it, at my own house, and found that they flourished perfectly' (Pierotti, 1864, p. 207).

40 *Cart. des Hosp.*, no. 150; *RRH*, no. 215.

41 The name 'Akeldama' also appears on the sixth-century Madaba Map.

42 See Levy, 1991, p. 502.

43 Pierotti, 1864, pp. 206–07; Schick, 1892b, pp. 283–89.

44 A forthcoming paper by Amit Re'em will describe this site. From this survey see reconstruction in Boas, 2001, fig. 20.2.

45 *Cart. des Hosp.*, no. 20; Riley-Smith, 2001, p. 111.

46 *Cart des Hosp.*, no. 112; *RRH*, no. 155

47 *Cart des Hosp.*, no. 972; *RRH*, no. 717.

48 Riley-Smith, 2001, p. 111.

49 See p. 56.

50 The most recent work is two seasons of excavation carried out by the IAA under the direction of Eliezer Stern in 1995, 2000 and 2003. For the panorama see Kedar, 1997, p. 165.

51 Riley-Smith, 2001, p. 111, notes that the hall or refectory commonly known as the 'Crypt of St John' (an error dating to the period prior to the recent excavations when the hall was still believed to be a subterranean structure; see p. 55), which was built prior to 1187, is out of line with the adjacent thirteenth-century structures – a fact which suggests that it was part of the twelfth-century convent. The church, which is on an entirely different alignment to all of the surrounding buildings, including the refectory and the *domus infirmorum* to its south, could also be earlier than all the other structures; but more likely, though, it is later and all of the archaeological evidence supports a later date.

52 Theoderich, p. 186.

53 Riley-Smith, 1967, pp. 247–48.

54 *Cart. des Hosp.*, nos. 917, 938.

55 Riley-Smith, 2001, pp. 111–12.

56 *Cart. des Hosp.*, no. 2612.

57 Riley-Smith, 1967, p. 185.

58 *Cart. des Hosp.*, no. 3771.

59 Dichter, 1973, pp. 18, 21–24, 26.

60 An additional difficulty with this identification is the fact that the location of the Accursed Tower (Turris Maledicta/Tour Maudite) is also uncertain. It appears on most of the medieval maps on the north-eastern corner of the outer wall, but on others it appears on the corner of the inner wall. The description of the Mamluk siege by the Templar of Tyre supports the location on the inner wall. See Prawer's comments on this (Prawer, 1969/70, vol. II, p. 554 and n. 39).

61 The excavation of this site, known as 'the Courthouse Site', was conducted by Moshe Hartal on behalf of the IAA and was subsequently published in a series of papers in A. Roshwalb-Hurowitz (ed.), *Atiqot* XXXI, 1997, pp. 1–128.

62 Hartal, 1997, p. 6; Nir, 1997, p. 31.

63 Hartal, 1997, p. 22.

64 Stern, 1997, p. 37. For examples of this type see Figure 78.

65 See p. 201.

66 These bowls make up 20 per cent of the assemblage.

67 This was carried out by Michael Eisenberg on behalf of Haifa University; publication forthcoming.

68 Avissar and Stern, 1998, p. 13.

69 According to a published plan, the courtyard was created in the thirteenth century when the structures to the north, west and south were added to the twelfth-century palace on the east. The arched recesses on all four sides were later additions. However, the dating of these phases is still under consideration and may well be revised in future publications. See the coloured plan showing the four principal stages of construction published by E. Stern, 2000, pl. 1.

70 *Cart. des Hosp.*, no. 2612.

71 See p. 53.

72 This panorama is usually attributed to Gravier d'Ortières, captain of the ship *Jason* and commander of Louis XIV's reconnaissance mission from 1685 to 1687. See comments and the illustration (pp. 164–66) in Kedar, 1997, pp. 157–80.

73 See the etching by le Bruyn, 1698, p. 307. Dichter (1973, p. 39) dates this work to 1681 and Shur (1990, pp. 184–85) and Goldmann (1994, p. 62) date it to 1679.

74 These excavations have been carried out by the Israel Antiquities Authority under the direction of Eliezer Stern. See E. Stern, 2000, pp. 4–12.

75 From the 1686 panorama we might conclude that the building stood almost intact up to that date. It is tempting to speculate on the cause of the apparent collapse of most of this wall (possibly indeed of most of the structure) in the 12 years between 1686 and 1698. No major earthquake is recorded at this time (see Amiran and Turcotte, 1994, p. 272). It is generally believed that most stone robbing in Akko took place much later, in the eighteenth and nineteenth centuries, when the town and its fortifications were rebuilt by Dahr al-Umar (d. 1775), al-Jazzar (d. 1804) and his successors. The Templars' palace, for example, was still largely standing in 1748 (see Figure 4), but four years later was entirely dismantled by Dahr al-Umar, who had occupied the town in *c.* 1749.

76 One in Latin outside the apse of the chapel refers to the commencement of building on 15 June 1440, and a second inscription in French located above a small door giving onto the Street of the Knights records that building was completed in 1489.

77 Riley-Smith, 1967, pp. 308–09.

78 Ibid., p. 308.

79 E. Stern, 1999b, p. 13. On sugar moulds, see p. 93. On the involvement of the Military Orders in sugar cultivation and manufacture, see pp. 93–4.

80 Riley-Smith, 1967, pp. 308–09.

81 The excavators date this wing to the middle of the twelfth century, i.e., before the building of the auberge and the transfer of the brothers' quarters to Montmusard, which Riley-Smith dates to after the Third Crusade. See Riley-Smith, 1967, pp. 247–48. On the auberge, see p. 57, this volume.

82 See pp. 56–7.

83 Jacoby, 1993, pp. 88–91.

84 Mitchell and Stern, 2001, pp. 207–13.

85 Riley-Smith, 1967, p. 252, n. 2.
86 This name was given to the hall in the nineteenth century, when it was buried under close to eight metres of sand and could be reached only by a tunnel. With the excavations of the 1990s it became apparent that in the Crusader period this building was in fact not subterranean at all.
87 Goldmann, 1994, pp. 8–13. He suggests that the vaulting of the hall could date to 1149 and that it may have been raised in the Gothic style in honour of King Louis VII, a great patron of the Gothic style, who was at that time in the East and who visited Acre.
88 Riley-Smith, 2001, p. 111; Pringle 1986b; 2000, XII, p. 71, n. 55; E. Stern, 2000, plan facing p. 16. As noted on p. 270, n. 69, the dates on Stern's plan are being reassessed.
89 King, [1934] 1980, p. 151, no. 3.
90 While the Hospitaller Rule is very uninformative on confinement in prison, the Rule of the Temple makes frequent mention of the punishment referred to as being 'put in irons'. See, for example, Upton-Ward, 1992, nos. 177, 233, 234, 236, 241, 242, 249, 250, 260, 266, 267, 271, 336, 430, 432, 437, 438, 446, 452, 457, 554, 569, 573, 587, 589, 591, 593, 594, 600, 603, 606, 610, 611, 612 and 620. While this could refer to the chaining of prisoners to a wall in a prison, it could also have meant that they had their feet (and perhaps hands) shackled but were not confined to a prison. A clause in the Templar Rule (no. 266) notes: 'And when the habit is taken from a brother and he is put in irons, he should lodge and eat in the Almoner's house and does not have to go to chapel.'
91 John of Joinville, 1848, p. 475.
92 For Paris's map see Dichter, 1973, pp. 10–15. For Paulinos's map see Hartal, 1997, p. 110, fig. 2.
93 See, p. 270, n. 72. For the first publication of the entire Panorama see Kedar, 1997, pp. 164–66 and fig. 7. For an enlarged view of the Church of St John see Goldmann, 1994, pl. XVIII.
94 See Goldmann, 1994, pp. 23–24, fig. 10, pls. XII–XVI.
95 The excavations were conducted by Eliezer Stern on behalf of the IAA. See E. Stern, 1999a, pp. 11–12; 2004.
96 Ibid. For an illustration see Ben-Dov, 1999, p. 92, fig. 21.
97 For an illustration of this panorama see Kedar, 1997, p. 165.
98 See especially the map of Paulinus of Puzzeoli in Dichter, 1973, p. 29.
99 See p. 54.
100 *Cart. des Hosp.*, no. 3396.19; King, [1934] 1980, p. 77–78.
101 According to Ze'ev Goldmann, during clearance excavations carried out in 1954 (prior to the opening of the municipal museum which was housed in this building for over three decades), a subterranean room was discovered below the furnace of the *hammam*. It contained an earlier furnace which was dated to the Middle Ages, probably the Crusader period (Goldmann, personal communication). In support of this proposal, it has been suggested that a building with a decidedly medieval appearance that can be seen on the eighteenth-century map of the English traveller Richard Pococke, who visited Akko in 1739, may have been the Crusader bathhouse. The illustration shows a building with a destroyed dome and a façade with a blocked entrance which may represent the western face of the present *hammam*, in which a blocked entrance can still be seen. See Avissar, 1994, pp. 33–34. However, Eliezer Stern believes that there is no evidence for an earlier bathhouse on the site of the *hammam* (personal communication), and Riley-Smith suggests that the location of the Hospitaller bathhouse may have been to the east of the compound. See Riley-Smith, 1967, p. 246, n. 2.
102 Riley-Smith, 1967, p. 248 and n. 4; King, [1934] 1980, p. 54, n. 3. This was possibly also the Vigne Neuve.
103 *Gestes des Chiprois*, p. 253.
104 Riley-Smith, 1967, p. 248. The auberge was primarily a residence but, being a large and grand building (as was apparently true of the auberges at Caesarea and Jaffa as well), it served certain other important functions, not only in this instance but, for example, to house General Chapters. See King, [1934] 1980, p. 53.
105 King, [1934] 1980, p. 67; Dichter, 1979, p. 52; Riley-Smith, 1967, p. 235. For St Michael see also Marino Sanudo's map in Dichter, 1973, pp. 18, 22, 23.
106 For a description and illustration of this piece see De Sandoli, 1974, pp. 303–04, fig. 131.

107 Zeev Goldmann, 1962a, pl. IV.

108 King, [1934] 1980, p. 75; Riley-Smith, 1967, p. 309.

109 According to the excavator, Israel Roll, the brief activity of the Hospitallers here was chiefly related to certain structural additions and changes and in particular to the development of a kitchen/dining area in the north-western part of the courtyard.

110 The gate was defended by two round projecting towers, the presence of which suggests a thirteenth-century date.

111 See Pringle, 1993, pp. 60–61.

112 This grant, confirmed by his son Walter I in September 1131, included other property outside the town. See *Cart. des Hosp.*, no. 94.

113 Riley-Smith, 1967, p. 429, n. 4.

114 *RRH*, no. 57 (1110); no. 293 (1154); *RRH Add.*, no. 280b (1153).

115 See Pringle, 1993, pp. 268, 271 and map, p. 265, fig. 79.

116 *RRH Add.*, no. 1023a; no. 1084a.

117 King, [1934] 1980, p. 53.

118 Benvenisti, 1970, p. 165.

119 See recent plan by Matthew Pease, recent photographs by Pease and Pringle, and photographs by K.A.C. Creswell (1919) in Pringle, 1998a, pp. 105–06, fig. 26 and pls. LXX–LXXIV.

120 Ibid., p. 106.

121 De Sandoli, 1974, p. 271; Pringle, 1998a, p. 107.

122 *Les Gestes des Chiprois*, 1887, p. 131.

123 *Cart. des Hosp.*, no. 302; *RRH Add.*, no. 376b. This was confirmed by Balian, lord of Sidon, in May 1237. See *Cart. des Hosp.*, no. 2160; *RRH Add.*, no. 1076a.

124 Hiestand, 1984, pp. 199–201.

125 *Cart. des Hosp.*, nos. 79, 82.

126 Ibid., no. 82. See Luttrell, 1997, pp. 53–54.

127 Salamé-Sarkis, 1980, pp. 57–94; Pringle, 2004, pp. 36–38.

128 *Les Gestes des Chiprois*, p. 236.

129 Riley-Smith, 1967, pp. 131–32.

130 *Cart. des Hosp.*, no. 5.

131 Enlart, [1899] 1987, p. 20.

132 Ibid., p. 291, n. 89.

133 Riley-Smith, 1967, p. 249.

3 THE URBAN QUARTERS OF THE TEUTONIC KNIGHTS

1 Strehlke, [1869] 1975, no. 69. The German hospice in Jerusalem had been established in *c.* 1143 by German residents of Jerusalem, with the aim of setting up a similar (if considerably smaller) establishment to that of the Hospitallers where pilgrims of German origin could expect a warmer welcome than they appear to have received at the Frankish hospital. On the discrimination, imagined or real, felt by the German pilgrims, John of Würzburg writes with some emotion. See John of Würzburg, pp. 124–26.

2 Strehlke, [1869] 1975, no. 25.

3 See Dichter, 1973, pp. 9–30.

4 *Les Gestes des Chiprois*, p. 253.

5 Riley-Smith, 1967, p. 179.

6 Favreau-Lilie, 1982, p. 275.

7 Favreau-Lilie notes (ibid., p. 276) that the high price of this sale suggests that this was a large property. She also notes that by 1291 the citadel had a moat only on its northern side facing Montmusard (ibid., p. 275, n. 22). The apparent disappearance of the moat to the south of the citadel sometime between 1273 and 1291 seems to suggest that there was no longer a need to maintain a strong line of defence around the citadel. Possibly the new double line of city fortifications which appears on the medieval maps was already in place, and in addition the expansion and fortification of Montmusard placed the citadel well within the town's defences.

8 Strehlke, [1869] 1975, nos. 28, 29.
9 According to Klaus Militzer, the Order was required only to keep these defences in repair and not to defend them. See Militzer, 1998, p. 52. This would resolve the problem of the Teutonic Order being involved in military activity five years before they are known to have taken on military functions in 1198.
10 The *Turris Alamanorum* can be seen on the fourteenth-century maps just to the south of the German Quarter (Dichter, 1973, pp. 18–26).
11 The joint excavations aimed at finding evidence to support the tentative identification of this area as the site of the Quarter of the Teutonic Knights. The possible identification was founded on the earlier discovery of the remains of the two monumental buildings here and the suggested redrawing of the map of thirteenth-century Acre by Benjamin Ze'ev Kedar (Kedar, 1997, pp. 157–80). The excavations were carried out in two short seasons in the summers of 1999 and 2000, directed by Adrian Boas of Haifa University and Georg Philipp Melloni of the Deutscher Orden. Damage to the structures in 1291 and in the late seventeenth and early eighteenth centuries was so intense that only fragments of walls and living surfaces survive. Consequently, the results of the excavation were inconclusive. None the less, the presence of large quantities of unglazed ceramic bowls, probably used by pilgrims or brothers of the Military Orders, together with vessels used in the refining of sugar (see p. 93), lends support to the identification of these remains with a Quarter of one of the Military Orders. As the unglazed bowls (discussed on pp. 200–1) are a variant of the type found in Hospitaller sites within and outside Akko, the identification of this site with the Teutonic Order is a reasonable one. The presence of sugar vessels is also a factor strengthening this identification, as the Teutonic Knights, like the Hospitallers, were active in the cane sugar industry.
12 Amongst the coins was a gold *Hyperpyron Nomisma* of Emperor John III Ducas-Vatatzes (1222–54 CE), ruler of the Byzantine state of Nicaea.
13 The building excavated by Dotan is now buried under modern houses.
14 See IAA, Akko File D/1, 24 July and 8 August 1961.
15 Boas and Melloni, forthcoming.
16 Moshe Dothan, 'Akko', *IEJ* 24, 1974, p. 277.
17 Kedar, 1997, p. 173.
18 These excavations were carried out by Yotam Tepper of the IAA (personal communication).
19 Riley-Smith, 1967, p. 179.
20 It has been suggested, albeit on still fairly slender evidence, that enamel-decorated glass beakers known as Syro-Frankish beakers were manufactured for the Teutonic Order, perhaps by artisans whose workshops were located within the Order's Quarter. See Engle, 1976 (no. 6–7), p. 103; 1982 (13–14), pp. 39–64.
21 Eracles, vol. II, pp. 325–26; Pringle, 1993, p. 181; Strehlke, [1869] 1975, no. 40.
22 Dichter, 1979, p. 81.
23 Strehlke, [1869] 1975, no. 103; *RRH*, no. 1205.
24 Strehlke, [1869] 1975, nos. 32, 296.
25 Ibid., no. 128.
26 Ibid., nos. 31, 36, 45, 56, 57.
27 *Gestes des Chiprois*, p. 131.
28 Strehlke, [1869] 1975, nos. 44, 128.
29 Desimoni, 1884, no. 452.

4 THE URBAN QUARTERS OF THE LEPER KNIGHTS OF ST LAZARUS

1 The attitude of the Church towards lepers underwent a transformation in the Crusader period. Leprosy, which was already well established in Europe, increased considerably in the twelfth century. Prior to the Crusades it had been regarded as punishment for sin. The increase in the disease, which was attributed to contact with the 'Infidels' during the Crusades, necessitated a reassessment. It was unacceptable that Crusades be equated with sin. The prophesy of Isaiah: 'yet we did esteem him stricken, smitten of God' (Isaiah 53:4)

was reinterpreted to mean that Christ himself was to be considered leprous. Consequently the disease came to be regarded as a sacred disease and lepers as 'stigmatized' by God. See Wheatley, 1985, pp. 154–55.

2 See *RRH*, no. 269.
3 See Röhricht, 1891, map facing p. 137.
4 Michelant and Raynaud, 1882, p. 42.
5 Clermont-Ganneau, 1901, pp. 113–14.
6 Schick, 1895, p. 30.
7 Bresc-Bautier, 1984, no. 162.
8 'Quant Salahadin vint asseger Jerusalem, il se herberja devant la cité par un juesdi au soir. Le vendredi par matin il l'asseja de lez la maladerie des femes et par devant la maladerie des homes et devant la tor David jusques a la porte de saint Estiene' (Eracles, p. 82).
9 See Röhricht, 1891, p. 138.
10 See Maeir and Bahat, 2004, p. 185, figs. 7, 8.
11 See Bahat, *NEAEHL*, vol. 2, p. 796.
12 See Dunkel, 1902, pp. 403–5; Boas, 2001, p. 187.
13 The Third Lateran Council of 1179 permitted segregation of lepers, including their burial in separate sites from the general population. See Tanner, 1990, p. 222.
14 Dichter, 1973, pp. 10–16.
15 Ibid., pp. 17–30.
16 De Marsy, 1884, no. 18; *RRH*, no. 361; Pringle, 1993, p. 180.
17 Enlart, [1899] 1987, p. 79.
18 Ibid.

5 THE QUARTER OF THE KNIGHTS OF ST THOMAS

1 Dichter, 1973, p. 10–11.
2 Ibid.
3 Ibid., p. 136.
4 Enlart, [1899] 1987, p. 20.
5 Ibid., p. 139.
6 Ibid., p. 138.
7 Ibid., p. 99.

6 EXPANSION INTO THE COUNTRYSIDE

1 Riley-Smith, 1967, p. 434.
2 *RRH*, no. 57; *Cart. des Hosp.*, no. 20. See p. 5.
3 These included two villages named Beithsur, the villages of Irnachar, Irrasin, Charroubete, Deirelcobebe, Meimes, Hale, Bothme and Heltawahin, as well as four villages from the royal domain: Fectata, Sahalin, Zeita and Courcoza; *Cart. des Hosp.*, no 116. See Ellenblum, 1998, p. 142 and n. 63; Tibble, 1989, p. 10. Tibble notes that with this grant Fulk was establishing a new lordship (the lordship of Bethgibelin) on lands previously belonging to the lords of Hebron and thus was not only involving the Hospitallers in the defence of the south but was using them as a means of weakening one of the more powerful lay seigneuries (1989, pp. 10–11).
4 Referring to Bethgibelin's sister castle of Blanchegarde in a passage that equally applies to Bethgibelin, William of Tyre wrote: 'those who dwelt in the surrounding country began to place great reliance on this castle as well as on the other strongholds, and a great many suburban places grew up around it. Numerous families established themselves there, and tillers of the fields as well. The whole district became much more secure, because the locality was occupied and a more abundant supply of food for the surrounding countryside was made possible.' William of Tyre, 15.25; trans. Babcock and Krey, 1943, vol. 2, p. 132.
5 *Cart. des Hosp.*, no. 399.
6 Prawer, 1980a, pp. 120–21.
7 *Cart. des Hosp.*, no. 399.

8 On the *carrucae* see Ellenblum, 1998, pp. 98–99.
9 This was what is known as *heritage*, the legal institution under which free, non-noble Frankish settlers held property in or close to towns for cultivation and on which to build their houses.
10 Personal communication, Amos Kloner.
11 This suggestion was made by Michael Ehrlich. See Ehrlich, 1999, p. 203.
12 Pringle, 1998a, pp. 278–81.
13 See, for example, Bagatti, [1947] 1993; Boas, 1996a.
14 *Cart. des Hosp.* no. 2274.
15 See Petersen, 2001, pp. 141–43.
16 In a photograph taken in that year the bridge appears to have been destroyed but the mill was still intact and functioning. See Khalidi, 1992, p. 246.
17 It is recorded in *Cart. des Hosp.*, no. 263 (1158), which refers to land granted to the Hospitallers by Hugh of Ibelin. On the existing remains see Petersen, 2001, pp. 222–23.
18 See Kochavi and Beit-Arieh, 1994, p. 30, no. 31.
19 Benvenisti, 1970, p. 252.
20 *RRH*, no. 57.
21 Pringle, 1997a, pp. 28–9, pl. XVI.
22 *Cart. des Hosp.* no. 309. See Pringle, 1997a, p. 83.
23 Pringle, 1997a, p. 83.
24 The cistern, which consists of two well-constructed connected barrel vaults, was excavated by Zvi Greenhut in 2000 adjacent to the groin-vaulted structure.
25 These excavations were directed by the late Calsten Thiede of the Staatsunabhängige Teologische Hochschule, Basel and Egon Lass of the IAA.
26 On the likelihood that this church was built by the Hospitallers see Pringle, 1993, pp. 16–17.
27 The date of *c.* 1165 is the latest date for the text by Belard of Ascoli (1112–*c.* 1165), which is the earliest known reference to a church at Abu Ghosh. See *Itinera Hierosolymitana Crucesignatorum*, p. 46.
28 Clermont-Ganneau, vol. II, 1896, pp. 61–63.
29 *Itinera Hierosolymitana Saeculi III–VIII*, p. 110 (15).
30 Pringle, 1993, p. 16.
31 Two rock-cut staircases from the Roman cistern were originally prepared to give access to the crypt, but these were never used.
32 Kühnel, 1988, pp. 149, 177–80.
33 The numerous column paintings in the Church of Nativity in Bethlehem are not true frescoes. For an extensive discussion of the Abu Ghosh frescoes see ibid., pp. 149–80. This study was written before the recent restoration work.
34 *RRH*, no. 458.
35 Benvenisti, 1970, pp. 241–45; Enlart, 1928, pp. 103–06; Pringle, 1992, pp. 163–67; 1993, p. 250. More recently (Harper and Pringle, 2000, p. 215) Pringle has referred to both Aqua Bella and the inner ward at Belmont as manor houses. Pringle notes that the function of the former as a castle and the latter as an infirmary/priory date to after they were acquired by the Hospitallers (personal communication).
36 Pringle, 1992, p. 162; 1993, p. 248.
37 Ellenblum, 1998, pp. 112–13.
38 *Cart. des Hosp.*, no. 139; *RRH*, no. 201.
39 Riley-Smith 1967, pp. 392–93. See Bresc-Bautier, 1984, no. 107; *Cart. des Hosp.*, no. 192.
40 *RRH*, no. 433.
41 Ellenblum, 1998, pp. 104–05. For sources see *Cart. des Hosp.*, nos. 498, 1176. On the church see Pringle, 1998a, pp. 329–32.
42 Riley-Smith, 1967, map 2; Pringle, 1997a, p. 46.
43 Pringle, 1986a, pp. 28–76.
44 Ibid., p. 42.
45 For details see ibid.
46 Riley-Smith, 1967, p. 429, n. 4.
47 Pringle, 1986a, pp. 43–58.

48 Ibid., p. 56.
49 See illustration, originally by the *SWP*, in ibid., p. 53.
50 Ibid., p. 51
51 On these sites see Pringle, 1997a.
52 See, for example, the plan of Bait 'Itab in ibid., p. 26.
53 Pringle, 1986a, p. 54.
54 *RRH*, no. 611.
55 Luttrell, 1994, p. 67.
56 *Cart. des Hosp.*, no. 94; *RRH*, no. 57; Pringle, 1986a, p. 59.
57 *Cart. des Hosp.*, no. 168; *RRH*, no. 243.
58 *Cart. des Hosp.*, no. 223; *RRH Add.*, no. 298a.
59 King, [1934] 1980, p. 30, n. 2, identified it with Kefireh between Jaffa and Jerusalem.
60 *Cart. des Hosp.*, no. 494. Caphaer was purchased from Baldwin of Ramla in 1175.
61 *Cart. des Hosp.*, nos. 217, 497; *RRH*, no. 274, *RRH. Add.*, no. 539b.
62 *Cart. des Hosp.*, no. 350; *RRH*, no. 426.
63 *Cart. des Hosp.*, nos. 621, 645; *RRH*, nos. 618–19.
64 *SWP*, 1881, p. 33 (El-Helât).
65 *Cart. des Hosp.*, nos. 879, 2141.
66 Pringle, 1986a, pp. 37–39. On Tour Rouge see ibid.; also pp. 256–7 this volume.
67 *Cart. des Hosp.*, no. 1251; *RRH*, no. 819.
68 *Cart. des Hosp.*, no. 1400; *RRH Add.*, no. 859b; Pringle, 1986a, p. 72.
69 *RRH.*, no. 321.
70 *Ernoul*, p. 153.
71 For an illustration of this chapel see fig. 2 in Pringle, 2004, p. 29.
72 *Cart. des Hosp.*, no. 1250; *RRH.*, no. 818.
73 *Cart. des Hosp.*, nos. 1400, 1414; *RRH. Add.*, nos. 859b; *RRH*, no. 866.
74 Pringle, 1991a, p. 90; 1997, p. 104.
75 Riley-Smith, 1967, p. 415.
76 Pringle, 1998a, p. 68.
77 *Cart. des Hosp.*, no. 2714.
78 *Cart. des Hosp.* no. 2353.
79 Ellenblum, 1998, pp. 177–78; *Cart. des Hosp.*, no. 1313.
80 See pp. 86–7, 240.
81 '. . . casale Recordana . . . cum molendinis', *Cart. des Hosp.*, no. 225; *RRH*, no. 293.
82 The agreements date to 1201 (*Cart. des Hosp.*, no. 1144); revised in 1235 (*Cart. des Hosp.*, no. 2107; *RRH*. nos. 1061a) and in 1262 (*Cart. des Hosp.*, nos. 3026, 3027, 3032).
83 The various agreements of these disputes are recorded in *Cart. des Hosp.*, nos. 2107, 2117.
84 However, destruction was apparently not complete. The truce (*hudna*) signed two decades later between the Franks and Qalawun (Sultan al-Mansur) in Cairo on 3 June 1283 refers to 'Da'uq and its mill' and 'Kurdanah and its mill' (Dan Barag, 'A New Source Concerning the Ultimate Borders of the Latin Kingdom of Jerusalem', *IEJ* 29 (3–4), pp. 201–02, 205). Income from the mills was devoted to the mausoleum of Qalawun in Cairo, further evidence of their survival after the departure of the Franks (Ellenblum, 1998, p. 209). Benvenisti notes that the locals claimed that the (Templar) mills were in use until 1925 (Benvenisti, 1970, p. 251).
85 Shaked, 2000, pp. 61–72.
86 Benvenisti, 1970, p. 249.
87 Shaked, 2000, pp. 69–70.
88 In conjunction with the diagonal tooling, the date of this mill is supported by ceramic finds of the twelfth and thirteenth centuries uncovered during the dismantling of the structure. Ibid., p. 70.
89 *Cart. des Hosp.*, nos. 1383, 1526; *RRH*, no. 892.
90 *Cart. des Hosp.*, no. 3400.
91 See Stern, 2001, pp. 277–308.
92 Frankel and Stern, 1996, pp. 89–123. See fig. 4, photo 1.
93 See p. 93.

94 Stern, 2001, pp. 282–99.
95 *Cart. des Hosp.*, no. 1354.
96 King, [1934] 1980, p. 114, no. 20.
97 Ludolf of Suchem, p. 39, n. 1.
98 Ibid., pp. 39–40.
99 Saladin spent the night here on 14 October 1192. See Imad ad-Din al-Isfahani, p. 397; Abû Shâmâ, p. 87; *SWP* 1881, vol. II, p. 302; Guérin, 1874, vol. II, p. 36.
100 *Cart. des Hosp.*, nos. 2107, 2117, 3032; *RRH*, no. 1062; *RRH. Add.*, nos. 1061a, 1062.
101 The use of double or multiple arches is more typically Ottoman than Frankish, although it is not unknown in Frankish building (Pringle, 1997a, pls. XC, XCVI).
102 Ibid., p. 62.
103 Ellenblum, 1998, p. 206.
104 Pringle, 1997a, p. 47. However, Ellenblum, 1998, p. 206, gives dimensions of 55.70/58 (e.–w.) by 54 (n.–s.) metres.
105 Ellenblum, 1998, p. 208. There is no visible evidence for fortification on either of these sites, but both require excavation to establish their layout.
106 Benvenisti, 1970, p. 252.
107 Ellenblum, 1998, p. 205.
108 *RRH*, no. 1212.
109 Pringle, 1998a, p. 333; *RRH*, no. 1413.
110 *RRH*, no. 1413, n.1.
111 Ellenblum, 1998, pp. 209–11, pl. 12; Pringle, 1997a; Weinberg, 1968, pp. 198–99.
112 Ellenblum, 1998, p. 209.
113 Pringle, 1997a, pp. 96–97.
114 Weinberg, 1987.
115 For an illustration of this type of beaker see Boas, 1999, pl. 6.4.
116 Ralph of Diss, p. 28.
117 Abû Shâmâ, p. 246. It was destroyed twice more in the following years, in September 1184 (Ralph of Diss, p. 28) and in July 1187 following the Battle of Hattin (Abû Shâmâ, p. 301). It never returned to Frankish hands.
118 This was in vain, as six years later Beaufort fell to Baybars.
119 Prawer, 1980a, p. 150.
120 After this the Commandery was apparently held by the Hospitallers until it was destroyed by the Mamluks in 1426.
121 Enlart, [1899] 1987, p. 487.
122 Ibid., p. 337.
123 Ibid., pp. 336–37.
124 Strehlke, [1869] 1975, no. 29.
125 Ibid., no. 32.
126 Ibid., no. 25.
127 Ibid., no. 34.
128 Ibid., no. 38.
129 Ibid.
130 Ibid., nos. 53, 58; *RRH*, nos. 934.
131 Strehlke, [1869] 1975, nos. 63, 65.
132 See pp. 126–30, 248.
133 Pringle, 1986b, pp. 52–81.
134 Ibid., p. 62.
135 Ibid., p. 63.
136 Strehlke, [1869] 1975, no. 66.
137 Ibid., nos. 119, 121.
138 Ellenblum, 1998, pp. 41–53.
139 Strehlke, [1869] 1975, nos. 52, 58; *RRH*, nos. 934.
140 See Pringle, 1993, p. 25 and, for a plan of this complex, Ellenblum, 1998, p. 171.
141 Strehlke, [1869] 1975, no. 65. '*Castro Novo quod dicitur Montfort . . . firmavit in territoria Trefile*' 'the new castle of Montfort was built on the land of Trefile'.

142 Frankel, 1988, p. 269.
143 See pp. 108–9.
144 Frankel, 1988, p. 254; Strehlke, [1869] 1975, no. 53, 58; *RRH*, no. 934.
145 See text B in Michelant and Raynaud, 1882, p. 198. See Ellenblum, 1998, p. 148.
146 This latter Saphet was located in the territory of Toron (Tibnin). See Strehlke, [1869] 1975, no. 84 (Pringle, personal communication).
147 Ibid., no. 31; *RHH*, no. 722.
148 Strehlke, [1869] 1975, no. 85; *RRH*, no. 1086.
149 Strehlke, [1869] 1975, nos. 108, 109, 111; letters of grant from January 1257 and no. 117; letter of grant of March 1261; *RRH*, nos.1252, 1253.
150 Strehlke, [1869] 1975, nos. 114, 115, 118; letters of confirmation from the lord of Sidon on 20 March and 11 June 1258 and March 1261.
151 Ibid., nos. 46, 71, 83, 128; *RRH*, no. 859.
152 Ludolf of Suchem, *PPTS* 12, p. 40.
153 *AOL*, IIB, no. 16.
154 Ibid., no. 1, dated 1130–45.
155 Ibid., no. 10.
156 Ibid., no. 31.

7 SUGAR-CANE CULTIVATION AND THE SUGAR INDUSTRY

1 See p. 246.
2 E.J. Stern, 1999b, p. 77.
3 King, [1934] 1980, p. 37; *Cart. des Hosp.*, no. 627.
4 Lev and Amar, 2002, p. 204.
5 E.J. Stern, 1999b, pp. 75–76.
6 Stern, 2001, pp. 284, 286–87, figs. 7, 19.
7 Boas and Melloni (forthcoming).

8 CASTLES AND THE DEFENSIVE ROLE OF THE MILITARY ORDERS

1 Langeais in the Loire Valley dates from 993–94.
2 Smail, 1956, p. 228.
3 Ernoul, pp. 27–28.
4 Lawrence, 1988, p. 70.
5 For the rebuilding of Saphet Castle from 1240 onwards (it is said to have taken three years to build), the King of Navarre, the Duke of Burgundy and other counts and barons offered to pay the Templars some 7,000 marks. How much of this amount was in the event paid by these nobles is unclear, but it is known that, in addition to the revenues and income of the castle itself, the Templars spent an enormous sum of 101 million Saracen bezants on its construction in the first two and a half years and around 40,000 bezants in each following year! It should of course be remembered that this was an exceptionally large castle. Another hint at the value of a castle is given by Saladin's offer to pay Baldwin IV 100,000 dinars if he would demolish the incomplete Templar castle of Vadum Jacob (Jacob's Ford) in 1178.
6 William of Tyre 12.7, p. 554; Babcock and Krey, 1943, p. 525.
7 Upton-Ward, 1992, no. 121.
8 Pringle, 1998b, pp. 94–102.
9 Barber, 1992, p. 315; Pringle, 1998b, pp. 94–102.
10 Lawrence, 1988, pp. 70.
11 Johns, 1997, I–VI; Deschamps, 1939, pp. 177–210.
12 To date (2005) most of the finds post-date the Crusader period.
13 See Boase, 1977, p. 157. The same could be said of Tortosa.
14 Kennedy, 1994, p. 124.
15 On the form of towers in this regard, see comments by Fedden and Thomson, 1957, pp. 48–49.

16 Ibid., p. 48.
17 Smail, 1956, pp. 204–05.
18 Ibid., p. 205.
19 Riley-Smith, 1967, p. 55; *Cart. des Hosp.*, no. 144.
20 Riley-Smith, 1969, p. 279.
21 On these castles see Edwards, 1987, pp. 221–29.
22 For the chief Templar castles on these two passes see ibid., pp. 99–102, 253; also Edwards, 1983.
23 See Edwards, 1987, pp. 58–62, 143–45; also pp. 145–7, 223, 243, this volume.
24 See Boase, 1978, p. 114.
25 Edwards, 1987, p. 39.
26 In fact, the Teutonic Knights may not have been the only Military Order that sought a haven from the hostile atmosphere of Acre. Although their reasons were somewhat different, the Templars may also have wished to remove themselves from Acre. Oliver of Paderborn believed that the Templars built Chateau Pelerin not only for military reasons but also to distance the brothers from the sin and filth of the port city. See Oliver of Paderborn, 1894, p. 171.

9 THE CHOICE OF PLAN

1 Lawrence, 1988, p. 37.
2 Kennedy, 1994, pp. 54–55.
3 While there is logic in the idea that the brothers in castles of the Military Orders were housed in the central ward, isolated from the lay members who occupied the outer Quarters, it is stretching the point to suggest that the use of concentric defences was developed by the Military Orders specifically to meet the needs of monastic life; see for example Nicholson, 2002, p. 61.
4 Prawer, 1972, p. 121.
5 Pringle, 1994c, p. 335.
6 Lawrence suggests that the design may have originated in tenth-century Provence (Lawrence, 1988, p. 22, n. 47) although, as Pringle notes, one of the example he cites, Les Baux, is in fact probably of thirteenth-century date. According to Lawrence (ibid., pp. 22–23), the idea was developed and popularised by William the Conqueror, who built the White Tower in London which served as a model for over fifty keeps in England and nearly as many in northern France. Pringle notes that Frankish keeps in the East have much more in common with western towers of the eleventh and twelfth centuries than with either Byzantine towers or Syrian tower-houses (Pringle, 2000, VIII, pp. 1–2). However, one cannot entirely rule out the possibility of an Eastern influence. The tenth-century keep at Philippi, although not apparently a domestic structure (Lawrence, 1983, p. 215), having a domed rather than vaulted ground floor and having three storeys whereas most Frankish keeps in the East have only two storeys, is none the less similar to the Frankish keeps in its size, massive construction and general appearance and function.
7 Not included here are towers which were an element in a larger castle, except for those where the tower may have stood alone in an earlier stage, for example at Beaufort and probably at Latrun.
8 Oliver of Paderborn, 1894, p. 169.
9 William of Tyre, 10.25 (26).
10 Johns, 1947, pp. 94–98.
11 See p. 164.
12 Johns, 1997, I, p. 97.
13 See pp. 91–2.
14 In the documents recording the sale of Jacques Mandelée's property to the Teutonic Order, the new castle of Montfort was referred to as being 'in the territory of Trefile' (Frankel, 1988, p. 266).
15 Pringle, 1997a, p. 108; 1998b, pp. 92–94.
16 The use of barrel-vaulting for the ground floor and basement levels and groin-vaulting for upper storeys is typical of Frankish keeps. The barrel vault is a massive, heavy construction and consequently forms a solid support for a tall building but is less practical for upper

levels. The thickness of its lateral walls makes it ideal for defensive structures. For living Quarters, which in most medieval buildings are relegated to upper storeys, the lighter groin vault is more appropriate, being more attractive in appearance and enabling the insertion of more and larger windows in its walls.

17 Benvenisti, 1970, p. 313; 1982, p. 144, figs. 12–13.
18 Pringle, 1998b, p. 94.
19 Ibid., p. 92 and n. 12.
20 The name 'Latrun' derived from the Spanish word for tower, *toron*. Benjamin of Tudela refers to the castle as 'Toron de los Caballeros': Benjamin of Tudela, n.d., vol. 1, p. 78; vol. 2, pp. 94–95, n. 178. (Adler refers to the reference to Toron de Los Caballeros and its identification with Shunam as 'corrupt'. Benjamin of Tudela, 1907, p. 26, n. 2.) A seemingly early (pre-Crusader) appearance of the name 'Latrun' in the English translations of Nasir i-Khusrau's eleventh-century account of his travels ('On the 3rd of Ramadan (3rd March) we left Ramleh, and travelled to a village, called Latrun . . .') appears to be erroneous, the original form in Khusrau actually having been 'Khatun'.
21 For this castle in its expanded form, see pp. 114–16.
22 Pringle, 1998b, pp. 94–95 and n. 19.
23 Theoderich, p. 175.
24 Personal communication, Y. Magen.
25 See Pringle, 1994b, pp. 162–65.
26 Theoderich, p. 177.
27 See pp. 256–7.
28 Pringle, 1986a.
29 Ibn al-Qalanisi, 1932, p. 127.
30 This earthquake is recorded as having caused considerable damage in Syria on 29 June. See Amiran, *et al.*, 1994, p. 270.
31 This is the well-known earthquake of 1202; ibid.
32 The only information on this castle in the Rule of the Temple is a reference to the sheepfold; Upton-Ward, 1992, no. 556, p. 144.
33 See illustration in Pringle, 1997a, pl. LXXVIII.
34 Benvenisti, 1970, pp. 314–15; Pringle, 1997a, pp. 106–07.
35 Albert of Aachen, 10.10–14.
36 William of Tyre, 14.8; Babcock and Krey, 1943, vol. 2, p. 58.
37 *Cart. des Hosp.*, no. 558; Delaville le Roulx, 1882, no. 7, p. 19; *RRH*, no. 572.
38 Benvenisti, 1970, p. 315.
39 Pringle, 1997a, pp. 106–07.
40 See p. 111.
41 We can judge the quality of its decoration from the capitals found on the site. See p. 210, Fig. 82.
42 D. Bellamy, unpublished plans drawn in 1938. Redrawn with new survey material by M. Pease. Published by Pringle, 1997a, p. 65.
43 See for example the illustrations in Le Bruyn, 1698, facing p. 296.
44 The two coastal castles, Cafarlet (Kafr Lamm, now called by its Hebrew name, Habonim) and Castellum Beroart (Minat al-Qal'a; in Hebrew, Ashdod Yam), originally built in the Umayyad period, were both used by the Franks. See Nachlieli *et al.*, 2000, pp. 101–03; Barbé, *et al.*, 2002, pp. 30–33.
45 Edwards has suggested that three *quadriburgia* east of Silifke in Armenian Cilicia (Kütüklu, Tumil and Yaka) may have been Crusader constructions. See Edwards, 1987, pp. 32, 267. This is based on the design, but also on the type of masonry used in the three castles as well as in Hospitaller Silifke.
46 See p. 73.
47 Kloner and Cohen, 2000, p. 34.
48 Ibid., pp. 34–35.
49 Ibid., p. 35.
50 This would be the appropriate location in a monastic arrangement for a fountain in which the brothers would wash prior to meals.

51 Burchard, 1896, p. 26. Marino Sanudo (1896, p. 24) gives a similar account.

52 Strehlke, [1869] 1975, nos. 53, 54, 58 59.

53 They were probably less. The height of preservation is not easy to establish since much of what can be seen today is in fact later terracing.

54 See Ellenblum, 1996a, pp. 104–22; 1998, pp. 41–53. See Strehlke, [1869] 1975, no. 128.

55 Gibb, 1969, pp. 515; Baldwin, 1969, p. 532; Kennedy, 1994, pp. 70–71.

56 Ibn al-Qalanisi, 1932, p. 288.

57 According to Kennedy (1994, p. 73), Saladin apparently did not take Arima and it passed to the Templars only in the thirteenth century.

58 For François Anus's plan, see Deschamps, 1934, p. 49, fig. 4.

59 Müller-Weiner, 1966, p. 53.

60 Deschamps, 1973, facing p. 315.

61 The problem of knowing which plan was reliable was largely solved for me by Ross Burns, who kindly provided first-hand information and several photographs of the site. Directions for some of the published illustrations of the eastern bailey are also erroneous. For example Kennedy, 1994, pl. 26, which claims to show the south-west tower of the inner (eastern) bailey, actually shows the north-east outer tower facing east, Müller-Weiner, 1966, pl. 43 shows the north-west corner of the same tower rather than the main tower on the western side of the eastern bailey as the description on p. 98 suggests. Deschamps (album), 1973, pl. LXVIII gives a good view taken by Anus of the south-west tower of the eastern bailey seen from the south-east.

62 The finest example of this type of castle, which constitutes an important advance in twelfth-century military architecture, the 'marriage of *turris* and *castrum*' (Smail, 1956, p. 228), is the castle of Gibelet, north of Beirut.

63 Kennedy, 1994, p. 78.

64 However, the castle did have some additional protection in the form of a rock-cut ditch which does not appear on Deschamps' plan.

65 Kennedy, 1994, p. 38.

66 The description by Theoderich suggests that the Hospitallers built their castle immediately after purchasing the existing castle in 1168. Theoderich, writing a year later, notes that the Hospitallers had built a very large and strong castle. See Theoderich, p. 189.

67 See plan of the *SWP*; Conder and Kitchener, 1882, vol. 2, p. 117.

68 For a reliable plan and description see Biller, 1989, pp. 121–27, figs. 4–6, 13, 18–19. Ben-Dov (1993a, p. 184) inappropriately calls this inner ward a donjon, the principal tower in a castle. He possibly is comparing its form to the shell keeps of the West, which also have salient corner turrets and a central open space (but hardly a courtyard). However, here we have not a donjon but a *quadriburgium*. Rey thought that there was an internal keep (how-ever, he thought the same of the tiny castle of Blanchegarde, which is unlikely as the whole castle measures only *c.* 16 by 16 metres). Lawrence dismissed this and referred to the large eastern tower at Belvoir as its keep. This tower does not appear on the plan on which he relied, which was drawn by C.H.C. Pirie Gordon in 1908. Like Rey and others who described Belvoir prior to the excavations, Lawrence clearly had a rather confused idea of the design of this castle. See Lawrence, 1988, p. 66, n. 52, p. 128 and fig. 47.

69 Chevedden, 2000, pp. 90–91.

70 Ibid., pp. 92–93.

71 Ibid., pp. 94, 95.

72 *Itinerarium Peregrinorum et Gesta Regis Ricardi*, ed. Stubbs, 1864, 1: 218–19 (quoted in Chevedden, 2000, p. 97).

73 Personal communication from Rabei Khamissy.

74 The nearest comparison to this situation is the castle of Cursat, south of Antioch, which like Montfort has a limited view and is located far from any road. Like Montfort, the site of Cursat was chosen for this very reason, in order to serve as the secluded residence of the Patriarch of Antioch.

75 Burchard of Mount Zion, p. 21.

76 Measurements made by Rabei Khamissy.

77 See pp. 151–3.

78 Lawrence, 1988, p. 77; Boase, 1967, p. 52.
79 Boase sees this change as a confusion with the word for fortress in Arabic (*karak*); Boase, 1977, p. 152. He notes that the name Krak des Chevaliers (Crac des Chevaliers) is a later embellishment.
80 Personal communication from Denys Pringle.
81 Beaufort castle was surveyed by the *SWP*, vol. 1, 1881, pp. 128–33. For Deschamps' survey see Deschamps, 1934, pp. 177–208. It has never undergone systematic excavation and has suffered greatly as a result of recent hostilities in the region.
82 Deschamps, 1939, pp. 176–208.
83 *SWP*, vol. 1, 1881 p. 129.
84 For the same reason, when the Crusaders built the remarkable double defences of Acre in the late twelfth or early thirteenth century they did not defend the sea approaches of the city with walls, since there was simply no threat from that direction.
85 In addition, as noted, in the Middle Ages the sea level was about 1.5 metres lower than at present.
86 Johns, 1997, IV, pp. 152–53. Consequently the area to the east of the counterscarp retains the original height of the tell and is more or less level with the inner courtyard of the castle
87 Ibid., I, fig. 13.
88 Deschamps, 1973, p. 265.
89 Lawrence, 1988, p. 88.
90 On this text see Pringle, 1985, p. 141.
91 This was exposed by Moshe Dothan. See *Bulletin of the Department of Antiquities of the State of Israel*, 3, 1951, p. 13. Other minor excavations were carried out by Adam Druks, 1962, p. 17.
92 Ongoing excavations carried out since 2001 by the IAA under the direction of Hervé Barbé and Emanuel Damati have uncovered parts of the Frankish work, together with Mamluk and Ottoman work. See Barbé and Damati, forthcoming.
93 Ellenblum *et al.* (forthcoming).
94 Wilbrandus de Oldenborg, p. 174.
95 Imad ad-Din al-Isfahani, quoted here from Upton-Ward, 1994, p. 181.
96 See p. 167.
97 Deschamps, 1973 (album), pl. 83.
98 A few courses of a tower (J on Edwards's plan) on the east may belong to the Byzantine fortification. See Edwards, 1987, p. 226.
99 Boase, 1978, p. 180.
100 The most detailed and accurate description of the castle is that of Edwards, 1987, pp. 221–29, fig. 66, pls. 200a–300b).
101 See p. 176.
102 See p. 166.
103 Edwards, 1987, p.226.
104 Ibid.
105 Ibid., p. 227.
106 Ibid., p. 224.
107 Kedar and Pringle, 1985, pp. 164–79.
108 Ibid., pl. 20b.
109 Harunia was originally built in the eighth century AD by Hārūn ar-Rashīd.
110 Edwards, 1987, p. 143.
111 Ibid. Though Harunia has only one tower, its two gates, one at either end, are possibly related to the design of the two castles built by the Germans in the western Galilee, Montfort and Judin, which have a tower at either end. This makes it worth while to re-examine Edwards's comment that 'none of the architectural features in the garrison fort [Harunia] indicate that any significant German construction is present'.
112 I can attest to this from personal experience: A fear of heights frustrated my own attempts to reach the castle.
113 For this castle see Deschamps, 1939, pp. 210–20; Kennedy, 1994, p. 54.

10 NON-DEFENSIVE COMPONENTS OF A CASTLE

1 Upton-Ward, 1992, p. 55, no. 146. See also nos. 281, 282, 284, 295, 300, 304, 308, 341, 348, 357, 362–64, 425, 468, 469, 503, 682.
2 Pringle, 1993, p. 72, fig. 24; Johns, 1997, I, pp. 52–58, fig. 16.
3 See p. 156.
4 For the frescoes, see p. 214.
5 A belfry is shown on the reconstruction of the castle published by Ben-Dov, though whether this suggestion is founded on archaeological data is unclear. See Ben-Dov, 1993a, p. 183.
6 Pringle, 1985, pp. 147–48; 1993, pp. 207–09.
7 See pp. 210–11.
8 The same perhaps applies to the carved and inscribed marble panel which was recovered in the grounds of the adjacent monastery. See De Sandoli, 1974, pp. 249–50, fig. 99.
9 Pringle, 1998a, p. 6.
10 Guérin, 1868, vol. I, p. 309.
11 Edwards, 1987, p. 60. Edwards suggests that the form is 'not especially suited for an apse, nor is there any division between a potential apse and nave'. However, angular apses are not unknown in Crusader churches, often with no division from the nave. See for example the castle chapel and parish church in Chateau Pelerin, the chapel in the sea castle at Sidon, St Catherine, Nicosia and St George the Latin, Famagusta.
12 See Kalayan, 1973, pp. 82–83, figs. (plans) II, III, pl. IV.
13 Pringle, 1998a, pp. 325–26.
14 Kalayan, 1973, fig. II.
15 Boas, 1999, p. 100.
16 Pringle, 1993, pp. 60–61.
17 Ibid., pp. 95–101; Kloner, 1983, pp. 52; Kloner and Chen, 1983, pp. 12–13.
18 Pringle, 1993, p. 97.
19 Ibid., p. 100.
20 This is a good reason to regard the settlement or faubourg of Bethgibelin as having been nearby, perhaps within the outer fortification walls or possibly, as the excavator suggests, across the modern road to the south (where there are some Frankish remains), rather than at a distant site such as the Byzantine church of Santa Anna near Tel Maresha, as has been suggested elsewhere (see pp. 73–4; also Ehrlich, 1999, p. 203).
21 See p. 35.
22 Barber, 1995, p. 199.
23 Johns, 1997, I, 44.
24 See Müller-Wiener, 1966.
25 Kennedy, 1994, p. 128.
26 Deschamps, 1939, pp. 206–07, fig. 19.
27 Kalayan, 1973, pl. V 1–3, fig. (plan) I.
28 Ben-Dov, 1972, p. 28.
29 Personal communication.
30 Though most dormitories were large vaulted halls, at Saranda Kolones the garrison may have slept in small, simply constructed rooms built against the wall of the outer ward. These rooms appear to have been flat-roofed and some of them had corner fireplaces. See Megaw, 1994, p. 45. However, as already noted there is no clear evidence for this being a castle of the Military Orders.
31 Upton-Ward, 1992 (The Primitive Rule), no. 21. See also the later clause, no. 680.
32 These measures would assist the brothers in rising for the night offices, but another reason for leaving a light in the dormitory is referred to in clause no. 37: '[they] should not be without light at night, so that shadowy enemies may not lead them to wickedness, which God forbids them'.
33 King, [1934] 1980, p. 169 (Esgarts), no. 73.
34 Kennedy, 1994, pp. 190–8.
35 ibid., pp. 194–95.
36 Benvenisti, 1970, p. 201.

37 Theoderich, p. 189.
38 See Taha, 2000, pp. 1587–613; Pringle, 1993, pp. 106–07; 1998a, pp. 29–30; 2004, p. 29.
39 Information from Denys Pringle. For an illustration of the old latrines see Deschamps, 1934 (album), pl. CIII.C.
40 See Hartal, 2001, pp. 36–40, 46–47.
41 See p. 144.
42 Pringle *et al.*, 1994, pp. 140–41, figs. 8, 13, 15, 18.
43 Ibid., pp. 140–41.
44 At Saranda Kolones there were 12 latrines, six in three of the four corner piers of the ground floor of the inner ward (two latrines in each pier) and an additional six in the floor above them. They drained via chutes through the piers into the sewage drains below which passed under the floor of the east moat, and from there no doubt to the sea (Megaw, 1994, p. 44). There are several contemporary Muslim examples.
45 Benvenisti, 1970, p. 299.
46 Rosser, 1986, p. 47. However, see comment in Rosser, 1985, p. 91.
47 Johns, 1997, II, pp. 124–29, pl. LI.1–3.
48 King, [1934] 1980, p. 47.
49 Upton-Ward, 1992, no. 23.
50 King, [1934] 1980, p. 71
51 Ibid., no. 22.
52 See plan on p. 134.
53 Kloner and Cohen, 2000, p. 35.
54 The refectory tables at the monastery of St Euthymius were also of stone. It was clearly easier to obtain stone than wood in these regions, but the use of stone tables may also have become a local tradition in monastic houses. In a twelfth-century Frankish farmhouse at Har Hozevim near Jerusalem a large stone table was used in the bakery, possibly for preparing the dough.
55 On these boards, also found in the kitchen at Belvoir and in many other castles, see p. 203.
56 Johns, 1997, vol. I, p. 60, fig. 24.
57 Ibid., p. 17.
58 Bashford Dean, [1927] 1982, p. 22, figs. 42, 44, 45.
59 See Ben-Dov, 1993a, p. 184.
60 Ibid. The outer bailey had a separate cistern capable of holding 650 cubic metres of water.
61 Roll, *et al.*, 2000, p. 30.
62 Ibid.
63 The lack of Crusader finds or evidence of the Mamluk attack (mangonel balls for example) on the kitchen floor have led to the suggestion that this part of the castle was in fact post-Crusader (ibid., p. 30). Considering that the castle and town were completely destroyed by Baybars, this seems improbable. It is highly unlikely that a kitchen would have been built in the ruins of a castle. It has been suggested by the excavator that these changes date to the end of Crusader rule, possibly the period between 1261 and 1265 when the Hospitallers held the castle. Israel Roll, personal communication.
64 Deschamps, 1934, p. 269.
65 Kennedy, 1994, p. 197.
66 Megaw, 1982, pp. 215–16, figs. 2, 3.
67 Deschamps, 1934 (text), pp. 269–74, fig. 57 (album) pl. CIV.B.
68 Roll, *et al.*, 2000, p. 29.
69 Ibid. The archaeologists suggested that this installation originally served as a flour mill, a suggestion that would strengthen the identification of the adjacent domed structure as a bakery oven. More likely, however, it functioned as another oven.
70 See Rosser, 1985, p. 83.
71 Bashford Dean, [1927] 1982, p. 22.
72 Ibid.
73 Johns, 1997, I, p. 98.
74 Kloner and Hübsch, 1996, p. 97.

11 ELEMENTS OF FORTIFICATION

1 Creswell, 1952, p. 101ff.
2 Deschamps, 1932, figs. 10, 13, 14.
3 Kloner and Cohen, 2000, p. 35.
4 Boas and Maeir, forthcoming.
5 See Edwards, 1987, fig. 66.
6 Personal communication from Denys Pringle.
7 Lawrence, 1979, p. 338.
8 See plan in Ben-Dor, 1993a, p. 183.
9 Creswell, 1952, p. 111, n. 4. Polybius (X.33.8) and Livy (XXVI.28) mention the use of the portcullis at Salapia in 208 BC. Creswell (1989) records that there are grooves for a portcullis in each of the three gates at Ukhaider (p. 249), and at 'Atshan, a khan-like building about half way between Ukhaider and Kufa (p. 258).
10 Polybius, X.33.viii.
11 Vegetius, *Epitoma Rei Militaris*, IV.4.
12 These are similar in design to the timber hoardings found in other regions.
13 See for example in the palace of Ukhaydir in Iraq, which dates from the eighth century (Lawrence, 1988, p. 83, n. 82). Another eighth-century example, the earliest in Islam, can be seen above the gate of the lesser enclosure of the Umayyad desert palace, Qasr al-Heïr al-Sharki. The idea derived from machicolation on the monastic tower of al-Mundhir which was incorporated into Qasr al-Heïr al-Gharbi. Box machicolation is also found in Tunisia on the ninth-century *ribat* of Burj Yunqa, and it is also present in the eleventh century when it was employed on the walls of Cairo. However, the earliest examples of stone machicolation occur in pre-Islamic northern Syria. Creswell notes at least ten examples (of which seven were not over entrances and in fact served as latrines). The earliest defensive machicolation is at Dar Qita in what was apparently an isolated watch tower dated AD 551. Creswell notes that still earlier written evidence relates to the use of box machicolation at Amida (Diyarbakr) in AD 504, where according to Joshua Stylites (AD 515): 'It was difficult [for the Byzantine army] to fight with them [the Persians] because, being on the crest of the wall, and having built themselves little houses all along the rampart in which they hid themselves, they could fight without being seen by those who were outside'; Creswell, [1958] 1989, p. 163. However, this description may in fact refer to wooden hoarding.
14 One of the earliest surviving examples is on a house called Umm al-Jamal on the edge of the Jordan desert which is dated to the early fifth century (*c.* 412). See Nicolle, 1996, vol. 2, p. 46.
15 Edwards, 1987, p. 15.
16 Ibid., pp. 15, 33–37, 68, 271.
17 Ibid., p. 15, n. 11.
18 Kalayan, 1973, pls. II 3, III 5; Johns, 1997, I, pp. 40–41; 1997, IV, p. 158, fig. 8.
19 Lawrence, 1988, p. 83. According to Pringle these were actually latrines. Thus, he notes (personal communication), they were in fact relieving the knights!
20 Lawrence, 1988, p. 74 and n. 66.
21 Johns, 1997, I, pp. 41, 51–52, fig. 15.
22 Kennedy, 1994, p. 116, n. 49.
23 For Aleppo see Müller-Wiener, 1966, pp. 66–67, 102, pl. 91; Kennedy, 1994, p. 157, pl. 61; for 'Ajlun see Johns, 1997, p. 28.
24 Kennedy, 1994, pp. 115–16, n. 44.
25 However, there may on occasion have been an arrangement similar to that found in the Crusader castle of Saone in the Principality of Antioch, where defensive considerations led the planners of at least one part of the defences to build a wall-walk which could only be reached via stairs from the courtyard. If there was no access to the wall-walk from the tower, the enemy breaching one part of the wall or a tower had immediate access not to the entire defences but only to the section or tower that he had taken.
26 Johns, 1997, IV, pp. 153–57.
27 For a good example of this see the arrow-slits on the walls of Caesarea.

28 See for example those in the towers of Castellum Regis (Fig. 33).

29 See Kennedy, 1994, p. 195.

30 Ibid.

31 The latter was the case in the great keep of Margat. This was not an ideal form, as it resulted in walls which were excessively massive in places and consequently wasted much of the internal space. The walls of the keep at Margat varied in thickness up to 10 metres at their centre!

32 Philo (I.2–5) referred to the disadvantage of corners, which could be damaged by a ram or by stones.

33 Fedden and Thomson, 1957, p. 48.

34 Kennedy, 1994, p. 158.

35 Ibid., p. 195. Kennedy notes that the canna is 2.2 metres. It is hoped that these measurements will be confirmed (or otherwise) in the excavations that are ongoing at the time of writing.

36 See Ben-Dov, 1993a, p. 182.

37 At Crac des Chevaliers the reservoir also played a role in enhancing the defences.

38 Edwards, 1987, p. 224.

12 STONEMASONRY AND CONSTRUCTION TECHNIQUES

1 Deschamps, 1934, pp. 225–74; 1934 (album), pls. CXVIII, CXX, CXIX.

2 Edwards, 1987, pp. 18–24.

3 Since Saladin was worried about the effect a prolonged and perhaps unsuccessful siege would have on his prestige, he left Crac after a single day's reconnaissance. At Margat in July, the Muslim army had been made to run the gauntlet of a Sicilian fleet which was able to enfilade the Ayyubid army as it moved along the road that passed through the narrow coast to the west of the castle. This took him north of Margat, but most probably its formidable appearance was the decisive factor in his decision not to besiege the castle. See Lyons and Jackson, 1997, p. 286.

4 Mining had been used with great effect by Zengi at Edessa (1144) and by Saladin at Vadum Jacob (1179), Tiberias (1187), Jerusalem (1187) and Belvoir (1189). In the thirteenth century Baybars employed mining at Arsuf (1265), Safed (1266), Crac des Chevaliers (1271) and Montfort (1271). It was later used at Marqab (1285) and Acre (1291).

5 The core usually has a random consistency, showing that it was poured from above into the space between the two faces of the wall. However, at least in one site the fill appears to have been carefully constructed. This can be observed in the southern and eastern walls of Vadum Jacob (Ellenblum *et al.*, forthcoming). In this case, it is possible that the rubble was placed in position in a neat fashion and the liquid cement poured in from above.

6 Edwards, 1987, pp. 18–24.

7 Ibid., p. 18.

8 In castles such as Lampron and Çandir the use of diagonally tooled ashlars and masons' marks is evident. The source of these techniques in Armenian building is not known and it is interesting to consider the possible explanation for this. Whereas we occasionally hear of the Franks employing Armenian masons, in certain instances it would seem that the Armenians either adopted Western stone-working techniques themselves or employed Western masons in the construction of their castles. These were perhaps masons already working in the region in the building of castles of the Military Orders in Cilicia.

9 Edwards, 1987, pp. 18–19.

10 Clermont-Ganneau, vol. 1, 1899, pp. 38–47.

11 Kalayan, 1973, pls. III.5 and IV.3.

12 William of Tyre makes occasional reference to this practice; see for example 15.24.

13 In later periods the tie-column became a purely decorative feature. In Ottoman architecture (the sixteenth-century walls of Jerusalem, for example), round, decoratively carved bosses were carved on stones to give the appearance of tie-columns. However, even in medieval architecture these columns were sometimes not true ties; although partly intended to be decorative, their function was to make the construction appear more massive than it in fact

was. At Maiden's Castle (Korykos), in south-western Cilicia, the antique columns are short, extending only through the outer face of the wall but giving the false impression of very massive construction.

14 A similar use of the amphitheatre seats is found in the local lord's tower at Baisan (Bait She'an).
15 Clermont-Ganneau, vol. 1, 1899, pp. 1–38; Pringle, 1981, pp. 173–99.
16 See Clermont-Ganneau, vol. 1, 1899, pp. 14, 17.
17 Ibid., p, 26.
18 See Johns, 1997, fig. 20.
19 Deschamps, 1939, vol. 1, p. 204; Clermont-Ganneau, vol. 1, 1899, p. 27.
20 Burgoyne and Richards, 1987, p. 116; Boas, 2001, pl. 13.1.
21 This information was communicated to me by Rabei Khamissy. Similar marks are found at Teutonic sites outside the Latin East, for example at Torre Alemanna in Apulia.

13 WEAPONS, ARMS AND ARMOUR

1 On the motivation behind the expedition of the Metropolitan Museum of Art see Bashford Dean, 1982, pp. 5–6.
2 The finds from Montfort were very fragmentary. Indeed, no major hoards of Crusader armour have come to light anywhere in the Near East and the same is true of Crusader period weapons, with the exception of arrowheads which have been found in large quantities at several sites. It would seem that the victorious side in any military encounter was careful to collect all of this valuable equipment for its own use. Armour was far too expensive to leave in the field.
3 Personal communication from Kate Raphael.
4 Roll and Tal, 1999, p. 50.
5 Information supplied by Kate Raphael. Details of a study on the Arsuf catapult stones will be published in a paper by Raphael and Teper, forthcoming.
6 Upton-Ward, 1992, no. 138.
7 Ibid., no. 82.
8 Ibid., no. 317.
9 Ibid., no. 607.
10 Ibid., no. 562.
11 Ibid., no. 427.
12 Ibid., no. 324.
13 Ronen and Olami, 1978, pp. 37–38, fig. 5.
14 Rozenberg, 1999, p. 129, pl. 4.
15 Upton-Ward, 1992, no. 138.
16 Ibid., no. 327.
17 Ibid., no. 55.
18 Lions are specifically mentioned; ibid, p. 181.
19 Ibid., no. 562.
20 Ibid., p. 181.
21 Dean, 1927, p. 37, figs. 53.n–q. See also Nicolle, 1988, vol. 1, p. 324; vol. 2, fig. 821e.
22 Johns, 1997, VI, p. 48, fig. 15.1–4.
23 Boas, 1999, fig. 6.3; Raphael, in Rozenberg, 1999, p. 154, pl. 8.
24 Dean, [1927] 1982, fig. 53v; Boas, 1999, pl. 6.17:4.
25 Raphael, in Rozenberg, 1999, p. 156, pl. 11; Dean, [1927] 1982, fig. 54I.
26 See illustrations in Rozenberg, 1999, p. 131, pl. 10.
27 Nicolle suggests this may in fact be part of a filter bucket; Nicolle, 1988, vol. I, p. 324.
28 Ibid, p. 321; vol. II, fig. 812; Schlumberger, 1943, p. 248, p. XIII.1.
29 Dean, [1927] 1982, p. 36, figs. 53c–e; Nicolle, 1988, vol. I, p. 324; vol. 2, figs. 821b–d.
30 Dean, [1927] 1982, p. 36, fig. 53u.

14 DAILY LIFE OF THE MILITARY ORDERS

1 See pp. 149–64.
2 Lawrence, 1997, pp. 209, 212.
3 See pp. 159–60 for a discussion of the location of refectories in castles.
4 King, [1934] 1980, p. 76; Upton-Ward, 1992, nos. 23, 288.
5 King, [1934] 1980, p. 47, statute 8. See also Upton-Ward, 1992, no. 289.
6 King, [1934] 1980, p. 47, statute 8.
7 Upton-Ward, 1992, no. 26.
8 Cartledge, in Pringle, 1986a, pp. 176–86.
9 Pringle 1986a, pp. 85–86, 128; table 12, p. 177.
10 Ibid., p. 178.
11 Croft, in Harper and Pringle, 2000, p. 174.
12 Ibid., p. 184.
13 Ibid., p. 185.
14 Upton-Ward, 1992, p. 101.
15 Mitchell and Stern, 2001, pp. 207–13; also p. 55, this volume.
16 Upton-Ward, 1992, nos. 187, 192.
17 Hubbard and McKay, in Pringle, 1986a, pp. 187–91.
18 King, [1934] 1980, p. 30.
19 Upton-Ward, 1992, nos. 319, 609.
20 Ibid., no. 609.
21 See pp. 74, 83–4.
22 See p. 160.
23 *AOL*, IIB, no. 10.
24 Pringle, 1986b, pp. 68–71.
25 Strehlke, [1869] 1975, no. 61.
26 King, [1934] 1980, pp. 29–30.
27 See descriptions of examples on p. 162.
28 King, [1934] 1980, p. 30, n. 3.
29 Upton-Ward, 1992, no. 25.
30 See Johns, 1997, I, p. 89, fig. 32; II, pp. 122, 129, fig. 20, pls. XLIV.3–4, LIII.1–2; III, pp. 137–44, figs. 1–2, Pls. XLIX–LVII; VI, pp. 46–48, 51, 53–54, figs. 13, 14, 19, pls. XXVI.2, XXVII–XXVIII. See also Pringle, 1982a, pp. 104–17.
31 See plates published in E.J. Stern, 1999a, pp. 259–65; 2000, pp. 52–60. Also E.J. Stern, 'The Hospitaller Order in Acre and Manueth: the Ceramic Evidence', forthcoming.
32 King, [1934] 1980, pp. 20, 22.
33 See p. 85; also Stern, 1997, pp. 37–39; 2001, p. 286; and Boas and Melloni, forthcoming.
34 Stern, 1997, p. 37. One may perhaps suggest that the latter came from the Hospitallers' compound in Tyre or Sidon.
35 Ibid. As noted on p. 273, n. 11, a variant form was found in excavations carried out in the east of Akko, possibly the Teutonic Quarter.
36 Stern, 2001, p. 826.
37 Upton-Ward, 1992, p. 129, no. 493.
38 Ibid., p. 66, no. 193.
39 Weinberg, 1987, pp. 305–15.
40 Dean, [1927] 1982, figs. 55–58.
41 Johns, 1997, I, p. 80, fig. 27; VI, p. 51, fig. 18.
42 Upton-Ward, 1992, no. 138.
43 Boas, 1999, p. 163, fig. 6.2.
44 Ibid., no. 140.
45 Dean, [1927] 1982, p. 30, fig. 45.D. Similar spoon parts found in the Red Tower excavations postdate the Crusader period, although they might possibly have survived from the Military Order phase; Pringle, 1986a, p. 163, fig. 54.6, 7.
46 It is also useful to take a look at the layout of the medieval monastery, the Military Order castle having been, to some degree, a fortified monastic compound. The typical monastery in

the Middle Ages was laid out around the cloister. On one side (often on the north) was the church, in the wing to its right were the chapter house and dormitory, in the wing opposite the church were the kitchen and refectory, and in the wing to the left of the cloister was the cellar. If we compare this layout with the castles and urban headquarters of the Military Orders, we can see how the chapels, kitchens, refectories, dormitories and lavatories are ranged around the cloister, albeit with some leeway as to their location in relation to one another. For example, in Acre the refectory and church are south of the cloister, the other domestic buildings to the north, west and east. At Belvoir the chapel is to the west (on an upper level), the refectory is to the south and the kitchen is on the south-east side of the cloister.

47 King, [1934] 1980, p. 69.
48 Ibid., p. 181.
49 Sterns, 1985, p. 343.
50 King, [1934] 1980, p. 107 (Statutes of Fr. William de Villaret, Chapter General of 1300).
51 See Usamah ibn-Munqidh (1964, pp. 165–6) for an example.
52 James [Jacques] de Vitry, LXXII, 1896, p. 64.
53 See pp. 20 and 35.
54 See pp. 46, 57, 159.
55 Ben-Dov, 1975, p. 104.
56 Dean, [1927] 1982, p. 30, fig. 54.A.
57 Upton-Ward, 1992, no. 317; King, [1934] 1980, p. 78.
58 King, [1934] 1980, p. 64.
59 Johns, 1997, IV, pl. LX.2; Rozenberg, 1999, p. 290, fig. 4.
60 Johns, 1997, VI, pl. XXV.1–2. A second stone board was found in the south-east fort of the faubourg.
61 Kloner and Cohen, 2000, p. 35.
62 Johns, 1997, VI, p. 54, fig. 20; Kool, 2002, pp. 83–84, fig. 6, pl. 1; Harper and Pringle, 2000, pp. 84–85.
63 De Sandoli, 1974, fig. 37.
64 Schlumberger, 1943, pl. XIII.1.2; Upton-Ward, 1992, p. 104, no. 379.
65 Schlumberger, 1943, pls. XIII.11, 12, XIV.1–8. See also King, 1932.
66 Menache, 1999, fig. 5.
67 Clermont-Ganneau, 1901, pp. 109–14.
68 See drawing in Dichter, 1979, p. 117.
69 Upton-Ward, 1992, no. 52.
70 King, [1934] 1980, p. 70.
71 Ibid., pp. 92–93.
72 Johns, 1997, VI, p. 43.
73 Boas and Melloni, forthcoming.
74 Ben-Dov, 1975, p. 106. Those from the forge were unfinished.
75 Ibid., pp. 43, 48, 51; figs. 8, 15.8, 13, 17, 18; pls. XXVI.1.
76 Harper and Pringle, 2000, p 134, no. 38, fig. 11.3.38.
77 De Vaux and Stéve, 1950, p. 148.
78 Johns 1997, VI, pp. 42–43, fig. 15.12.

15 WORKS OF ART IN URBAN SITES AND CASTLES OF THE MILITARY ORDERS

1 See for example Folda, 1995; Kühnel, 1994; Kühnel, 1988.
2 As noted on p. 27, the existence of such a workshop is disputed by some scholars.
3 Jacoby, 1982, p. 326. Regarding the artistic sources for the work produced in this workshop, Folda has suggested that Italian sculptors (or artists of Italian parentage) who had previously worked on the Church of the Holy Sepulchre and other projects in Jerusalem would have been employed in this workshop from the 1160s on, alongside local sculptors. Regarding the distinctive 'Wet-Leaf Acanthus' style of these works, he writes that its origins

appear to have been in the Roman, Byzantine and Umayyad works that these artists could have seen in Jerusalem, as well as their own Italian traditions.

4 Ibid. On the descriptions of John of Würzburg and Theoderich see pp. 20–1. For al-Idrisi's description see *PEFQS*, 1888, p. 33.
5 Folda, 1995, p. 451. For a discussion of the various works of the Templar workshop reused in the al-Aqsa Mosque and elsewhere see pp. 441–56 and pls. 10.13a–16g.
6 For these examples see Jacoby, 1979, pp. 3–14.
7 See Buschhausen, 1978, pp. 234–36, pls. 298, 299, 304.
8 Jacoby, 1987, p. 20.
9 Jacoby, 1979, pp. 4–7 and figs. 2–8.
10 Pringle, 1993, pl. LXXXVIII; compare to Folda, 1995, pl. 10.14b.
11 Clermont-Ganneau, vol. 2, 1896, p. 101.
12 Jacoby, 1982, pl. 19.
13 Ibid., p. 377, fig. 97.
14 Barbé, 2003, pp. 252–55.
15 E. Stern, 2000, p. 12., pl. 2. See also a capital from the Bosta in Goldmann, 1994, pl. XVII.2
16 Goldmann, 1994, pp. 9–10, pl. III.1–2.
17 See pp. 129, 215.
18 Deschamps, 1934, album pl. C.
19 Barash, 1971, pp. 191–97, pl. 46. It was not apparently unusual for sculpture, even non-figurative pieces, to be decorated with paint, even non-figurative pieces as is evident from recent finds from the Hospitaller complex at Acre; will be published by Eliezer Stern.
20 Barash, 1971, pp. 199–207; Folda, 1995, p. 397, pl. 9.36f.
21 Jacoby, 1987, p. 22.
22 Ibid.
23 Ibid., pp. 15–16.
24 Folda, 1977, pl. XXIV.a.b.c.d.
25 Kühnel, 1988. See also Diehl, 1924, pp. 226–29; De Sandoli, 1974, pp. 41ff., figs. 93–95; Folda, 1977, pp. 259–61, pls. XXXIV, b, XXV, b; 1995, pp. 382–90, pls. 934a–9.35g; Weyl-Carr, 1982, pp. 215–43.
26 Kühnel, 1988, p. 158.
27 Folda, 1995, p. 403.
28 Folda, 1982b, pp. 198–209.
29 Nickel, 1989, pp. 42–43, figs. 19–21.
30 Clermont-Ganneau, 1898, pp. 234–39; Enlart, 1925 (text, vol. 1), pp. 197–98; Vincent and Abel, *Jérusalem*, fasc. III, p. 667, n. 1, pl. LXVI; Folda, 1995, pp. 297–99.
31 Folda, 1995, pp. 299, 561, n. 60.

CONCLUSION

1 See Kedar and Pringle, 1985.

BIBLIOGRAPHY

Primary sources

Abû Shâmâ, *Le Livre des deux jardins*, in *RHCr. Or.*, vols. IV–V.

Albert of Aachen (Albertus Aquensis) *Liber Christianae expeditionis pro emundatione Sanctae Hierosolymitanae ecclesiae*, in *RHCr. Occid.*, vol. VI.

Beha ad-Din, *The Life of Saladin*, ed. C.W. Wilson, trans. C. Conder, in *PPTS*, vol. 13.

Benjamin of Tudela, *The Itinerary of Benjamin of Tudela*, trans. and ed. M.N. Adler, London, 1907.

Benjamin of Tudela, *The Itinerary of Benjamin of Tudela*, trans. and ed. A. Asher, 2 vols., New York, n.d.

Bresc-Bautier, G. (ed.) (1984), *Le Cartulaire du Chapitre du Saint-Sépulcre de Jérusalem*, in *DRHC*, vol. XV.

Le Bruyn, C. (1698), *Reizen van Cornelis de Bruyn, Door de Vermaardste Deelen van Klein Asia . . . Aegypten, Syrien en Palestina*, Delft.

Van Bruyn, C. (1725), *Travels in Palestine*, 2 vols., London.

Burchard of Mount Zion, *Descriptio Terrae Sanctae*, ed. J.C.M. Laurent, *Peregrinatores Medii Aeui Quatuor*, Leipzig (1864), pp. 1–100.

Burchard of Mount Zion, trans. A. Stewart, in *PPTS*, vol. 12.

Chronique d'Ernonl et de Bernard le Trésovier, ed. M.L. de Mas Latrie, Paris, 1871.

Cronica S. Petri Erfordiensis moderna, ed. O. Holder-Egger, *MGH SS*, vol. 30, pp. 424–25.

De Curzon, H. (ed.) (1886), *La Règle du Temple*, Société de l'Histoire de France, Paris.

—— (1977), *La Règle du Temple*, edition Champion, Paris.

Daniel of Kiev, *Pilgrimage of the Russian Abbot Daniel in the Holy Land 1106–1107*, trans. C.W. Wilson, in *PPTS*, vol. 4.

Delaville Le Roulx, J. (1881), 'Trois chartes du XIIe siècle concernant l'ordre de Jean de Jérusalem', in *AOL* 1, pp. 409–15.

—— (1882), *Documents concernant les Templiers*, Paris.

—— (ed.) (1894–1905), *Cartulaire général de de l'Ordre des Hospitaliers de Saint-Jean de Jérusalem, 1100–1310*, 4 vols., Paris.

—— (1895), 'Inventaire de pièces de Terre Sainte de l'Ordre de Hospital', *ROL* 3, pp. 36–106.

Desimoni, C. (1884), 'Quatre titres de propriétés des génois à Acre et à Tyr', ed. Comte de Riant, *AOL* 2, B, pp. 213–30.

Eracles, *L'Estorie d'Eracles empereur et la conquête de la Terre d'Outremer*, in *RHCr. Occid.*, vol. II, Paris, 1859.

Ernoul, *L'estat de la Cité de Iherusalem*, in Henri Michelant and Gaston Raynaud, *Itinéraires à Jérusalem et descriptions de la Terre Sainte rédigés en français aux XIe, XIIe & XIIIe siècles*, *SOL*, *SG* 3, Genève, 1882, pp. 31–52; trans., C. Conder, in *PPTS*, vol. 6.

Fulcher of Chartres, *Gesta peregrinantium francorum*, *RHCr. Occid.*, vol. III, pp. 311–485, ed.

H. Hagenmeyer, *Historia Hierosolymitana (1095–1127)*, Heidelberg, 1913; trans. F.R. Ryan, *History of the Expedition to Jerusalem*, New York, 1969.

Les Gestes des Chiprois, ed. G. Raynaud, Publications de la Société de l'orient latin, Série historique, vol. V, Genève, 1887.

Huygens, R.B.C. (ed.) (1965), 'De constructione castra Sapher: construction et functions d'un château fort franc en Terre Sainte', *Studi medievali* ser. 3, 6; trans. in H. Kennedy, *Crusader Castles*, Cambridge, 1994.

—— (ed.) (1994), *Peregrinationes Tres. Saewulf, John of Würzburg, Theodericus*, Turnholti.

Ibn al-Qalanisi, *The Damascus Chronicle of the Crusades*, trans. H.A.R. Gibb, London, 1932.

Imad ad-Din al-Isfahani, *Conquête de la Syrie et de la Palestine par Saladin*, trans. H. Massé, in *DRHC*, vol. X.

Itinera Hierosolymitana Crucesignatorum (saec. XII–XIII), ed. S. de Sandoli, vol. II, Studium Biblicum Franciscanum, Collectio maior, vol. II, xxiv, Jerusalem, 1988.

Itinera Hierosolymitana Saeculi III–VIII, ed. P. Geyer, Vienna, 1896.

Itinerarium Peregrinorum et Gesta Regis Ricardi, in *RS*, vol. 38.1, ed. W. Stubbs (1864), London.

James de Vitry, *Lettres de Jacques de Vitry*, ed. R.B.C. Huygens, Leiden, 1960.

—— Historia Orientalis (Historia Hierosolymitana), ed. J. Bongars, *Gesta Dei per Francos*, vol. 2, Hanau 1611, pp. 296–391.

James (Jacques) de Vitry, trans. A. Stewart, in *PPTS*, vol. 11.

John of Joinville, *Memoirs of Louis IX, King of France*, in *Chronicles of the Crusades*, London, 1848.

—— *Histoire de Saint Louis*, trans. R.B. Shaw, *Chronicles of the Crusades*, New York, 1963.

John of Würzburg, *Descriptio Terrae Sanctae*, ed. R.B.C. Huygens, *CCCM*, vol. 139, pp. 78–141; trans. A. Stewart, in *PPTS*, vol. 4.

King, E.J. ([1934] 1980), *The Rule, Statutes and Customs of the Hospitallers, 1099–1310, with Introductory Chapters and Notes*, London.

Ludolf of Suchem, *Description of the Holy Land*, trans. A. Stewart, in *PPTS*, vol. 12.

Marquis d'Albon (ed.) (1913), *Cartulaire général de de l'Ordre du Temple 1119.?–1150. Recueil des chartes et des bulles relatives à l'ordre du Temple*, Paris.

De Marsy, A. (ed.) (1884), 'Fragment d'un cartulaire de l'ordre de Saint-Lazare en Terre Sainte', in *AOL*, 2.2, pp. 121–58, Paris.

Marino Sanurdo, *Secrets for the Crusaders* (abstract – Part XIV of Book III), trans. A Stewart, in *PPTS*, vol. 12.

Matthew Paris, *Chronica Maiora*, in *RS* (57), 7 vols.

Michelant, M. and G. Raynaud (eds) (1882), *Itinéraires á Jérusalem et descriptions de la Terre Sainte rédigés en français aux XIe, XIIe et XIIIe siècles*, Geneva.

Oliver of Paderborn (*Oliveri Paderbornensis*), *Historia Damiatina*, ed. O. Hoogweg, *Die Schriften des Kölner Domscholasters*, in Bibliothek des Litterarischen Vereins in Stuttgart 202, Tübingen, 1894.

Paoli, S (ed.) (1733–37), *Codice diplomatico del sacro militare ordine gerosolimitano oggi di Malta*, 2 vols., Lucca.

Röhricht, R. (ed.) (1893–1904), *Regesta regni Hierosolymitani*, 2 vols., Innsbruck.

Ralph of Diss, *Opera historica*, in *Rerum Britannicarum medii aeui scriptores or Chronicles of Great Britain and Ireland in the Middle Ages*, *RS*, vol. LVII, 2 vols.

Saewulf, *Peregrinatio*, ed. R.B.C. Huygens, *CCCM*, vol. 139, pp. 59–77; trans. Canon Brownlow, in *PPTS*, vol. 4.

Simon de St Bertin, 'Gesta abbatum Sancti Bertini Sithensium', ed. O. Holder-Egger, in *Monumenta germaniae historica scriptores*, ed. G.H. Pertz, *et al.*, vol. 13, 1826–1934, p. 649.

Strehlke, E. (ed.) (1869, repr. 1975), *Tabula Ordinis Theutonici*, Berlin, Toronto.

Theoderic (Theoderich), *Libellus de locis sanctis*, ed. R.B.C. Huygens, *CCCM*, vol. 139, 1976, pp. 142–97; trans., A. Stewart, in *PPTS*, vol. 4.

Upton-Ward, J.M. (trans. and ed.) (1992), *The Rule of the Templars: The French Text of the Rule of the Order of the Knights Templar*, Woodbridge.

Usamah Ibn-Munqidh, *Memoirs of an Arab-Syrian Gentleman*, trans. Philip K. Hitti, Beirut, 1964.

Walter Map, *De nugis curialium*, ed. T. Wright, Camden Society, 1850.

Wilbrandus de Oldenborg, in Johann C.M. Laurent (ed.), *Peregrinatores medii aevi quatuor*, Leipzig, 1864.

William of Tyre (Guillaume de Tyr), *Chronique*, ed. R.B.C. Huygens, 2 vols., *CCCM* vols. 63 and 63A; trans. E.A. Babcock and A.C. Krey, *A History of Deeds Done beyond the Sea*, 2 vols., New York, 1943.

Secondary sources

Abel, F.M. (1926), 'Chronique: Lettre d'un templier trouvée récemment à Jérusalem', *RB* 35, pp. 288–95.

—— (1927), 'Yazour et Beit Dedjan ou le Chastel des Plains et le Chastel de Maen', *RB* 36, pp. 83–89.

—— (1946) 'Jaffa au moyen-âge', *JPOS* 20.1, pp. 6–28.

Amiran, D., E. Arieh and T. Turcotte (1994), 'Earthquakes in Israel and Adjacent Areas: Macroseismic Observations since 100 B.C.E.', *IEJ* 44, pp. 260–305.

Aristidou, E. (1983), *Kolossi Castle Through the Centuries*, Nicosia.

Avissar, M. (1994), 'The Hammam in Old Akko', in *Twentieth Archaeological Conference in Israel, March, 1994: Abstracts*, Jerusalem, pp. 33–34.

—— (1995), 'Tel Yoqne'am: The Crusader Acropolis', *ESI* 15, pp. 41–42.

Avissar, M. and E. Stern (1998), 'Akko, the Old City', *ESI* 18, pp. 13–14.

Bagatti, B. (1947, trans. R. Bonanno, 1993), *Emmaus-Qubeibeh*, Jerusalem.

—— (1982), 'Crusader Church on Mount Tabor', in E. Schiller (ed.), *Mount Tabor and its Vicinity, Kardom* 20, pp. 30–37.

Bahat, D. (1991), 'Topography and Archaeology', in Prawer and Ben-Shammai (eds), 1991, pp. 68–134.

Balard, M. (ed.) (1996), *Autour de la première croisade. Actes du colloque de la Society for the Study of the Crusades and the Latin East (Clermont-Ferrand, 22–25 juin 1995)*, Paris.

Baldwin M.W. (1969), 'The Latin States Under Baldwin III and Amalric I, 1143–1174', in Setton (ed.), vol. 1, pp. 528–62.

Barash, M. (1971), *Crusader Figural Sculpture in the Holy Land: Twelfth Century Examples from Acre, Nazareth and Belvoir Castle*, Ramat Gan.

Barbé, H. (2003), 'Recherches archéologiques sur la forteresse de Safed: Découverte récente d'une tête sculptée d'époque franque', *Bulletin Monumental* 161-III, pp. 252–55.

Barbé, H. and E. Damati (2004), 'La forteresse médiévale de Safed: Données récentes de l'archéologie', *Crusades* 3, pp. 171–73.

—— (forthcoming), 'Safed – The Fortress', *Atiqot*.

Barbé H., Y. Lehrer and M. Avissar (2002), 'Ha-Bonim', *HA/ESI* 114, pp. 30–33 (illustrations in Hebrew section, pp. 34–38).

Barber, M. (1970), 'The Origins of the Order of the Temple', *Studia Monastica* 12, pp. 219–40.

—— (1992), 'Supplying the Crusader States: The Role of the Templars', in Kedar (ed.), 1992, pp. 314–26.

—— (ed.) (1994a), *The Military Orders: Fighting for the Faith and Caring for the Sick*, Aldershot.

—— (1994b), 'The Order of St Lazarus and the Crusades', *CHR* 80, no. 3, pp. 439–56.

—— (1995), *The New Knighthood: A History of the Order of the Temple*, Cambridge.

Battista, A. and B. Bagatti (1976), *La fortezza saracena del Monte Tabor (AH 609–15: AD 1212–18). SBF, Coll. Min.*, vol. XVIII, Jerusalem.

Ben-Dov, M. (1969), 'The Excavations at the Crusader Fortress of Kokhav- Hayarden (Belvoir)', *Qadmoniot* 2.1, pp. 22–27 (Hebrew).

—— (1972), 'The Crusader Castle of Belvoir', *CNI* 23.1, pp. 26–28.

—— (1974), 'The Fortress of Latrun', *Qadmoniot* 7.3–4, pp. 117–20 (Hebrew).

—— (1975), 'Crusader Fortresses in Eretz-Israel', *Qadmoniot* 8.4, pp. 102–13 (Hebrew).

—— (1976), 'Crusader Castles in Israel', *CNI* 25, p. 216.

—— (1983), *Jerusalem's Fortifications: The City Walls, the Gates and the Temple Mount*, Tel-Aviv (Hebrew).

—— (1985), *In the Shadow of the Temple*, Jerusalem.

—— (1986), 'The Sea Fort and Land Fort at Sidon', *Qadmoniot* 19.3–4, pp. 113–19 (Hebrew).

—— (1993a), 'Belvoir', in *NEAEHL*, vol. 1, pp. 182–86.

—— (1993b), 'Latrun', in *NEAEHL*, vol. 3, pp. 911–13.

—— (1993c), 'The Restoration of St. Mary's Church of the German Knights in Jerusalem', in Yoram Tsafrir (ed.), *Ancient Churches Revealed*, Jerusalem, 1993, pp. 140–42.

—— (1999), 'Churches in the Crusader Kingdom of Jerusalem', in Silvia Rozenberg (ed.), *Knights of the Holy Land: The Crusader Kingdom of Jerusalem*, Jerusalem, pp. 82–93.

Ben-Dov, M. and Y. Minzker (1968), 'Kokhav Ha-Yarden (Belvoir)', *RB* 75, pp. 419–20.

—— (1982), *In the Shadow of the Temple*, Jerusalem.

Ben-Tor, A., M. Avissar and Y. Portugali (1996), *Yoqneʿam I* (*Qedem Reports* 3), Jerusalem, pp. 20–23.

Benvenisti, M. (1970), *The Crusaders in the Holy Land*, Jerusalem.

—— (1982), '*Bovaria–babriyya*: A Frankish Residue on the Map of Palestine', in Kedar, *et al.* (eds), 1982, pp. 130–52.

Van Berchem, M. and E. Fatio (1914), *Voyage en Syrie: Mémoires de l'Institut Français d'Archéologie Orientale du Caire*, Cairo.

Bessac, J.C and J. Yasmine (2001), 'Étude préliminaire des chantiers de construction du château de Beaufort', *BAAL* 5, pp. 241–320.

Biller, T. (1989), 'Die Johanniterburg Belvoir am Jordan: zum frühen Burgenbau der Ritterorden im Heiligen Land', *Architectura: Zeitschrift für Geschichte der Baukunst/Journal of the History of Architecture*, pp. 105–36.

Boas, A.J. (1996a), 'A Recently Discovered Frankish Village at Ramot Allon, Jerusalem', in M. Balard (ed.), 1996, pp. 583–94.

—— (1996b), 'Survey of Crusader Structures in Caesarea', *ESI* 17, pp. 77–79.

—— (1999), *Crusader Archaeology: The Material Culture of the Latin East*, London and New York.

—— (2001), *Jerusalem in the Time of the Crusades*, London and New York.

Boas, A.J. and R. Lewis (forthcoming), 'Latrun (Toron des Chevaliers) in the Light of Recent Research'.

Boas, A.J. and A.M. Maeir (forthcoming), 'The Crusader Castle of Blanche Garde and the Medieval and Modern Village of Tell es-Safi in the Light of Recent Discoveries'.

Boas, A. and G.P. Melloni (forthcoming), *Akko, Western Galilee Bakery Site*.

Boase, T.S.R. (1967), *Castles and Churches of the Crusading Kingdom*, London.

—— (1971), *Kingdoms and Strongholds of the Crusaders*, London.

—— (1977), 'Military Architecture in the Crusader States in Palestine and Syria', in Setton (ed.), vol. 4, pp. 140–64.

—— (1978) (ed.), *The Cilician Kingdom of Armenia*, Edinburgh and London.

Bradbury, J. (1992), *The Medieval Siege*, Woodbridge.

Braune, M. (1985), 'Die mittelalterliche Befestigungen der Stadt Tortosa/Tarsus: Vorbericht der Untersuchungen 1981–1982', *Damaszener Mitteilungen* 2, pp. 45–54.

Burgoyne, M. and J. Folda (1981), Review of Buschhausen, 1978, *AB* 63, pp. 321–24.

Burgoyne, M. and D.S. Richards (1987), *Mamluk Jerusalem: An Architectural Study*, London.

Burns, R. (1999), *The Monuments of Syria: An Historical Guide*, London and New York.

Buschhausen, H. (1978), *Die süditalienische Bauplastik im Königreich Jerusalem von König Wilhelm II. Bis Kaiser Friedrich II.* (Österreichische Akademie der Wissenschaten, Philos.-histor. Kl., *Denkschriften*, 108. Band), Wien.

Cadei, A. (1999), 'Castellum quod dicatur Baffes', *Arte d'Occidente: temi e metodi: Studi in onore di Angiola Maria Romanini*, Rome, pp. 131–42.

Cahen, C. (1940), *La Syrie du nord à l'époque des croisades*, Paris.

Canning, R. (trans.) (1984), *The Rule of Saint Augustine: Masculine and Feminine Versions* (with introduction and commentary by Tarsicius J. van Bavel), London.

Cathcart King, D.J. (1949), 'The Taking of Crac des Chevaliers in 1271', *Antiquity* 23, pp. 83–92.

Chéhab, M. (1975), *Tyr à l'époque des croisades, I. Histoire militaire et diplomatique*, 2 vols. = *BMB*, pp. 27–28.

—— (1979) *Tyr à l'époque des croisades, II. Histoire sociale, économique et religieuse*, 2 vols. = *BMB*, pp. 31–32.

Chevedden, P.E. (2000), 'The Invention of the Counterweight Trebuchet: A Study in Cultural Diffusion', *DOP* 52, pp. 71–116.

Clermont-Ganneau, C. (1896–99), *Archaeological Researches in Palestine During the Years 1873–1874*, 2 vols., London.

—— (1898), 'Un reliquaire des croisades', *RAO* II, pp. 234–39.

—— (1901), 'Archaeological and Epigraphic Notes on Palestine', *PEFQS*, pp. 109–23 and 235–50.

Conder, C.R. (1874), Lieut. Claude R. Conder's Reports, *PEFQS*, pp. 11–24.

—— (1875), 'The Muristan', *PEFQS*, pp. 77–81.

—— (1882), 'Jerusalem: Newly Discovered Church', *PEFQS*, pp. 116–20.

Conder, C.R. and H.H. Kitchener (1881–83), *The Survey of Western Palestine: Memoirs of the Topography, Orography, Hydrography and Archaeology*, 3 vols., London.

Creswell, K.A.C. (1952), 'Fortification in Islam before A.D. 1250', *Proceedings of the British Academy* 38, pp. 89–125.

—— (1958, revised and enlarged 1989), *A Short Account of Early Muslim Architecture*, Harmondsworth.

Dailliez, L. (1996), *Règle et statuts de l'Ordre du Temple*, Paris.

Dalman, G. (1925), *Hundert deutsche Fliegerbilder aus Palästina*, Gütersloh.

Damati, E. (1986), 'Safed', *ESI* 5, pp. 93–94.

Dar, S and J. Mintzker (1987), 'Qaqun, Turris Rubea and Montidier: Three Crusader Sites in Emeq Hefer', *ZDPV* 103, pp. 192–213.

Dean, B. (1982), *The Crusaders' Fortress of Montfort*, Jerusalem, facsimile edition of Bashford Dean, *A Crusaders' Fortress in Palestine, Bulletin of the Metropolitan Museum of Art*, New York, September 1927.

Deschamps, P. (1932), 'Les entrées des châteaux des croisés en Syrie et leurs défenses', *Syria*, pp. 369–87.

—— (1934) *Les châteaux des croisés en Terre Sainte*, vol. I, *Le Crac des Chevaliers*, 2 vols. (text and album), Bibl. Archéol. et Hist., vol. XXXIV, Paris.

—— (1937), 'Les deux Cracs des croisés', *Journal Asiatique* 209, pp. 494–500.

—— (1939), *Les châteaux des croisés en Terre Sainte*, vol. II, *La défense du royaume de Jérusalem*, 2 vols. (text and album), Bibl. Archéol. et Hist., vol. XXXIV, Paris.

—— (1964), *Terre Sainte romane*, La Pierre-qui-vire.

—— (1973), *Les châteaux des croisés en Terre Sainte*, vol. III, *La défense du Comté de Tripoli et de la Principauté d Antioche*, Paris.

DeVries, K.R. (1992), *Medieval Military Technology*, Lewiston, N.Y.

Dichter, B. (1973), *The Maps of Acre: An Historical Cartography*, Acre.

—— (1979), *The Orders and Churches of Crusader Acre*, Acre.

Dickie, A.C. (1899), 'The Lower Church of St John, Jerusalem', *PEFQS*, pp. 43–45.

Diehl, Ch. (1924), *Les fresques de l'église d'Abou-Gosch, comptes-rendus de l'Académie des Inscriptions et Belles-Lettres*, Paris.

Druks, A. (1962), 'Excavations in the Crusader Castle of Safed', *HA* 2, p. 17 (Hebrew).

Dunkel, P. (1902), 'Excavations at Jerusalem' (trans. J.E. Hanauer), *PEFQS*, pp. 403–05.

Dussaud, R. (1927), *Topographie historique de la Syrie antique et médiévale*, Paris.

Edbury, P.W. (1991), *The Kingdom of Cyprus and the Crusades, 1191–1374*, Cambridge.

—— (1994), 'The Templars in Cyprus', in Barber (ed.), 1994a, pp. 189–95.

—— (1996), *The Conquest of Jerusalem and the Third Crusade (The Old French Continuation of William of Tyre cxli, cxliii)*, Aldershot.

—— (1997), *John of Ibelin and the Kingdom of Jerusalem*, Woodbridge.

Edbury, P.E. and J.G. Rowe (1988), *William of Tyre: Historian of the Latin East*, Cambridge.

Edgington, S. (1998), 'Medical Care in the Hospital of St John in Jerusalem', in Nicholson (ed.), 1998, pp. 27–33.

Edwards, R. (1983), 'Bagras and Armenian Cilicia: A Reassessment', *Revue des Etudes Arméniennes* 17, pp. 415–55.

—— (1987), *The Fortifications of Armenian Cilicia*, Georgetown.

Ehrlich, M. (1999), 'The Inland Towns in Twelfth Century Palestine', Unpublished Ph.D. dissertation, Bar-Ilan University, Ramat Gan.

Ellenblum, R. (1996a), 'Colonization Activities in the Frankish East: The Example of Castellum Regis (Mi'ilya)', *EHR* 111, pp. 104–22.

—— (1996b), 'Three Generations of Frankish Castle-Building in the Latin Kingdom of Jerusalem', in Balard (ed.), 1996, pp. 517–51.

—— (1998), *Frankish Rural Settlement in the Latin Kingdom of Jerusalem*, Cambridge.

Ellenblum R. and A. Boas (1999), 'Mezad Ateret', *HA/ESI* 109, pp. 5–6.

Ellenblum, R., A.J. Boas, A. Agnon and S. Marco (forthcoming), *Vadum Iacob*, vol. I.

Engle, A. (1976), *Readings in Glass History* 6/7, p. 103.

—— (1982), *Readings in Glass History* 13/14, pp. 35–69, 71–74.

Enlart, C. (1860, reprinted Jerusalem 1973), *Les églises de la Terre Sainte*, Paris.

—— ([1899] 1987), *Gothic Art and the Renaissance in Cyprus*, trans. and ed. D. Hunt, London.

—— (1925–28), *Les monuments des croisés dans le royaume de Jérusalem: architecture religieuse et civile*, 2 vols. + 2 albums, Bibliothèque archéologique et historique, VII–VIII, Paris.

Eydoux H.-P. (1982), *Les châteaux du soleil: forteresses et guerres des croisés*, Paris.

Favreau-Lilie, M.-L. (1982), 'The Teutonic Knights in Acre after the Fall of Montfort (1271): Some Reflections', in Kedar, *et al.* (eds), 1982, pp. 272–84.

Fedden, R. and J. Thomson (1957), *Crusader Castles*, London.

Fino, J.-F. (1970), *Forteresses de la France médiévale*, Paris.

Folda, J. (1977), 'Crusader Art and Architecture: A Photographic Survey', in Setton (ed.), vol. IV, pp. 251–354.

—— (ed.) (1982a), *Crusader Art in the Twelfth Century*, British Archaeological Reports (BAR), International Series, vol. CLII, Oxford.

—— (1982b), 'Crusader Frescoes at Crac des Chevaliers and Marqab Castle', *DOP* 36, pp. 177–210.

—— (1995), *Crusader Art in the Twelfth Century*, Cambridge.

Forey, A.J. (1977), 'The Military Order of St. Thomas of Acre', *EHR* XCII, pp. 481–503.

—— (1984), 'The Militarization of the Hospital of St John', *Studia Monastica* 26, pp. 75–98.

—— (1985), 'The Emergence of the Military Order in the Twelfth Century', *Journal of Ecclesiastical History* 36, pp. 175–95 (republished in A. Forey, *Military Orders and Crusades*, Aldershot, 1994).

—— (1992), *The Military Orders: From the Twelfth to the Early Fourteenth Centuries*, London.

—— (1994) *Military Orders and Crusades*, Aldershot.

Foss, C. and D. Winfield (1986), *Byzantine Fortification: An Introduction*, Pretoria.

Fournier, G. (1976), *Les châteaux dans la France médiévale: essai de sociologie monumentale*, Paris.

France, J. (1999), *Western Warfare in the Age of the Crusades 1000–1300*, London.

Frankel, R. (1980), 'Three Crusader Boundary Stones from Kibbutz Shomrat', *IEJ* 30, pp. 199–201.

—— (1988), 'Topographical Notes on the Territory of Acre in the Crusader Period', *IEJ* 38, pp. 249–72.

—— (1998), 'Some Notes on the Work of the Survey of Western Palestine in Western Galilee', *PEFQS* 130, pp. 99–105.

Frankel, R. and N. Gatzov (1986), 'The History and Plan of Montfort Castle', *Qadmoniot* 19.1–2, pp. 52–57 (Hebrew).

Frankel, R. and E.J. Stern (1996), 'A Crusader Screw Press from Western Galilee – The Manot Press', *Techniques and Culture* 27, pp. 89–123.

Frankel, R., N. Gatzov, M. Aviam and A. Dagani (2001), *Settlement Dynamics and Regional Diversity in Ancient Upper Galilee. Archaeological Survey of Upper Galilee*, IAA Reports 14.

Friedman, E. (1971), 'The Medieval Abbey of St Margaret of Mount Carmel', *Ephemerides Carmeliticae* 22, p. 295–348.

—— (1979), *The Latin Hermits of Mount Carmel: A Study in Carmelite Origins*, Rome.

Friedman, Y. (1982), 'Mount Tabor in the Crusader Period', in E. Schiller (ed.), *Mount Tabor and its Vicinity*, Kardom XX, pp. 26–30 (Hebrew).

Gabrieli, F. ([1969] 1989) *Arab Historians of the Crusades*, trans. E.J. Costello, New York.

Gibb H.A.R. (1969), 'The Career of Nur ad-Din', in Setton (ed.), vol. I, pp. 513–27.

Gibson, S. and D.M. Jacobson (1996), *Below the Temple Mount in Jerusalem: A Sourcebook on the Cisterns, Subterranean Chambers and Conduits of the Haram al-Sharîf*, Oxford.

Glüksmann, G. and R. Kool (1995), 'Crusader Period Finds from the Temple Mount Excavations in Jerusalem', *Atiqot* 26, pp. 87–104.

Goldmann, Z. (1962a), 'Newly Discovered Crusaders' Inscription in Acre (Preliminary Report)', *CNI* 13, no. 1.

—— (1962b), 'The Refectory of the Order of St John in Acre', *CNI* 12, pp. 15–19.

—— (1967), 'The Hospice of the Knights of St John in Akko', in *Archaeological Discoveries in the Holy Land*, Archaeological Institute of America, New York.

—— (1974), 'Le Convent des Hospitaliers à Saint Jean d'Acre', *Bible et Terre Sainte*, 160, pp. 8–18.

—— (1987), *Akko in the Time of the Crusades: The Convent of the Order of St. John*, Jerusalem.

—— (1993), 'Acco: Excavations in the Modern City [II]', in *NEAEHL*, vol. 1, pp. 24–27.

—— (1994, 2nd edition), *Akko in the Time of the Crusades: The Convent of the Order of St. John*, Jerusalem.

Gough, M. (1952), 'Anazarbus', *Anatolian Studies* II, pp. 85–150.

Guérin, V. (1868, 1874, 1880), *Description géographique, historique et archéologique de la Palestine*, 7 vols. (Judée, Samarie and Galilée), Paris.

Hamilton, R.W. (1949), *The Structural History of the Al-Aqsa Mosque. A Record of Archaeological Gleanings from the Repairs of 1938–1942*, London.

Hanna, Z. (1994), *Syria: The Castles and Archaeological Sites in Tartous*, Damascus.

Harper, R.P. (1988), 'Belmont (Suba)', *RB* 95, pp. 277–79.

—— (1989a), 'Belmont Castle (Suba) – 1987', *ESI* 7–8 (1988–89), pp. 13–14.

—— (1989b), 'Belmont Castle (Suba) – 1988', *HA* 94, pp. 48–49 (Hebrew).

—— (1990), 'Belmont Castle (Suba) – 1988', *ESI* 9 (1989–90), pp. 57–58.

Harper, R. and D. Pringle (1988), 'Belmont Castle: A Historical Notice and Preliminary Report of the Excavations in 1986, *Levant* 20, pp. 101–18.

—— (1989), 'Belmont Castle 1987: Second Preliminary Report of Excavations', *Levant* 21, pp. 47–61.

—— (2000), *Belmont Castle: The Excavation of a Crusader Stronghold in the Kingdom of Jerusalem*, Oxford.

Hartal, M. (1997), 'Excavation of the Courthouse Site at 'Akko: The Architecture and Stratigraphy in Area TA', *Atiqot* XXXI, pp. 3–30.

—— (2001), *The Al-Subayba (Nimrod) Fortress: Towers 11 and 9*, IAA Reports 11, pp. 36–40, 46–47.

Hazard, H.W. (1975), 'Caesarea and the Crusades', in R.J. Bull and D.L. Holland (eds), *The Joint Expedition to Caesarea Maritima*, vol. 1, Montana.

Hiestand, R. (1984), *Papsturkunden für Templar und Johanniter*, Göttingen.

Hubatsch, W. (1966), 'Montfort und die Bildung des Deutschordensstaates im Heiligen Lande', *Nachrichten der Akademie der Wissenschaften in Göttingen*, 1st series, Phil.-hist. Klasse, 51, pp. 161–99, Göttingen.

Huygens, R.B.C. (1965), 'Un nouveau texte du traité "De constructione castri Saphet" ', *Studi Medievali*, third series, 6 (I), pp. 355–87.

Jacoby, D. (1993), 'Three Notes on Crusader Acre', *ZDPV* 109.1, pp. 88–91.

Jacoby, Z. (1979), 'The Tomb of Baldwin V, King of Jerusalem (1185–1186) and the Workshop of the Temple Area', *Gesta* 18, pp. 3–14.

—— (1982), 'The Workshop of the Temple Area in Jerusalem in the Twelfth Century: Its Origin, Evolution and Impact', *Zeitschrift für Kunstgeschichte* 45, pp. 325–94.

—— (1985), 'The Provençal Impact on Crusader Sculpture in Jerusalem: More Evidence on the Temple Area Atelier', *Zeitschrift für Kunstgeschichte* 48, pp. 442–50.

—— (1987), *A Display of Crusader Sculpture at the Archaeological Museum (Rockefeller)*, Jerusalem.

Jacquot, J. (1929), *L'Etat des Alouites*, Beirut.

Johns, C.N. (1932), 'Excavations at Pilgrims' Castle, 'Atlit: The Faubourg and its Defences', *QDAP* 1, pp. 111–29.

—— (1934), 'Excavations at Pilgrims' Castle, 'Atlit (1932): The Ancient Tell and the Outer Defences of the Castle', *QDAP* 3, pp. 145–64.

—— (1936), 'Excavations at Pilgrims' Castle, 'Atlit (1932–3): Stables at the South-West of the Suburb', *QDAP* 5, pp. 31–60.

—— (1947), *Guide to Atlit*, Jerusalem.

—— (1975), ''Atlit', in *EAEHL*, vol. I, pp. 130–40.

—— (1993), ''Atlit', in *NEAEHL*, vol. I, pp. 112–17.

—— (1997), *Pilgrims' Castle ('Atlit), David's Tower (Jerusalem) and Qal'at ar-Rabad ('Ajlun)*, ed. D. Pringle, Aldershot.

Kalayan, H. (1973), 'The Sea Castle at Sidon', *BMB* 26, pp. 81–89.

Kedar, B.Z. (ed.) (1992), *The Horns of Hattin*, Jerusalem.

—— (1996), 'The Frankish Period: "Cain's Mount" ', in Ben-Tor, *et al.*, 1996, pp. 3–7.

—— (1997), 'The Outer Walls of Frankish Acre', *Atiqot* XXXI, pp. 157–80.

—— (1998), 'A Twelfth-Century Description of the Jerusalem Hospital', in Nicholson (ed.), 1998, pp. 3–26.

—— (1999) *The Changing Land between the Jordan and the Sea. Aerial Photographs from 1917 to the Present*, Jerusalem.

Kedar, B.Z. and D. Pringle (1985), 'La Fève: A Crusader Castle in the Jezreel Valley', *IEJ* 35, pp. 164–79.

Kedar, B.Z., H.E. Mayer and R.C. Smail (eds) (1982), *Outremer: Studies in the History of the Crusading Kingdom of Jerusalem Presented to Joshua Prawer*, Jerusalem.

Kedar, B.Z., J. Riley-Smith and R. Hiestand (eds) (1997), *Montjoie. Studies in Crusade History in Honour of Hans Eberhard Mayer*, Aldershot.

Kennedy, H. (1994), *Crusader Castles*, Cambridge.

Khalidi, W. (ed.) (1992), *All That Remains: The Palestinian Villages Occupied and Depopulated by Israel in 1948*, Washington, DC.

King, D.J.C. (1951), 'The Defences of the Citadel of Damascus: A Great Mohammedan Fortress of the Time of the Crusades', *Archaeologica* XCIV, pp. 57–96.

King, E.J. (1931), *The Knights Hospitallers in the Holy Land*, London.

—— (1932), *The Seals of the Order of St. John of Jerusalem*, London.

—— (1934, repr. 1980), *The Rule, Statutes and Customs of the Hospitallers 1099–1310*, London.

Kloner, A. (1983), 'Bet Govrin: A Medieval Church and Fortifications', *HA*, 83, pp. 52–53 (Hebrew).

Kloner, A. and D. Chen (1983), 'Bet Govrin: Crusader Church and Fortifications', *ESI* 2, pp. 12–13.

Kloner, A. and E. Assaf (1996), 'Bet Govrin – 1993', *ESI* 17, pp. 144–50.

Kloner, A. and M. Cohen (1996a), 'Bet Govrin – 1994', *ESI* 17, pp. 151–53.

—— (1996b), 'Bet Govrin – 1994–1996', *ESI* 19, pp. 77–79.

—— (2000), 'The Crusader Fortress at Bet Govrin', *Qadmoniot* 33.1, pp. 32–39 (Hebrew).

Kloner, A. and A. Hübsch (1996), 'The Roman Amphitheater of Bet Guvrinn: A Preliminary Report on the 1992, 1993 and 1994 Seasons', *Atiqot* XXX, pp. 85–106.

Kloner, A., M. Cohen and A. Hübsch, (2001), 'Bet Guvrin, 1998–1999', *HA/ESI* 113, pp. 105–106.

Kochavi, M. (ed.) (1972), *Judaea, Samaria and the Golan: Archaeological Survey, 1967–1968. Archaeological Survey of Israel*, vol. I, Jerusalem.

Kochavi, M. and I. Beit-Arieh (1994), *Map of Rosh Ha-ʿAyin*, Jerusalem.

Kool, R. (2001), 'The Crusader Mint of Vadum Jacob: New Implications for the Minting of Coins in the Latin Kingdom during the Second Half of the 12th Century', in *I luoghi della moneta: Le sedi dellezecche dall'antichità all' età moderna. Convegno internazionale, Milano Università degli Studi – 22/23 ottobre 1999*, Milan, pp. 329–33.

—— (2002), 'Coins at Vadum Jacob: New Evidence on the Circulation of Money in the Latin Kingdom of Jerusalem during the Second Half of the Twelfth Century', *Crusades* 1, pp. 73–88.

Kühnel, B. (1994), *Crusader Art in the Twelfth Century*, Berlin.

Kühnel, G. (1988), *Wall Painting in the Latin Kingdom of Jerusalem*, Berlin.

Lawrence, A.W. (1978), 'The Castle of Baghras', in T.S.R. Boase (ed.), *The Cilician Kingdom of Armenia*, Edinburgh and London, pp. 34–83.

—— (1979), *Greek Fortification*, Oxford.

—— (1983), 'A Skeletal History of Byzantine Fortification', *ABSA* 78, pp. 171–227.

Lawrence, C.H. (1997), *Medieval Monasticism*, London and New York.

Lawrence, T.E. (1988), *Crusader Castles*, Oxford.

Lee, G. (1996), *Leper Hospitals in Medieval Ireland with a Short Account of the Military and Hospitaller Order of St Lazarus of Jerusalem*, Dublin and Portland, Oreg.

Lev, E. and Z. Amar (2002), *Ethnic Medicinal Substances of the Land of Israel*, Jerusalem.

Levy, M. (1991), 'Medieval Maps of Jerusalem', in J. Prawer and H. Ben-Shammai (eds), *The History of Jerusalem: Crusaders and Ayyubids (1099–1250)*, Jerusalem, pp. 418–518 (Hebrew).

Luttrell, A. (1994), 'The Hospitallers' Medical Tradition: 1291–1530', in Barber (ed.) 1994a, pp. 64–81.

—— (1997), 'The Earliest Hospitallers', in Kedar, *et al.* (eds), 1997, pp. 37–54.

Lyons, M.C. and D.E.P. Jackson (1997), *Saladin: The Politics of the Holy War*, Cambridge.

Maeir, M. and D. Bahat (2004), 'Excavations at Kikkar Safra (City Hall), Jerusalem 1989', *Atiqot* 47, pp 169–92.

Marcombe, D. (2003), *Leper Knights: The Order of St Lazarus of Jerusalem in England, c. 1150–1544*, Woodbridge.

Marshall, C. (1992), *Warfare in the Latin East, 1192–1291, Cambridge Studies in Medieval Life and Thought, 4th series*, vol. XVII, Cambridge.

Masterman, E.G.W. (1914), 'Safed', *PEFQS*, pp. 169–79.

—— (1919), 'A Visit to the Ruined Castles of the Teutonic Knights', *PEFQS*, pp. 71–75.

—— (1928), 'A Crusaders' Fortress in Palestine', *PEFQS*, pp. 91–97.

Mayer, H.E. (1975), Introduction to the photographic reprint of *Tabula Ordinis Theutonici*, Toronto, pp. 75–77.

—— (1988), *The Crusades*, Oxford.

Mayr, L. (1782), *Reisebeschreibung nach Jerusalem in Palestina*, Landshut, Munich Staatsbibliothek Ms CGM2967.

Megaw, A.H.S. (1964), *A Brief History and Description of Kolossi Castle*, Nicosia.

—— (1971), 'Excavations at Saranda Kolones, Paphos: Preliminary Report on the 1966–67 and 1970–71 Seasons', *RDAC*, pp. 117–46.

—— (1972), 'Supplementary Excavations on a Castle Site at Paphos', *DOP* 26, pp. 322–43.

—— (1977), 'Cyprus: Military Architecture', in Setton (ed.), vol. IV, pp. 196–207.

—— (1982), 'Saranda Kolones 1981', *RDAC*, pp. 210–216.

—— (1984), 'Saranda Kolones: Ceramic Evidence for the Construction Date', *RDAC*, pp. 333–40.

Megaw, P. (1994), 'A Castle in Cyprus Attributable to the Hospital?', in Barber (ed.) 1994a, pp. 42–51.

Menache, S. (1999), 'The Military Orders in the Crusader Kingdom of Jerusalem', in Rozenberg (ed.) 1999, pp. 137–41.

Mesqui, J. (2001), *Châteaux d'Orient*, Milan.

Metcalf, D.M., R. Kool and A. Berman (1999), 'Coins from the Excavations at 'Atlit', *Atiqot* 37, pp. 89–164.

—— (2000), 'The Coins and Tokens', in Harper and Pringle (eds), 2000, pp. 81–85.

Michaud, J.F. (1822), *Histoire des croisades*, 7 vols., Paris.

Militzer, K. (1998), 'The Role of the Hospitals in the Teutonic Order', in Nicholson (ed.), 1998, pp. 51–59.

Mitchell, P. (1998), 'The Archaeological Approach to the Study of Disease in the Crusader States, as Employed at Le Petit Gerin', in Nicholson (ed.), 1998, pp. 43–50.

Mitchell, P.D. and E. Stern (2001), 'Parasitic Intestinal Helminth Ova from the Latrines of the 13th Century Crusader Hospital of St John in Acre, Israel', in M. La Verghetta and L. Capasso (eds), *Proceedings of the XIIIth European Meeting of the Paleopathology Association, Chieti, Italy: 18th–23rd September 2000*, Teramo, pp. 207–13.

Molin, K. (1997), 'The Non-Military Functions of Crusader Fortifications, 1187-circa 1380', *Journal of Medieval History* 23:4, pp. 367–88.

—— (2001) *Unknown Crusader Castles*, London and New York.

Müller-Wiener, W. (1966), *Castles of the Crusaders*, trans. J.M. Brownjohn, London.

Nachlieli, D., Y. Masarawah, M. Ein-Gedi and F. Sontag (2000), 'Ashdod-Yam', *ESI* 112, pp. 101–03.

Nicholson, H. (1993), *Templars, Hospitallers and Teutonic Knights: Images of the Military Orders, 1128–1291*, Leicester.

—— (ed.) (1998), *The Military Orders. Vol. II, Welfare and Warfare*, Aldershot.

—— (2001), *The Knights Hospitaller*, Woodbridge.

—— (2002), *The Knights Templar: A New History*, Phoenix Mill.

Nickel, H. (1989), 'Some Heraldic Fragments Found at Castle Montfort/Starkenberg in 1926, and the Arms of the Grand Master of the Teutonic Knights', *Metropolitan Museum Journal* 24, pp. 42–43.

Nicolle, D.C. (1988), *Arms and Armour of the Crusading Era 1050–1350*, 2 vols., New York.

—— (1996), *Medieval Warfare Source Book*, 2 vols., London and New York.

Nir, Y. (1997), 'The Crusader Well in Area TA', *Atiqot* XXXI, pp. 31–34.

Oman, C.W.C. (1924), *A History of the Art of War in the Middle Ages* (2nd edition), 2 vols., London.

Ovadiah, A. (1973), 'A Crusader Church in the Jewish Quarter of the Old City of Jerusalem', *EI* 11, pp. 208–12 (Hebrew).

Patrich, J. (1984), 'The Structure of the Muristan Quarter of Jerusalem in the Crusader Period', *Cathedra* 33, pp. 3–16 (Hebrew).

Peilstöcker, M. (2000), 'Yafo, Rabbi Yehuda Me-Raguza St.', *ESI* 20, p. 48.

Perez, N.N. (1988), *Focus East: Early Photography in the Near East (1839–1885)*, Jerusalem.

Perlbach, M. (1890), *Die Statuten des Deutschen Ordens*, Halle.

Petersen, A. (2000), 'The Fortress of Shafr ʿAmr and Related Buildings', *Levant* 32, pp. 77–96.

—— (2001), *A Gazetteer of Buildings in Muslim Palestine (Part 1)*, Oxford.

Pierotti, E. (1864), *Jerusalem Explored*, 2 vols., trans. T.G. Bonney, Cambridge.

Prawer, J. (1967), 'History of the Crusader Castle of Kaukab al-Hawa', *Yediot* 31, pp. 236–49 (Hebrew).

—— (1969/70) *Histoire du royaume latin de Jérusalem*, 2 vols., Paris.

—— (1972), *The Latin Kingdom of Jerusalem. European Colonialism in the Middle Ages*, London.

—— (1977), 'Crusader Cities', in H.A. Miskimin, D. Herlihy and A.L. Udovitch (eds), *The Medieval City*, New Haven, Conn. and London, pp. 179–99.

—— (1980a), *Crusader Institutions*, Oxford.

—— (1980b), 'Military Orders and Crusader Politics in the Second Half of the XIIIth Century', in J. Fleckenstein and M. Hellmann (eds), *Die geistlichen Ritterorden Europas* (Vorträge und Forschungen, 26; *Sigmaringen*), pp. 217–29.

—— (1991), 'Geo-Ethnography of Crusader Jerusalem', in Prawer and Ben-Shammai (eds), 1991, pp. 1–67.

Prawer, J. and M. Benvenisti (1970), 'Crusader Palestine', sheet 12/IX of *Atlas of Israel*, Jerusalem and Amsterdam.

Prawer, J. and H. Ben-Shammai (eds) (1991), *The History of Jerusalem. Crusaders and Ayyubids (1099–1250)*, Jerusalem (Hebrew).

Pringle, D. (1981), 'Some Approaches to the Study of Crusader Masonry Marks in Palestine', *Levant* 13, pp. 173–99.

—— (1982a), 'Some More Proto-Maiolica from ʿAtlit (Pilgrims' Castle) and a Discussion of its Distribution in the Levant', *Levant* 14, pp. 104–17.

—— (1982b), 'Church Building in Palestine before the Crusades', in J. Folda (ed.), *Crusader Art in the Twelfth Century*, Oxford, pp. 5–46.

—— (1985), 'Reconstructing the Castle of Safad', *PEQ* 117, pp. 139–49.

—— (1986a), *The Red Tower (al-Burj al-Ahmar): Settlement in the Plain of Sharon at the Time of the Crusaders and Mamluks (AD 1099–1516)*, London.

—— (1986b), 'A Thirteenth Century Hall at Montfort Castle in Western Galilee', *The Antiquaries Journal* 66, pp. 52–81.

—— (1989a), 'A Templar Inscription from the Haram al-Sharif in Jerusalem', *Levant* 21, pp. 197–201.

—— (1989b) 'Crusader Castles: The First Generation', *Fortress* 1, pp. 14–25.

—— (1991a), 'Survey of Castles in the Kingdom of Jerusalem, 1989: Preliminary Report', *Levant* 23, pp. 87–91.

—— (1991b), 'Crusader Jerusalem', *BAIAS* 10, pp. 105–13.

—— (1992), 'Aqua Bella: The Interpretation of a Crusader Courtyard Building', in Kedar (ed.), 1992, pp. 147–67.

—— (1993), *The Churches of the Crusader Kingdom of Jerusalem*, vol. I, Cambridge.

—— (1994a), 'Burj Bardawil and Frankish Settlement North of Ramallah in the Twelfth Century', in K. Athamina and R. Heacock (eds), *The Frankish Wars and their Influence on Palestine*, Bir Zeit, pp. 30–39.

—— (1994b), 'Templar Castles on the Road to the Jordan', in Barber (ed.), 1994a, pp. 148–66.

—— (1994c), 'Towers in Crusader Palestine', *Château-Gaillard: études de castellogie médiévale. vol.*

xvi. Actes du colloque internationale tenu à Luxembourg (Luxembourg), 23–29 août 1992, Caen, pp. 335–40.

—— (1995), 'Town Defences in the Crusader Kingdom of Jerusalem', in I. Corfis and M. Wolfe (eds), *The Medieval City under Siege*, Woodbridge, pp. 69–121.

—— (1996), 'Belvoir Castle', in S.J. Turner (ed.), *The Dictionary of Art*, London.

—— (1997a), *Secular Buildings in the Crusader Kingdom of Jerusalem: An Archaeological Gazetteer*, Cambridge.

—— (1997b), 'The Investigation of a Medieval Pit in the Muristan, Jerusalem, by Fr Charles Coüasnon OP, Mr Leonidas J. Collas and Mrs Crystal-M. Bennett in May 1963', *Levant* XXIX, pp. 201–215.

—— (1998a), *The Churches of the Crusader Kingdom of Jerusalem*, vol. II, Cambridge.

—— (1998b), 'Templar Castles between Jaffa and Jerusalem', in Nicholson (ed.), 1998, pp. 89–109.

—— (2000), *Fortification and Settlement in Crusader Palestine*, Aldershot.

—— (2004), 'Castle Chapels in the Frankish East', in N. Faucherre, J. Mesqui and N. Prouteau (eds), *La fortification au temps des croisades*, Rennes, pp. 25–41.

Pringle, D., A. Petersen, M. Dow and C. Singer (1994), 'Qal'at Jiddin: A Castle of the Crusader and Ottoman Periods in Galilee', *Levant* 26, pp. 135–66.

Pryor, J.H. (1988), '*In Subsidium Terrae Sanctae:* Exports of Foodstuffs and War Materials from the Kingdom of Sicily to the Kingdom of Jerusalem, 1265–1284', *Asian and African Studies* 22, pp. 127–46.

Raban, A. (1986), 'The Ports of Acre', in M. Yedaya (ed.), *The Western Galilee Antiquities*, Tel-Aviv, pp. 180–94 (Hebrew).

Raphael, K. and Y. Teper (forthcoming), 'The Archaeological Evidence from the Mamluk Siege of Arsuf, 1265', in *Mamluk Studies Review*.

Rey, G.E. (1871), *Études sur les monuments de l'architecture militaire des croisés en Syrie et dans l'île de Chypre* (Collection de Documents Inédits sur l'Histoire de France), Paris.

—— (1877), *Recherches géographiques et historiques sur la domination des Latins en Orient*, Paris.

—— (1883), *Les colonies franques de Syrie aux XIIme et XIIIme siècles*, Paris.

Richard, J. (1982), 'Hospitals and Hospital Congregations in the Latin Kingdom during the First Period of the Frankish Conquest', in Kedar, *et al.* (eds), 1982, pp. 89–100.

—— (1999), *The Crusades c. 1071–c. 1291*, trans. J. Birrell, Cambridge.

Riley-Smith, J. (1967), *The Knights of St John in Jerusalem and Cyprus c. 1050–1310*, London.

—— (1969), 'Notes and Documents: The Templars and the Castle of Tortosa in Syria: An Unknown Document Concerning the Acquisition of the Fortress', *EHR* 84, pp. 278–88.

—— (1978), 'The Templars and Teutonic Knights in Cilician Armenia', in Boase (ed.), 1978, pp. 92–117.

—— (1987), *The Crusades: A Short History*, London.

—— (1999), *Hospitallers: The History of the Order of St John*, London and Rio Grande.

—— (2001), 'Guy of Lusignan, the Hospitallers and the Gates of Acre', in Riley-Smith, *et al.* (eds), 2001, pp. 111–15.

Riley-Smith, J., M. Balard and B.Z. Kedar (eds) (2001), *Dei gesta per Francois: études sur les croisades dédiées a Jean Richard*, Aldershot.

Roberts, D. (1842), *The Holy Land: Syria, Idumea, Arabia, Egypt and Nubia*, 3 vols., London.

Rogers, R. (1992), *Siege Warfare in the Twelfth Century*, Oxford.

Röhricht, R. (1891), 'Karten und Pläne zur Palästinakunde aus dem 7. bis 16. Jahrhundert', *ZDPV* 14, pp. 137–41.

Roll, I. (1996), 'Medieval Apollonia-Arsuf: A Fortified Coastal Town in the Levant of the Early Muslim and Crusader Periods', in Balard (ed.), 1996, pp. 595–606.

Roll, I. and E. Ayalon (1982), 'Apollonia–Arsuf – A Coastal Town on the Southern Sharon Plain', *Qadmoniot* 57.1, pp. 16–22 (Hebrew).

—— (1989), *Apollonia and Southern Sharon: Model of a Coastal City and its Hinterland*, Tel Aviv (Hebrew, with English summary, pp. iv–ix).

—— (1993), 'Apollonia–Arsuf', in *NEAEHL*, vol. I, pp. 72–75.

Roll, I. and O. Tal (eds) (1999), *Apollonia–Arsuf: Final Report of the Excavations*. Vol. I, *The Persian and Hellenistic Periods*, Tel Aviv.

Roll, I., H. Yohana, Y. Tepper and T. Harpak (2000), 'Apollonia–Arsuf. During the Crusader Period in the Light of New Discoveries', *Qadmoniot* 33, no. 1 (119) (Hebrew), pp. 18–31.

Ronen, A. and Y. Olami (1978), *The Israel Archaeology Survey: Atlit Map*, Jerusalem.

Roshwalb-Hurowitz, A. (ed.) (1997), 'Akko (Acre): Excavation Reports and Historical Studies', *Atiqot* XXX1, pp. 1–128.

Rosser, J. (1985), 'Excavations at Saranda Kolones, Paphos, Cyprus 1981–1983', *DOP* 39, pp. 81–95.

—— (1986), 'Crusader Castles in Cyprus: Recent Excavation of the Castle of the Forty Columns in Paphos', *Archaeology* 39, pp. 40–49.

—— (1987), 'The Lusignan Castle at Paphos Called Saranda Kolones', *Studies in Mediterranean Archaeology* 77, pp. 185–98.

—— (1999), 'The Castle of the Forty Columns: Excavating a Crusader Castle in Cyprus', *Minerva* 8.1, pp. 26–29.

Rozenberg, S. (1999), *The Knights of the Holy Land*, Jerusalem.

Runciman, S. (1952–54), *A History of the Crusades*, 3 vols., Cambridge.

Salamé-Sarkis, H. (1980), *Contributions à l'histoire de Tripoli et de sa région à l'époque des croisades: problèmes d'histoire, d'architecture et de céramique*, Paris.

De Sandoli, S. (1974), *Corpus inscriptionum crucesignatorum terrae sanctae*, Jerusalem.

—— (1979), 'Iscrizione latina su pietra medievale', *La Terra Santa* 55, pp. 19–20.

Schick, C. (1872), 'Church of the Knights of St John', *PEFQS*, p. 100.

—— (1873), 'Muristan', *PEFQS*, p. 72.

—— (1887), 'Notices on the Dome of the Rock and the Church of the Sepulchre by Arab Historians Prior to the First Crusade', transl. Guy Le Strange, *PEQ* 1887, pp. 90–103.

—— (1889), 'Recent Discoveries in Jerusalem, II. The Muristan', *PEFQS*, pp. 113–14.

—— (1891), 'Reports from Jerusalem', *PEFQS*, pp. 198–204.

—— (1892a), 'The Buildings South of the Double Gate', *PEFQS*, pp. 19–24.

—— (1892b), 'Aceldama', *PEFQS*, pp. 283–89.

—— (1894a), 'Notes', *PEFQS*, pp. 146–47.

—— (1894b), 'Jerusalem Notes', *PEFQS*, pp. 261–66.

—— (1895), 'Reports from Herr Baurath Von Schick, A Stair and Postern in the Old Wall', *PEFQS*, p. 30.

—— (1901), 'The Ancient Churches of the Muristan', *PEFQS*, pp. 51–53.

—— (1902), 'The Muristan, or the Site of the Hospital of St. John at Jerusalem', *PEFQS*, pp. 42–56.

Schiller, E. (ed.) (1979), *The First Photographs of the Holy Land*, Jerusalem.

Schlumberger, G.L. (1943), *Sigillographie de l'Orient Latin*, Paris.

Setton, K.M. (gen. ed.) (1969–89), *A History of the Crusades*, 6 vols., Madison.

Shaked, I. (1997), 'Margaliot Fortress', *ESI* 16, pp. 17–18.

—— (2000), 'Identifying the Medieval Flour Mills at Doq and Recordane', *Cathedra* 98, pp. 61–72 (Hebrew), English summary, p. 172.

Shavit, J. and E. Galili (2002), 'Akko West, Coastal and Underwater Surveys', *Hadashot Arkeologiyot (ESI)* 114, pp. 10–12.

Shur, N. (1990), *A History of Acre*, Tel Aviv.

Sinclair, T.A. (1990), *Eastern Turkey: An Architectural and Archaeological Survey*, vol. IV, London.

Smail, R.C. (1956), *Crusading Warfare*, Cambridge.

Stark, H. (1999), 'A Crusader-Period Building at Latrun', *Atiqot* 38, pp. 215–18.

Stern, E. (1999a), 'Akko, the Old City', *HA/ESI* 109, pp. 10–13.

—— (1999b), Old 'Akko, the Fortress', *HA/ESI* 110, pp. 13–14.

—— (2000), 'The Centre of the Order of Hospitallers in Acre', *Qadmoniot* 33.1, pp. 4–12 (Hebrew).

—— (2004), 'The Church of St John in Acre', *Crusades* 3, p. 183.

Stern, E.J. (forthcoming), *The Hospitaller Order in Acre and Manueth: the Ceramic Evidence.*

Stern, E. and M. Avissar (1994), 'Akko, the Citadel', *ESI* 14, pp. 22–25.

—— (1996), 'Akko, the Old City', *ESI* 18, pp. 13–14.

Stern, E., K. Raveh, S.A. Kingsley and A. Raban (1993), 'Dor', in *NEAEHL*, vol. I, pp. 357–72.

Stern, E.J. (1997), 'Excavation of the Courthouse Site at Akko: The Pottery of the Crusader and Ottoman Periods', *Atiqot* 31, pp. 35–70.

—— (1999a), 'Ceramic Ware from the Crusader Period in the Holy Land', in Rozenberg (ed.), 1999, pp. 259–65.

—— (1999b), 'The Sugar Industry in Palestine during the Crusader, Ayyubid and Mamluk Periods in the Light of Archaeological Finds', Unpublished MA thesis, Hebrew University of Jerusalem, Jerusalem (Hebrew with English abstract).

—— (2000), 'Crusader Period Pottery in Palestine: New Discoveries', *Qadmoniot* 33.1, pp. 52–60 (Hebrew).

—— (2001), 'The Excavations at Lower Horbat Manot: A Medieval Sugar-Production Site', *Atiqot* XLII, pp. 277–308.

Sterns, I. (1969), 'The Statutes of the Teutonic Knights: A Study of Religious Chivalry', Unpublished Ph.D. dissertation, University of Pennsylvania, Philadelphia.

—— (1985), 'The Teutonic Knights in the Crusader States. A: Foundation and Organization of the Order', in Setton (ed.), vol. V, pp. 315–56.

Taha, H. (2000), 'Excavation of the Water Tunnel at Khirbet Belameh, 1996–1997', in P. Matthiae, *et al.* (eds), *Proceedings of the First International Congress on the Archaeology of the Ancient Near East, Rome, May 18th–23rd 1998*, Rome, pp. 1587–613.

Tanner, N.P. (ed.) (1990), *Decrees of the Ecumenical Councils.* Vol. 1, *Nicaea I to Lateran V*, London and Washington D.C.

Tibble, S. (1989), *Monarchy and Lordships in the Latin Kingdom of Jerusalem 1099–1291*, Oxford.

Toy, S. (1955), *A History of Fortification from 3000 BC to AD 1700*, London.

Tristram, H.B. (1865), *The Land of Israel: A Journal of Travels in Palestine*, London.

Upton-Ward, J.M. (1994), 'The Surrender of Gaston and the Rule of the Templars', in Barber (ed.), 1994a, pp. 179–88.

Ussishkin, D. and J. Woodhead (1992), *Excavations at Tel Jezreel 1990–1*, Tel-Aviv.

—— (1994), 'Excavations at Tel Jezreel 1992–1993: Second Preliminary Report', *Levant* 26, pp. 1–48.

De Vaux, R. and A.M. Stéve (1950), *Fouilles à Qaryet el-'Enab, Abu-Ghosh, Palestine*, Paris.

Vincent, H. and F.M. Abel (1914–26) *Jérusalem: recherches de topographie, d'archéologie et d'historie, vol. II. Jérusalem nouvelle*, 4 fasces and album, Paris

Vincent, L.-H. (1925), 'Garden Tomb', *RB*, 34, pp. 401–31.

De Vogüé, M. ([1860] 1973), *Les Églises de la Terre Sainte*, 1st edition, Paris; reprint, Toronto.

Vriezen, K.J.H. (1977), 'Jérusalem: Quartier du Muristan', *RB* 84, pp. 275–78, pl. 12.

Warren, C. and C. Conder (1884), *Survey of Western Palestine, Jerusalem*, London.

Weinberg, G.D. (1968), 'Es-Samiriya', *IEJ* 18, pp. 198–99.

—— (1987), 'A Glass Factory of Crusader Times in Northern Israel (Preliminary Report)', *Annales du 10ᵉ Congrès de l'Association internationale pour l'Histoire du Verre, Madrid-Sérgovie, 23–28 septembre 1985*, Amsterdam, pp. 305–17.

Weyl-Carr, A.-M. (1982), 'The Mural Paintings of Abu Ghosh and the Patronage of Manuel Comnenus in the Holy Land', in Folda, 1982a, pp. 215–43.

Wheatley, M.A. (1985), 'Leprosy – A Disease Apart: A Historical and Cross Cultural Analysis of Stigma', Unpublished Ph.D. thesis, Carleton University.

Wightman, G.J. (1993), *The Walls of Jerusalem from the Canaanites to the Mamluks*, Mediterranean *Archaeology Supplement* 4, Sydney.

Wilkinson, J. with J. Hill and W.F. Ryan (1988), *Jerusalem Pilgrimage 1099–1185* (Hakluyt Society, vol. 167), London.

Winter, P.H. (1944), *Preservation and Reconstruction of Acre, Survey and Report*, Acre.

Wojtowicz, R.T. (1991), *The Original 'Rule of the Knights Templar'* (no place of publication).

Yeivin, Z. (1973), 'Archaeological Activities in Samaria', in *Eretz Shomron: The Thirteenth Archaeological Convention, September 1972*, p. 150, pl. 19.1, 2, p. xix (English summary), Jerusalem.

Youngs, G.R. (1965), 'Three Cilician Castles', *Anatolian Studies* XV, pp. 113–34.

INDEX